Responsible Pleasure

Responsible Pleasure

The Brook Advisory Centres and Youth Sexuality in Postwar Britain

CAROLINE RUSTERHOLZ

Great Clarendon Street, Oxford, OX2 6DP,
United Kingdom

Oxford University Press is a department of the University of Oxford.
It furthers the University's objective of excellence in research, scholarship,
and education by publishing worldwide. Oxford is a registered trade mark of
Oxford University Press in the UK and in certain other countries

© Caroline Rusterholz 2024

The moral rights of the author have been asserted

Some rights reserved. No part of this publication may be reproduced, stored in
a retrieval system, or transmitted, in any form or by any means, for commercial purposes,
without the prior permission in writing of Oxford University Press, or as expressly
permitted by law, by licence or under terms agreed with the appropriate
reprographics rights organization.

This is an open access publication, available online and distributed under the terms of a
Creative Commons Attribution – Non Commercial – No Derivatives 4.0
International licence (CC BY-NC-ND 4.0), a copy of which is available at
http://creativecommons.org/licenses/by-nc-nd/4.0/.

Enquiries concerning reproduction outside the scope of this licence
should be sent to the Rights Department, Oxford University Press, at the address above

Published in the United States of America by Oxford University Press
198 Madison Avenue, New York, NY 10016, United States of America

British Library Cataloguing in Publication Data

Data available

Library of Congress Control Number: 2023952569

ISBN 978–0–19–286627–1

DOI: 10.1093/oso/9780192866271.001.0001

Printed and bound in the UK by
Clays Ltd, Elcograf S.p.A.

Links to third party websites are provided by Oxford in good faith and
for information only. Oxford disclaims any responsibility for the materials
contained in any third party website referenced in this work.

For Matthieu, Louis, and Samuel

Acknowledgements

I am deeply grateful to my oral history respondents who kindly shared their stories with me. Thank you for your trust. I would also like to thank Brook for their support with my research.

I am also indebted to the Wellcome Trust for their support through a Research Fellowship (209726/Z/17/Z) from 2018 to 2022 and for open access funding which has made this book freely available online. My editor at Oxford University Press, Cathryn Steele, has shown enthusiasm for this project from the early stages. Nadine Kolz at Oxford University Press also provided guidance and help. Sincere thanks also to the three anonymous reviewers for their useful feedback. I am truly grateful to Kate Errington who brilliantly did the index at short notice.

I wrote this book while on a fellowship at Cambridge University. I would like to thank my wonderful colleagues at Cambridge University who supported this project. All my gratitude goes to Simon Szreter, Lucy Delap, Helen McCarthy, Yuliya Hilevych, and George Severs for inspiring conversations and friendship.

The archival research for this project was conducted at a number of libraries and archives. I am grateful to the staff at the Wellcome Collection, National Archives, Bishopsgate Institute, and British Library.

In addition, I feel extremely lucky to be surrounded by fantastic friends and colleagues who supported me through this research and read the book proposal or chapter drafts. Special thanks to Nicole Bourbonnais, Helen McCarthy, Flurin Condreau, Jenny Crane, Lucy Delap, Hannah J. Elizabeth, Anne Hanley, Kristin Hay, Yuliya Hilevych, Agata Ignaciuk, Laura Kelly, Tracey Loughran, Penny Tinkler and Simon Szreter, as well as the members of the writing group I created during the pandemic.

I am also lucky to be surrounded by friends and colleagues who inspired me with their own work. Special thanks to Jenny Bangham, Nicole Bourbonnais, Maud Bracke, Helen McCarthy, Jenny Crance, Lucy Delap, Hannah J. Elizabeth, Lesley Hall, Alana Harris, Laura Kelly, Wendy Kline, Tracey Loughran, Ben Mechen, Jesse Olzynko-Gryn, Bibia Pavard, George Severs and Christabelle Sethna. The title of this book was decided while having dinner with Nicole Bourbonnais, Christabelle Sethna, and George Severs. I am grateful to the three of them for the brainstorming.

Some chapters of this book are partially based on articles and chapters published in the *Journals of British Studies*, *Medical Humanities*, and the *Journal of the History of Sexuality*, and in edited collections and are reprinted with permission.[1]

It took me five years to write this book. Over this period, I have experienced the joy of becoming the mother of two wonderful boys, Louis and Samuel. I embarked on this writing journey during the pandemic when the nurseries were closed. I feel privileged that I was able to work from home, part-time, while sharing childcare responsibilities with my husband at a time when key workers were risking their lives. During this period, I also underwent treatment for breast cancer. The journey through cancer has left me with many scars, and I am still in the process of physical, emotional, and mental recovery. This experience significantly impacted my ability to write the book and maintain proper focus. Yet, writing also provided me with a semblance of normality when I returned to work after a year-long hiatus, as my brain slowly found its own rhythm again. Writing became a goal that helped me momentarily forget my status as a cancer patient.

Both motherhood and cancer illuminated for me how dependent we are on the support of others. Without a strong support network, completing this project would have been impossible. As such, my greatest debt is to my husband Matthieu Chavaz. He has been an unwavering pillar of strength throughout this challenging and difficult period. During the pandemic, we divided our worktime equally. During the cancer treatment, he remained a positive, supportive, and caring force in my life. I cannot express how invaluable his love and support has been throughout this journey.

I would also like to thank my parents Marc and Chantal, my sister Sophie, my brother Charles Rusterholz, and my family-in-law Jacques, Annemarie,

---

[1] Caroline Rusterholz, 'Youth sexuality, responsibility, and the opening of the Brook advisory centres in London and Birmingham in the 1960s', *Journal of British Studies* 61.2 (2022): 315–42; Caroline Rusterholz, '"If we can show that we are helping adolescents to understand themselves, their feelings and their needs, then we are doing [a] valuable job": Counselling young people on sexual health in the Brook Advisory Centre (1965–1985)', *Medical Humanities* 49.2 (2023): 154–62; Caroline Rusterholz, '"A mechanical view of sex outside the context of love and the family": Contraception, censorship and the Brook Advisory Centre in Britain (1964–1985)', *Journal of the History of Sexuality*, 33.1 (2024): 33–55; Caroline Rusterholz, 'Teenagers, sex and the Brook Advisory Centres (1964–1985)', in Sian Pooley and Jono Taylor (eds) *Children's Experiences of Welfare in Modern Britain* (Institute of Historical Research, 2021): 247–73 and Caroline Rusterholz, 'A Private Matter? The Brook Advisory Centre and Young People's Everyday Sexual Health in the 1960s–1980s', in Hannah Froom, Tracey Loughran, Kate Mahoney, and Daisy Payling (eds), *'Everyday Health': Embodiment, and Selfhood since 1950* (Manchester University Press, forthcoming).

Julien, and Leo Chavaz. Special thanks go to my mother Chantal and mother-in-law Annemarie who travelled all the way from Switzerland to help us with the newborn baby. I am also deeply indebted to the dedicated nursery staff who took exceptional care of my children during this period.

My friends have also been a constant source of support. Thanks to Emilie Baierlé, Léonie Chiquet, Jean-Baptise Deleze, Laure Perret, Paz Irrarazabel, Suzanna Reyes, Ermioni Xanthopoulou, Delphine Monnard, Anne-Sophie De Weck, Sofia Suarez, Cathy Herbrand, Pauline Milani, Tiphaine Robert, Anne-Francoise Praz, Dominique Lasseur, Laura Hickman, Julie Petard, and Franck Sébastien.

Contents

List of Figures	xiii
List of Tables	xv
Introduction	1
Periodization and the history of sexuality	3
Monitoring youth sexuality	10
History of expertise and the voluntary sector	14
'Race' and sexual politics	16
Sources and methodology	18
The structure of the book	21
1. The Context: Youth, Sex, and Public Anxieties in the 1950s–1960s	25
The postwar years and young people	26
Debating youth sexuality: doctors and social scientists	27
Cultural and mass media representation of youth sexuality	32
Sexual health services before Brook	36
The setting up of Brook Advisory Centres and the role of Helen Brook	40
Conclusion	46
2. Locality and Controversy: The Opening of Brook Centres across Britain	48
The establishment of the centres	50
Motivations to establish the centres	56
Opposition to the centres	60
Challenging the opposition: Medical authority and sexual responsibility	63
Conclusion	68
3. Activism and the Shaping of Sexual Politics	69
A network of birth control activism	71
Financial issues	76
Lobbying politicians to expand contraceptive services	82
In defence of the Abortion Act	88
Campaigning against Gillick, 1980–1986	92
The Health of the Nation	101
Conclusion	103
4. The Centres: Location, Materiality, and Sensory Aspects	106
The checklist for creating a centre	107
Location and clientele	109
Layout of the centres	116
Conclusion	127

5. 'It's an excellent service for a lot of young people and a place of
   trust for them': The Clients and the Shaping of Brook Centres   128
   Demographics over time   130
   Race and ethnicity   137
   Clients' lived experiences with the centre   141
   Clients' influence on the services   161
   Conclusion   165

6. Counselling Young People Towards Sexual Maturity   167
   Good counselling practices   168
   Counselling in practice   177
   Counselling for contraception   181
   Counselling for pregnancy   191
   Counselling for psychosexual problems   194
   Conclusion   200

7. Education and Information on Contraception   203
   Information on services   204
   Sex education materials   210
   Inclusive sexual health information   228
   Young men and contraception   234
   Confidentiality   238
   Teenage magazines   240
   Conclusion   244

   Conclusion   246

References   253
Index   267

List of Figures

4.1	Tottenham Court Road Centre late 1960s	118
4.2	Liverpool in the mid-1980s	120
4.3	Brixton Centre 1984	121
4.4	Tottenham Court Road Centre 1980s	122
5.1	Age of new clients	135
7.1	Safe sex contraception	215
7.2	A look at safe sex: Contraception, birth control, family planning, 1978	218
7.3	Brook, *Cool it*, 1993	224
7.4	Brook, *Do you come here often?* 1993	225
7.5	Brook, *Whatever turns you on*, 1993	226
7.6	Brook, *Penis model pack*, 1991	237

List of Tables

3.1	Teenage pregnancy among under-16s in England and Wales, trends in conception among girls under 16 (the rate is per 1,000 girls 13–15)	101
5.1	Teenage sexual experience, 1964 and 1974–1975	132
5.2	Contraception used on occasion of first heterosexual intercourse, by date of birth	134
5.3	Methods of contraception for new clients by percentage	137
5.4	Ethnic description of clients of London Brook (10 centres) by percentage	141

Introduction

In a 1964 article published in the *Daily Mirror* newspaper, the pioneer family planning advocate and director of the Marie Stopes Memorial Foundation Clinic, Helen Brook, defended and explained her creation of the Brook Advisory Centre (Brook thereafter). First opened in London, Brook was the first centre to cater specifically for young, unmarried people and to provide contraceptive and sexual counselling in postwar Britain. Helen Brook justified her endeavour as follows: 'We want to give young people a place where they can come to discuss all of their problems of love and sex, singly or in pairs. We will not moralise but we'll try to teach them responsibility about their sex life.'[1] Instilling a sense of responsibility in the young, and discussing their feelings and emotions in a non-judgmental way, were the central values of Brook.

Five years after the first centre opened in London, John, a white 19-year-old university student, related his experience of attending Birmingham Brook in 1969 with his girlfriend to the journalist Wendy Cooper. John first explained that taking precautions was usually linked to the way he felt about the relationship. 'If it is a casual affair, a man seldom bothers to take precautions. But if you get fond of a girl, as I am with my girl Jean, you want to take care of her.'[2] Jean first attended a family planning clinic, but she was turned down because she was not married. She then went to Brook, first alone, then with John. John stressed what he valued most about Brook: 'they don't moralise or judge. They talk things over and do something practical to help.' John ended by highlighting that the hypocrisy of society made him sick and that his bitterness was shared by other university students.

Some 30 years later, in 1997, the journalist June Southworth from the *Daily Mail* reported on the death of Helen Brook at the age of 90, with the headline, 'Did this woman really liberate a generation or did she create the promiscuous society?'[3] She emphasized the key role that Helen Brook played in providing contraception for young people and the resistances this service triggered.

---

[1] 'Full mark to this sex-help clinic for the teenage lovers', *Daily Mirror*, 2 June 1964, 7.
[2] Wendy Cooper, 'Give our daughter the pill', *The People*, 13 September 1969.
[3] June Southworth, 'Did this woman really liberate a generation or did she create the promiscuous society?', *Daily Mail*, 8 October 1997, 34–5.

To her detractors, Helen Brook came to embody the 'permissive' society and what they perceived as its negative consequences: 'Though she had largely solved the problem of abortion by birth control, she had conversely contributed to the promiscuity that followed as a result of the availability of the pill.' Southworth tapped into the enduring controversy over the confidentiality of the service for under-16s—whereby contraception could be prescribed without a parent's consent—in order to criticize Helen Brook's achievement: 'To many parents, Helen Brook was the woman who stole their children's innocence.' Young people's access to contraception remained a controversial issue, even 30 years after the creation of Brook. These examples illustrate some of the central themes running through this book: the fact that personal and social responsibility became the key lexicon for supporters of a new sexual culture in the debate around youth and contraception; young people's experience with Brook and the fact that they valued its non-judgmental approach; and the enduring controversies around contraceptive access for young people.

This book is a sociocultural history of young people's sexuality in postwar Britain from the 1960s to 2000, using Brook as a case study to explore the way youth sexuality was institutionally and locally handled, debated publicly, and experienced individually. It takes an intersectional perspective to explore the development of Brook's service in different localities and to account for the disparities in access to contraception and sexual health services. The book examines how and why cultural and social norms about young people's sexuality changed over a period associated with growing 'permissiveness' and sexual liberation. It assesses how far these norms were aligned with the subjective experience of young people and the extent to which the two were mutually constitutive. It does so by focusing on a pioneering sexual health charity operating on the cusp of voluntary and state-financed sectors. From the opening of its first centre in London—followed by other centres in Birmingham (1966), Cambridge (1966), Bristol (1968), Edinburgh (1968), and Liverpool (1972), to name a few—to the present day, Brook has been the first and one of the major provider of contraceptive advice and sexual counselling to unmarried people and teenagers. Until 1964, contraceptive advice was only given to married women and brides-to-be; for the latter, this was conditional on formal proof of their engagement, in Family Planning Centres, Marie Stopes clinics, and Marriage Guidance Centres, as well as with General Practitioners.[4] Brook broke with the tradition of counselling only married people and extended their service to young and unmarried people. In

---

[4] On the history of birth control clinics and family planning centre see Audrey Leathard, *Fight for Family Planning* (Springer, 1980).

so doing, it pioneered an initiative that would form the primary model for the provision of advice on contraception for teenagers in Britain. The charity is still active today and remains a key player in sexual health services. Although Brook has provoked fierce opposition and triggered recurrent public debates on teenage sexuality, little is known of its history. As a non-governmental organization that nevertheless had clear connections with the Family Planning Association (FPA) and the National Health Service (NHS), Brook is an important organization through which we might nuance our understanding of the economics of healthcare, on the one hand, and the relationship between changing sexual cultures, sexual politics, and young people's sexual experiences, intimacy, and subjectivities on the other hand. This book provides a substantial and original contribution to scholarship on the forging of the modern sexual subject in Britain. Brook was also one of the first institutions to specifically cater for young people in Europe. In France, the first family planning clinics opened in the early 1960s and there were some resistances to counselling young people under the age of majority.[5] In Switzerland too, providing contraceptive information and devices to young people was controversial, even more in a society marked by striking differences in sexual health services across cantons. Sexual health information to young people started to be given because young people attended regular family planning centres, originally opened to counsel married people.[6] In Sweden, Swedish youth guidance centres opened from the early 1970s as place where young people could discuss their sexual needs.[7] In the Netherlands too, centres for young people were created by the Rutgers Foundation. This Foundation even took an international turn with the development of international sexual health policy. Therefore, other countries were facing a similar demand for contraceptive information for young people, but it seems that Britain was one of the first countries to specifically open a centre for young, unmarried people.

Periodization and the history of sexuality

The forty-year period (1960s–2000) that this book covers was characterized by dramatic socio-economic and cultural changes that refashioned the face of

---

[5] Marie-Françoise Lévy, 'Le mouvement français pour le planning familial et les jeunes', *Vingtième siècle Revue d'histoire* 75 (2002): 75–84.

[6] Anne-Françoise Praz, 'Gérer la sexualité des jeunes. Stratégies familiales et institutionnelles en Suisse romande (1960–1977)', presentation given at the Society for the History of Children and Youth Ninth Biennial Conference, Rutgers University, Camden, NJ, June 21–3 2017.

[7] Anna-Karin L Larsson, 'Girls' responsibilities, boys' needs: Sexual health, gender and youth in Sweden 1970-1999', *European Journal for the History of Medicine and Health* 80.1 (2022): 96–118.

Britain. Traditionally, the history of postwar Britain has been divided into three distinct periods, based on political trends.⁸ The first period (1945–1968) saw the advent of the social democracy, with a rise in the standard of living, the democratization of secondary education, and full employment and the arrival of the Windrush generation. The second period (1968–1979) was characterized by the threat to social democracy from internal contradictions. This period, which stood between the 'swinging sixties' and Margaret Thatcher's divisive 1980s, is said by its detractors to mark Britain's entry into economic and social decline.⁹ The third period was marked by the triumph of 'neoliberalism' (1979–1995).¹⁰ The 1980s was a decade of cuts in public expenditure, the polarization of political forces, rising unemployment and inflation, racial tensions, and increasing neoliberalism through privatization and the primacy of market forces. The 1990s saw a growing disillusion with the Conservative party, notably due to increasing social inequalities and 'declining community sense'. However, the decade ended with a renewed period of growth in prosperity and the advent of New Labour.¹¹

A similar periodization has been applied to the deep changes in the social and sexual culture, sexual politics, and sexual subjectivities of ordinary people that took place between the 1960s and 1990s. This book starts in the 1960s, but makes some incursions into the preceding decade as there were several relevant debates and controversies that occurred in the 1950s. Historians generally refer to society in Britain from the Lady Chatterley publication trial in 1960 to the end of the 1960s as the 'permissive society'.¹² Historian

---

⁸ Brian Harrison, *Seeking a Role: The United Kingdom, 1951–1970* (Oxford University Press, 2009); Brian Harrison, *Finding a Role: The United Kingdom, 1970–1990* (Oxford University Press, 2010). Recently, this periodization has been severely criticized by Matthew Hilton, Chris Moores, and Florence Sutcliffe-Braithwaite, ''New Times' revisited: Britain in the 1980s', *Contemporary British History* 31.2 (2017): 145–65.

⁹ Alwyn W. Turner, *Crisis? What Crisis?: Britain in the 1970s* (Aurum Press, 2009). Recent research has revisited the myth of the 1970s as a time of crisis. See Robinson Emily et al., 'Telling stories about post-war Britain: Popular individualism and the "crisis" of the 1970s', *Twentieth Century British History* 28.2 (2017): 268–304; Lawrence Black and Hugh Pemberton, 'Introduction. The Benighted Decade? Reassessing the 1970s?', in Lawrence Black, Hugh Pemberton, and Pat Thane (eds), *Reassessing 1970s Britain* (Manchester, 2013): 1–24.

¹⁰ Hilton, Moores, and Sutcliffe-Braithwaite, *New Times* revisited; Andy McSmith, *No Such Thing as Society: A History of Britain in the 1980s* (Constable, 2010); Alwyn W. Turner, *Rejoice! Rejoice!: Britain in the 1980s* (Aurum Press, 2010).

¹¹ Kenneth O. Morgan, *Twentieth Century Britain: A Very Short Introduction* (Oxford University Press, 2000).

¹² Anthony Aldgate, *Censorship and the Permissive Society: British Cinema and Theatre, 1955–1965* (Oxford University Press, 1995); Marcus Collins (ed.), *The Permissive Society and its Enemies: Sixties British Culture* (Rivers Oram Press, 2007); Mark Donnelly, *Sixties Britain: Culture, Society and Politics* (Routledge, 2014); Jeffrey Weeks, *Sexuality and its Discontents: Meanings, Myths and Modern Sexualities* (Routledge, 1985): 17–21; Dominic Sandbrook, *White Heat: A History of Britain in the Swinging Sixties* (ABrookus, 2006).

Arthur Marwick described the 1960s period as a cultural and material revolution in terms of family relationships, opportunities, and moral and personal freedom for ordinary people.[13] He also noticed a new permissiveness and a more relaxed and tolerant attitude toward sexual mores, perceptible through the passing of 'permissive' legislation, to borrow from Marxist sociologist Stuart Hall.[14] Such legislation encompassed the decriminalization of abortion and of sex between men in England and Wales (1967), as well as the Family Planning Act (1967) that enabled but did not require Local Health Authorities to give birth control advice, regardless of marital status, on social as well as medical grounds, using voluntary organizations such as the Family Planning Association and Brook as their agents if they wished. But contraception was not freely available for single women until 1974. From the 1950s, a rising incidence of premarital intercourse—or at least increasing recognition thereof—led to new anxieties around illegitimacy (see Chapter 1). New reliable contraceptive technologies arrived on the British market in the 1960s. Until then, methods for controlling fertility had ranged from coitus interruptus and abstinence to diverse substances ingested or placed into the vagina and barrier methods such as the cap, pessary, diaphragm, condoms, and early forms of intra-uterine devices, alongside more traditional methods of birth control authorized by the Catholic Church, such as the rhythm method.[15] Nevertheless, despite the availability of mechanical and modern methods of birth control, individuals relied mainly on coitus interruptus and less often on the condom.[16] In 1961 the contraceptive pill became available on prescription for married women, and from 1963, new forms of IUD started to be prescribed. However, hormonal and mechanical methods of birth control remained difficult to obtain for young and unmarried people prior to the 1967 Family Planning Act. Condoms had to be bought in pharmacies, which did not place them on display; they had to be requested by the purchaser.

---

[13] Arthur Marwick, *Britain in the Century of Total War: War, Peace, and Social Change, 1900–1967* (Atlantic Little, Brown, 1968); Arthur Marwick, *The Sixties: Cultural Revolution in Britain, France, Italy, and the United States, c.1958–c.1974* (Bloomsbury, 1998); Arthur Marwick, 'The 1960s: Was there a 'cultural revolution?', *Contemporary Record* 2.3 (1988): 18–20.

[14] Stuart Hall, 'Reformism and the Legislation of Consent', in *Permissiveness and Control: The Fate of the Sixties Legislation* (Macmillan, 1980): 1–43.

[15] On the development of contraceptive methods and the role of the Family Planning Association in this see Caroline Rusterholz, *Women's Medicine, Sex, Family Planning and British Female Doctors in Transnational Perspective (1920–1970)* (Manchester University Press, 2020), chapter 1. On the relationship between birth control and Catholicism in Britain see David Geiringer, *The Pope and the Pill: Sex, Catholicism and Women in Post-War England* (Manchester University Press, 2020).

[16] Kate Fisher, *Birth Control, Sex, and Marriage in Britain 1918–1960* (Oxford University Press, 2006); Simon Szreter and Kate Fisher, *Sex Before the Sexual Revolution: Intimate Life in England 1918–1963* (Cambridge University Press, 2010).

Advertisements did become more obvious after the pill was released. The barber shop was another option, but not all young people had the financial means to go to the barber regularly.[17]

Historians have discussed the alleged peculiarity of a British sexual revolution, debating its scope, timing, reasons, and even its existence.[18] There is today a growing consensus that broad sexual changes occurred during the long twentieth century and that a large-scale acceleration of sexual changes happened in the period 1962 to 1969.[19] As a result, the notion of 'permissiveness' has been nuanced. Frank Mort, in particular, has warned against the use of 'permissiveness', pointing out that it obscures more than it reveals. He qualifies the term as 'slippery' and challenges the idea of the 1960s as a 'watershed break'.[20] Several studies have foregrounded the continuity of certain traditional values such as the double standard that young women, but not men, were still expected to be virgins when entering marriage and that marriage, not a career, remained the key goal for teenage girls.[21]

As a growing body of scholarship has shown, overall, the 1960s were not the decade of sexual experimentation in the young usually described by the contemporary tabloids and moralizers. While the 1960s could have seen more experimentation in sex behaviours among the educated married, the principal novel transgression for the unmarried was (protected) intercourse before marriage. Premarital sex did increase but young people remained fairly conventional in their social and moral attitudes towards sex, and marriage continued to be the key goal for a majority of young women. As recalled by Stevi Jackson and Sue Scott:

---

[17] Claire Jones, *The Business of Birth Control: Contraception and Commerce in Britain Before the Sexual Revolution* (Manchester University Press, 2020).

[18] Callum G. Brown, 'Sex, religion, and the single woman: The importance of a "short" sexual revolution to the English religious crisis of the sixties', *Twentieth Century British History* 22.11 (2011): 189–215; Sam Brewitt Taylor, 'Christianity and the invention of the sexual revolution in Britain, 1963–1967', *Historical Journal* 60.2 (2017): 519–46; Hera Cook, *The Long Sexual Revolution: English Women, Sex, and Contraception 1800–1975* (Oxford University Press, 2004); Dominic Sandbrook, *White Heat: A History of Britain in the Swinging Sixties* (Abacus, 2006): 9; Jeffrey Weeks, *Sexuality and its Discontents: Meanings, Myths and Modern Sexualities* (Routledge, 1985); Szreter and Fisher, *Sex Before the Sexual Revolution*. On Catholicism and female sexuality, see David Geiringer, 'Catholic understandings of female sexuality in 1960s Britain', *Twentieth Century British History* 28.2 (2017): 209–38.

[19] Jeffrey Weeks, *The World We Have Won: The Remaking of Erotic and Intimate Life* (Routledge, 2007); Lesley A. Hall, *Sex, Gender and Social Change in Britain since 1880* (Bloomsbury, 2017).

[20] Frank Mort, *Capital Affairs: London and the Making of the Permissive Society* (Yale University Press, 2010): 3.

[21] Carol Dyhouse, *Girl Trouble: Panic and Progress in the History of Young Women* (Bloomsbury, 2014); Claire Langhamer, 'Adultery in post-war England', *History Workshop Journal* 62.1 (2006): 86–115.

We had been teenagers in the 1960s when, despite the hype to the contrary, girls were expected to guard their "reputations" and remain virginal and when there was little information available on female desire and pleasure. Each of us, in different ways, had to negotiate the double standard and tensions between our own desires on the one hand and fears of pregnancy and damage to 'reputation' on the other, while also managing pressures from boyfriends to 'go all the way'.[22]

This increase in premarital sex was driven by new norms about emotional intimacy and romantic love. These norms took shaped in the preceding decades. Indeed, Claire Langhamer has shown that by the 1950s love became tightly bound with sex within the widely 'promoted notion of modern marriage'.[23] In addition, in a modern marriage, spouses were expected to plan and space the births of their children, showing sexual responsibility. This book takes Langhamer's argument further by arguing that love and sex were also bound together in order to justify young people's sexual initiation from the 1960s. Therefore, this book engages with the debate over sexual change in the 1960s and asks what role Brook played in shaping norms around youth sexuality and young people's sexual behaviours.

A common assumption is that the 1970s saw an increased 'liberalization' of sexual behaviours, albeit accompanied by push-back from right-wing governments and politicians.[24] Since the 1970s, new narratives around the self, sexuality, and the body emerged in Western societies, contributing to the advent of the sexual citizenship characterized by those who 'claimed for equal rights under the law, in politics, in economics, in social matters and in

---

[22] Stevi Jackson and Sue Scott, 'A Sociological History of Researching Childhood and Sexuality: Continuities and Discontinuities', in E. Renold Ringrose and R. D. Egan (eds), *Children, Sexuality and Sexualization* (Palgrave Macmillan, 2015): 39–55. In addition, on the complexities of this and social class differentiated biological knowledge in an era before effective sex education in schools, see Szreter and Fisher, *Sex Before the Sexual Revolution*, chapters 2–3.

[23] Claire Langhamer, *The English in Love: The Intimate Story of an Emotional Revolution* (Oxford University Press, 2013). Claire Langhamer, Matthew Thomson, and Thomas Dixon have all argued that the 1950s marked a cultural, emotional, and social milestone where new definitions and understandings of the self took place. Similarly, Lynn Abrams has noted a shift in the understanding of the feminine self from self-abnegation and respectability to self-development and self-fulfilment. See Thomas Dixon, *Weeping Britannia: Portrait of a Nation in Tears* (Oxford University Press, 2015); Matthew Thomson, *Psychological Subjects: Identity, Culture and Health in Twentieth Century Britain* (Oxford University Press, 2006); Matthew Thomson, *Lost Freedom: The Landscape of the Child and the British Post-War Settlement* (Oxford University Press 2013); Lynn Abrams, 'Liberating the female self: Epiphanies, conflict and coherence in the life stories of post-war British women', *Social History* 39.1 (2014): 14–35. Some of Abrams' interviewees came from working-class families, but most of these women enjoyed social mobility early in life via grammar school and university.

[24] Jeffrey Weeks, *Sexuality and its Discontents: Meanings, Myths and Modern Sexualities* (Routledge, 1985).

sexual matters'.²⁵ The decade witnessed the creation of the Gay Liberation Front and the Women's Liberation movement in 1970.²⁶ The latter campaigned for free contraception and abortion on demand, highlighting the need for better access to contraception.²⁷ More generally, women's voices started to be heard on the political stage as well as within public discourses. Germaine Greer's *The Female Eunuch*, published in 1970, criticized the traditional nuclear family and the sexual repression of women, while the Virago publishing house, created in 1973, gave a voice to new feminist thinking and to marginalized women of colour.²⁸ Labour implemented the 1970 Equal Pay Act and the 1975 Sex Discrimination Act. Women also entered higher education in far greater numbers. In 1974, contraception became free under the 1974 Family Planning Amendment Act, while DHSS guidelines encouraged the development of services specifically aimed at young people. Sexuality was increasingly perceived and presented as a source of self-realization, and new norms of sexual behaviours were defined.²⁹ Similarly, Anthony Giddens has contended that since the 1970s there has been a democratization of the self, where plastic sexuality has become paramount. By plastic sexuality, he refers to the ways individuals lived their sexuality, liberated from traditional constraints and based on the idea of 'love', whereby love is contingent, subject to continuous negotiation, and built on an ideal of equality and mutual satisfaction.³⁰ Focusing on youth sexuality, I argue, partly challenges this narrative.

The 1970s ended with a growing contestation against young people's access to sexual health services. A Conservative government was elected in 1979 on a platform emphasizing morality and values. The 1980s saw a 'moral regeneration' through a return to 'Victorian values' and the key role played by the New Right in debates over sexual morality and the negative consequences of the 'permissive society'.³¹ Contraceptive advice for young people under 16 without parental consent became hotly debated in the mid-1980s in the House

---

[25] Jeffrey Weeks, 'The sexual citizen?', *Theory, Culture & Society* 15.3 (1998): 47.
[26] Lucy Robinson, *Gay Men and the Left in Post-war Britain: How the Personal got Political* (Manchester University Press, 2013).
[27] Anna Coote and Beatrix Campbell, *Sweet Freedom: The Struggle for Women's Liberation* (John Wiley, 1987).
[28] Lorna Stevens, '13 Telling Tales of Virago Press', in Stephen Brown (ed.), *Consuming Books: The Marketing and Consumption of Literature* (Routledge, 2006): 160.
[29] Ben Mechen, *Everyday Sex in 1970's Britain* (unpublished PhD dissertation, University College London, 2016).
[30] Anthony Giddens, *The Transformation of Intimacy: Sexuality, Love and Eroticism in Modern Societies* (Stanford University Press, 1992).
[31] James Hampshire and Jane Lewis. '"The ravages of permissiveness": Sex education and the permissive society', *Twentieth Century British History* 15.3 (2004): 290–312.

of Lords; the Gillick case contested whether GPs' could prescribe birth control to under-16s and was settled in favour only on appeal to the supreme court (the House of Lords at this date).[32] The following years saw the rise of AIDS and the passing of the infamous Section 28.[33] In the late 1980s, the Conservative government made teenage pregnancy a key issue, a concern that culminated with the 1992 *Health of the Nation* initiative.[34] With the advent of the web in the (very) late 1990s; digital sexual information became increasingly available and changed the way that young people learnt about sex. Our story ends at the point that the Labour government launched a 10-year 'Teenage Pregnancy Strategy' for England, to tackle the country's high rates of such pregnancies and to reduce social exclusion.[35] This saw the establishment of teenage pregnancy as a major social public health problem.

By using youth as a 'useful category of historical analysis',[36] this book challenges several ideas about the period, in particular its periodization into three distinct eras and the whiggish view of a progressive liberalization of sexual mores and behaviours. This book argues that shifting the focus from adults to young people reveals a different reading of the period, a reading in which continuities are as important as ruptures and changes. As this book demonstrates, anxieties and enduring resistance towards young people's sexuality remained key markers across the decades. Exploring youth sexuality involves analysing its shifting and historically contingent boundaries, as well as exploring its social regulations and intimate practices. This book contributes to bringing the history of youth, the history of sexuality, the history of expertise, and the history of race and reproductive politics into close conversation.

---

[32] Martin Durham, *Sex and Politics: Family and Morality in the Thatcher Years* (Macmillan International Higher Education, 1991); Jane Pilcher, 'Gillick and After: Children and Sex in the 1980s and 1990s', in Jane Pilchner and Stephen Wagg (eds), *Thatcher's Children? Politics, Childhood and Society in 1980 and 1990* (Falmer Press, 1996): 77–93.

[33] Virginia Berridge, *AIDS in the UK: The Making of Policy, 1981–1994* (Oxford University Press, 1996); Matt Cook, '"Archives of feeling": The AIDS crisis in Britain 1987', *History Workshop Journal* 83.1 (2017): 51–78; Matt Cook, 'AIDS, Mass Observation, and the fate of the permissive turn', *Journal of the History of Sexuality* 26.2 (2017): 239–72; Hannah J. Elizabeth, *[Re]inventing Childhood in the Age of AIDS: The Representation of HIV Positive Identities to Children and Adolescents in Britain, 1983–1997* (unpublished PhD dissertation, University of Birmingham, 2016); Hannah J. Elizabeth, '"Private things affect other people": *Grange Hill*'s critique of British sex education policy in the age of AIDS', *Twentieth Century British History* 32.2 (2021): 261–84.

[34] Lisa Arai, *Teenage Pregnancy: The Making and Unmaking of a Problem* (Policy Press, 2009).

[35] Alison Hadley, Roger Ingham, and Venkatraman Chandra-Mouli, 'Implementing the United Kingdom's ten-year teenage pregnancy strategy for England (1999–2010): How was this done and what did it achieve?', *Reproductive Health* 13.1 (2016): 139.

[36] Joan Scott, 'Gender: A useful category of historical analysis', *American Historical Review* 91.5 (1986): 1053–75.

Monitoring youth sexuality

Youth is a difficult term to define, as its boundaries vary historically and culturally.[37] In this book, youth is defined by the age range of Brook clients, which was 13 to mid-20s. Since the 1960s and 1970s, historians have tried to identify the emergence of this age category, distinct from childhood and adulthood, by analysing its treatment and representations.[38] They have emphasized that the start and end points of youth can be flexible and shifting, and have concentrated on the institutional constraints that bring about this distinct phase of life. They have also shown that youth became an object of growing regulation at the end of the nineteenth century amid increasing concerns over juvenile delinquency due to a lack of control between the point when young people left school and the point when they entered employment, joined the army, or got married.[39] Similarly, 'adolescent' appeared as a distinctive category around 1900, when medical and scientific discourses revealed that the years between puberty and the 20s were characterized by emotional and physical changes experienced by every adolescent.[40] Adolescence was therefore a period and stage of life when young people needed guidance from adults to help them navigate this tumultuous and emotionally highly charged time. This guidance was deemed essential to transform young people into respectable and responsible citizens. As a result, the terminological variation partly reflects a disciplinary boundary—'adolescence' is widely used in

---

[37] Barbara A. Hanawalt, 'Historical descriptions and prescriptions for adolescence', *Journal of Family History* 17.4 (1992): 341–51; Giovanni Levi and Jean-Claude Schmitt, *L'Histoire des Jeunes en Occident* (Seuil, 1996): 7–19.

[38] John R. Gillis, *Youth and History: Tradition and Change in European Age Relations, 1770–Present* (Academic Press, 1974).

[39] Jean-Claude Caron, Annie Stora-Lamarre, and Jean-Jacques Yvorel, *Les âmes mal nées. Jeunesse et délinquance urbaine en France et en Europe (XIXe–XXIe siècles)* (Presses Universitaires de Franche-Comté, 2008); Pamela Cox and Heather Shore (eds), *Becoming Delinquent: British and European Youth, 1650–1950* (Ashgate, 2002); Pamela Cox, *Gender, Justice and Welfare: Bad Girls in Britain, 1900–1950* (Macmillan, 2003); Harry Hendrick, *Images of Youth. Age, Class, and the Male Youth Problem, 1880–1920* (Clarendon Press, 1990); John Springhall, *Coming of Age: Adolescence in Britain, 1860–1960* (Gill and Macmillan, 1986); John Springhall, *Youth, Popular Culture and Moral Panics: Penny Gaffs to Gangsta-rap, 1830–1996* (Basingstoke, 1996); Agnès Thiercé, *Histoire de l'adolescence (1950–1914)* (Belin, 1999); Louise Jackson, 'Childhood and Youth', in H. G. Cocks and Matt Houlbrook (eds), *Palgrave Advances in the Modern History of Sexuality* (Springer, 2005): 231–55; Matthew Waites, *The Age of Consent: Young People, Sexuality and Citizenship* (Palgrave Macmillan, 2005); Judith R. Walkowitz, *City of Dreadful Delight: Narratives of Sexual Danger in Late-Victorian London* (University of Chicago Press, 1992). Similar trends have been noted outside Britain, in particular in the USA: Mary Odem, *Delinquent Daughters: Protecting and Policing Adolescent Female Sexuality in the United States, 1885–1920* (University of North Carolina Press, 1995); Stephen Robertson, 'Age of consent law and the making of modern childhood in New York City, 1886–1921', *Journal of Social History* 35.4 (2002): 781–98.

[40] Stanley Hall, *Adolescence: Its Psychology and its Relations to Physiology, Anthropology, Sociology, Sex, Crime, Religion and Education* (Sydney Appleton, 1904).

psychological and medical literature while sociologists use 'youth'—and partly a divide in conceptualization. In the latter, psychologists employ 'adolescence' to refer to a psychosocial stage of development characterized by the psychological process of puberty, whereas 'sociologists focus on young people's experiences, their position in society and their unique sub-cultures'.[41]

Historians of nineteenth and twentieth-century Britain have recognized that gender, class, and race impacted the way young people's sexuality was perceived and experienced. Young male sexuality was usually deemed less problematic than that of their female counterparts, and met with greater tolerance.[42] Up until the mid-twentieth century, girls who willingly engaged in sexual intercourse outside marriage or displayed any sexual knowledge were heavily pathologized and labelled as sexual 'delinquents'.[43] Illegitimacy and precocious female sexuality was perceived as a threat to the social order and this was primarily analysed through the prism of social class.[44] Adolescent and youth sexuality was therefore intensely monitored through close, albeit informal, control by parents, relatives, and neighbours and increasingly by the state.[45]

The Second World War was said to have increased the immorality of young women, especially those from the working class, the 'good time girls', and

---

[41] Ofra Koffman, *Towards a Genealogy of Teenage Pregnancy in Britain* (PhD submitted to Goldsmith College, University of London, 2008).

[42] Hera Cook, *The Long Sexual Revolution*. Melanie Tebbutt, *Making Youth: A History of Youth in Modern Britain* (Macmillan Education, 2016): 106; Dyhouse, *Girl Trouble*.

[43] Dyhouse, *Girl Trouble*; Meg Gomersall, *Working-class Girls in Nineteenth Century England: Life, Work and Schooling* (St Martin's Press, 1997); Linda Mahood and Barbara Littlewood, 'The "vicious" girl and the "street-corner" boy: Sexuality and the gendered delinquent in the Scottish child-Saving movement, 1850–1940', *Journal of the History of Sexuality* 4.4 (1994): 549–78.

[44] Dyhouse, *Girl Trouble*; Pat Thane and Tanya Evans, *Sinners? Scroungers? Saints? Unmarried Motherhood in Twentieth-Century England* (Oxford University Press, 2013). By the beginning of the twentieth century, the respectability and sexual passivity of young girls were important elements in middle-class and working-class families. The oral history studies of Simon Szreter and Kate Fisher have shown that sexual puritanism remained very pervasive in the first half of the twentieth century, especially for working-class women, who needed to pretend to be ignorant of sexual knowledge as a sign of respectability. See Szreter and Fisher, *Sex Before the Sexual Revolution*.

[45] Besides this focus on control and repression, historians have also explored the advent of a 'youth culture'. In the course of the twentieth century, youth became increasingly regarded as a specific phase of life with shared experiences referred to as youth culture, identifiable through common 'rites of passage', leisure activities, lifestyle, clothing, music, behaviour patterns, and consumer goods. See, for instance, among other works: Stanley Cohen, *Folk Devils and Moral Panics: The Creation of the Mods and Rockers* (MacGibbon & Kee, 1972); David Fowler, *The First Teenagers: Young Wage-Earners in Interwar Britain* (Woburn Press, 1995); Stephen Humphries, *Hooligans or Rebels? An Oral History of Working Class Childhood and Youth, 1889–1939* (Blackwell, 1981); Claire Langhamer, *Women's Leisure in England, 1920–1960* (Manchester University Press, 2000); Angela McRobbie, *Feminism and Youth Culture: From Jackie to Just Seventeen* (Macmillan, 2000); Chris Tarrant, *Ready Steady Go!: Growing Up in the Fifties and Sixties* (Hamlyn, 1994); Penny Tinkler, *Constructing Girlhood: Popular Magazines for Girls Growing up in England, 1920–1950* (Taylor & Francis, 1995); Penny Tinkler, 'Are you really living? If not, get with it!', *Cultural and Social History* 11.4 (2014): 597–619.

concerns about race spread due to increasing media coverage, often with a racist orientation, of mixed-race sexual relationships.⁴⁶ Gender, age, class, and race remained defining markers of potentially 'problematic sexual behaviours' in contemporary commentators' views, a legacy inherited from the previous century. Even though, by the mid-twentieth century, adolescent heterosexuality was understood as being a normal stage of physical and emotional development, young women's attraction to young men was only accepted as long as they remained virgins.⁴⁷ The age of consent was 16 for heterosexual young people, and following the 1929 Marriage Act, young men and women over 16 could get married. Marriage was still many young girls' main dream for the future.

Historians of youth have also emphasized that from the 1950s onwards, new moral and personal freedom was extended to young people with the advent of teenagers as consumers and new forms of leisure activities.⁴⁸ In postwar Britain, secondary education became the norm (the compulsory school-leaving age was raised to 15 in 1947, and not to 16 until 1972), better employment opportunities for teenagers became available, and the number of young women living in bedsits rose drastically.⁴⁹ From the 1950s, there were renewed anxieties about illegitimacy and premarital sex, and growing concerns around the spread of venereal disease. The 1950s and 1960s saw the emergence of teenage pregnancy as an object of policy intervention and this new focus was partly due to the growing influence of psychology on government work.⁵⁰ The teenage birth rate in England and Wales had risen steadily until, at its peak in the early 1970s, 'it was three times the rate in the early 1940s'.⁵¹ The rate then decreased until 1977, rose again for three years, then

---

⁴⁶ Lucy Bland, 'White women and men of colour: Miscegenation fears in Britain after the Great War', *Gender & History* 17.1 (2005): 29–61; Lucy Bland, *Britain's 'Brown Babies': The Stories of Children Born to Black GIs and White Women in the Second World War* (Manchester University Press, 2019).

⁴⁷ Louise A. Jackson, '"The coffee club menace": Policing youth, leisure and sexuality in post-war Manchester', *Cultural and Social History* 5.3 (2008): 293; Hall, *Sex, Gender and Social Change in Britain*, 167–84.

⁴⁸ Langhamer, *Women's Leisure in England*; McRobbie, *Feminism and Youth Culture*; Jackson, 'The coffee club menace'; John Springhall, *Youth, Popular Culture and Moral Panics: Penny Gaffs to Gangsta-rap, 1830–1996* (Basingstoke, 1996).

⁴⁹ Madeleine Arnot, Miriam David, and Gaby Weiner, *Closing the Gender Gap: Post-war Education and Social Change* (Cambridge University Press, 1999).

⁵⁰ This concern led the government to offer ways of alleviating teenage unmarried motherhood; for instance, the setting up of the St Christopher's Mother and Baby Home in Lambeth by London County Council in 1961. Ofra Koffman, 'Children having children? Religion, psychology and the birth of the teenage pregnancy problem', *History of the Human Sciences* 25.1 (2012): 119–34. Ofra Koffman, *Fertile Bodies, Immature Minds?: Morality, Psychology and the Birth of Teenage Pregnancy* (PhD dissertation, 2008).

⁵¹ Judith Bury, *Teenage Pregnancy in Britain* (Birth Control Trust, 1984): 7.

reduced again. In 1981, the birth rate among teenagers in Britain was the lowest for more than 20 years.[52] The rate then rose sharply again and teenage pregnancy became a matter of public health concern, amounting to a 'subdued moral panic' about unemployed teenagers who became pregnant during this time. This panic had much to do with the fact that these young women did not enter the labour market but instead lived on state support benefits, a particular focus of the Conservative government.[53] Class was a central facet of this debate; race also played a pivotal role in the shaming of teenage mothers.

From the 1950s, there was also a renewed interest in adolescence as a period of transition between childhood and adulthood in the sociological and medical literature. Drawing heavily on Freud's theory of psychosexual development, psychoanalysts like Anna Freud and Peter Blos published major studies on the subject.[54] Adolescence was perceived as a transitional stage, an essential process where young people became more mature. However, adolescents needed guidance throughout this process, and adults were responsible for the smooth transition to sexual maturity, especially for young women. The growing body of advice-based literature during this period that aimed to prepare young girls for marriage and motherhood testifies to this new concern. At a time when marriage was idealized as an intimate, emotional relationship that contributed to personal fulfilment and where mutual sexual pleasure was central, it was believed that young girls had to learn the basics of sex and reproduction—the facts of life—to ensure that they properly matured into good wives and mothers.[55] As a result, sex education in school became increasingly valued.[56]

As this overview illustrates, historians have been researching youth sexuality for some time. However, they have mainly concentrated on 'problem youth', that is, sexual delinquents, unmarried mothers, and so on. Therefore, there exists a lack of research on 'normal' teenagers, with the exception of Hannah Charnock's work on female teenagers' sexuality and friendship.[57] She

---

[52] Ibid. [53] McRobbie, *Feminism and Youth Culture*, 220.

[54] Peter Blos, *On Adolescence: A Psychoanalytic Interpretation* (Free Press, 1962), chapter 7; Anna Freud, 'Adolescence', *The Psychoanalytic Study of the Child* 13.1 (1958): 255–78.

[55] On marriage as an emotional and intimate relationship see: Langhamer, *The English in Love*; Janet Finch and Penny Summerfield, 'Social Reconstruction and the Emergence of Companionate Marriage, 1945–59', in David Clark (ed.), *Marriage, Domestic Life and Social Change: Writings for Jacqueline Burgoyne* (Routledge, 1991): 6–27. On the new prevalence of mutual sexual pleasure see Caroline Rusterholz, '"You can't dismiss that as being less happy, you see it is different": Sexual therapy in 1950s England', *Twentieth Century British History* 30.3 (2019): 375–98.

[56] Lesley A. Hall, 'Eyes Tightly Shut, Lying Rigidly Still and Thinking of England?: British Women and Sex From Marie Stopes to Hite 2000,' in Claudia Nelson and Michelle H. Martin (eds), *Sexual Pedagogies: Sex Education in Britain, Australia, and America, 1879–2000* (Palgrave Macmillan, 2004): 53–71.

[57] Hannah Charnock, 'Teenage girls, female friendship and the making of the sexual revolution in England, 1950–1980', Historical Journal 63.4 (2020): 1032–53.

has shown that knowledge about sex became increasingly valued among young people in the 1970s and that peer opinions were key to young people's sexual subjectivity. While Charnock offers fresh insights into young people's experiences and networks, she does not address the role of the voluntary sector in fostering sexual knowledge. This book is therefore the first of its kind that looks at the history of young people's sexuality, its monitoring in postwar Britain, and its relationship with sexual politics and health. In addition, this study focuses on the ways that Brook adapted to changes in youth sexual culture and experiences.

A note is needed here about terminology. Contemporary commentators used the terms 'young people' or 'girls and boys' for any unmarried people between 18 and 25 years old. At first, unmarried sexuality was an object of debate and a source of anxiety in the 1960s, due to the debate around whether unmarried people should have access to family planning services in a context where the FPA still favoured married people. Once this was resolved in 1974 when contraception became free for individuals, single or married, the focus shifted, and teenagers became an object of anxiety over the following decades.

History of expertise and the voluntary sector

This book makes also a key contribution to the literature around the role that charities and the voluntary sector held in the sexual politics and sexual culture of postwar Britain. Brook members played a significant role in shaping public policy and mediating public discussions about young people's sexual experiences. Broadly, over this period, access to sexual health services evolved from being provided privately through Brook, to being partially financed by local authorities and the Department of Health and Social Security, to becoming a major target of government policy in the 1990s. As experts, Brook members acted as mediators between the state and young people's needs. Following the pioneering work of Michel Foucault, many historians have stressed that experts became central social and political actors in the so-called 'liberal governmentality'.[58] According to Foucault, the notion of 'governmentality' encompasses the questions of ' how to govern oneself, how to be governed, by

---

[58] Michel Foucault, *La Volonté de Savoir: Histoire de La Sexualité 1* (Gallimard, 1976); Michel Foucault, *Security, Territory, Population: Lectures at the Collège de France 1977–1978* (Palgrave Macmillan, 2007); Ludovine Bantigny, Christina Bard, and Claire Blandin (eds), 'L'expertise face aux enjeux biopolitiques. Genre, jeune, sexualité', Special Issue of *Histoire@Politique* 14.2 (2011), online; Mitchell Dean, *Governmentality: Power and Rule in Modern Society* (Sage, 2010).

whom the people will accept being governed, how to become the best possible governor'. In the 'liberal governmentality' that has characterized Western societies since the turn of the nineteenth century, new intermediaries between the state and the individual, such as the psy-profession and other 'expert professions', have played an active role in guiding individuals towards a 'better' management of the self.[59] They regulate the 'conduct of the self'.[60] These experts were and still are purveyors of differentiated norms of conducts and behaviours based on gender, age, class, and race. Nikolas Rose has argued that the development of 'psy knowledge and practices' played a pivotal role in creating a choosing, willing, and self-governing self in the second half of the twentieth century.[61] Similarly, Mathew Thomson has shown the reach and variety of popular psychology of the mid-century where the 'development of self' was perceived as a 'psychological, interiorised journey towards integration of personality'.[62]

Moreover, recent research has emphasized the continuous role played by voluntary organizations in Britain during the long twentieth century.[63] It has shown that in the mixed economy of welfare, charities and non-governmental organizations were crucial in filling the gaps left by the state's welfare provision. A strand of scholarship has paid attention to the nature of the relationship between the state and voluntary sectors.[64] Other historians have emphasized the paradoxical role of voluntary agencies in both support and control.[65] For instance, Pat Thane and Tanya Evans have explored the experiences of unmarried mothers over the twentieth century, foregrounding the relative disadvantage they experienced and the essential work done by

---

[59] It is not to say that psy-disciplines were not useful in non-liberal governmentality. On the contrary, research has shown the use and dismissal of psychology by the Nazi and communists.

[60] Nikolas Rose, *Inventing Our Selves: Psychology, Power, and Personhood* (Cambridge University Press, 1998): 29.

[61] Ibid.; Nikolas Rose, *Governing the Soul: The Shaping of the Private Self* (Free Association Books, 1999).

[62] Mathew Thomson, *Psychological Subjects: Identity, Culture and Health in Twentieth-century Britain* (Oxford, 2006): 266; Michael Shapira, *The War Inside: Psychoanalysis, Total War, and the Making of the Democratic Self in Postwar Britain* (Cambridge, 2012).

[63] Jane Lewis, 'Family provision of health and welfare in the mixed economy of care in the late nineteenth and twentieth centuries', *Social History of Medicine* 8.1 (1995): 1–16; Matthew Hilton et al., *The Politics of Expertise: How NGOs Shaped Modern Britain* (Oxford University Press, 2013); Jennifer Crane, *Child Protection in England, 1960–2000: Expertise, Experience and Emotions* (Palgrave Macmillan, 2018).

[64] John Davis, 'Reshaping the Welfare State? Voluntary Action and Community in London, 1960–1975', in Lawrence Goldman (ed.), *Welfare and Social Policy in Britain Since 1870: Essays in Honour of Jose Harris* (Oxford University Press, 2019): 198–212; Julie Grier, 'A Spirit of "Friendly Rivalry"?: Voluntary Societies and the Formation of Post-War Child Welfare Legislation in Britain', in Jon Lawrence and Pat Starkey (eds), *Child Welfare and Social Action in the Nineteenth and Twentieth Centuries: International Perspectives* (Liverpool University Press, 2001): 234–55.

[65] Cox, *Gender, Justice and Welfare*.

voluntary agencies in supporting them. They identified a discrepancy between the public condemnations of unmarried motherhood and the more complex and messy experiences of unmarried mothers, who were often supported by their families.[66] However, what remains somehow hidden in this history, is the role of sexual health charities and their relationship with the National Health Service and local authorities. This book explores the relationship between Brook and local authorities, as well as the aims behind the charity. It examines whether Brook resulted from the traditional will to monitor teenage female sexuality due to fears over young women's increasing autonomy—Helen Brook hence positioning herself as a 'moral entrepreneur'—or from the will to value young people's search for sexual pleasure.

'Race' and sexual politics

This book makes a contribution to the understudied history of race and reproductive politics in postwar Britain. While race is a central category of analysis in many recent works focusing on postwar Britain, from studies looking at Enoch Powell and his notorious anti-immigration narrative, to works on citizenship, belonging, and race and what it meant to be British in the postwar period, to anti-Black racism, the grassroots activism of the minoritized population, and their lived experience in a decolonized Britain, little is known about race and sexual politics in Britain.[67] By providing a historical perspective on disparities in sexual health services, this study gives voice to criticisms of the persistent racism that have characterized British sexual politics.

Following the Second World War, Britain faced a labour shortage. Despite a publicity campaign designed by the government to draw workers to 'essential' but unattractive industries, the main industries still faced an acute labour shortage. As a result, the government started to consider immigration and

---

[66] Thane and Evans, *Sinners? Scroungers? Saints?*
[67] On Enoch Powell see Camilla Schofield, *Enoch Powell and the Making of Postcolonial Britain* (Cambridge University Press, 2013); Sally Tomlinson, 'Enoch Powell: Empires, immigrants and education', *Race Ethnicity and Education* 21.1 (2018): 1–14; Shirin Hirsch, *In the Shadow of Enoch Powell: Race, Locality and Resistance* (Manchester University Press, 2020). On anti-racism resistances see Kennetta Hammond Perry, *London is the Place for Me: Black Britons, Citizenship and the Politics of Race* (Oxford University Press, 2016); Rob Waters, *Thinking Black: Britain, 1964–1985* (University of California Press, 2018); Kieran Connell, *Black Handsworth: Race in 1980s Britain* (University of California Press, 2019); Jordanna Bailkin, *Afterlife of Empire* (University of California Press, 2012); James Hampshire, *Citizenship and Belonging: Immigration and the Politics of Demographic Governance in Postwar Britain* (Palgrave Macmillan, 2005); Kathleen Paul, *Whitewashing Britain: Race and Citizenship in the Postwar Era* (Cornell University Press, 1997).

citizenship as a potential solution to the economic crisis. European and Irish workers were encouraged to move to Britain. In 1948, the British Nationality Act conferred citizenship on Commonwealth subjects, granting them the right to settle in Britain. As a result, more than half a million non-white migrants journeyed to Britain from different parts of the British Commonwealth between the late 1940s and the early 1960s.[68] This mass migration created many anxieties. Fears that 'foreigners' were reproducing at a far greater rate than the 'local' population emerged, giving rise to a new definition of what it meant to be 'British'.[69] At that time, a race discourse emerged that focused on the alleged hyper-fertility of the Black population. This discourse helped to create an ideal representation of home and family to which Black families did not belong.[70] Black male sexuality was depicted as a threat to white women. Similarly, recent research by Anne Hanley has shown the advent of racial stereotypes around Black male sexuality and promiscuity between the 1950s and 1960s in the service of a nationalist anti-immigrant agenda.[71] Black men were accused of spreading venereal diseases. In 1962, with the Commonwealth Immigrants Act, restrictions were imposed on the rights of entry for individuals from South Asia, Africa, and the Caribbean. In addition, racism shaped the delivery of NHS services. The first research undertaken in order to denounce the racism in the healthcare system was carried out by Black feminist activists who were heavily involved with the Organization of Women of African and Asian Descent (OWAAD). Authored by Beverley Bryan, Stella Dadzie, and Suzanne Scafe, *The Heart of the Race: Black Women's Lives in Britain* was and still is a powerful book that gave voice to Black women's experiences in postwar Britain.[72] It exposed the daily racism they faced and emphasized doctors' and politicians' obsession with their fertility. Black women's bodies were a site of forced experimentation through birth control, as illustrated by the widely prescribed Depo-Provera and its dramatic effects on women's health.[73] In addition, sterilization was widely

---

[68] Hammond Perry, *London is the Place for Me*, 7: Roberta Bivins, *Contagious Communities: Medicine, Migration, and the NHS in Post-war Britain* (Oxford University Press, 2015).

[69] Paul, *Whitewashing Britain*.

[70] Wendy Webster, *Imagining Home: Gender, Race and National Identity, 1945–1964* (Routledge, 1998).

[71] Anne Hanley, 'Migration, racism and sexual health in postwar Britain', *History Workshop Journal* 94 (2022): 202–22.

[72] Beverley Bryan, Stella Dadzie, and Suzanne Scafe, *The Heart of the Race: Black Women's Lives in Britain* (Virago, 1985).

[73] Caitlin Lambert, '"The objectionable injectable": Recovering the lost history of the WLM through the Campaign Against Depo-Provera', *Women's History Review* 29.3 (2020): 520–39.

encouraged. Recently, Cecily Jones has argued that 'race and reproductive politics have been intimately entwined in Britain over centuries of colonialism and imperialism'.[74]

While this body of scholarship has stressed the use of racial stereotypes, there have been no studies considering the ways that race played out in the public debate about youth sexuality and the expansion of sexual health services for young people. By taking age, race, class, and gender as categories of analysis, the book recognizes that the availability of contraception through Brook did not affect young people equally. Age was also a central issue of contention. Under-16s were welcome and provided for in the centre, but conservative lobbies relentlessly campaigned to assert parental authority over medical confidentiality.

Sources and methodology

This book combines the history of youth, the history of sexuality, the history of expertise, and the history of race and reproductive politics through a case study that explores the changing landscape of young people's intimate lives in postwar Britain and takes their lived experiences seriously. The sources used in the book are varied and reflect different points of view, all illuminating different facets of young people's sexual history. Taken together, they offer an insight into cultural, political, and medical ideals and norms around young people's sexuality as well as individual attitudes and subjectivities. Five types of sources constitute the backbone of the book's narrative.

First, the official archives of Brook offer fascinating material about the scope of the clinic's work. Held at the Wellcome Library, they contain the minutes of the board and sub-committees, annual reports of the local centres, and published and educational material created by Brook. These archives allow for detailed documentation of the evolution of the centres and their activities. Nevertheless, they also contain some gaps. Early reports about the work of the local clinics are missing, while access to files containing information on clients is restricted due to data protection, limiting the scope of this book and preventing the analysis of significant material that explores young people's experiences. This lack of sources for documenting clients' lived experiences

---

[74] Cecily Jones, '"Human weeds, not fit to breed?": African Caribbean women and reproductive disparities in Britain', *Critical Public Health* 23.1 (2013): 49–61.

could be partially addressed using the case stories mentioned in the annual reports, articles written by Brook staff that mentioned case stories and articles published in the mass media that covered the running of the centres. Case stories are not neutral examples but instead problematic sources; though they were presented as 'reflecting typical clients', they were seemingly selected for their potential to attract attention and provoke emotion. Furthermore, they are few in number; this is mainly due to the fact that Brook members acknowledged the unethical aspect of presenting cases to the press:

> We are constantly being asked to provide 'cases' for interviews with journalists, radio, and TV producers, and though we would welcome the opportunity to show the kind of work we do, we cannot ask young people to expose themselves to the public even though it might result in more understanding and support. They are too vulnerable and public reaction can be pitiless.[75]

Second, this book makes use of social science surveys on sex and sexual relationships carried out during the period under study. Sex surveys have recently attracted increasing attention. Historians of sexuality, social historians, and even historians of religion have carried out detailed analyses of the 'Little Kinsey' survey in Britain, reassessing the idea of a sexual revolution. However, sex and social surveys carried out in the 1970s, 1980s, and 1990s have received less attention. While social surveys tend to dilute the individual experience into aggregated data, they are nevertheless essential in providing a broader picture of changes in sexual norms and behaviours and cultural attitudes to sexuality. In addition, surveys carried out by Brook members, as well as statistics from the centres, provide rich insights into clients' sexual behaviours.

Third, this book relies heavily on newspapers and teenage magazines in order to understand public debate on the subject. Newspapers reflect and shape norms around young people's sexuality. Many recent studies have analysed the press in order to assess changes and continuities in topics including fatherhood, motherhood, working mothers, sex and family life, understanding of health, and sexuality.[76] Adrian Bingham has emphasized the role played by the mass media in shaping individuals' perceptions of

---

[75] 'Brook London Annual reports, 1981', in SA/BRO/D/10/1/2, Wellcome Library, London.
[76] Laura King, *Family Men: Fatherhood and Masculinity in Britain, c.1914–1960* (Oxford University Press, 2015).

'legitimate' or 'illegitimate' topics of discussion. Mass media helped redefine the borders of what was acceptable and legitimate, thus positioning sexuality at the fore of public debates in the mid-twentieth century.[77] This book used the major broadsheets and tabloids, namely the *Guardian*, the *Observer*, the *Daily Mirror*, the *Daily Telegraph*, the *Daily Mail*, the *Daily Express*, the *Birmingham Post*, the *Evening Standard*, the *Sunday Mercury*, the *Sunday Telegraph*, *The People*, and the *Times*. The digital archives of five of these—the *Daily Mirror*, the *Telegraph*, the *Guardian*, the *Birmingham Post*, and the *Times*—have been extensively researched, while I refer to the other newspapers at specific points of debate. In addition, the Brook archives contained clippings of articles covering the work of the clinic and related controversies. Complementing these sources, two young people's magazines have also been extensively analysed: *Just Seventeen* and *Nineteen*. Their problem pages offered two types of information: young people's sexual anxieties and problems which helped us to determine why some visited Brook, and the answers and categories used by experts in their replies. Agony aunts regularly advised readers to turn to Brook for help with contraception and unwanted pregnancies. Dr Fay Hutchinson, medical officer of one of the London Brook centres, worked as an agony aunt for *Nineteen* magazine. These teenage magazines are especially interesting since they featured articles on sexual health written by Brook staff. For instance, press officer Suzie Hayman wrote several articles for *Just Seventeen* on sexual health. In addition to these sources, a small number of topical films, novels, and memoirs, as well as sex advice literature, have been used to gauge public debate on youth sexuality.

Fourth, government papers and parliamentary debates, Medical Officer of Health reports, and medical journals complement this picture, exploring official views on teenage sexuality and helping to understand its 'problematization'.

Finally, 16 oral history interviews with former counsellors (nine) and clients of Brook (seven) have been conducted in line with best practice, with support on ethical issues provided by the Cambridge Research Ethics Office, to document young people's experience with Brook. Existing oral history interviews with staff of Brook as well as with former clients held at the Wellcome Library and British Library complement these sources. The value of oral history for exploring intimate subject, for understanding the feelings, views, and experiences of women and men who would not otherwise enter the historical record and for reassessing common assumptions about the period does not need to be

---

[77] Adrian Bingham, *Family Newspapers?: Sex, Private Life, and the British Popular Press 1918–1978* (Oxford University Press, 2009).

proven any longer.[78] Oral history interviews are rich sources for analysing individual subjectivity and allow for the exploration of lived experiences with sexual health services.

The structure of the book

Drawing on a wide range of sources, this study is divided into seven chapters, and traces chronologically and thematically the many ways through which youth sexuality was publicly perceived, monitored, and individually experienced.

Chapter 1 sets the stage for a study of teenage sex. It provides an overview of the social, cultural, and political context that made young people's sexuality an object of sociological inquiry and public discussion, and paints a picture of youth sexual behaviour through statistics and data gathered in sexual health surveys during the period under study. It then turns to the way youth sexuality was perceived and debated by experts and the mass media. It argues that a new sexual openness in mass media was noticeable in the 1950s, giving rise to a new permissiveness in the 1960s, and this resulted in generational tensions. The chapter then turns to the key players in sexual health services before the opening of Brook, namely the Family Planning Association and Marie Stopes Foundation, and highlights their main values. It shows their reluctance to engage with young, unmarried sexuality. Finally, it focuses on the key role played by Helen Brook in expanding sexual health services to unmarried young women. In constructing the need for a service for unmarried people, Brook faced being accused of encouraging promiscuity. This resulted in the production of a narrative that emphasized the notion of responsibility and moral guidance for unmarried people to avoid unwanted babies. This framework retained and fused the old FPA's argument of having desired children within the family with the new argument that unmarried girls should therefore be given the means to avoid illegitimate births and in so doing they were acting responsibly.

Chapter 2 describes the conditions under which a selection of centres were implemented. It takes the opening of five Brook branches in Britain and their local centres (London, Birmingham, Bristol, Edinburgh, and Liverpool) as case

---

[78] Fisher, *Birth Control*; Laura Kelly, *Contraception and Modern Ireland: A Social History c.1922-1992* (Cambridge University Press, 2023); Szreter and Fisher, *Sex Before the Sexual Revolution*; Caroline Rusterholz, *Deux enfants c'est deja pas mal, Famille et fecondite en Suisse, 1955-1970* (Antipodes, 2017).

studies to illuminate the impact of locality on the controversy about young people's sexuality and shows the intertwining of local and sexual politics. Each case study reveals the discursive and political boundaries of the definition of legitimate sexuality, and sheds light on the key players behind the centres and their opponents.

Chapter 3 focuses on the way that Brook members shaped reproductive politics, the alliances they formed, and the lobby strategies they developed in order to expand the provision of contraception for young people over time. The chapter argues that Brook members should be considered activists, and explores the resources on which they drew and the networks they mobilized in order to advance their political and sexual agenda of providing free contraception and sexual advice to young, unmarried people. The chapter first focuses on the microcosm of advocacy for contraception, which saw individuals, such as founder Helen Brook, Chairman Caroline Woodroffe, Press Officer Suzie Hayman, Brook Board member and Chair Dilys Cossey, Chief Officer Alison Frater, and Policy Director Alison Hadley, navigating between different health charities and organizations such as the Family Planning Association, the Abortion Law Reform Association, the Birth Control Trust, and the Pregnancy Advisory Services. It then moves to address the ways Brook members dealt with issues around fundings. Finally, it explores the various key sexual health policies that Brook fought or helped to implement over the years. Taking a chronological approach, it shows how Brook members increasingly capitalized on their expertise in order to influence policy makers. Over the years, they moved from an outsider position to one of prominence in the British landscape of sexual politics. This chapter concentrates on landmark legislations and Brook's role in the debate, from the 1974 DHSS guidance to the setting up of the *Health of the Nation*.

Chapter 4 considers the setting up of the centre from material and sensory angles. It shows the criteria that were taken into consideration when opening a centre, and underlines the importance of the location, its accessibility, and the layout of the centre in enabling the smooth running of the latter. In addition to the materiality of the centre, the sensory element was key to making sure young people felt welcome. Brook recognized that an agreeable atmosphere depended as much on the staff as it did on the centre's decoration and ambience. Staff were recruited based on their attitude towards young people's sexuality. Music, biscuits, tea, and coffee were all elements that contributed to creating a relaxed and friendly environment. In addition, the chapter looks at the location of the centres and what this reveals about regional inequalities and about who was thought to be in need of sexual help (and monitoring). It shows that in the 1970s and 1980s, Brook opened some centres in deprived and mixed-race neighbourhoods such as Brixton in London and Handsworth in Birmingham. In so doing, they targeted minoritized young people, who were defined as a vulnerable category, while at the same time believed to be extremely hard to reach.

Chapter 5 provides an overview of the demographics of the clients and how they changed over time. It shows that an increasing number of under-16s attended the services over the years and discusses the impact that restrictive policies, such as restricting the provision of contraception to over-16s, had on the demographics of the clinic's attendees. In addition, the chapter explores the absence of data on ethnicity and its related implications for addressing the needs of specific communities. Focusing again on the five case studies of London, Birmingham, Bristol, Edinburgh, and Liverpool, the chapter explores young people's lived experiences with the centres and the impact their visits had on their lives, future perspectives, and opportunities. Drawing on case histories, oral history interviews, and media coverage of these centres, the chapter argues that finding a friendly, non-judgmental and confidential service—a place where anxieties, fears, and emotions could be expressed— was central for young people. They valued self-determination and praised the service for taking them seriously. Some even went on to work for Brook. In addition, this chapter explores the impact that clients had on the development of sexual counselling through the references made to clients' needs in the development of sexual health guidelines. From the start, Brook valued clients' experiences with the centre. However, with the advent of the idea of the patient as a consumer in the 1980s, the client's experience became paramount in the way Brook envisaged their work. They devised several ways of assessing the quality of their services and set the standard for a client-centred approach to sexual health services in the 1990s.

Chapter 6 looks in particular at the details of the services from an intersectional perspective, focusing on the content and evolution of counselling services. This chapter explores what Brook members defined as the key components and values underpinning counselling. It argues that Brook pioneered a new form of counselling where trust, confidentiality, and a non-judgmental attitude (at least in front of the client) were paramount elements. It then moves on to analyse in detail the three types of counselling offered in the centres. By looking closely at the content of the sexual counselling and medical guidance, it identifies norms around a model of 'good' and 'bad' sexual behaviours and how these norms were class-based and racialized. Particular attention is paid to the categories used to frame the individuals

24   RESPONSIBLE PLEASURE

seeking sexual health advice, or perceived as needing sexual health intervention. In addition, the chapter looks at the methods prescribed to the patients and what they were told about 'responsible' sexual behaviours.

Chapter 7 evaluates the outreach activity of Brook through case studies on public health and education campaigns over time. Taking a chronological approach, it focuses on several campaigns that reveal broader contemporary concerns. In the 1970s, following the Chronically Sick and Disabled Person Act of 1970, Brook pioneered a new initiative in improving access to sexual health information and services for young people with disabilities. In the 1980s, Brook worked closely with the FPA to try to encourage boys to share responsibility for birth control. Similarly, in the 1980s, they tried to encourage young people from ethnic minority backgrounds to attend Brook centres. From the 1980s to the 1990s, they developed visual and creative material to inform young people about AIDS. The 1990s were also the decade where the centrality of confidentiality became paramount in the advertising of sexual health services, and Brook played a key role in informing public health policy on the matter. In addition, this chapter explores instances of resistance and censorship that hindered the work of the charity. Finally, this chapter explores the way Brook worked with the mass media. From the time of Brook's creation, its members were quick to understand the power of media in tackling prejudices against unmarried sexuality. They worked in close connection with several newspapers and teenage magazines.

The book ends with a Conclusion that reviews the book's main findings. This book therefore provides the first study of young people's sexuality and their relationship with sexual health services in postwar Britain. While many young people did not use sexual health services and relied on other forms of support, those who did and the reasons for their choice tell us a lot about young people's expectations and fears connected to sexuality.

1
The Context

Youth, Sex, and Public Anxieties in the 1950s–1960s

There existed a core of assumptions around British young people in the 1960s. Contemporary commentators presented them as leisurely and materially oriented, permissive, free, rebellious, promiscuous, sexually precocious, delinquent, and in a perpetual clash with their parents. These were and remain part of the popular memory of the 1960s.[1] It was against this backdrop of moral panic around young people's behaviour and sexual morality that the first Brook Advisory Centre opened in 1964 in London.

This chapter provides an overview of the major changes that impacted young people's lives in the postwar years and led to their sexuality becoming the object of increasing scrutiny. Indeed, to understand Brook's significance and impact, it is important to replace its opening in the historical context of the 1950s and 1960s and in the longer history of what we today call 'sexual and reproductive health services'. This chapter first offers a brief overview of the social, cultural, and political changes that affected young people and then moves on to analyse the ways through which social investigators, doctors, and journalists framed young people's sexuality. It then focuses on the major players in sexual health services and sheds light on the reasons for creating a new charity specifically dedicated to providing contraception to young unmarried people.

---

[1] See in particular Helena Mills, 'Using the personal to critique the popular: Women's memories of 1960s youth', *Contemporary British History* 30.4 (2016): 463–83; John Clarke, Stuart Hall, Tony Jefferson, and Brian Roberts, 'Subcultures, Cultures and Class: A Theoretical Overview', in Stuart Hall and Tony Jefferson (eds), *Resistance through Rituals: Youth Subcultures in Post-war Britain* (Routledge, 1996): 9–74; Mark Donnelly, 'Sixties Britain: The Cultural Politics of Historiography', in Trevor Harris and Monia O'Brien Castro (eds), *Preserving the Sixties* (Palgrave Macmillan, 2014): 10–30.; Hall, *Sex, Gender and Social Change*; Louise Jackson and Angela Bartie, *Policing Youth* (Manchester University Press, 2014).

The postwar years and young people

The postwar years saw a new emphasis on young people. This was partly because young people were more visible, given that they were more numerous. A postwar baby boom had meant that the number of live births rose substantially in 1945–1947, and this new cohort reached adolescence in the late 1950s and 1960s. This public concern about young people was also closely associated with the advent of the teenager as a consumer. The end of rationing, the opening up of the market, and a new postwar economic affluence were all factors conducive to new leisure activities and growing consumerism. Average real wages increased by 25% between 1938 and 1958, but those of adolescents increased by 50%.[2] This greater disposable income was spent on a variety of new consumer goods, such as record players, cinema tickets, clothes, and magazines. This rising affluence also altered peer dynamics; new forms of inclusions and exclusions were created along the lines of 'material markers of social status'.[3] In addition, peer values and opinion became paramount to adolescence, as many contemporary sociological studies argued.[4] This peer interaction was reinforced by compulsory school attendance; the school-leaving age rose from 14 to 15 in 1947 and then to 16 in 1972. In addition, co-educational comprehensive secondary education became increasingly common from the 1960s, which reinforced opportunities for mixing between sexes. With rising prosperity in the 1950s, young couples were increasingly able to establish their own home, which resulted in a drop in the average age of marriage. Age at marriage fell from 27 for men and 24.5 for women in 1945–1950 to 24.6 for men and 22.5 for women in 1966–1970; this led many historians to consider this period as the golden age of marriage.[5] Physical maturity also occurred earlier in young people. On average, girls reached menarche by the age of 13.5 in the 1960s, compared with age 16–17 a century earlier.[6]

Historians have also shown that the generation of women who grew up after the Second World War participated in major social, cultural, and demographic changes. An increasing number of women undertook higher

---

[2] Jeffrey Weeks, *Sex Politics and Society: The Regulation of Sexuality since 1800* (Routledge, 2018): 276.

[3] See also Christian Bugge, '"Selling Youth in the Age of Affluence": Marketing to Youth in Britain since 1959', in Lawrence Black and Hugh Pemberton (eds), *An Affluent Society? Britain's Post-War 'Golden Age' Revisited* (Ashgate, 2004): 185–202.

[4] James Hemming, *Problems of Adolescent Girls* (Heinemann, 1960). On the impact of peers on sexual knowledge see Charnock, 'Teenage girls, female friendship and the making of the sexual revolution in England, 1950–1980', *Historical Journal* 63.4 (2020): 1032–53.

[5] Several demographers have insisted that the baby boom was before anything else a marriage boom.

[6] Tebbutt, *Making Youth,* 127.

education; women were married at a younger age than the previous generation; early marriage was more common among working-class girls, and they were married in greater numbers; and women grew up in a relatively affluent society and with a wider range of professional opportunities than the previous generation. This new relative independence for young women created anxieties, as Carol Dyhouse has shown. In particular, sexual precocity among young women raised concerns.[7] As Louise Jackson and Angela Bartie have argued, 'the "problem girl", the "good time girl" and the "wayward girl" were terms that were widely used across the period to describe the sexual delinquent'.[8] Young girls who engaged in sexual relationships were accused of spreading venereal diseases. In 1960s Scotland, as historian Roger Davidson has shown, medical experts continued to blame adolescent girls for the rise in the venereal disease (VD) rate.[9] As Penny Tinkler has shown, there was also a new emphasis on self-realization for young single girls through young people's magazines in the late 1950s and early 1960s. These new cultural expectations for young women enjoined them to 'be themselves' and live fun and fulfilling lives, opening up alternative paths to the abrupt and traditional trajectory of living at home until marriage; however, heterosexual love and marriage still remained the most attractive means of self-actualization.[10] Youth magazines were central in the diffusion of the new model of self-expression and self-realization and this early form of individualism. However, these competing visions of the self created anxieties for young single women, who struggled to conform to ideal notions of independence.[11]

In addition to this focus on increasing independence, historians have demonstrated that there were also concerns about migration and romantic relationships between young men from the West Indies and white girls. Indeed, young Black men were accused of seducing white young women and of spreading venereal diseases.[12]

Debating youth sexuality: doctors and social scientists

Political and medical anxiety over young people's sexuality was not new. The difference in postwar Britain was the fact that young people's sexual

---

[7] Dyhouse, *Girl Trouble*.   [8] Jackson and Bartie, *Policing Youth*, 117.
[9] Roger Davidson, *Dangerous Liaisons: A Social History of Venereal Disease in Twentieth-Century Scotland* (Rodopi, 2000): 249.
[10] Tinkler, 'Are you really living?'.
[11] Dyhouse, *Girl Trouble*; Jackson, 'The Coffee Club menace'.
[12] Webster, *Imagining Home*; Bivins, *Contagious Communities*; Adrian Bingham, *Family Newspapers?: Sex, Private Life, and the British Popular Press 1918–1978* (Oxford University Press, 2009).

behaviours were scrutinized intensely. Indeed, these behaviours attracted growing attention in the second half of the twentieth century due to anxieties around increasing illegitimacy, incidence of venereal diseases, young people's growing freedom, and alleged generational tensions. Sexual mores were said to be loosening for young people, which caused concern about a moral collapse in traditional values. These concerns were also partially class-based, since it was mostly the births outside marriage among young middle-class women that caused alarm. Mass media and contemporary commentators, such as religious authorities, doctors, and sexual health advocates, debated the reasons behind these trends and offered diverging solutions. This testified to the fact that young people's sexuality and premarital sex had become an area of concern, especially young women's sexual behaviour. These competing views show a lack of consensus among authorities, revealing that there was neither a single understanding of the problem of youth sexuality nor a single solution to it.

Teenage sexual activity, the illegitimacy rate, and sexual activity outside marriage have been the objects of several sociological and statistical investigations and surveys during the period under study, offering a glimpse into the sexual behaviours of young people. In 1939, official statistics about premarital pregnancy were collated for the first time: almost 22.5% of brides were pregnant at marriage. Among mothers under 20, at least 42% of first births had been premaritally conceived; the figure was 31% among those aged 21, 22% at 22, 10% at 25–29, and 8% at 30–34. The rate of premarital conception among women under 20 was 47.9% in 1945, 56.4% in 1955, and 57.1% in 1965.[13] The number of live births registered as illegitimate remained at a low level until the end of the 1950s—50.1 per 1,000 births in 1956–1960. However, from the early 1960s this number rose rapidly: 69 in 1961–1965, 86.8 in 1971–1975, and 104.6 in 1976–1980.[14] In particular, between 1962 and 1972, illegitimate births among women under 20 years as a percentage of all live births among this age group increased from 20.7% to 27.5%.[15]

The age of first sexual intercourse fell from a range of 19–23 years in 1951–1955 to 17–21 years in 1966–1970. Hera Cook, Adrian Bingham, and Callum Brown, among others, have analysed sexual surveys and highlighted some defining trends.[16] Callum Brown in particular has argued that there was

---

[13] Pat Thane, *Happy Families?: History and Family Policy* (British Academy, 2011). [14] Ibid.
[15] Christine Farrell, *My Mother Said... the Way Young People Learned about Sex and Birth Control* (Routledge & Kegan Paul, 1978).
[16] Bingham, *Family Newspapers?*; Brown, 'Sex, Religion and the Single Woman'; Cook, *The Long Sexual Revolution*.

a gradual change in tolerance in attitudes towards premarital sex from the early 1960s.[17]

Mass Observation's 'Little Kinsey' report of 1949 offered interesting information on the perception of 2,052 ordinary individuals chosen at random from the streets of various British cities. Much has been written about it and its reception in the mass media. According to the results, 44% felt that 'standards of sexual morality' were 'declining', and only 17% thought they were improving, while 63% disapproved of extra-marital relations, which led the researchers to conclude that 'There is certainly no easy or widespread acceptance of sex relations outside marriage in the population as a whole.'[18] Some seven years after the Little Kinsey report, Eustace Chesser's study *The Sexual, Marital and Family Relationship of the English Woman* argued that premarital intercourse had become more common between 1900 and the Second World War, especially among young engaged couples. His study was based on 6,000 responses from women between ages 18 and 60 to questions about their family and sexual life. The questionnaires were distributed by 1,500 medical practitioners to their female patients. The sample was unrepresentative and biased towards the under-40s, and included a large proportion of upper-middle-class women. The results showed that 19% of women born before 1904 had had sexual intercourse before marriage, compared to 36% of women born between 1904 and 1914, 39% of women born between 1914 and 1924, and 43% of those born between 1924 and 1934.[19]

This alleged increase in premarital sex was said to result in an increase in the prevalence of venereal diseases and illegitimacy, which attracted the attention of the medical profession. Some medical professionals publicly called for contraceptive information to be made widely available to young people. For instance, in 1959, the Harley Street psychologist Eustace Chesser published an article entitled 'Is Chastity Outmoded? Outdated? Out?' in a special issue of *Family Doctor*, a magazine issued by the BMA. In 1956, the magazine had published a special issue entitled *Getting Married*, a guide to matrimonial life. The pamphlet was such a success that they decided to renew the issue each year. In 1959, however, the fourth issue provoked a fierce debate, forcing the BMA to withdraw it four days after publication. The 1959 booklet, under the direction of the family planning doctor Winifred de Kok, who later became a broadcaster for *Tell Me Doctor* on the BBC, instigated several articles. Chief

---

[17] Brown, 'Sex, Religion and the Single Woman'.
[18] Quoted in Brown, 'Sex, Religion and the Single Woman'.
[19] Eustace Chesser, *The Sexual, Marital and Family Relationship of the English Woman* (Hutchinson's Medical Publications, 1956).

targets for criticism were Chesser's article and an article by a lecturer in genetics, Roger Pilkington, entitled 'Marrying with a baby on the way'. Chesser was accused of promoting premarital sex by writing that 'pre-marital intercourse, despite the fact that it is a limited relationship, can also be more than ordinarily pleasant'.[20] He affirmed that choosing between being chaste or unchaste should be the citizen's right as long as this decision 'was not detrimental to the society of which he was part'.[21] He suggested that contraception was a solution to the negative consequences of premarital sex. Pilkington's article opened with the sentence: 'So you are a bride. And you are pregnant, too',[22] emphasizing the rise in premarital sex and resulting births. He suggested that women who married while pregnant had made an 'understandable mistake'.[23] Condemnations were quick to follow, with letters of indignation pouring into the BMA and criticisms from religious circles. For instance, the *Church Times* described the booklet as an un-Christian publication and urged doctors to express their outrage to the BMA. Similarly, Canon R. H. Preston from Manchester condemned the booklet as 'irresponsible and non-Christian'.[24] Following the withdrawal of the leaflet, Chesser and de Kok resigned from the BMA in protest.

Contraception as a solution to unwanted pregnancies for premarital sexuality was also suggested by George M. Carstairs, Professor of Psychomedicine at the University of Edinburgh, in his 1962 annual BBC Reith Lecture. In his lecture, he asked, 'Is chastity the supreme virtue?', and then went on to explain that charity, the consideration of and concern for others, should come first. In his view, sexual experience before marriage when precautions were taken could be 'a sensible preliminary' that might lead to better chances of a 'considerate and mutually satisfying partnership'. Therefore, premarital sex should be understood as an expression of charity. Other stances supporting access to contraception for young people were expressed the following year. In 1963, the British scientist and physician Alex Comfort was invited by the BBC to present the re-edition of his book, *Sex and Society,* in which he publicly defended premarital sex. He argued that 'ideally older adolescents should be allowed to decide for or against coitus for themselves (which they are doing already in any case), and given contraceptive facilities on which freedom of choice depends'. He called for widespread access to information about

---

[20] 'Getting Married', *Family Doctor,* special issue (British Medical Association, 1959): 38.
[21] Ibid., 41.   [22] Ibid., 54.   [23] Ibid., 56.
[24] 'Article on chastity irresponsible', *The Manchester Guardian,* 13 April 1959, 5.

contraception, since 'adolescent intercourse is already becoming commoner and commoner without benefit of contraceptive education'.[25]

However, not all medical professionals shared the opinion that making contraceptive information available to young people was the solution to tackling unwanted pregnancies and venereal disease. In 1961, the British Medical Association appointed a committee with representatives from churches, the medical, nursing, and educational professions and social services, in order 'to consider practical measures for combatting venereal disease, particularly among young people'. This report showed an increase in sexually transmitted diseases and attributed its origin to promiscuous behaviour. Both premarital and extramarital sexual relations were said to be common and 'most of the witnesses thought they had increased, believing there was a radically altered attitude towards sexual morality and morality in general'.[26] The report claimed that promiscuity had become 'fashionable'. It was widely publicized in the mass media; for instance, the *Daily Express* summarized its main elements by emphasizing the sensational results. The newspaper highlighted that a new love game called King's Command in which 14-year-olds were said to have intercourse as 'a kind of forfeit' had been reported by a social worker.[27] The main recommendation of the report was the establishment of a concerted public campaign between churches, social workers, and teachers to reaffirm the value of chastity. Improved education on the facts of life at school, it was thought, could also contribute to slowing down the spread of VD.

Debates about young people's sexuality were not limited to medical professional circles. The BMA report motivated Michael Schofield to undertake a study on the sexual behaviours of young people in 1963, surveying nearly 2,000 teenagers. The aim of this study was to 'obtain facts about the sexual attitudes and behaviours of young people aged fifteen to nineteen'. The object of the research was to 'provide the basic and scientific information which is the essential first step before suitable education measures can be developed'. More specifically, he linked the need for this research with a statement made by the BMA Report on Venereal Disease and Young People (1964).

This report was mainly based on observations by professionals, and Schofield stressed that there existed no historical information to back up the statement of increasing promiscuity. Therefore, his research filled a need for a 'realistic assessment of adolescent sexual experience'.[28] His results were

---

[25] Alex Comfort, *Sex in Society* (Duckworth, 1963).
[26] 'Venereal disease and young people', *British Medical Journal*, 7 March 1964, 576.
[27] 'Teenage love, sex for kicks and party games', *Daily Express*, 6 March 1964, 8–9.
[28] Michael Schofield, *The Sexual Behaviour of Young People* (Little, Brown, 1965): 7.

revealing, showing that young people were much more traditional than publicly acknowledged. The study showed that they were considerably less promiscuous than many imagined. Premarital sexual relations remained the behaviour of a minority. Age played a role: 11% of boys and 6% of girls had had intercourse by the age of 17, and 30% and 16%, respectively, had done so by the age of 19. The sexually experienced girls had had an average number of 2.3 partners, while the experienced boys had an average of 6.3. Less than half the boys always used some form of birth control, and a majority of girls neither took precautions nor insisted that their partner should do so. He showed that only 40% of boys and 22% of girls were in favour of sex 'with your fiance' before marriage. On the proposition that 'sexual intercourse before marriage is wrong', 35% of boys and 61% of girls agreed. Most of the young people were in favour of better sex education and the majority said they were dissatisfied with the information they had received.

Nevertheless, there were some signs of more liberal attitudes. He showed that the proportion of illegitimate births to women aged 15–19 years had remained largely static at around 17–18% from 1938 until the late 1950s, but rose sharply to 18.6 in 1960 to 19.8 in 1961 and 20.5 in 1962.

Cultural and mass media representation of youth sexuality

Debates about youth sexuality were numerous and occurred in different spaces. The mass media, young women's magazines, and cinemas were all channels for conveying the changing and contradictory attitudes towards youth sexuality. Much has been written about sexual morality and the press during the postwar years. Adrian Bingham has argued that there was a growing public appetite for sexual content in the press.[29] As a result, sex became increasingly frankly discussed in the mass media, pushing back the discursive boundaries of what was 'legitimate'. This new focus was driven by financial profit, but not only that. Journals that featured straightforward and 'scientific' information on sex, challenging the hitherto usual moral treatment of the subject, saw their circulation increase. In addition to this financial gain, there also existed a democratic mission to provide sex education that would enlighten a readership often ignorant on sexual matters. Advice columns became a channel for conveying sexual health information. However, these remained framed in a moralistic tone, where premarital sex was still

[29] Bingham, *Family Newspapers*.

condemned and the double standard that young women had to be virgins until marriage was prevalent.

In the late 1950s and early 1960s, the public debate about young people's sexuality intensified. There had been a spate of articles in British newspapers warning about the increase in venereal disease, illegitimacy, backstreet abortions, and premarital sex. Two main attitudes dominated: a down-to earth attitude that recognized changes in the moral state of society and suggested ways of adapting to them; and strong condemnations of the dismantlement of British society and its values. This brief section briefly highlights some articles that revealed these tensions.

In 1961, *The Guardian* published a piece on unmarried mothers. The journalist interviewed the former secretary of the National Council for the Unmarried Mother and Her Child, Isabel Granger. Granger attributed the increase in teenage mothers to the increase in the number of teenagers as a whole. She thought that ignorance about contraception was not a key factor: in her view, 'boys and girls know all about this thing'. What they lacked was the privacy to use contraceptives as well as 'the sense of responsibility to use their knowledge'. Even more problematic and significant, in Granger's opinion, was the 'double think' that led to girls not carrying contraceptives in order to avoid being indecent. The solution for tackling promiscuity? It lay, according to Granger, in a non-judgmental attitude that taught responsible sexual behaviour to young people.[30]

The same year, again in *The Guardian*, the British writer and Labour politician Wayland Young wrote a column on abortion. He gave the example of a 16-year-old girl who went to a backstreet abortionist and made multiple attempts to abort. As a result, she haemorrhaged and ended up in hospital. Young drew two main conclusions about the case: the first was that social class played a key role in the outcome. If the girl had had more money she would have been able to afford a private doctor. The second was that it was ignorance about contraception that resulted in this dramatic outcome. The best means to prevent botched abortions was therefore to provide information on contraception to young people and, in Young's view, 'at long last to get over the furtive mentality over contraceptives: if we could admit their existence and explain their use to our children'.[31] Unsurprisingly, his stance provoked a number of reactions also published within the journal that pivoted around the supporters of better sex education and provision of contraception and their

---

[30] 'Unmarried mothers need guidance: Lack of real family life', *The Guardian*, 16 December 1961, 4.
[31] Wayland Young, 'Abortion', *The Guardian*, 2 June 1961.

opponents, who saw contraception as a Pandora's box that would encourage young people to 'behave immorally without having to face the consequences'.[32] In 1963, another article published in *The Guardian*, entitled 'Decline in teenage morality', underlined the spread of venereal disease and the increasing rate of illegitimacy.[33]

Newspapers also carried out their own smaller surveys about the alleged relaxation of sexual mores among young people. For instance, the *Sunday Pictorial* interviewed several young people and found that only one of them disapproved of premarital sex. Following George M. Carstairs' BBC Reith Lecture, *Sunday Pictorial* readers were also asked whether 'chastity was out of date'; a small majority opined that it was not.[34] Discussing the results of a survey of students at a London university in the *Sunday Mirror*, the journalist Anne Allen pointed out that one-third of student couples 'were living together as man and wife' and 'almost all had sexual experience before marriage'. These contrasting answers highlighted the fact that sexual mores were in flux at the beginning of the 1960s.

In September, Dr Richard Fox, consultant psychiatrist to the Severalls Hospital, co-authored a booklet entitled 'Towards a Quaker view of Sex'. *The Daily Mirror* covered the talk he gave at the Conference of the Royal Institute of Public Health, highlighting the 'frankness' of the speech. Fox underscored the fact that premarital sex was a given of society and that either society would adapt to it and change its moral condemnation or 'it will have to permit and prepare people for much earlier marriage'.[35] Fox held the view that individuals are curious about 'what there is in sex' and consequently, it was better to experiment before marriage than after. These liberal attitudes to youth sexuality were seen as encouraging premarital sex. Outrageous reactions were rapidly voiced. At the Convocation of York in October 1963, Canon Richard Norburn of Bolton suggested the reaffirmation of the Church position on chastity, which was an 'ideal to be seriously aimed at'. He considered the public endorsement of premarital sex a 'formidable attack in what they are trying to achieve'.[36] Two years later, the British Council of Churches' report 'Sex and Morality' stated its condemnation of premarital sex by emphasizing

---

[32] 'Letters to the editors: Contraception or abortion', *The Guardian*, 6 June 1961.
[33] 'The decline in teenage morals', *The Guardian*, 6 May 1963, 5.
[34] Quoted in Bingham, *Family Newspapers*, 120.
[35] 'A doctor made a speech yesterday and he forecast the headline the *Mirror* would put on it. This is it: Doc backs teenage sex, but we think this headline is better... You can't ban teenage sex says doctor', *Daily Mirror*, 28 September 1963, 3.
[36] 'Chastity a serious ideal', *The Guardian*, 10 October 1963, 4.

the precept of 'abstinence before marriage and fidelity within it',[37] showing less openness than the Quaker publication.

Besides this emphasis on young people's sexuality, throughout the 1950s and early 1960s, the press, social investigators, and many politicians presented teenage behaviour as both the cause and the consequence of a generational clash. For instance, in 1957, the *Daily Mirror* wrote, 'This is the year of the war on parents'.[38] As we will see, supporters of young people's right to sexual knowledge and contraception drew on this generational tension to explain adults' reluctance to provide information about contraception, attributing this attitude to feelings of jealousy from the parental generation towards a freedom that they had not enjoyed, or the taboo surrounding sex that prevented mothers from talking to their daughters.

Cultural representations of young people in theatre plays and movies were also ambivalent, sometimes presenting condemnation and sometimes alternative models where young girls enjoyed growing freedom and went on the move, travelling and migrating to cities. As Penny Tinkler has argued when analysing movies and magazines, this new mobility opened up new opportunities for young women but also came 'at a cost'.[39] Indeed, 'teenage girls are portrayed at even greater sexual risk when out of place, be it on the move or living away from home because of work, leisure opportunities or demands for independence'.[40] Similarly, several movies and theatre plays addressed the issues of inter-racial relationships, teenage pregnancy, homosexuality, and venereal disease and presented these topics as 'social realities'. In 1963, for instance, the movie *That Kind of Girl* (1963) tackled the issue of venereal disease and presented a compassionate attitude towards the 18-year-old Eva, an Austrian au pair, who contracted VD when she lost her virginity. Her situation was handled sensitively by the medical profession and her employers, who continued to employ her.

These various representations testify to the fact that public views on young people's sexuality were in flux during the 1960s, oscillating between condemnation and support for growing sexual freedom. The context was therefore one of increasing public debate on youth sexuality, with those taking a pragmatic approach to youth sexuality pitted against those with a conservative and moral

---

[37] 'The Morality Report', *The Times,* 25 October 1966, 5.
[38] 'Revolt against parents', *Daily Mirror*, 9 December 1957, 12.
[39] Penny Tinkler, 'Going places or out of place? Representations of mobile girls and young women in late-1950s and 1960s Britain', *Twentieth Century British History* 32.2 (2021): 212–37.
[40] Janet Fink and Penny Tinkler, 'Teetering on the edge: Portraits of innocence, risk and young female sexualities in 1950s' and 1960s' British cinema?', *Women's History Review* 26.1 (2017): 9–25.

approach. A consensus was nevertheless perceptible, and rested on the recognition that illegitimacy and the spread of venereal disease were increasing and that something had to be done to counter these trends. It was in this context of fears around unwanted pregnancies and rising illegitimacy that the first Brook Advisory Centre opened in London in 1964.

Sexual health services before Brook

From the interwar years up until 1974, when the National Health Service incorporated family planning under the NHS Reorganization Act, multiple charities, agencies, and spheres of activity conglomerated to form a network of what would today be called sexual health services. Key players among them were the National Birth Control Association (NBCA) which became the Family Planning Association (FPA), the Marie Stopes Clinic, and the Marriage Guidance Council.[41] These voluntary services focused on providing contraceptive advice to married women or mothers only, as well as counselling couples on their marital difficulties. While counselling married couples on contraception and sexual problems was becoming more accepted in postwar Britain, counselling teenagers and unmarried people remained highly controversial. Some doctors, such as Joan Malleson, Norman Haire, and Helena Wright, had counselled and fitted unmarried women with contraceptives in their private practice since the interwar years but not via the FPA.[42] In 1952, the FPA decided to formalize a practice that, until then, occurred informally in several FPA clinics, namely the provision of contraceptive advice to about-to-marry people.[43] In addition to this focus on the affianced, there was also a growing interest among FPA members in determining whether providing contraceptive advice to unmarried people was a good idea. In 1954, Helen Brook, a family planning member of the Islington FPA clinic and newly elected to the FPA Executive Committee, suggested as a topic of discussion 'the best way to treat patients outside matrimony'.[44] This demand was

---

[41] On these organizations see, for instance Jane Lewis, David Clark, and David Morgan (eds), *'Whom God Hath Joined Together': The Work of Marriage Guidance* (Routledge, 1992); Deborah A. Cohen, 'Private lives in public spaces: Marie Stopes, the Mothers' Clinics and the practice of contraception', *History Workshop Journal* 35.1 (1993): 95–116. Leathard, *Fight for Family Planning*; Caroline Rusterholz, *Women's Medicine: Sex, Family Planning and British Female Doctors in Transnational Perspective 1920–70* (Manchester University Press, 2020).

[42] I am grateful to Lesley Hall who shared this information with me.

[43] 'Premarital advice', in SA/FPA/A3/14/14, Wellcome Library, London.

[44] 'Letter from General Secretary to Helen Brook, 14 April 1954', in SA/FPA/A4/A8/2, Wellcome Library, London.

connected to two key elements. The first was the arrival of men from the West Indies who were frequently recruited to work on London's trains and buses. The men's partners often came with them to England, but these couples were not married. They often had children that they left with their relatives in the West Indies when they moved, and sent money back home. Many of these 'respectable women' became pregnant and could not be seen in family planning clinics. Helen Brook explained:

> 'And that seemed to be very foolish to me, because these poor women had come here to earn money, and once they were pregnant and got children here there were no mothers to look after the children for them so they could go out to work. They all seemed to me to be so ill-thought through, you know; London Transport had brought most of these people over, it was, you know, their main idea, and though they thought of a lot of things they didn't think of what I would call practical things.'

She decided to do something about the situation and contacted the Foreign Office, the West Indies High Commissioner, and finally the FPA; the latter consequently allowed unmarried West Indian women to be seen in FPA clinics as long as they were in a 'stable relationship'. Interestingly, the FPA's policy to advise only married women was changed for 'migrant' women, as these women were perceived as in need of intervention and monitoring. While Helen Brook framed this new initiative as helping these women, which was certainly the case, the fact that the FPA, despite strong opposition against letting unmarried people come to the clinics, did allow unmarried West Indian women to be seen and helped by the doctor testified to the fact that West Indian people's fertility was certainly perceived as undesirable.

In 1962, following Professor G. M. Carstairs' BBC Reith Lecture, members of the North Kensington Women Welfare Centre wondered whether they should extend the provision of contraception to unmarried and young people. While mentioning the 'uproar' that this talk would without doubt cause among members of the church and council for social hygiene, they nevertheless recognized that 'sex experience amongst the teenagers has come to stay and that therefore they must seek protection in birth control'. The FPA Executive Committee would have to be consulted, but some support was already perceptible among high-profile members.[45]

---

[45] 'Unmarried', in SA/FPA/SR7, Wellcome Library, London.

Meanwhile, in 1963, Dr John McEwan, member of the FPA, started to contact different personalities to submit a resolution for the Annual General Meeting of the FPA in 1964 'to admit all women to clinics for contraceptive advice whether they are married or not'. He gained the support of the radical birth control advocate and family planning doctor Helena Wright. McEwan's resolution underlined the urgency of taking a rational approach to unwanted pregnancies. Unwanted pregnancies still occurred despite the work done by the FPA, he explained. A high proportion of these unwanted pregnancies were among 'unmarried women', and, he added, 'it seems right to doubt the principle by which the FPA constitution divides the notional offsprings of women into those from married mothers whose conception it will help to prevent and those from unmarried mothers whom it will allow to be conceived without hindrance. Are such children not family in our sense of family planning? [...] If it is women who [are] to be helped by the FPA then surely it ought to be the prerogative of all women to have access to the clinical services.'[46] This statement was sent to Leah Manning, who explained that she would submit a resolution that demanded that doctors be free to see and advise whoever turned to the clinics for help.[47] In the columns of *Family Planning*, several letters were sent by members expressing their outrage at Manning's proposition, drawing on the argument that providing information and means to avoid pregnancy would be detrimental to the moral state of the country and encourage promiscuity. For instance, Agnes Bowman, who helped to found the Halifax FPA, felt that 'young people should be urged to hold to a higher standard of moral behaviour rather than make excuses for their promiscuity for if this latter is encouraged I fear we may unleash psychological results in the choice and continued cherishing of a final marriage partner which far outweigh the short lived pleasure of an affair'.[48] Another letter presented Manning's values as 'all wrong' and called for the stopping of the 'drift to the country's total moral degradation' by the putting in place of action aimed at 'protecting the minds of the children from the vice perverts'.[49] The choice of wording reflected the view that young people were perceived as children that needed protection. Information and advice about contraception and sex were considered a perversion that 'poisoned' young people's minds. Instead, sexual morality and chastity should be reaffirmed.

---

[46] 'Proposed changes in policy for family planning clinics', in PP/MEW/C/2/1, Wellcome Library, London.
[47] Ibid.
[48] Agnes Bowman, 'Family planning for the unmarried?', *Family Planning* 12.4 (1964): 105.
[49] Walter and Katherine Hague, 'Sexual morality and the young', *Family Planning* 13.1 (1964): 20.

A few letters supported Manning's suggestion. In particular, one letter from a teacher stressed that the teaching of the church on chastity before marriage came from the early fathers who 'were prejudiced against women, against earthly enjoyments in general and love in particular'. She supported the giving of contraceptive advice to all who asked for it, especially since she had found that the young people she taught were ready to listen to practical advice 'and they are not promiscuous and want to lead decent lives'.[50] These letters were a taste of the controversy that would be unleashed at the General Assembly of the FPA in 1964.

At the General Assembly, more than 850 delegates, visitors, and press members gathered in Westminster. Manning presented her resolution as an answer to the rising level of illegitimacy and illegal abortions and to the fact that 'pre-marital sexual intercourse is something which has begun to establish itself'.[51] She quoted cases of girls at universities who 'had sought abortion to avoid being sent down'. She therefore linked the need to provide contraceptive advice with the new opportunities that were opening up for girls. Contraception, as a preventive measure against abortion, was presented as a means to avoid narrowing girls' future career prospects. She tried to downplay fears of promiscuity by specifying that she was not asking that every 15-year-old who 'does it for kicks' should be given contraceptive advice, but she wanted to help the girl who, 'deeply in love', could not get married yet. She appealed to delegates to put away 'self-righteousness' and to let 'kindness rule their minds'.[52] Members of the FPA were divided about Manning's resolution. A minority were completely against it, fearing that such a resolution would 'open the doors to wholesale national fornication'.[53] Fear of pregnancy had traditionally worked as a deterrent to young people having sex before marriage, since the consequences of an illegitimate pregnancy were dramatic for young women's social status and prospects. Removing this fear by giving young people the means to protect themselves against unwanted pregnancy would, it was believed, encourage them to have sex.

Many delegates felt that the role of the FPA was to deal with family and married people and were afraid of losing members and the support of the churches if the association broadened the scope of its responsibility. Present

---

[50] Mrs B. L. Lustig, 'Family planning for the unmarried?', *Family Planning* 13.1 (1964): 20.

[51] 'Resolution 11, The Family Planning Association, Minutes of Annual General Meeting and conference held on Wednesday and Thursday 3 and 4 June, 1964', p. 14, in SA/FPA/A2/13, Wellcome Library, London.

[52] 'The Family Planning Association, Minutes of Annual General Meeting and conference held on Wednesday and Thursday 3 and 4 June, 1964', p. 14, in SA/FPA/A2/13, Wellcome Library, London.

[53] John Prince, 'Birth control for the unmarried approved', *Daily Telegraph*, 5 June 1964.

during the debate was Reverend Kenneth Greet, the chairman of the British Council of Churches' Advisory Group on Sex, Marriage, and the Family and secretary of the Methodist Christian Citizenship Department, who stated that 'if the resolution increased the general permissive atmosphere it might do more harm than good'.[54] He reminded the delegates that the FPA had a responsibility to provide more comprehensive sex education to young people as part of a wider education 'in human relations involving values and attitudes'.[55] As an alternative, an amendment was put forward by the Islington Branch, which stated that unmarried people should be referred for advice about birth control and sex problems to the Youth Advisory Centre, the creation of which the FPA should encourage.[56] Spicer was present during the General Assembly and briefly described the clientele of the centre as 'good people who wanted to make good marriage'.[57] She thereby tried to inscribe her work within the marital framework so cherished by the FPA. However, the FPA, aiming to distance itself from youth sexuality and keep its hard-won legitimacy and financial support, declined this new responsibility and tasked the Youth Advisory Centre, which later became the Brook Advisory Centre, with developing this service.

The setting up of Brook Advisory Centres and the role of Helen Brook

Until 1964, contraceptive advice was only given to married women and the affianced, conditional on formal proof of their engagement, in FPA centres, Marie Stopes Clinics, Marriage Guidance Centres, and by General Practitioners. The opening of Brook changed this situation. The tactic devised by Helen Brook was efficient in that she used a loophole in the Marie Stopes constitution to experiment, and then presented her experiment to the Marie Stopes members as a fait accompli.

When the birth control activist Marie Stopes died in 1958, she left her centre to the Eugenics Society, provided that her clinic was not, under any circumstances, to be taken over by the FPA. Stopes had a conflicting relationship with FPA members; she had once been a member of the NBCA but left the committee in hostile circumstances, arguing that no one listened to her despite

---

[54] 'The Family Planning Association, Minutes of Annual General Meeting and conference held on Wednesday and Thursday 3 and 4 June, 1964', p. 15, in SA/FPA/A2/13, Wellcome Library London.
[55] Ibid.   [56] Ibid.   [57] Ibid.

the pivotal role she played in creating the movement. In 1958, Helen Brook was asked to reorganize and direct the Marie Stopes Clinic in Whitfield Street, London.

Helen Brook was an interesting character. She was born in 1907, the daughter of an artist who owned a gallery in Chelsea. She was first married, aged 18, to a violinist, and had a daughter. After a few years of marriage, she asked for a divorce on infidelity grounds.[58] She then went to Paris and studied art. She later married Robin Brook, an economist in London; the couple wanted to have a child. Helen Brook recalled, 'So, I then decided we'd better have a child, and then of course I was unable to conceive. And this was awful, but it was also good in a way for what was to come later, because I understood then how terrible it was for women who wished to have a family, not to have a child when they thought they could easily.'[59] This experience made her particularly aware and sensitive to the experiences and difficulties faced by women. After tubal insufflation, she had two children. When her daughters were both in high school, Helen Brook felt the need 'to do something with her life'. An acquaintance, who worked at the Islington FPA clinic, suggested that she should work there as an interviewer. She recalled, 'And of course I loved it, I absolutely adored it. And this relationship with the patient, and of course it was nice for the patients, because they found a lot of relaxed people there, who talked to them, and they weren't doctors. Of course in those days people were really nervous of doctors, and our patients were coming from quite lowly homes, and many of them, you know, from extremely poor surroundings.'[60] Brook then became chairman of the Islington FPA clinic for twelve years, following which she moved to the Marie Stopes Clinic. She explained that she had begun to realize that something needed to be done for unmarried women, for two main reasons. The first was that 'she couldn't bear to see children being brought up without a proper family background'.[61] She followed the FPA ideology that each child should be a wanted child. The second reason was the arrival of West Indian women in London, as mentioned above. Brook's empathy drove her to act on a pressing issue; she started to realize that it was not only women from the West Indies, but also unmarried women in England, who needed access to birth control. When she was asked to reorganize the Brook Centre, she took the opportunity to try a new experiment in one of the Stopes offices, hence avoiding the self-imposed limitation of the FPA to

---

[58] Helen Brook, interviewed by Rebbeca Adams, in C408/014 British Library.   [59] Ibid.
[60] Ibid.   [61] 'A singular lady: Helen Brook', *The Guardian*, 19 June 1974.

married mothers only.⁶² She used a loophole in the Marie Stopes constitution to expand the scope of the clients:

> 'I became deeply aware of the fact that here was the opportunity to start a session for the unmarried woman. Because we were not under the rules of the FPA, you see. Because it didn't belong to the FPA, it was quite separate. And Marie Stopes had made it quite clear that it was never to be run by the FPA. Although they had to have somebody from the FPA, and FPA doctors, to work in it, because they were the people who knew how to do it you see. But I was still part of the FPA, but I was doing this other as well, but it all worked and fitted in.'⁶³

The new memorandum of the Marie Stopes Foundation did not state that married women were the only clients, but instead flagged clients generally as those with ill-health, who were poor, or in distress.⁶⁴ In November 1962, the Clinic Committee included unmarried girls, brought to the clinic by social and health workers, in the clinic's clientele.⁶⁵ The Clinic Committee, carefully chosen by Brook, was made up essentially of 'forward-looking'⁶⁶ members of the FPA: Brook herself; her husband Robin Brook; the birth control activist Margaret Pyke, a founding member of the FPA and its chairwoman in 1954; Dr Evelyn Fisher, who had worked with Marie Stopes for the previous 30 years and was a member of the Abortion Law Reform Association; Mrs D. Gibson; Mrs Rotha Peers, who was the secretary of North Kensington Marriage Welfare Centre, one of the first FPA clinics in London; the British author Jean Medawar, a member of the executive committee of the FPA, joint editor of *Family Planning*, and wife of Nobel laureate Peter Medawar; Faith Schenk, the secretary of the clinic; and Joan Windley, the administrator of the clinic under Marie Stopes. The restriction on unmarried girls brought to the clinic by social workers was soon to be abandoned; in March 1963, Brook proposed an early evening doctor's session to which 'girls and young men, often still at school or university'⁶⁷ could come for discussion and advice on problems with

---

⁶² Ibid. ⁶³ Ibid.
⁶⁴ 'Amendments to the Memorandum of the Marie Stopes Foundation Limited, 25 January 1960', in SA/EUG/K37, Wellcome Library, London.
⁶⁵ 'Minutes of the Clinic Committee, 14 November 1962', in SA/EUG/K.42:Box 79, Wellcome Library, London.
⁶⁶ Helen Brook, 'In the club', p. 14, in GC/105/4, Wellcome Library, London.
⁶⁷ 'Minutes of the Clinic Committee, 20 March 1963', in SA/EUG/K.42:Box 79, Wellcome Library, London.

sexual relationships. Practical instruction in birth control was left to the doctor's discretion.

The members of the Clinic Committee unanimously supported this suggestion, provided the Board agreed, and it was decided that Dr Faith Spicer, a mother of three who had experience working with young people and had worked in a FPA clinic, would be asked to run the session. The Marie Stopes Foundation Board consisted of six members: Marie Stopes' executor, Alan Wyborn; the British zoologist and general secretary of the Eugenics Society, Dr Colin Bertram; the physician and geneticist, former general secretary of the Eugenics Society, and member of the Medical Research Council's Clinical Genetics Unit (of which he became the director in 1964), Dr Cedric Carter;[68] the paediatrician and psychiatrist, member of the Eugenics Society, Medical Advisor of the Children's Society, and executive member of the Standing Conference of Societies Registered for Adoption, Lady Hilda Lewis;[69] and Margaret Pyke. Aware that this move could trigger resistance from the Board, the letter asking for approval emphasized the discreet character of the endeavour, stating that the session 'would not be publicized but would be made known by word of mouth'.[70] On 27 March, the Board, by correspondence, formally agreed to hire Dr Faith Spicer.[71] Despite the absence of publicity, within weeks the word spread rapidly among women:

'[W]e saw our first... And it was very interesting, we didn't say a word to anybody, it was deadly secret. And this went on, and by... I suppose it must have been by March, we were absolutely... well we had to have more than one session a week, and so I had to get somebody else in to help, and, you know, the whole thing began to get almost too much for us. Because by some extraordinary... I don't know how it happened, but the news got round England... [LAUGHING]... like wildfire. You didn't have to say anything, extraordinary.'[72]

Letters were also sent to London FPA centres to inform them of the 'special consultation service for young people', urging them to ask young people in

---

[68] 'Professor Cedric Carter', *Journal of Medical Genetics*, 21(1984): 401–3.
[69] 'Hilda Lewis Memorial Fund', *British Medical Journal*, 1 (1967): 701.
[70] 'Minutes of the Clinic Committee, 20 March 1963', in SA/EUG/K.42:Box 79, Wellcome Library, London.
[71] 'Minutes: The tenth meeting of the Board of the Marie Stopes Memorial Foundation Limited, 11 December 1963', in SA/EUG/K.39, Wellcome Library, London.
[72] Ibid.

need of advice to 'write, phone or call for an appointment'.[73] In December, the Board were seemingly cautious, as they asked to be 'more fully informed on procedure at this stage before consideration was given to any expansion of this service'.[74]

A special meeting was therefore arranged for early January. Two newly elected members of the Board were present: Helen Brook and James Meade, a professor of economics at Cambridge. The president of the foundation—the neurologist Lord Russell Brain, who was a former president of the Royal College of Physicians, fellow of the Royal Society, and president of the Family Planning Association—was invited, as was Dr Spicer, so she could present her work. A background circular to aid the discussion, written by Bertram, warned that the special session would either harm or increase the reputation of the clinic, and if there were 'harmful repercussions, such as bad press, it could extend to the Eugenics Society itself'.[75] He therefore explained that the setting up of an ad hoc trust, using the clinic premises, for a few years would mitigate the risks of bad publicity for the Foundation and the Eugenics Society. Dr Spicer gave a brief account of her work and stressed the high demand for the sessions, which had resulted in an increase to two sessions a week and the hiring of a new doctor.[76] She framed the need for these sessions around the type of clients the sessions targeted: young students—18–19 years old on average—who were in stable relationships but unable to marry due to financial reasons, and had come for birth control advice (70%). Schoolgirls and students from university were thought to be especially in need of advice since living away from home opened up space for sexual experimentation.[77]

As Helen Brook later explained, class and race were central in creation of Brook. Her motivation for holding such sessions, as she reflected four years after their creation in 1966, was to tackle the issue of rising rates of illegitimate births. She attributed this increase to several factors, namely the larger population of young people, earlier puberty, the greater freedom and mobility of the young, and immigration from Ireland and what she called 'backwards

---

[73] 'Letter from J. Windley, clinic secretary of the Marie Stopes Memorial Clinic, to Mrs Windett, North Kensington Marriage Welfare Centre, 31 May 1963,' in SA/FPA/NK34, Wellcome Library, London.

[74] 'Minutes: The tenth meeting of the Board of the Marie Stopes Memorial Foundation Limited, 11 December 1963', in SA/EUG/K.39, Wellcome Library, London.

[75] 'Bertram, "Consultation Sessions for Young People", 16th January 1964', in SA/EUG/K/38/45, Wellcome Library, London.

[76] 'A special meeting of the Board of the Marie Stopes Memorial Foundation Limited, called for the purpose of considering the Clinic's consultation session for young people, 16th January 1964', in SA/EUG/K39, Wellcome Library, London.

[77] See Dyhouse, *Girl Trouble*, 162.

countries'.⁷⁸ Brook's main target clientele was young white women brought in by social workers, usually from deprived working-class backgrounds, who were deemed in need of monitoring, as well as white middle-class and upper-class young couples at university who were said to be in committed relationships 'but unable to marry due to financial reasons'.⁷⁹ These young couples were presented as in need of advice, rather than control, in order to avoid unwanted pregnancies that would jeopardize their future. She would later add 'it's the public school girl who is the absolute target',⁸⁰ since they were still being raised with the idea that respectability meant sexual ignorance and they were 'totally innocent, they've never heard about anything'.⁸¹ In 1969, when reflecting on the reasons behind Brook, she explained 'It's so sad, isn't it, when you see nice girls just going up to university and for (some) dotty reason they have got themselves pregnant just before. [...] We're here to prevent unnecessary conception.'⁸² This focus on preventing young women to drop out of education functioned alongside another key driver for Helen Brook: that of women's equality with men. In an *Everyman* TV show in 1994, Helen Brook reflected on her motivations and asserted that 'I was determined that women should have the same chance as their brothers to go...should have the same chance for further education and be regarded as equal human beings.' In 1974 she would also explain that contraception was 'only one little bit of women's fight for freedom'.⁸³

Irish immigrants and those from 'backwards countries', most likely immigrants from the West Indies, South Asia, and Africa based on postwar migration trends, were also potential clients. As many studies have shown, young Black boys from the West Indies were usually presented by the mass media and social scientists and experts as sexual predators, allegedly bringing venereal diseases to Britain, while white working-class girls were always thought to be more promiscuous than white middle-class girls.⁸⁴ Both groups were therefore perceived as vulnerable populations that needed to be educated in order to behave responsibly. This meant that, from the start, the

---

⁷⁸ 'Helen Brook, Address to Westminster social workers 5 September 1966', in SA/BRO/J/1/7, Wellcome Library, London.
⁷⁹ 'Marie Stopes Memorial Foundation, A special meeting of the Board of the Marie Stopes Memorial Foundation Limited, called for the purpose of considering the Clinic's consultation session for young people, 16 January 1964', in SA/EUG/K39. Wellcome Library, London.
⁸⁰ 'A Maureen Cleave interview', *The Evening Standard*, 16 January 1967, 7.
⁸¹ 'Helen Brook, interviewed by Rebecca Abrams,' in C408/014, British Library, London.
⁸² 'Look !', *Sunday Times*, 15 June 1969, 52.
⁸³ Patricia Ashdown-Sharp, 'A singular lady', *The Guardian*, 19 June 1974.
⁸⁴ Bingham, *Family Newspapers?*; Bivins, *Contagious Communities*; Dyhouse, *Girl Trouble*; Webster, *Imagining Home*.

white/middle-class norm of committed young people in steady relationships functioned as the model of 'good' sexual behaviour.

Spicer strategically emphasized the commitment of young people and their desire to marry in a foreseeable future to align her work with the older sexual values of the FPA and Marie Stopes around counselling married women and mothers. The Board unanimously agreed on the worth of the sessions, but recommended that they were to be held not as a normal part of the work of the clinic but instead as an experimental research project called Advisory Centre for Young People, under Spicer's direction. The Board subsidized the project through free accommodation and a grant of £500. In addition, it asked that the project be 'brought to the attention of social welfare organisations and referral agencies but not publicised in the Press or otherwise'.[85] In the following months, complying with Bertram's advice to set up a separate organization, Helen Brook sought legal advice to create a Trust, which would coordinate the openings of other clinics. She received an anonymous donation of £5,000 a year over three years to expand this work, and, as a result, the Brook Advisory Centre officially opened in July 1964.

Conclusion

The 1950s and early 1960s saw increasing scrutiny of young people's sexual behaviours, with anxieties about illegitimacy, venereal diseases, and abortion conflated in order to portray unmarried and young people's sexual behaviours as problematic. Two main opposing positions attempted to offer solutions to what were considered deeply worrying trends. Partisans of the provision of contraception to young people presented it as a practical and pragmatic solution that would mitigate the negative effect of increasing sexual activity among young people, while opponents of contraception perceived it as an encouragement to promiscuity and worried that the removal of the fear of pregnancy would lead to increasing fornication among young people. Instead, they urged the teaching of the virtue of chastity.

It was in this context that Brook opened as a prophylactic centre to help prevent abortions and unwanted pregnancy for unmarried young people. While this opening was, at the time, perceived as a radical move and sometimes criticized through the lens of promiscuity, this chapter argues that the

---

[85] 'The eleventh meeting of the Board, 18 March 1964', in SA/EUG/K39, Wellcome Library, London.

main justification for opening a centre specifically dedicated to the unmarried was an emphasis on instilling a sense of sexual responsibility.

The opening of Brook broke with the long-established tradition, maintained by sexual and reproductive health charities such as the FPA and Marie Stopes Clinic, to advise married women only. Despite making a departure from these charities' clientele, Brook members drew on familiar ideas developed by the FPA, namely the idea of committed and loving relationships and the fact that each child should be a wanted child. The Brook therefore continued the legacy of the FPA in that they encouraged steady relationships and responsible sexual behaviours and they also held some continuity in racial and classist prejudices. However, this story of continuity should not obscure the fact that Brook reconfigured the notion of responsibility to include young unmarried people, paving the way for increasing autonomy and sexual freedom in the subsequent decades.

2
Locality and Controversy
The Opening of Brook Centres across Britain

In 1964, the first article covering the official opening of Brook was published in the *Daily Mirror*. The Labour-supporting tabloid had been a pioneer in the spread of information on sexual matters since World War Two.[1] Entitled 'Full mark[s] to this sex-help clinic for the teenage lovers',[2] the article welcomed the work of Brook. The female journalist and agony aunt Marjorie Proops, who held progressive views on sex,[3] acknowledged the subversiveness inherent in the subject but nevertheless recognized the social benefit of the endeavour: 'It is certain it will provoke a great big noisy uproar. [. . .] But a new birth control organisation whose specific aim will be to give contraceptive advice to the unmarried gets full mark[s] from me.' Proops presented Helen Brook as a rational woman who was taking realistic measures by offering 'practical help' with avoiding the bad consequences of 'irresponsible sex', such as unwanted babies, illegitimacy, and dramatic fallout for 'unwed teenage mothers'. Proops depicted the centre as a place where young people could discuss 'all their problems of love, sex and marriage'. Having recognized the urgency of the situation, the journalist praised Brook's initiative and quoted Helen Brook, who said that Brook 'will try to teach them (the young) responsibility about their sex lives'.[4]

This positive reception of Brook's work contrasted drastically with the reaction of the Birmingham local newspapers when they covered a similar suggested scheme for Birmingham. An intense debate began when the *Sunday Mercury* opened its columns to supporters and opponents of Brook in August

---

[1] According to historian Adrian Bingham, the *Daily Mirror* claimed 'that being sexually informed was an essential element of modern citizenship, and that therefore, popular papers had a duty to play their part in the fight against ignorance', Bingham, *Family Newspapers?* 53.

[2] Marjorie Proops, 'Full mark[s] to this sex-help clinic for the teenage lovers', *Daily Mirror*, 2 June 1964, 7.

[3] On Marjorie Proops and her role in advising readers about sex see Bingham, *Family Newspapers*, 75–95.

[4] Marjorie Proops, 'Full mark[s] to this sex-help clinic for the teenage lovers', *Daily Mirror*, 2 June 1964, 7.

1965; the Public Opinion Action Association sponsored a meeting on the subject in November. In particular, opponents argued that the scheme would be 'a prescription for fornication without tears'.[5]

This chapter focuses on the role played by locality in the controversies surrounding the openings of Brook centres in five different cities: London, Birmingham, Bristol, Edinburgh, and Liverpool. Lesley Hall and Adrian Bingham have argued that the discursive boundaries of what constitutes 'acceptable' sexuality have shifted over time.[6] There was now a way to frame the need for birth control while staying within the remits of respectability. Historians Clare Debenham, Lesley Hall, Audrey Leathard, and Stephen Brooke have all contended that in order to be seen as respectable, birth control advocates needed to emphasize that birth control helped working-class mothers through the improvement of their health and economic conditions, rather than pushing for women's rights and sexual freedom.[7] Building on this work, this chapter explores the discursive boundaries used by Brook and its opponents through an analysis of the correspondence between Brook and local leaders, the memories of Brook funders, and the media coverage of the centres. It first identifies the main leaders, their motivations, and the opposition they faced in opening centres. Talking about young people's sexuality and recognizing that they did engage in premarital sex was still an antagonistic issue in the 1960s. There was an accepted view that premarital sex was dangerous for various reasons. As mentioned in Chapter 1, some pointed out that engaging in premarital sex without the means to protect oneself could result in unwanted pregnancy, illegal abortions, and venereal diseases. Others believed that providing birth control information would only encourage young people to have sex and therefore increase the trend of illegitimacy and contribute to the moral decline of Britain. The solutions proposed differed drastically. For the former, better access to birth control facilities and information to sexual knowledge through sex education was essential; for the latter, a reaffirmation of the values of traditional family life was paramount.

In this context, Brook supporters needed to develop strategies that would mitigate criticism and appease, to a certain extent, the fears and anxieties of opponents. These strategies were the resort to the support of medical authorities and to a narrative focused on sexual responsibility. The only acceptable

---

[5] Ibid.   [6] Hall, *Sex, Gender and Social Change*; Bingham, *Family Newspapers?*
[7] Stephen Brooke, *Sexual Politics: Sexuality, Family Planning, and the British Left from the 1880s to the Present Day* (Oxford University Press, 2011); Clare Debenham, *Birth Control and the Rights of Women: Post-Suffrage Feminism in the Early Twentieth Century* (I. B. Tauris, 2014); Leathard, *Fight for Family Planning*; Hall, *Sex, Gender and Social Change*.

way of presenting a scheme for providing contraception to young people was to stress the educational dimension of Brook's work, namely the fact that Brook members were trying to instil a sense of sexual responsibility in the young. Any deviation from this narrative was met with strong opposition. However, this is not to say that this narrative was accepted; resistance was still powerful and shaped the ways that local politicians, doctors, and moral campaigners reacted to Brook.

The establishment of the centres

Officially opened in July 1964 in London, the aims of the first Brook Advisory Centre were 'the prevention and the mitigation of the suffering caused by unwanted pregnancy and illegal abortion by educating young persons in matter[s] of sex and contraception and developing among them a sense of responsibility in regard to sexual behaviours'. The justification behind the creation of the centre, namely the fight against unwanted pregnancy and illegal abortion, was very similar to that underpinning the creation of FPA centres. Following the opening of London Brook, similar schemes were launched in different cities around Britain. This shows that the concerns about young people's sexuality and lack of information and access to contraception were widespread. The setting up of these local centres more or less always followed the same stages. First, a small group of liberal individuals joined forces to start the process. Second, the launch group contacted London Brook for practical help and advice and sometimes financial help. Third, this small group of committed individuals tried to keep their plan low-key and away from press attention as long as possible, therefore avoiding fierce debate.

In 1965, a Brook centre opened in Birmingham after a few months of intense public debate and significant opposition. The personalities behind the centre were Dr Martin Cole, a lecturer in genetics at Birmingham University and active member of the Abortion Law Reform Association, Prof François Lafitte, Dean of the Faculty of Social Studies and author of the FPA 1963 report *Family Planning in the Sixties,* and Mrs Audrey Court, the Birmingham FPA association's chairwoman. As was the case with London Brook, the founders of Birmingham Brook were closely connected to the FPA. Following the opening of Brook in London, Cole and Lafitte wrote the memorandum 'A Birmingham Centre for family planning advice for the unmarried' in April 1964. They highlighted the need to open a centre for unmarried people, 'especially the young, who rightly or wrongly, are engaging in sexual relations',[8] in order to complement the services offered by the FPA. The memorandum took the work done by Helen Brook in the Marie Stopes Memorial Clinic as an example and recognized that it was just as important to discuss personal, physical, emotional, and moral problems as to provide information about and instruction in contraceptive technique. The centre would differ from the FPA, they argued, in that it would cater for the unmarried only, avoid a one-sex approach, adopt an 'educative-permissive attitude', which was a way of saying they would not moralize young people and allow its staff to work at their own pace by relying on appointments. Cole and Lafitte received financial backing from Brook to set up the administrative machinery[9] and create an informal consultative body.[10] Despite strong criticism and opposition, the Birmingham Brook centre finally opened in premises rented from the FPA in September 1966. Due to fears about protests, two guards were hired to make sure everything went smoothly; this was unnecessary.

A similar staged process characterized the opening of Brook in Bristol. In 1966, several individuals started to consider providing contraception to young people. In November of that year, anxious about the increase in the illegitimacy rate among young women, Labour Councillor Roy Morris tried to persuade the Health Committee of Bristol to agree to birth control advice for single girls in FPA clinics.[11] At the same time that Roy Morris first voiced his opinion, the Humanist Society at Bristol University was also trying to stimulate interest in the topic, as university students were becoming vocal about their needs and asking for birth control.[12] In a similar fashion to Birmingham, three of the Humanist Society's members, Leigh Chapman, Martin Lambert, and Elizabeth McMeekan, produced a report entitled *The Arguments For and Against a Brook Advisory Centre in Bristol*.[13] The report was intended as a survey of attitudes towards the setting up of Bristol Brook. The authors contacted 'as many people as they could whose occupational position had a bearing on this issue'. They interviewed social workers, doctors, and clergy members. The report argued in favour of the opening of the centre, based on key arguments, as we will see in the next section.

---

[8] 'A Birmingham Centre for Family Planning Advice for the unmarried, preliminary suggestions by Prof Lafitte and Dr Martin Cole, April 1964', in COLE 55, Bishopsgate Institute, London.
[9] 'Clinic to advise older teenagers', *Birmingham Post*, 9 August 1965, 1.
[10] Audrey Court and Cynthia Walton, *1926–1991: Birmingham Made a Difference: The Birmingham Women's Welfare Centre, the Family Planning Association in Birmingham* (Barns Brook, 2001): 54.
[11] Helen Reid, 'Sex and the single girl', *Western Daily Press*, 16 November 1966.
[12] Ruth Cole, 'The beginning of Avon Brook', in PP/MEW/C/3/6, Wellcome Library, London.
[13] Leigh Chapman, Martin Lambert, and Elizabeth McMeekan produced the report *The Arguments For and Against a Brook Advisory Centre in Bristol*, in SA/BRO/D/1/2/1, Wellcome Library, London.

In January 1967, a Working Party was formed from members of the Humanist Society,[14] the FPA, and Roy Morris, including the FPA doctor Betty Orton, the Humanist Society member Elizabeth McMeekan (one of the authors of the report), and the journalist for the *Evening Post* Barbara Buchanan.[15] The group wrote to London Brook to ask for financial help and advice about devising a successful strategy. Leigh Chapman and Martin Lambert were invited to visit the London centre and talk with Helen Brook. The latter advised them to set up a committee quietly and to 'try to get a clinic established in a small way without a lot of publicity'.[16] Chapman and Lambert recounted their experience to the Working Party in March. During that session, the decision was made to turn the Working Party into the Bristol Brook Clinic Campaign Committee (BBCCC).[17] Councillor Roy Morris was elected chairman and Dr Anthony Flood, consultant psychiatrist, vice chairman. The BBCCC decided to apply to use the Health Committee's premises free of charge in order to hold a contraceptive and counselling session for young people once a week. This was refused by the Health Committee on the ground that new powers were likely to be given to local authorities to extend family planning provision through the Edwin Brooks Family Planning Bill if the bill was successful. In August 1967, following the success of the Bill, the Health Committee announced they would consult the FPA and informed the BBCCC that they would not enter discussion with them at this stage. The BBCCC made several attempts to join the consultation without success. Despite these drawbacks, the BBCCC continued with the plan of finding suitable premises and affiliated itself as a branch of the Brook Advisory Centre. It elected a new president, Edwin Brooks, the MP for Bebington, and new vice presidents, Mr Arthur Palmer, Labour MP, and his wife Dr Marion Woollaston consultant psychiatrist to Fulham General Hospital. The BBCCC also set up a newsletter to inform its supporters of its advance and raise funds. The BBCCC applied to the Gloucestershire Health Committee, who granted them permission to use a Filton Clinic in January 1968. Once the Brook centre in Filton was accepted, some members of the BBCCC visited the Brook centre in London to gather knowledge and see how a Brook was run in practice. In

---

[14] Callum Brown has shown that the Humanists were key actors in the debate about the liberalization of contraception and abortion. See Callum Brown, *The Battle for Christian Britain: Sex, Humanists and Secularisation, 1945–1980* (Cambridge University Press, 2019): 216–50.

[15] 'Letter from Elizabeth McMeekan to secretary of Brook Betty Hunter, 15 January 1967', in SA/BRO/D/1/2/1, Wellcome Library, London.

[16] 'Letter from Betty Hunter to Dr Cornes, 7 February 1967', in SA/BRO/D/1/2/1, Wellcome Library, London.

[17] 'Clinic campaigners for Bristol talks', *Bristol Evening Post*, 8 January 1968.

January 1968, Morris declared in the press 'We know there is a need for such a clinic in Bristol.'[18] In March 1968, the first Bristol Brook session was provided to clients. In June 1968, after the national FPA decided it would advise the unmarried, the FPA started its first session for unmarried people in Bristol.

In Liverpool, the Merseyside Young People's Advisory Clinic (MYPAC) opened in October 1967 as an affiliate to Brook. There was a long tradition in the city of offering contraceptive advice to married women. Indeed, a Mother's Welfare Clinic, providing birth control to married women, had opened in 1926 as a result of the efforts of middle-class women and men. The setup of the clinic went smoothly because it received support from the 'informal networks among the Liverpool elite and was a testimony to the city's philanthropic traditions', as historian Emma Jones has argued. The impetus therefore came from well-off individuals with the social and financial capital to open a clinic. The City Council financially supported the clinic from 1935 onwards in spite of Catholic opposition. By 1960, three branch clinics existed in the city.[19] While Liverpool had a strong Catholic community, Emma Jones has shown that this did not have any bearing on the opening of the Mother's Welfare Clinic or its subsequent expansion. Jones demonstrates that the establishment of the Liverpool Mother's Welfare Clinic was done independently of the local authority and as such was kept away 'from the political interference of religion'. Analogous to what had happened in Birmingham and Bristol, the impetus to open a Liverpool Brook centre came from individuals who shared concerns about the need to advise young people. These individuals were members of the FPA and the Socialist Medical Society. Dr Margaret Smyth, a Medical Officer at the FPA clinic in Liverpool, was the first to contact London Brook. She was supported by Mrs Gregory, a member of the executive committee of the Liverpool FPA, who was married to a professor of physiology.

In January 1967, Smyth and Gregory decided to write to Helen Brook to ask for help and advice. In her letter, Smyth explained that her private practice was not suitable for many young people and that her working pattern was also inconvenient for them due to their work hours.[20] She felt that there was an urgent need to open a centre for young people. Soon after Smyth's letter to Helen Brook, she was contacted by the Socialist Medical Society to attend a

---

[18] Ibid.
[19] Emma L. Jones, 'The establishment of voluntary family planning clinics in Liverpool and Bradford, 1926–1960: A comparative study', *Social History of Medicine* 24.2 (2011): 352–69.
[20] 'Letter from Margaret Smythe to Helen Brook, 31 January 1967,' in SA/BRO/D/12/2, Wellcome Library, London.

meeting where Edwin Brooks MP was presenting the Parliamentary Bill Family Planning Act. At the meeting, she met Edith Levy, secretary of the Society and wife of a GP in the south area of the city, who offered her help. The latter invited Smyth and Gregory to her home; at the meeting, it was decided they would establish a Working Party to assess the need to open a centre for the unmarried. Once the Working Party was set up, Cllr Taylor publicly announced the plan to open an Advisory Centre.[21] After a few months, premises were found and the first session took place in October 1967.[22] At first, MYPAC had no premises of their own and operated inside the office of a GP practice. However, soon afterwards, the FPA provided them with free premises in their building and MYPAC were able to run two centres. In 1972, its centre in the GP office closed. MYPAC officially became a Brook branch in 1974.

In Edinburgh, discussions around the establishment of a Brook centre started in 1967. Historians Roger Davidson and Gayle Davis have argued that the 1960s saw a significant development in family planning services in Scotland, boosted by the arrival of the pill. In addition, they have stressed that the expansion of family planning provision was also fuelled by 'the rapid expansion in the female student population, a group more sexually active and determined to obtain access to the pill as part of a "wider flouting of traditional conventions" and a "permissive" shift in youth culture and moral rebellion'.[23] The push to open an Edinburgh Brook clinic originated from women involved with the local FPA. Moya Woodside, a committed FPA member with the help of June Bedford and Janet Jackson—who had both worked in the premarital clinic of the FPA, and Jill Jansen, a psychiatric social worker who worked with Woodside at the Royal Edinburgh Hospital, set up the 'Social Aspects of Contraception' Group to discuss the opportunity to open a Brook centre. Woodside had helped Marie Stopes to set up a Mother's Clinic for Constructive Birth Control in Belfast in 1938.[24] She became honorary secretary in 1939. In 1943, she qualified as a psychiatric social worker. Her first appointment at the Maudsley Hospital was as a research assistant to Dr Eliot Slater, a leading psychiatrist, conducting interviews for a study on marriage relationships among soldiers. She gathered substantial information on birth control practices and knowledge and as a result published a couple of

---

[21] 'Advice Centre planned for the unmarried', *Liverpool Echo*, 23 February 1967, 7.
[22] 'First session of Advisory Centre', *Liverpool Echo*, 3 October 1967, 7.
[23] Roger Davidson and Gayle Davis, *The Sexual State: Sexuality and Scottish Governance, 1950–80* (Edinburgh University Press, 2012): 132.
[24] Moya Woodside, 'Family planning, connections and recollections', in SA/MEW/C/3/2, Wellcome Library, London.

articles on the subject. Her publications attracted the attention of Dr Clarence Gamble, who was an American doctor, heir to Proctor and Gamble, convinced eugenicist, and ardent supporter of birth control. He offered Woodside a post at the Institute of Social Science at the University of North California, where she would study the effectiveness of the 1933 Sterilization Act in that state. She interviewed a sample of sterilized women to learn how they felt about the operation. The majority were African-American women. Woodside's study stressed the enthusiasm of these women for sterilization. In the USA, she attended several conferences on population and fertility control and met with renowned family planners such as Dr Abraham Stone, the Director of the New York Planned Parenthood Federation. These encounters would prove essential in setting up a Brook centre in Edinburgh.

In the 1950s, Woodside returned to London and became a member of the FPA and a Fellow of the Eugenics Society. She then worked as a psychiatric social worker at Holloway Prison where she conducted research on women convicted for criminal abortions. In 1963, she settled in Edinburgh to work at the University Department of Psychiatry, before moving to the Royal Edinburgh Hospital's social work department. She became a member of the Executive Committee of the FPA.

Once the 'Social Aspects of Contraception' Group was set up, lecturers from the Social Medicine Department of the University of Edinburgh expressed interest in joining. They urged for some action to be taken in light of the growing demands from students for answers to the problems of abortions and contraception. Despite repeated calls from the students, the Student Health Centre still refused to provide contraceptive advice. As a result, the lecturer Dr Margaret Gilmore opened a contraceptive service at her own home. These lecturers joined the group and pressed for the opening of a Brook centre.

In the meantime, university students were also facing confrontation with the Rector of the University of Edinburgh, Malcolm Muggeridge. Elected by the student representative committee on the basis of his past rebellion against the British establishment, he had since become a Catholic believer, and a critic of the 'permissive society'. He opposed the students' demand for the University Health Centre to provide information concerning the contraceptive pill and the pill itself if requested by any student.[25] Muggeridge's stubborn opposition to the pill, in what was then called 'the pill and pot' scandal,

---

[25] Charlie Lynch, *Scotland and the Sexual Revolution c.1957–1975: Religion, Intimacy and Popular Culture* (PhD dissertation, University of Glasgow, 2019): chapter 2, 'The Muggeridge Affair. 1968, Moral Controversy and the University'.

triggered student protests and led to his resignation in January 1968, coincidentally at the same moment as the opening of Edinburgh Brook.[26]

While students were campaigning for access to the birth control pill, the 'Social Aspects of Contraception' Group received additional support from individuals interested in the international dimension of the population problem. In 1967, June Bedford was asked to set up a Scottish Branch of the Family Planning International Committee, which was renamed the World Population Crisis Campaign because 'the innocuous name Family Planning International was too brutally frank for Scottish consumption',[27] as she remembered. Many high-profile members of the WPCC joined the 'Social Aspects of Contraception' Group, where they discussed the necessity of opening a Brook centre. Among them was the advocate Nicholas Fairbairn, who had become interested in family planning because of the many cases of divorce he dealt with that had been instigated by unintended pregnancies.[28] June Bedford and Janet Jackson turned to Fairbairn for legal advice, and he became the chairman of Edinburgh Brook. Dr Elizabeth Rose, a member of the World Population Crisis Campaign, was recruited as a doctor at the Brook. In addition, Moya Woodside utilized her relations with Clarence Gamble to secure some funding for the opening of the Brook. Nicholas Fairbairn managed to find premises in a house in Lower Gilmore Place, which was relatively discreet and central, not far from the University. In addition, they received financial help from London Brook. The centre opened in January 1968, at the same time as a controversy was arising within the University of Edinburgh. This gave the centre some adverse publicity; until that point, the endeavour had remained low-key in order to avoid opposition from moral conservatives, in particular the churches. As a *Telegraph* article underscored: 'to those who know Edinburgh, one astonishing fact is that Fairbairn et al. have manged to organise the centre without the opposition of the City Fathers, or the knowledge of the Scottish press'.[29]

Motivations to establish the centres

In the archival materials covering the setting up of centres, Brook members referred to the motivations that underpinned their work: a desire to fight

---

[26] For more information on the Muggeridge affair, see Lynch, *Scotland and the Sexual Revolution c.1957–1975*.
[27] June Bedford, 'The origin of the Brook Clinic in Edinburgh', in SA/MEW/C/3/2, Wellcome Library, London.
[28] Nicholas Fairbairn, *A Life is Too Short: Autobiography Volume 1* (Quartet Books, 1987): 153.
[29] Mandrake, 'Next phase in the battle of Edinburgh', *The Sunday Telegraph*, 21 January 1968, 5.

unwanted pregnancies, illegal abortions, and rising illegitimacy. As explained in Chapter 1 since the 1950s there had been a shift of the incidence of illegitimate births from the over-20s to the under 20s.[30] In 1976, about 37% of illegitimate births were to girls under 20 compared with 15% in 1951. However, from the early 1970s the rate of illegitimacy in the under-20s had begun to drop. In addition, the reasons for creating centres were also grounded in activist's personal experience of working in FPA clinics or with young people.

In London, Helen Brook interviewed in 1963, in the Labour-supporting tabloid, the *Daily Mirror*, presented her work as a responsible move to help reduce the rate of illegitimacy and the number of backstreet abortions.[31] Anticipating criticisms and accusations that the Brook centre was encouraging promiscuity, Helen Brook played on the 'modernism' of her vision by qualifying plausible opponents as 'backward looking and narrow-minded people' and emphasizing that her approach answered a real need, since 'tut-tutting will not bring down the illegitimate birth rate figures. Contraceptive and correct sex knowledge will.' She added that moral speeches 'are not getting us anywhere'. What was needed was a practical initiative.

In Birmingham, Martin Cole, who was deeply supportive of expanding access to legal abortions to young women, realized that the prevention of pregnancies would also be a useful weapon in the fight against illegal abortions.[32] Cole and Lafitte in their report on the need to open a Brook centre in Birmingham presented the centre as an effective way of 'preventing the greater evils of unwanted pregnancy, unwanted children and unwanted and illegal abortions'. From the start, Cole and Lafitte used the word clients instead of patients and stressed that one of the key goals of the centre was to respect clients' wishes in their choice of birth control methods, instead of insisting on the doctor's preferred method. The goal was to encourage informed choice by the client.

In Bristol, reducing the number of unwanted pregnancies was also a key driver for the creation of a centre. In the report *The Arguments For and Against a Brook Advisory Centre in Bristol*, the authors presented the extent of the problem Bristol Brook was aiming to remedy; they reviewed illegitimacy rates in Bristol, which stood at 9.8% of all live births in 1965. They also pointed that 36% of brides under 20 years old were pregnant at the time of their marriage. In addition, they estimated the number of illegal abortions to be

---

[30] Dilys Cossey, *Safe sex for teenagers*, 1978, in SA/BRO/E/7, Wellcome Library, London.
[31] Christine Whiting, 'Would you let your teenage daughter go to a birth control clinic?', *Daily Mirror*, 8 November 1963, 9.
[32] Court and Walton, *Birmingham Made a Difference*, 53.

around 1,000 per year. The authors argued that if young people were properly advised and instructed about contraception when young, they would be sexually responsible later in life, which would reduce the number of illegal abortions and rushed marriages. The centre would therefore function as a preventive measure to reduce the hazards of unwanted pregnancies and the physical damage caused by illegal abortions. In its first newsletter published by the BBCCC to gain support for opening a Brook centre, the authors reaffirmed their commitment to tackle the increase in sexual intercourse outside marriage, especially among young people, and to take 'some action to deal with this problem rather than give no alternative to unwanted pregnancy or abortion'.[33] The centre was therefore presented as a preventive measure. Moreover, in the *Bristol Evening Post* Cllr Roy Morris presented the reason behind a Brook centre as 'an attempt to deal with the problem of illegitimate children before it occurs'. Trying to convince a wider audience, he also played out on the economic benefit of such centres for public finances: 'we have a large number of children in care in this city, costing a great deal of money to support. If contraceptive advice to all women can reduce abortion figures and the number of children in care, then the sooner we have it the better.'[34]

Besides fighting unwanted pregnancies and reducing the hazard of illegal abortions, the centres were also deemed essential in filling a gap in the services. In Bristol, the report underlined the necessity of opening a Brook centre by giving an overview of the types of resources available for young people; existing facilities for counselling young people were desperately lacking. Parents would be the obvious providers of advice, but the topic of sex and contraception was shrouded in embarrassment and secrecy. Most young people did not know they could turn to GPs; those who did feared that their GP would inform their parents. A confidential counselling service was deemed necessary in order to offer essential knowledge to young people. In Liverpool too, the inquiry carried by the Committee reported that 'none of the local family planning services were willing to provide contraceptive advice to the unmarried'.[35] Once the FPA and local health authorities started providing advice to the unmarried in 1972, the MYPAC Committee felt that a special

---

[33] 'Bristol Brook Campaign Fund, Newsletter August 1967', in SA/BRO/D/1/2/1, Wellcome Library, London.
[34] Cllr Roy Morris, in 'We'd be happy to close down—chairman', in *Bristol Evening Post*, 15 January 1968.
[35] 'Merseyside Young People Advisory Clinic, First report, 1967–68', in SA/BRO/D/12/2, Wellcome Library, London.

clinic 'geared to the needs of young people was still a necessity'. The Committee stressed that young people did not want to attend FPA clinics, fearing that they might see their mothers or someone else who knew them, and they did not trust their GP as the latter was often the family doctor.[36]

Finally, the motivations to open the centre came from members' dissatisfaction with the position of the FPA and from their experience in working with young people. In London, Helen Brook opened the first centre because she witnessed the misery of unmarried clients who were turned down at FPA clinics. In Bristol, Labour Councillor Roy Morris had first tried to convinced the FPA to catered for the unmarried by arguing that sexual mores were changing rapidly and that even theologians were questioning traditional beliefs of chastity, but, he emphasized, medical and voluntary bodies were still dominated by such beliefs.[37] His remark was aimed specifically at the Family Planning Association, who were refusing to provide contraceptive advice to young people.

In Edinburgh, the catalyst for opening a centre came from FPA members who were dissatisfied with the position of the Association. The FPA members, Moya Woodside, Mrs June Bedford, and Janet Jackson—who had both worked in the premarital clinic of the FPA[38] and had challenged the strict attitudes of nurses and doctors who were sending patients away because they could not prove that they were soon to be married,[39] believed that the association should do more to meet the needs of 'socially deprived women' and 'girls about to get married'.[40] Together, they formed a 'Social Aspects of Contraception' Group. The FPA had made it clear that they would not become involved with providing contraceptive advice to young unmarried people.

Finally, in Liverpool, founding member Margaret Smyth was moved to action as a result of her experience in general practice. Indeed, she had established a small private contraceptive consultation practice and had started to see the unmarried. As her interest in the subject increased, she collected information and contacted Dr Faith Spicer from London Brook and Dr Libby Wilson from a FPA clinic in Sheffield, asking them to refer clients to her. She

---

[36] 'Brook Advisory Centre Merseyside, Annual report 1974', in SA/BRO/D/12/1/1, Wellcome Library, London.
[37] 'Birth control for unmarried – plea', *Bristol Evening Post*, 2 November 1966.
[38] Premarital advice was first given in some FPA clinics from 1952 on the basis that the couple would be married in the following six weeks.
[39] June Bedford, 'The origin of the Brook Clinic in Edinburgh', in SA/MEW/C/3/2, Wellcome Library, London.
[40] Ibid.

explained in a letter to Helen Brook that 'the more I see of these young people the more I realise how urgent and important this work is'.[41]

Opposition to the centres

The opening of the clinics triggered opposition from various players and individuals. One source of opposition came from some FPA doctors, who fought the provision of contraception to unmarried people out of fear of the charity losing its hard-won respectability and financial support.

For instance, as already mentioned in Chapter 1, the creation of Brook in London resulted from the FPA refusal to allow unmarried people into its clinics. In Birmingham too, FPA members opposed Brook. In June 1965, an intense controversy occurred within the Birmingham branch of the FPA over whether to support and endorse Cole's endeavour. Professor of Economics Philip Sargant Florence, vice-president of the Birmingham branch, feared that an official endorsement of Brook would break up the unity enjoyed by the Birmingham Association.[42] Indeed, several Birmingham FPA members were already opposed to the existence of these centres, since they had publicly condemned the resolution taken during the 1964 FPA General Assembly. Mrs E. Clews of the West Midland Federation of the FPA stated that giving the green light to sexual intercourse between young people would strike 'a blow at the very foundation of the association'.[43] Mrs Joyce Child, chairwoman of the Sutton Coldfield FPA clinic, shared Clews' disapproval of the setting up of the clinic: 'We must strive to work for the preservation and enrichment of family life, not the degradation and unhappiness that would surely follow from condoning this so-called new pattern of premarital behaviour.'[44] She feared that condoning premarital sexuality would lead to an increase in promiscuity and therefore a rise in unwanted pregnancies and venereal diseases. In addition, the suggestion to establish a Brook centre in the premises of the FPA centre in the Calthorpe Estate, where the University of Birmingham was located, was first defeated by the FPA Executive Committee, but the Advisory Committee of the FPA persuaded the Executive Committee to reconsider their decision. The Birmingham branch of the British Medical

---

[41] 'Letter from Margaret Smyth to Helen Brook', 31.01.67, in SA/BRO/D12/2, Wellcome Library, London.
[42] 'Teenagers' clinic is proposed', *The Guardian*, 7 June 1965, 3.
[43] 'Plea for girls in love', *Daily Mail*, 5 June 1964, 3.
[44] Mrs Joyce Child, 'Teenage sex problems', *Birmingham Post*, 29 June 1964, 8.

Association was also opposed to the centre, fearing it would increase promiscuity.⁴⁵

Similarly, when the news broke that the BBCCC in Bristol had received the support of the Gloucestershire Health Committee to open a centre in Filton, this move was criticized by the chairwoman of the Bristol Committee of the Family Planning Association, Mrs Salt, who accused the BBCCC of rushing into opening a clinic without due preparation.⁴⁶ This was indicative of resistance from the local FPA to allowing Brook to deal with young people's sexuality. Opposition from the FPA was also present in Liverpool. In a letter sent to Helen Brook, Margaret Smythe underscored that Liverpool was 'very rigid in its morality', giving the example that the majority of Liverpool FPA members were opposed to advising the unmarried.

Opposition to Brook was not limited to the FPA branch; it came from various local bodies and politicians. In Birmingham Councillor Colin E. J. Franklin, chairman of the Birmingham Health Committee;⁴⁷ Nigel Cook, chairman of the Birmingham Education Committee; Mr Keith J. F. Simms, vice-president of the Birmingham Association of the National Union of Teachers; and Dame Edith Pitt, MP for Edgbaston (where the FPA clinic was located) and former Parliamentary Secretary for the Ministry of Health all opposed the scheme. Once the clinic opened, local political opposition to Brook nevertheless remained active. The City of Birmingham Health Committee voted against endorsing Brook and allowing its social workers to publicize Brook services.⁴⁸ Despite the Family Planning Act of 1967, which allowed local authorities to provide birth control to all women, married or single, the Health Committee continued to refuse to accept the work of the Centre as a 'vital and necessary part of the City's Family Planning Services'.⁴⁹ It was not until 1972, when the Labour Party gained control of the city council, that a full free contraceptive service for Birmingham residents was implemented on the order of the new Chairman of the Health Committee, John Charlton. The FPA and Brook were used as agents to widen contraceptive access. This move was referred to as 'sex on the rates' by opponents, among them the former Councillor Franklin.⁵⁰

---

⁴⁵ 'Doctors opposed contraceptive clinic plan', *Birmingham Post*, 16 October 1965, 1.
⁴⁶ 'We'd be happy to close down—chairman', *Bristol Evening Post*, 15 January 1968.
⁴⁷ 'Dr Cole's sex clinic: a moral confrontation', *Sunday Mercury*, 22 August 1965, 11.
⁴⁸ 'Committee will not help Brook', *Birmingham Post*, 12 November 1966, 1.
⁴⁹ '3rd Annual Report, Birmingham Brook, 1969', in SA/BRO/D3/1/1, Wellcome Library, London.
⁵⁰ 'Conflict over free family planning scheme', *Birmingham Post*, 29 September 1972, 18.

Church leaders were also vocal in their opposition to Brook. Birmingham in the 1960s was a fertile ground for traditional values and criticisms of the 'permissive society'. Indeed, Mary Whitehouse and Norah Buckland launched their campaign to 'clean up the BBC' from Birmingham Town Hall in 1964. Moreover, the West Midlands was famous for its vocal opposition to abortion; this was led by the Catholic Hugh MacLaren, who was Professor of Obstetrics and Gynaecology at the University of Birmingham and fiercely against the liberalization of abortion.[51] Canon Bryan Green of the Church of England, the Rector of Birmingham, wrote columns for the local newspaper, the *Birmingham Post* against the scheme.[52] Moreover, the Reverend John Good lamented the suggestion that a Brook should be opened in Birmingham: 'We are in favour of planned families but this is not right at all. This clinic will encourage a completely free attitude towards sex. I can only describe it as a revolutionary step backward.'[53] In Liverpool too, religious leaders were presented as potential opponents. Indeed, in a letter to Helen Brook describing the difficulties she faced, Margaret Smyth explained that 'Liverpool has its Roman Catholic problem.'[54] The Roman Catholic community constituted an important section of the voters and had influence on potential donors, which might mean that it would be difficult to find backing and funding for opening a Brook centre.

In Edinburgh, leaders of Brook kept their plan secret to avoid moral religious opposition. Historians Davidson and Davis have explained that Scotland was very morally conservative and quoted the co-founder of Edinburgh Brook, Margaret Gilmore, who described Scotland as 'struggling to emerge from a spiritual ice-age in which our main adversary is an antisexual puritanism shot through with an overwhelming spiritual sadism'.[55] Davidson and Davis have further underlined the religious opposition to providing contraceptive advice to the young and unmarried from the Church of Scotland's Committee on Temperance and Morals—even though the Church of Scotland accepted family planning more generally—and the Roman Catholics, who condemned premarital and unmarried sex.

Finally, the last source of opposition came from individuals involved in universities. In Liverpool, the Medical Officer of the University Student Health

[51] David Paintin, *Abortion Law Reform in Britain (1964–2003): A Personal Account* (London, 2015): chapter 7.
[52] 'Millionaire backs new clinic: Birth control tuition for all comers', *Birmingham Sunday Mercury*, 6 June 1965, 3.
[53] Ibid.
[54] 'Letter from Margaret Smyth to Helen Brook', 31.01.67, in SA/BRO/D12/2, Wellcome Library, London.
[55] Margaret Gilmore, 'Counselling at the Brook Centre', *The Scotsman*, 2 February 1968, 8.

Service did not want to support Smythe's work. In Edinburgh, when the news broke of the opening of the clinic, opposition was fierce. The principal of the University of Edinburgh, Professor Swann, disagreed with the opening of Brook, asserting that such a service would be best provided by general practitioners.[56] Similarly, local newspapers reported negatively on the endeavour. Letters sent by the public condemned the scheme, arguing that the centre would undermine the 'status of marriage' and that the centre would act as a contraceptive shop, with a 'policy of the deliberate withholding of counselling'.[57]

Challenging the opposition: Medical authority and sexual responsibility

In order to counter the opposition and calm down potential critics Brook members relied on two strategies: attracting the backing of respectable individuals, mainly medical men, and putting forward a narrative of sexual responsibility.

All Brook centres were created thanks to a campaigning committee, that generally gathered male experts, very often doctors. This was meant to legitimize the setting up of the centre by showing that this endeavour was respectable since it attracted the backing of experts, all respectable men. In Birmingham, the committee that pushed to open a Brook was made up of five esteemed Birmingham personalities. In addition to Cole and Lafitte, these included: Professor Douglas Vernon Hubble, a paediatric endocrinologist and Dean of the Faculty of Medicine at Birmingham University; Mr George Jonas, a solicitor, former city councillor, prospective Parliamentary Labour candidate for Hail Green and member of the Abortion Law Reform Association; and Dr Peter Eckstein, a senior lecturer in anatomy.[58] In Bristol too medical doctors were invited to be part of the Bristol Brook Clinic Campaign Committee in order to impart a sense of respectability. Morris was elected chairman; Dr Anthony Flood, consultant psychiatrist, was elected vice-chairman; and the married couple Mr Arthur Palmer MP and Marion Woollaston, a psychiatrist and consultant to the Fulham General Hospital, were both made vice-presidents.

The establishment of Liverpool Brook was underpinned by a comparable strategy of gathering prominent well-off and respectable individuals. These

---

[56] 'New pill clinic opens as don disagrees', *Daily Express*, 22 January 1968, 7.
[57] 'The Brook Centre', Letter from Eileen Walsh, *The Scotsman*, 26 January 1968.
[58] 'The clinic controversy', *Birmingham Post*, 27 November 1965, 10.

individuals invited in the campaigning committee included: Dr Edwin Brooks who passed the Family Planning Act; Dr Cyril Taylor, who was a Labour councillor and member of the Socialist Medical Association and chairman of the Liverpool Welfare Committee; and several social workers, general practitioners, gynaecologists, and psychiatrists.

The backing from medical individuals was also key in gaining legitimacy in Edinburgh. Two senior University of Edinburgh academics, Professor Walter Perry, the Vice Principal and Professor of Pharmacology, and Lord Peter Richie Calder, Professor of International Relations and a humanist peace activist became sponsors of Brook. Sir Derrick Dunlop, the Scottish physician and pharmacologist behind the Dunlop Committee—which investigated the side effects of new drugs in the UK, also joined the committee.

Alongside the presence of respectable individuals in the campaigning group leading to the opening of the centre, Brook established a board of directors at the national level, who oversaw the organization of the different centres. This board was made up of esteemed individuals to give the charity respectability. In 1964, Helen Brook, Margaret Pyke, the British family planning activist and Lord Brain, a British neurologist, baron, fellow of the Royal Society were all board members. In 1966, Brain and Pyke passed away and were replaced by Robin Brook (Helen Brook's husband), Sir Theodore Fox, a quaker. In addition, a Medical Advisory Committee was also set up made of renowned doctors and professors at different British universities and hospitals. Its aim was to evaluate the latest medical advancements pertaining to contraception, to organize clinical trials, and devise the medical policy of the centres.

The other strategy utilized by Brook members to downplay criticism was to put forward a narrative that emphasized sexual responsibility. This narrative explained why the London centre was generally positively received by the broadsheet and tabloid press. Indeed, Helen Brook and Faith Spicer, the doctor who worked in the first sessions dedicated to unmarried women 'sold' their achievement to an expert audience and the public by emphasizing the expert counselling dimension of the centre, whereby young people would be educated and taught about responsible sexual behaviour. In addition, they portrayed their clients as young people in steady relationships. Their strategy was to show that the centre would not encourage promiscuity but instead promote, if not monitor, responsible behaviour among young people and prepare them for marriage. In so doing, they acted realistically and aligned the centre with the aim of the FPA in the sense that they were supporting committed young people in avoiding backstreet abortions and unwanted children, and thus helping them to have a wanted child once married. In addition, this emphasis on sexual responsibility was aimed to address, to a certain extent, the anxieties expressed by opponents about the new morality. Responsibility in sexual behaviour stood in contrast to promiscuity.

The two reports on the activity of the centre in its first two years (1963–1964), written by Spicer and published in the journal *Family Planning*, clearly deployed this strategy.[59] The reports presented the centre's clients as committed young people: out of 177 who visited the centre in the first year, 70 were engaged, while 90 were in a steady relationship. This number clearly demonstrates that promiscuity was not widespread and that, on the contrary, the self-selected group of young people who made use of the service displayed responsible behaviours. Patients fell into two groups: the first were 'the mature, sensible people [who] have made their decision to have intercourse with the partner they love and perhaps wish to marry'. The second group included young people who were undecided or confused or who had made mistakes in the past but wanted to live their future lives more wisely. Spicer drew on the FPA argument that each child should be a wanted child in order to justify the work of the centre: 'any action designed to prevent unhappy marriage and unwanted and deprived children should be encouraged'. In addition, her narrative promoted the idea that a protected steady relationship would lead to a successful marriage. In so doing, Spicer presented the work as a continuation of the FPA's work on preserving the stability of the marital relationship. Similarly, the first report on the Brook centre did not portray promiscuous young people but rather responsible young people in steady relationships who needed advice: 'The greatest proportion of people coming to the centre are young women, quite sure at the time that they have a steady relationship who wish to discuss, often in great detail and sometimes together with their young men, methods of birth control. They make a sincere effort to be responsible, listen objectively to what is said.'[60] Importantly, the picture chosen to illustrate this report depicted two hands held together, therefore emphasizing the commitment of young people, an implicit reference to a possible future marriage. Here, again, Brook's work was aimed to be preventative, preparing young people for marriage.

In Birmingham, the news that a Brook centre was to be opened triggered massive opposition. This opposition was very much the result of the way Cole framed his narrative. Indeed, a fierce debate about the 'sex clinic' took place within the columns of two local newspapers, the *Sunday Mercury* and the

---

[59] Faith Spicer, 'The Marie Stopes advice centre for young people', *Family Planning* 13 (1964): 31.
[60] 'Annual Report of the Brook Advisory Centre', *Family Planning* 15 (1966): 47–50.

Birmingham Post, with the founders of Brook confronting their opponents. The initial cause of outrage was Cole's defence of young people's right to enjoy their sexuality. His justification for opening a Brook centre rested on two main reasons: 'Firstly, the need to stem the appalling tide of illegitimate births. Secondly, to produce a society which will allow young people to enjoy sexual experience free of feelings of guilt and free of fear of disease.'[61] He added that he was convinced he was 'doing something that is morally right' and iterated the fact that he was not in favour of 'a sexual free-for-all' but considered it a very good thing that young people learnt about sex in order to avoid illegitimate babies and venereal diseases and to have what he defined as this 'wonderful experience' without hurting themselves or other people. This emphasis on sexual experimentation as an enjoyable experience provoked a very strong reaction, with opponents making the argument that the centre would encourage promiscuity and degrade young people's morality.

Cole was aware that his opinion had triggered strong opposition; he tried to temper his stance at a public debate organized by the Public Opinion Action Association in November 1965. He stressed the fact that young people were emotionally more mature than the previous generation and used sex as a means of communication. In his view, it was a valuable means 'as long as it is used properly, as long as there is a measure of information and a measure of emotional maturity to go with it'.[62] The aim of the centre was therefore to make sure that young people were informed and could thus avoid illegitimacy, shotgun marriages, and abortions. Moreover, it was of utmost importance to Cole that the centre would enable young people to find solutions with help from 'carefully chosen professional people, all medically qualified, who will be there to answer questions and to lead a conversation so that the girl or the boy, preferably together, will talk about their problem'.[63] Cole's underscoring of the medical component of the centre and its counselling dimension was an attempt to appease the voices that were accusing him of damaging young people's morality. Dr Faith Spicer also took part in the debate and sought to rectify the narrative by highlighting the counselling nature of the centre and the way it worked to preserve marital life by advising young people in steady relationships. As shown by this example, the boundaries of legitimate public debate on youth sexuality encompassed the notion of responsibility, but sexual experimentation remained very much outside of these boundaries.

---

[61] 'Man behind the teenage sex clinic', *Sunday Mercury*, 15 August 1965, 10.
[62] 'Sex clinic controversy: The big debate', *Birmingham Post*, 30 November 1965, 7.
[63] 'Morals and the young: The great debate', *Sunday Mercury*, 5 December 1965, 10.

In Bristol too, the emphasis on sexual responsibility was key in the promotion of the clinic. In line with Helen Brook's strategy, the Bristol report first underlined the counselling and educational dimension of the centre, the aim of which was to impart a sense of sexual responsibility in the young, and stressed that these centres treated young people's problems in a realistic and pragmatic way by providing professional advice about emotional, sexual, and birth control issues. The Bristol report focused on the potential harmful effects that might result from establishing a Brook. The main negative effect referred to the well-trodden narrative that providing contraception would encourage promiscuity by removing the fear of pregnancy, which had allegedly historically acted as a deterrent to sexual intercourse. However, the report underlined that Brook encouraged a responsible attitude to sex and birth control and that this would have positive outcomes. Finally, the ethical considerations were put forward, consisting mainly of the argument that sex before marriage was considered by many to be morally wrong. As a whole, the report offered a nuanced approach, arguing that while the setting up of a Brook did entail risks, as a preventive measure it would help to remedy the problem posed by the increase in premarital sex. The report was sent to London Brook for advice. Once the Brook centre was up and running, in its first annual report, the medical director Dr Ruth Coles again emphasized the counselling dimension of her work: 'It should be stressed that the service provided is not an automatic prescription service. Counselling forms a large part of the interview with the doctor.'[64] This, again, shows how the narrative around counselling was key in Brook's public image. Similarly, in 1977, the chairman of Bristol Brook, Charles Hannam—who had arrived in Britain as a Jewish child seeking refuge from Nazi Germany and had eventually become a teacher—stressed that Brook's distinctive quality was the ability not only to provide a medical service but also to counsel its clients.[65]

Nicholas Fairbairn, in Edinburgh, also tapped into the narrative about sexual responsibility. In an attempt to circumvent potential critics and to give the centre an air of respectability, he asserted in the local newspaper that the centre 'is providing for people who have a stable sexual relationship and are not married'. The aim of this assertion was to emphasize that the centre was not encouraging promiscuity but instead offering a needed service for responsible young people in committed relationships. Fairbairn framed this scheme within the controversy surrounding students and the pill by

[64] 'Brook Wessex Branch, Annual Report, 1971', in SA/BRO/D/1/1/1, Wellcome Library, London.
[65] 'Brook Wessex Branch, Annual Report, 1977', in SA/BRO/D/1/1/1, Wellcome Library, London.

asserting that the centre was the alternative to forcing young people 'to try to have pills on the black market, which is happening at the university, and is extremely dangerous'.[66] Similarly, these assertions were refuted by Margaret Gilmore, who wrote to the *Scotsman* defending Brook by arguing that its policy was precisely to advise young people and that there would be an 'opportunity for any girl with an emotional, sexual or birth control problem to discuss this with one of the doctors'.[67]

As illustrated by these local examples, the strategy of countering criticism and making contraception acceptable for young people was shared between the different working groups that set up local Brook branches in different cities.

Conclusion

The creation of Brook centres in different cities followed a similar trend and faced the same opposition. Individuals became concerned about the fate of the unmarried through their work in either FPA clinics or in university settings. They joined forces to open a Brook and usually formed a working group to assess the need for such a centre. They contacted London Brook for financial help and advice and tried to keep their plan under wraps from the media for as long as possible.

Opposition to the plans came mainly from FPA members and conservatives who believed the provision of contraceptive advice to young people would encourage promiscuity. As a way to mitigate these criticisms, local leaders emphasized the counselling dimension of the centres and the fact that they were trying to instil a sense of sexual responsibility in young people by promoting protected intercourse in a committed relationship. In Birmingham, Martin Cole deviated briefly from this narrative by underlining sexual pleasure; his position was met with fierce opposition. The emphasis on counselling and responsibility provided the discursive boundaries within which young people's sexuality could be discussed. This discursive strategy functioned as a continuity of the family planning movement's emphasis on responsible parenthood.

---

[66] 'Clinic opens to help problem with the unmarried', *Edinburgh Evening News*, 22 January 1968.
[67] Margaret Gilmore, 'Counselling at the Brook centre', *The Scotsman*, 2 February 1968.

3
Activism and the Shaping of Sexual Politics

In the witness seminar marking the 50th anniversary of Brook, Caroline Woodroffe, secretary of Brook from 1970 onwards, reflected on her work at the centre. She recalled how much fun she had with other Brook members.

> I was greeted in Birmingham and in Bristol and Edinburgh and Belfast and Liverpool by friends, stayed in everybody's houses. It was just super. For one thing, we were self-selected, we weren't in it for our careers, it wasn't going to do anybody's career any good, we weren't in it for money as you may imagine. We were in it because we all agreed with what we were doing and that was very uniting.[1]

This feeling of unity and shared conviction of doing something important are defining features of activism. As Gleen Laverack defines it, activism is an 'action on behalf of a cause, action that goes beyond what is conventional or routine'.[2] Health activism typically involves challenging the existing order with a view to improving individual health and reducing health disparities among populations. Birth control and family planning activism focused on improving access to contraceptive methods and information about what we would call today sexual and reproductive health, an idiom unknown at the time.[3] By drawing on archival materials from Brook (annual reports and board minutes), as well as archives of other voluntary organizations, parliamentary

---

[1] Caroline Woodroffe, Wellcome Witness Seminar: 50 Years of Brook on Friday 6 February 2015.
[2] Glenn Laverack, *Health Activism: Foundations and Strategies* (Sage, 2013): 1.
[3] Laura Kelly, *Contraception and Modern Ireland: A Social History, c.1922-92* (Cambridge University Press, 2023); Stephen Brooke, '"A new world for women"? Abortion law reform in Britain during the 1930s', *American Historical Review* 106.2 (2001): 431–59; Stephen Brooke, 'The sphere of sexual politics: The Abortion Law Reform Association, 1930s to 1960s', in Nick J. Crowson, Matthew Hilton, and Dr James McKay (eds), *NGOs in Contemporary Britain* (Palgrave Macmillan, 2009): 77–94; Hannah J. Elizabeth, '"If it hadn't been for the doctor, I think I would have killed myself": Ensuring adolescent knowledge and access to healthcare in the age of Gillick', in Jennifer Crane and Jane Hane (eds), *Posters, Protests, and Prescriptions* (Manchester University Press, 2022): 255–80; Leathard, *Fight for Family Planning*; Rusterholz, *Women's Medicine*.

debates, newspapers articles, and oral history interviews with Brook members, this chapter explores the role that Brook members played in the shaping of local and national reproductive politics around teenage sexuality. It asks what strategies they deployed and alliances they formed to expand contraceptive provisions to young people. By answering these questions, this chapter offers rich insights into the broader terrain of sexual politics between the 1960s and 1990s.

In so doing, this chapter adds to the growing body of scholarship that has addressed the relationship between voluntary organizations and state services, as well as the important contributions made by campaigner groups, activists, and charities to changing laws and policies on health.[4] By exploring the changing nature of activism and the voluntary sector over time, this chapter supports the argument made by Hilton et al. that the voluntary sector became more professionalized. Indeed, as I demonstrate, Brook members joined the charity with previous expertise in working and lobbying for birth control services, and the recruitment of new members became increasingly formalized. Yet, this chapter adds another layer to this argument about the professionalization of voluntary group by arguing that alongside it, voluntary activism around birth control also became more emotional, not least because of the subject itself and its targeted population; improving birth control services for young people. This chapter also shows that over three decades Brook fought to improve access to contraception for young people and their efforts came to fruition in the 1990s, with the *Health of the Nation* strategy. Finally, this chapter also makes a key contribution to the literature on the construction of the teenager. Brook played a key role in expanding access to contraceptive services for young people and constructed their clients as 'teenagers' and 'young people'.

This chapter first explores the factors that drove individuals to commit to Brook and the role that Brook members played in making birth control services and advice available to young people. It therefore focuses on Brook's campaigning strategies for attracting funding and for improving and expanding access to contraception; it covers this campaign from the NHS

---

[4] Berridge, *AIDS in the UK*; Crane, *Child Protection in England*; Mathew Hilton et al., *The Politics of Expertise: How NGOs Shaped Modern Britain* (Oxford University Press, 2013); Martin Moore, 'Food as medicine: Diet, diabetes management, and the patient in twentieth century Britain', *Journal of the History of Medicine and Allied Sciences* 73.2 (2018): 150–67; Alex Mold, *Making the Patient-Consumer: Patient Organisations and Health Consumerism in Britain* (Manchester University Press, 2015); Alex Mold and Virginia Berridge, *Voluntary Action and Illegal Drugs: Health and Society in Britain since the 1960s* (Palgrave Macmillan, 2010); Pat Thane and R. Davidson, *The Child Poverty Action Group, 1965 to 2015* (Child Poverty Action Group, 2015); Thane and Tanya, *Sinners? Scroungers? Saints?*

Reorganization Act of 1974 when the provision of contraception became free under the NHS, to the fight against restriction of the Abortion Act, the Gillick amendment, and the *Health of the Nation* strategy.

A network of birth control activism

This section sheds light on the reasons why individuals got involved in working for Brook. One of the main rationales given by Brook members for joining was their previous commitment to birth control and family planning. Indeed, many Brook members were involved in other committees; they all evolved in the same social network, revolving around family planning, lobbying, and fighting to improve access to abortion and contraception. The work of the various sexual and reproductive health charities of the time was therefore interrelated.

Helen Brook had opened a Brook centre due to her experience in working in a family planning clinic. This was also the case for Audrey Court, who was the chairwoman of Birmingham's Family Planning Association before leaving the position to become the chair of Birmingham's Brook Advisory Centre and one of its vice-presidents. Similarly, Dr Faith Spicer, who qualified as a doctor in 1944 from University College London and became a psychiatrist, also started working in the North Kensington Family Planning clinic before moving to the Marie Stopes Foundation and then Brook.

Caroline Woodroffe, the general secretary of Brook from 1970 to 1986, started at the FPA as a volunteer. She was also chair of the Birth Control Trust and Maternity Alliance. Her interest in birth control came from her family; her parents were both 'committed to women's rights and therefore family planning' and were active in the national and international sphere. Her mother, Lady Cadbury, had opened the first FPA centre in Canada, while Woodroffe's father worked at the International Planned Parenthood Federation (IPPF). She remembered:

> I was taken as a teen to a worldwide meeting of the IPPF in the Hague. I remember meeting all the people my parents were working with. No, Brook was not the beginning for me at all. It was just a very good next step. When my youngest child was five, I needed a job and Helen said, come and do the Brook job.[5]

---

[5] Private interview with Caroline Woodroffe, 20 September 2018.

Woodroffe then joined Brook and was instrumental in the development of Brook. As remembered by Alison Frater, press officer and then chief executive, Woodroffe 'was the primary driver of the Brook centres. Her values and insights drove what became an influential organization.'[6]

Dilys Cossey was another salient example of a Brook member who held different positions in various charities and organizations linked to birth control. She was the secretary for the Abortion Law Reform Association (1964 to 1968) and a member of the team that reformed the abortion law in 1967. She remembered: 'what was interesting about the people in the Abortion Law Reform Movement is they were all dedicated and devoted family planners [...] many of the people who were involved in the 1960s Reform Movement are now like myself have found a life in the family planning movement'.[7] She explained that she felt 'a camaraderie with the unmarried sex lobby—we were both on the fringes'.[8] From 1970–1974 she was the general secretary for the Birth Control Campaign and ran a successful parliamentary campaign for wider voluntary vasectomy and free NHS contraception. Subsequently, Cossey worked with the Birth Control Trust and was the founder and administrator/researcher for the UK Parliamentary Group on Population, Development, and Reproductive Health. She was a Brook board member during the years 1984 to 2001 and chair from 1995 to 2001. She also chaired the FPA (1987 to 1993). Before she officially joined Brook as a board member, she wrote two pamphlets for the organization, *Safe Sex for Teenagers* and *The Case for Condoms*.

Abortion rights was also what attracted Sheila Abdullah, a GP who volunteered at Brook Liverpool and was a Brook board member. Abdullah was a feminist socialist who had campaigned for abortion rights through the Merseyside Abortion Campaign. She was also part of the birth of the Women's Liberation Movement in Liverpool and took part in the first national conference held in Oxford in 1970. Martin Cole's interest in birth control for unmarried women also stemmed from his involvement with the Abortion Law Reform Association. He was a founding member of the British Pregnancy Advisory Services and considered, as did Dilys Cossey, that access to contraception was a preventive measure against abortions. Similarly, Joanna Brien, who worked at Brook as a counsellor, came to the organization from the British Pregnancy Advisory Services. Contraception and abortions were two faces of the same coin for many Brook members.

---

[6] Private phone interview with Alison Frater, 7 February 2020.
[7] Dilys Cossey, *In the Club*, in GC/105/5, Wellcome Library, London.
[8] Wellcome Witness Seminar: 50 Years of Brook, Friday 6 February 2015.

Other members were moved to action because of their prior more general involvement in women's or young people's health. Dr Faith Spicer explained in an interview in 1984 that she had started working with children in schools, running various groups for sex education. She had 'woken up to the fact' that she was providing baby clinic and ante-natal clinics but there was nothing for teenagers, a moment that she described for young people as the most 'critical stage of their lives'.[9] She felt that it was 'high time to start something for the young'. Helen Brook approached Spicer about working in the Marie Stopes Clinic because she was lecturing on adolescent sexuality.

Meanwhile, Pauline Crabbe came to Brook after having worked as the deputy national secretary of the National Council for Unmarried Mothers and their Children. In an interview conducted for the *History Workshop* television programme she explained:

> throughout all this time, the twelve years that I worked with these girls and young women and sometimes with the boys, the men as well, I had always felt oh what a pity that people cannot have the opportunity to choose when they wanted to be pregnant and planned for it and I had already left the National Council after twelve years and went for a little while to another area of work altogether, and then I'd always wanted to go back working with women—young women—and then I saw the job at Brook advertised and I went into it thinking that it was a marvellous opportunity to work with an organisation that was based on giving information about birth control because it would mean that I would be helping people to make a decision about whether or not they controlled their own fertility.[10]

This example also illustrates the way that Brook, as an organization, became more professionalized over the years. First, Brook staff were employees of the charity and were therefore paid on sessional fees. Moreover, new positions within the organization became advertised from the mid-1970s, instead of being filled by individuals approached by Brook members. Moreover, as the board minutes made it clear from the mid-1970s, there were discussions about which key criteria to include in the advertisement of positions, be it social workers, nurses, doctors, counsellors, or secretaries, showing how Brook set a standard of professional conduct. Alison Hadley first joined Brook as a nurse in 1983 after applying for the position. She explained that she had come to the

---

[9] Faith Spicer, *In the Club*, GC/105/5, Wellcome Library, London.
[10] Pauline Crabbe, *In the Club*, 1984, in GC/105/5, Wellcome Library, London.

organization because of her previous experience as a health visitor. After qualifying as a nurse in 1977, Hadley decided to leave hospital nursing and turned to health visiting. There, she witnessed the difficulties faced by teenage mothers, which prompted her to undergo family planning training:

> It was when I was doing the health visiting and looking after quite a lot of teenage mothers that I became interested in the isolation that they experienced and that most of them hadn't planned their pregnancy. So I got interested in family planning in this broader sense and how much better it would have been for them if they'd have managed to delay the pregnancy. So then I did my family planning training. [...] I thought, actually this is an area that I really feel passionate about, you know, to give young people particularly better choices about their reproductive health. So then I left health visiting and started doing some freelance journalism and I worked for Brook as a nurse in two of their London centres as well as a counsellor in British Pregnancy Advisory Services.[11]

She explained that she had been doing a 'combination of health journalism, pregnancy counselling and frontline Brook work'. In 1986, she became the press and information officer for Brook. This new position was particularly well-suited to Hadley, as she recalled: 'It just seemed to combine everything together because it was advocacy and journalism and bringing what I was seeing on the frontline into the press and information work.' In 1991, she became policy officer and stayed at Brook until 2000, when she moved to the national Teenage Pregnancy Unit which was established to lead and implement the Labour Government's 10-year Teenage Pregnancy Strategy.

Alison Frater, policy officer then chief officer, joined Brook because of her interest in women's health issues and in policy and advocacy work. In a private interview, Frater explained that before joining Brook she had experience in:

> research but with significant engagement in what was then called 'the women's movement'. I had a postgrad scholarship from University of London to study at UC Berkeley—in the early '80s prior to applying to work at Brook. The USA/Berkeley crucible of women's activism especially

---

[11] Private interview with Alison Hadley, 5 February 2019.

around women's reproductive rights was defining and inspiring for me—it was a great learning experience also by being exposed in postgrad work to brilliant epidemiology at UCB.[12]

This gave her good experience prior to working for Brook. She further reflected on what Brook meant to her and what Brook gave her. She really valued the fact that she was 'working on the issues in general but playing a major role in Gillick in particular was real training for activism, lobbying from a sound evidence base, informing public policy. For under 16s and for abortion rights we won and had a profound impact—some of which is now—alarmingly—eroding.' This quotation encompasses some key areas in which Brook campaigned: offering confidential services, even for under-16s, and maintaining access to abortion as defined in the 1967 Abortion Act.

Finally, one other key reason why individuals joined Brook was their drive to improve women's position in society. In an interview conducted in *National Life Stories*, Helen Brook emphasized that access to birth control was a way of providing women with the same opportunities as men:

> I suppose many of us coming to the conclusion that unless women had proper birth control, they were never going to make their way in the world, because many women still, even then, wanted to have a career of some sort... I also wanted to make it possible for women to be as free as men, and to be able to choose and not depend on intercourse as a way of life.[13]

In an interview with *The Guardian* in 1974 to commemorate ten years of Brook, Helen Brook again stressed that: 'Contraception is only one little bit of women's fight for freedom.'[14]

Similarly, Caroline Woodroffe recalled that Brook was set up for two reasons: mainly 'to ensure that every child was a wanted child, and, secondly, to improve the position of women by freeing them from the burden and fear of unwanted pregnancy. Access to contraception is essential for gender equality.'[15] She explained that she was 'brought up as a feminist',[16] and remembered that gender equality was a key issue for her. 'I was appointed a member of the Equal Opportunities Commission by the Labour government

---

[12] Private email exchange with Alison Frater, 29 November 2022.
[13] Interview with Helen Brook by Rebecca Abrams, *National Life Stories*: 66.
[14] 'A singular lady: Helen Brook', *The Guardian*, 19 June 1974, 9.
[15] Caroline Woodroffe, Wellcome Witness Seminar: 50 Years of Brook on Friday 6 February 2015.
[16] Private interview with Caroline Woodroffe, 10 September 2018.

in recognition of the importance of birth control in equal, meaning gender, opportunities. Access to contraception was essential for the improvement in the position of women and we played an important part.'[17] In the same fashion, Dilys Cossey also underlined the extent to which contraception was essential to freeing women:

> I thought that if women are gonna be free, they've gotta be free to express their sexuality and not to get pregnant because even today I know with the best will in the world, the major part or the most part of having a child will probably devolve upon the woman. And you have to be ready for, it was in my generation if you had a baby, because you gave up everything.[18]

As illustrated in these examples, the main Brook leaders identified there were drawn into birth control activism for young people because of previous experience working with different birth control charities, or past experience with young people as well as strong feminist views on providing contraception to young people to foster gender equality. These individuals held high-profile positions within the organization such as general secretary, chairwoman, press officer, policy officer. These positions were real leadership positions in that they required members to engage with the media, politicians, and local and national health authorities.

Financial issues

The activism of Brook members took many forms, depending on the circumstances and Brook's priorities. One key area where Brook members had to relentlessly campaign was funding. Indeed, the development of the centres was time and again restricted by financial issues. The charity status of Brook meant that attracting and securing this funding was a recurrent concern for the centre. The annual reports of Brook underlined this difficulty, which was hampering the centre's effort to meet its clients' needs. Brook lamented that due to underfunding, too much time was spent seeking to secure financial viability instead of expanding their services to meet the growing demand they faced. As a result, many centres could not hold more than a small number of sessions per week, sometimes at hours that did not fit with the schedule of

---

[17] Caroline Woodroffe, Wellcome Witness Seminar: 50 Years of Brook on Friday 6 February 2015.
[18] Private interview with Dilys Cossey, 20 April 2019.

young people. The funding to run the London centres was provided by charitable donations and the fees paid by clients—£3 per year—but many young people could not afford the fees and were thus seen without charges. This situation meant that Brook had to campaign to attract funding. During the first few years of Brook, in addition to a first grant of £15,000 donated by a banker colleague of Helen Brook's husband John Newton, the board of the Marie Stopes Memorial Foundation Ltd provided a three-year financial support donation of £500 and the use of rent-free premises at Whitfield Street. However, this money was not enough and Brook members struggled to keep their services afloat. Brook also gave grants and loans to help with the opening of other local centres.

At first, the centres mainly relied on donations. Brook organized events and used mass media to attract funding. In 1968, Brook made an appeal for funds and collected £10,000. In 1969, a new appeal was launched; it included a Week's Good Cause broadcast on BBC Radio 4, which featured Lord Ritchie Calder from Edinburgh, a Scottish journalist, writer, and academic. In his broadcast, he emphasized the importance of the work of Brook in avoiding unwanted pregnancies. Drawing on his own experience of reporting sexual crimes in criminal court cases and as a shorthand writer in civil court cases, dealing with paternity or affiliation cases, he stressed the 'tragedies, youthful ignorance and sanctimonious intolerance'[19] he had witnessed, which had prompted him at nineteen to engage in 'self-protection'. The Brook's work, he argued, prevented tragedies and was meant to 'help the young people help themselves by acquiring a mature and responsible attitude towards sex'.

In the 1970 annual report, Helen Brook expressed her approval of an expansion in the provision of birth control advice for the unmarried by general practitioners, local health authorities, hospitals, and FPA clinics (in 1969 the Association had decided to allow the unmarried to be seen in its clinics). However, this success also meant that there was a fall in income from donations and subscriptions, a trend attributed to the fact that Brook's aims were more 'widely accepted'.[20] The financial situation therefore remained precarious.

In London, several Area Health Authorities (AHA) provided financial support to Brook by paying per capita fees for their residents who visited the

---

[19] Lord Ritchie Calder, quoted in 'Brook Annual Report, 1969', in SA/BRO/E/1, Wellcome Library, London.
[20] 'Annual Report of Brook, 1970', in SA/ALR/F.1:box 93, Wellcome Library, London.

clinic; these authorities included Southwark, Camden, and Hackney in 1970.[21] By 1973, 25 of the 33 London Boroughs had made agency arrangements to finance a free or partly free service. However, this was not the case everywhere. In Birmingham, the Health Committee of the local council, which had a Conservative majority, flatly refused to support the work of the centre from its creation in 1966 until 1972, despite repeated applications by Brook. Birmingham Brook campaigned for free contraceptive advice and received the support of the local Women's Liberation group. Eventually, in 1972, a new city council with a Labour majority made birth control free and available.[22] From then on, Birmingham Brook received financial help. The refusal was connected to a concern about morality, with the committee fearing that funding the service would condone 'promiscuity'.[23] By the end of 1972, two-thirds of AHA were providing free consultation to all residents. In 1973, Edinburgh also provided free consultation and supplies.[24]

In 1974, under the NHS reorganization act, birth control became free and Brook retained a key role as an agent and service provider. From that point, the centres were financed by the NHS through AHA. Yet the free birth control services meant that AHA had to allocate their scarce resources to the entire range of health services, including birth control. Consequently, Brook were not able to expand their services to meet the growing demand. Indeed, underfunding became a recurrent concern. In Bristol, the Avon Health Authority announced in 1974 that a free service would not be available. Liverpool did not receive any financial help either. In 1976, these centres finally offered free contraceptive services following doctors' admission to the Family Practitioners Medical List for the provision of contraceptive services.[25] Despite these governmental funds, Brook still had to top up their income from AHA (which in 1980 became District Health Authorities) by asking clients and supporters for donations and raising grants for special projects. In addition, some Brook centres received local authority education or social service funding.

---

[21] London Borough of Southwark, *Annual Report of the Medical Officer of Health and Principal School Medical Officer* (1967): 31; London Borough of Camden, *Annual Report of the Medical Officer of Health and Principal School Medical Officer* (1967): 30; London Borough of Hackney, *Annual Report on the Health of the Borough* (1970): 29, in 'London's Pulse, The Medical Officer of Health Reports', online.

[22] 'Birmingham Annual Reports 1966–72', in SA/BRO/D3/1/1, Wellcome Library, London.

[23] 'Annual Report of Brook, 1978', in SA/ALR/F.1:box 93, Wellcome Library, London.

[24] 'Annual Report of Brook, 1973', in SA/ALR/F.1:box 93, Wellcome Library, London.

[25] 'Annual Report of Merseyside Brook, 1976', in SA/ALR/F.1:box 93, Wellcome Library, London.

In 1978, the Department of Health and Social Security decided to allocate a grant to Brook's new Education and Publication Unit to help them develop their work. In 1979, the Scottish Home and Health Department and the board of Brook carried out a one-year study, conducted by Edinburgh secretary Jean Malcolm, to assess the need for and reaction to additional Brook-type youth advisory services in Scotland. The report indicated support for the idea from the region's chief administrative medical officers and the Scottish Office. However, the necessary expansion could not be funded as there was no money.[26] In 1979, Judith Bury from Edinburgh wrote a report for the National Organization on the work of Brook and the direction that this work should take.[27] She emphasized the issue of accessibility for new clients. Since funding was limited and the majority of Brook centres lacked space as a result, the waiting time for new clients to be seen in centres continued to increase. It was recognized that the centres catered for unmarried people as a priority. This meant that clients over 25 were turning to Brook for contraception. Bury further stressed that what made Brook distinctive was its focus on young people. Therefore, one solution to the backlog of waiting time was to ask married clients and clients over 25 to move to another service provider. In 1981, despite a waiting list, the centre at Tottenham Court Road had to reduce its number of sessions due to financial hardship. In 1982, the Greater London Council granted the centre their request for money, allowing them to increase their number of clinic sessions again.

Brook members also campaigned to maintain their government funding. For instance, in 1981, the DHHS grant given to Brook for its Education and Publication Unit was being jeopardized by concerted action from conservative lobbies such as the Responsible Society—a moral conservative pressure group created in 1971 by Dr Stanley Ellison with the main goal of restoring traditional values and campaigning against school sex education and contraceptive information[28]—who were pressuring the Minister of Health, Dr Gerard Vaughan, to withdraw the DHSS funding. Indeed, the Responsible Society launched a public campaign against Brook in the mass media. Valerie Riches, general secretary of the Responsible Society, featured in an article published in

---

[26] Julie Davidson, 'Sex Education', article found in SA/BRO/F/1/16, Wellcome Library, London.
[27] Judith Bury, 1979 Report, in SA/BRO/B/1/6, Wellcome Library, London.
[28] Durham, *Sex and Politics*; Hampshire and Lewis, 'The Ravages of Permissiveness'; Lawrence Black, 'There Was Something About Mary: The National Viewers' and Listeners' Association and Social Movement History', in Nick Crowson, Matthew Hilton, and James McKay (eds), *NGOs in Contemporary Britain: Non-state Actors in Society and Politics since 1945* (Palgrave Macmillan, 2009): 182–200.

The Daily Telegraph on 13 March 1980 entitled 'The sex industry versus the parents'.[29] In the article, Riches complained about the 'sex lobby', which, she claimed, had the main motto that 'there are no rights or wrongs about any forms of sexual activity at any age provided only that no conception results'. Brook had a specific philosophy, she argued, whereby children should be liberated from the repressive attitudes of parents and teachers and that sex should be dissociated from emotions. Another attack was made in the Commons in May. John Stokes, the MP for Halesowen and Stourbridge, condemned the educational materials published by what he called the 'sex education industry',[30] namely Brook and the FPA. He described Brook as 'so revolutionary in their approach to sexual and family morality that there is not even a pretence of respectability'.[31] In particular, Stokes accused Brook of having triggered a revolution in teenage sexual behaviour, and further stressed that the centre's practical approach encouraged young people to 'indulge in sexual intercourse from an early age' and that sex was presented as the 'most normal and natural thing in the world. I call that damnable advice.' He called for the removal of the DHSS grant to the FPA and Brook.

This call was renewed by Jill Knight in August. As the chairman of the all-party Lords and Commons Family and Child Protection Group, she denounced the funding of family planning charities with public money. She claimed to have received a complaint from a father that his daughter's school was visited by doctors from the Brook centre during a sex education day course. In particular, she denounced the fact that 'first, a speaker from the family life association spoke about adult relationships, about love and marriage and the dangers of illicit sex. Then a doctor from the Brook clinic spoke on contraceptives, and all kinds of contraceptives were not only discussed but examined.'[32] Knight attacked the work done by the FPA and Brook, arguing that the latter undermined the family and encouraged promiscuity and that 'money is being used to break the law of the land and to weaken family ties and debase children'. She therefore urged the Minister of Health to reconsider providing DHSS funding to the FPA and Brook. During the same debate, Tory MP James Pawsey opined that 'parents should have the absolute right to withdraw their children from such

---

[29] Valerie Riches, 'The sex industry, versus the parents', *The Daily Telegraph*, 13 March 1980.
[30] 'MP John Stokes, on 14th May 1980', *20th Century House of Commons Hansard Sessional Papers*, Fifth Series, no. 984 (1980): 1516–23.
[31] Ibid.
[32] Jill Knight, 'Family planning group, 4th August 1980', *20th Century House of Commons Hansard Sessional Papers*, Fifth Series, no. 990 (1980): 196.

classes if they feel that it would have long term ill-effects, or any ill-effects, for that matter'.[33]

Caroline Woodroffe, aware of the pressure on Dr Vaughan, the Minister of Health, orchestrated a campaign of support for Brook to ensure that the DHSS renewed its financial aid. She wrote to many influential personalities who were long-time supporters of Brook, such as the Labour MPs Charles Morrison and William Hamilton, asking them to defend Brook in the Commons in order to maintain the grant.[34] Hamilton and Morrison closely followed the argument written by Woodroffe and took a stance against Knight in the Commons, underlining that Brook and the FPA were meeting 'the consequences of a lower standard of sexual morality'[35] rather than encouraging a lowering of moral standards. The emphasis on a pragmatic approach to youth sexuality, where Brook's work functioned as a response to young people's low sexual morals, testifies to the various and sometimes contradictory strategies that Brook members had to deploy in order to maintain their funding. Brook's campaign proved successful; the grant was allocated, though on the condition that Brook withdrew some teaching materials deemed too explicit.[36]

This constant battle for funding continued throughout the following decades. In 1989, London Brook received funding from Bloomsbury Health Authority for AIDS work. In 1990, public funding accounted for 84% of total branch income. In 1992, the report *The Health of the Nation* set out five priority areas in which the NHS and the Department of Health, as well as local community actors, should invest to improve people's health and well-being. These key areas were selected because the government identified them as having the greatest need and scope for cost-effective improvements in the overall health of the country.[37] AIDS and sexual health, especially for young people, were one of the priorities. As a result, Brook received increased financial support to set up additional centres across the country from 1992 onwards. For instance, in 1993, Brook received an additional grant of £20,000 from the government to support their targets, as outlined in *The Health*

---

[33] James Pawsey, 'Family planning group, 4th August 1980', *20th Century House of Commons Hansard Sessional Papers*, Fifth Series, no. 990 (1980): 196.
[34] 'Letter from Caroline Woodroffe to Charles Morrison, 1st August 1980', in SA/BRO/H/5, Wellcome Library, London.
[35] 'Mr Charles Morrison, answer to "Family planning group" on 4th August 1980', *20th Century House of Commons Hansard Sessional Papers,* Fifth Series, no. 990 (1980): 208.
[36] On the censorship of BAC's teaching materials, see Caroline Rusterholz, 'A mechanical view of sex outside the context of love and the family: Contraception, censorship and the Brook Advisory Centre in Britain (1964–1985)', accepted for publication, *Journal of the History of Sexuality*, 33.1 (2024): 33–55.
[37] Department of Health, *The Health of the Nation: A Strategy for Health in England*, 1992: 15.

of the Nation.[38] That year, public funding accounted for 89% of total branch income, a 5% increase since 1990.

Overall, uncertainty about funding and time dedicated to seeking out financial solutions without doubt affected Brook services, impairing their expansion, and leaving staff obliged to turn down some young people who came to the centres. Brook had to use different strategies to attract and maintain funding: they relied on donations, fundraising events, government grants, and funds from local health authorities. Sometimes, Brook had to tap into conservative arguments to secure their financial support. Moreover, this section demonstrates that locality did impact the amount of funding Brook centres received, but that Brook centres also worked together to raise money and campaign to maintain their funding.

Lobbying politicians to expand contraceptive services

The following sections examine the impact that Brook had on legislative changes. One of the key strategies used by Brook to foster political reform was ensuring that some of its members were affiliated with other campaigning groups and working parties that would lobby politicians for wider provision of contraception. Indeed, Brook fought alongside other bodies and voluntary agencies to make contraception free on the NHS, to maintain access to abortion, and to guarantee contraceptive advice for the under-16s. Moreover, they were increasingly called upon to give evidence and offer their views, testifying to the way they moved from an outsider position to one of prominence and importance in the British landscape of sexual politics. In so doing, Brook was able to carve out a territory for itself as the representative for young people, distinctly, in the broader landscape of sexual and reproductive health activism.

In 1974, the Department of Health memorandum for guidance on family planning services specifically retained a role for Brook as a service provider. It stated that:

> people of all ages, married and unmarried, attend ordinary clinic sessions and all should be made welcome at them. However, it may be advantageous to hold some separate sessions for young people either in health centres, hospital out-patient departments or similar settings, where a variety of health

---

[38] Brook Advisory Centre, *Annual Report, 1992-93: A Year of Expansion*: 15.

or social services are provided, or in a quite separate informal non-institutional setting whichever is thought likely to be most well attended. Whatever place is chosen for these sessions, an informal and friendly atmosphere is desirable, as is the choice of staff with whom the young can find it easy to communicate and who are sympathetic to their problems [...] Agency arrangement with the Brook Advisory Centres should continue for the time being as NHS agencies open to all.[39]

In addition, the memorandum advised that doctors could provide contraceptive advice to a girl under 16 without advising her parents, although they should always seek the girl's consent to tell her parents.[40] As historian Ben Mechen has argued, the passing of Clause Four was the result of a convergence of arguments and fears about population growth—both globally and nationally in Britain—as well as unwanted pregnancies (especially among unmarried young women), the resulting costs of these pregnancies for society and the high number of abortions.[41] Brook contributed to this change in legislation through different means. First, it signed the 1970 Birth Control Manifesto alongside the Family Planning Association, the Abortion Law Reform Association, the Simon Population Trust, the Conservation Society (a society focused on population policy), and the Pregnancy Advisory Service. The manifesto sent to the parliamentary candidates asked for birth control advice to be widely available 'under the Health Service from general practitioners and doctors working in local authority, hospital and voluntary birth control clinics'.[42] It also called for sterilizations and vasectomies to be free under the NHS, for the Abortion Act to be maintained, and for provision to be expanded under the NHS. Moreover, the manifesto requested recognition of the importance of education for responsible sexual relations and parenthood, along with funding for a nationwide government health education campaign for birth control, among other requests. The manifesto also connected the need to expand birth control advice with the issue of family planning overseas. It also drew on the idea of population boom and the need for Britain to keep its overseas aid.

---

[39] 'Family Planning Service, Memorandum of Guidance DHSS 1974', in SA/BRO/B/1/10, Wellcome Library, London.
[40] Department of Health and Social Security, *Family Planning Services. Memorandum of Guidance.* Issued with HSC(IS)32. DHSS, 1974.
[41] Mechen, *Everyday Sex.*
[42] 'Birth Control Manifesto, June 1970, sent out to parliamentary candidates', in SA/BBC/A/6, Wellcome Library, London.

Second, Brook members joined the Birth Control Campaign (BCC). Founded in 1971, the BCC brought together a wide range of individuals who shared the goal of making contraception freely available under the NHS. The campaign was set up to lobby politicians, the media, and civil servants; it gathered experts from different fields.[43] Caroline Woodroffe, the secretary of Brook, was elected a member of the management committee, alongside members of the Abortion Law Reform Association (such as Dylis Cossey), who would later work at Brook); Malcolm Pott, Medical Director of the International Planned Parenthood Federation; and Dr John Dunwoody, Labour MP and parliamentary under-secretary in the Department of Health and Social Security, among others. The central office of the BCC shared premises with the Brook Advisory Centre. Exchange between Brook and BCC was natural, as explained by Dylis Cossey, who acted as the secretary of the BCC: 'I got to know most people in the building, those running the clinics and those in the admin, and Caroline Woodroffe and I shared crises and confidences.'[44] Following the BCC advice, Brook wrote to MPs, sharing their request that contraception be made free under the new act.[45] This campaigning group was influential in the passing of the NHS Reorganization Act.

However, the work of Brook did not stop there. Indeed, Brook members submitted evidence to different working groups set up to assess ways of improving access to contraception. For instance, in 1975, Caroline Woodroffe wrote a letter to David Owen, Minister of State for Health, to recommend that 'nurses with suitable training should be able to prescribe oral contraceptives and that the government should arrange for any necessary statutory instrument to be put before Parliament'.[46] In parallel, a letter signed by 23 doctors, mainly from the FPA and published in the *British Medical Journal*, asked for the same expansion of the provision of the pill; this subsequently fostered the creation of a Working Group on Oral Contraceptives set up by the Central Health Services Council, the Committee on Safety of Medicine, and the Medicine Commission in order to consider the request made in the *BMJ* letter. In their response to Caroline Woodroffe, the DHSS invited Brook to submit its view to the Working Group on three issues relating to the expansion of the provision of oral contraceptives: 'on

---

[43] For a detailed analysis of this campaign see Mechen, *Everyday Sex*.
[44] Private interview with Dylis Cossey, April 2019.
[45] 'Various letters sent by Sally Price from Birmingham BAC and Helen Brook to MPs', in SA/BRO/D/3/2/4, Wellcome Library, London.
[46] 'Medical Advisory Committee, Minute, 23rd January 1976', in SA/BRO/C1/1, Wellcome Library, London.

prescription written by suitable trained state registered nurses, midwives and health visitors rather than by a doctor; on sale over the counter from retail pharmacies; more widely and in what manners'.[47] The annual report of 1976 mentioned that Brook had submitted evidence and been asked to give oral evidence to the group. The recommendations that Brook submitted suggested that:

> availability of oral contraceptives should be extended, new ways of obtaining oral contraceptives should be considered and women wishing to have a medical consultation before taking oral contraceptives should still have this service; pelvic examination should not be a prerequisite to obtaining oral contraception; access to oral contraceptives should be considered independently of other issues related to the medical screening of women and there should be a reduction in the number of oral contraceptives brands available.[48]

Caroline Woodroffe also tried to raise awareness of Brook's stance on the subject by publishing an opinion piece in *The Times* entitled 'Breaking the pill monopoly', in which she reiterated the pros of making the pill more widely available, in particular the fact that many young girls were running out of pills before they were able to renew their prescription at the doctors, thus increasing their risk of getting pregnant.[49] In spite of these recommendations, in 1980 the parliamentary under-secretary of state at the DHSS, Sir George Young, stated that the government had no intention of extending the arrangements for prescribing oral contraceptives.[50]

In 1985, Caroline Woodroffe wrote the DHSS to encourage them to update their memorandum of Guidance on Family Planning as to give 'maximum encouragement to Health Authorities to improve the family planning services for all young people'.[51] She situated her demand within the broader context of increasing abortion rates for young women aged 15–24.

Brook also devised strategies to pressurize the Department of Health and Social Security and Area Health Authorities to expand the services they

---

[47] 'Letter from C. T. Brown, Secretary of the DHSS, to Caroline Woodroffe, 24th July 1975', in SA/BRO/C/1/1, Wellcome Library, London.
[48] 'Brook Annual Report, 1976', in SA/ALR/F.1, Wellcome Library, London.
[49] Caroline Woodroffe, 'Breaking the pill monopoly', *The Times*, 27 October 1976.
[50] 'Sir George Young, Family Planning Clinic, 25th February 1980', in *Hansard, Commons*. https://hansard.parliament.uk/Commons/1980-02-25/debates/2ada2eb0-3b24-4dd5-91d9-f1939678c2f6/FamilyPlanningClinics?highlight=working%20group%20oral%20contraceptives#contribution-f1967640-bdae-4e03-97b7-2d1f9282efbc.
[51] 'Minutes of the Board meeting, 12 April 1985', in SA/BRO/B1/10, Wellcome Library, London.

provided to young people. One of their strategies was to gain the support of celebrities for their work. In 1990, for Valentine's Day, Brook designed an A3 poster displaying the names of politicians and celebrities (actors, singers, sports personalities) who had endorsed the centres, along with a press release to generate maximum publicity and show the 'widespread support for Brook as the organization calls on every district health authority to provide a youth advisory service to combat [the] rising teenage conception and abortion rate'.[52] Among these celebrities, Brook highlighted the support of agony aunts, who had expertise in dealing with young people's sexual problems. Marje Proops from the *Daily Mirror*, Deidre Sanders from *The Sun*, Angela Willans from *Woman's Own*, Virginia Ironside from the *Sunday Mirror*, Tricia Kreitman from *Mizz*, and Nick Fisher and Maroushka Monro from *Just Seventeen* were all signatories. In particular, Deidre Sanders, who received more than 1,000 letters a week, was portrayed as an 'expert' and quoted as urging for more Brook centres:

> The vast majority of young people who write to me for help are already involved in a sexual relationship but many are too afraid to get contraceptive help from their GP or family planning clinic. With so few services they feel confident to use, a heart-breaking number are already pregnant. What all teenagers desperately need is an approachable service like Brook around the corner.[53]

In addition to the endorsement of experts, Brook also highlighted the support of famous young people such as the all-female pop band Fuzzbox. The members explained that they had all been clients at Brook since 'none of us wanted to go to the GP in case he told our parents. It wasn't that we didn't get on at home, we did; we just wanted to keep that part of our lives private.'[54] The band then explained that FPA clinics were a bit 'off-putting' because of their association with older, married women, while Brook was geared towards the young. This kind of endorsement from famous personalities without doubt helped Brook to maintain its profile as the leading organization for young people; it also put pressure on Area Health Authorities to increase the number of services specifically dedicated to young people, given the stark regional

---

[52] Press release, 'Celebrities pledge support for Brook Advisory Centres on Valentine's Day', 9 February 1990, in SA/BRO/B1/12, Wellcome Library, London.
[53] Ibid.
[54] Press release, 'Fuzzbox join over 100 celebrities supporting BAC', 9 February 1990, in SA/BRO/B1/12, Wellcome Library, London.

variation in access to separate informal and contraceptive services, with only 50% of AHAs providing them.

Finally, the last strategy Brook used to call for an increase in services for young people was to showcase statistics and case studies to the press, highlighting the failure of public health services and the challenges that young people faced despite their efforts to behave responsibly. For instance, in 1990 Brook made the link between the financial cut in doctors sessions at Brook and family planning clinics and the rise in teenage conception rates. This was picked up by *The Independent* health correspondent after a visit to central office. The journalist quoted Brook statistics that showed that teenage conceptions had risen from 58.7 per thousand 15–19 years olds in 1980 to 66.6 in 1988, while the number of doctors sessions in Brook centres had fallen from 8,108 in 1980 to 6,880 in 1989, and in family planning clinics from 202,000 to 191,000 in 1987 (when the government stopped counting the sessions), due to financial restrictions in the district health authorities that fund family planning clinics and helped the Brook centres.[55]

In 1992, Brook issued a press release endorsing the new DHSS guidelines on family planning services that emphasized the need for confidential services to be easily accessible to teenagers. This statement holds significant importance as research conducted by Brook in 1991 revealed that 44% of young individuals seeking contraceptive help from the FPA were unable to secure an appointment within a week and subsequently turned to Brook service for assistance. For instance, a 17-year-old young woman had unprotected sex on a Friday night and required emergency contraception by Monday evening. Unfortunately, the FPA clinic was closed on Monday and there were no appointments available at her GP practice. Despite seeking help from four different GPS, she was unable to receive the assistance she needed. A 15-year-old girl sought to obtain the pill on the recommendation of her mother. However, when she went to the FPA, she was told that a parent must be present for her to receive help. A 20-year-old woman called Brook for assistance with an unwanted pregnancy. Her GP had refused to refer her for an abortion, and her local FPA clinic only offered pregnancy testing and counselling to existing clients.[56]

In each of these cases, individuals seeking sexual health services encountered barriers that prevented them from receiving the care they needed. These

---

[55] Celia Hall, 'Teenage pregnancies rises as cash cuts hit family planning', *The Independent*, 27 December 1990, quoted in SA/BRO/B1/12, Wellcome Library, London.

[56] Brook, Press release Government recommends provision of teenage birth control services, 3 February 1992, in PP/MEW/C/3/7, Wellcome Library, London.

situations highlighted the importance of ensuring that sexual health services were responsive to the needs of individuals and were able to provide timely and appropriate care in a non-judgmental and supportive manner. These examples also demonstrate a key strategy used by Brook throughout the years. Brook emphasized sexual responsibility not only in their promotional materials but also by drawing attention to the real-life experience of young people who tried to behave responsibly but had been failed by existing services.

In defence of the Abortion Act

In addition to contraception, Brook members were also committed to facilitating access to abortion services and defending the Abortion Act of 1967. In 1972, they submitted evidence to the Lane Committee, which reviewed the functioning of the Abortion Act in light of repeated accusations of abuse. The Lane Committee report underlined that there was no need to reform the Abortion Act and stressed 'the need for continuity, subject to some further regulation'.[57] Brook also sent a report to the Select Committee on Abortion, established in 1975, following James White's bill to reduce the upper time limit for most abortions to 20 weeks in order to control commercial exploitation, prevent foreign women from seeking abortion in Britain, and prohibit the treatment of overseas women 'lured into Britain' for abortion.[58] The centre wrote a memorandum on methods of pregnancy testing, outlets and costings,[59] and sent comments to the Secretary of State regarding the Report of the Select Committee on Abortion and the Abortion Amendment Bill, emphasizing their concern about the number of young girls having late abortions. The following statistics were provided to support access to late abortion: in 1973 in England and Wales, only 13% of abortions for girls under 16 and only 15% of abortion for girls aged 16–19 took place at nine weeks gestation or less, compared to 35% for women aged 30–34.[60] Brook argued that the many barriers suggested by White in order to regulate access to abortion would increase the proportion of late abortions 'with all the suffering that entailed'.[61] Instead, Brook stated that the Government should recognize that 'until the

---

[57] On the Abortion Act and the different attempts to restrain it, see Sally Sheldon, Gayle Davis, Jane O'Neill, and Clare Parker, *The Abortion Act 1967: A Biography of a UK Law* (Cambridge University Press, 2022).
[58] 'James White', in *Hansard, HC*, 7 February 1975, vol. 885, col. 1758.
[59] 'Pregnancy testing in relation to upper age limit', in 'James White Bill and Select Committee on Abortion', in SA/ALR/B.34, Wellcome Library, London.
[60] 'Brook Annual Report, 1976', in SA/ALR/F.1:box 93, Wellcome Library, London.   [61] Ibid.

NHS provides sufficient abortion facilities, women seeking abortion would benefit from the existence of the private sector'. Instead of introducing regulations that would inflate charges, the government, Brook suggested, should subsidize private abortions until NHS provision was increased. In addition, Brook called for agency arrangements to be made with approved nursing homes in order to facilitate abortion for women who qualified for free abortion when it was not possible to carry out the operation under the NHS. More importantly, Brook argued, approved referral agencies should similarly be financed in order to provide 'supporting unbiased counselling and information to women who don't know who to turn to for help', in a similar fashion to the service provided by Brook. Another recommendation was to publicize a list of nursing homes approved for abortions, with their addresses and costs to be made available in various public locations such as the Post Office, Citizen's Advice Bureau, clinics, and so on.

The Select Committee produced four reports and followed the recommendations of the Lane Committee for tighter regulation.[62] Following these reports, David Owen, Health Minister, took the issue into hand and 'devised a wide-ranging raft of regulatory measures that would both restrict abusive practices under the Abortion Act and protect it against more substantial challenge'.[63]

In addition, Brook participated in the Coordinating Committee in Defence of the Abortion Act set up in 1976, a group of 35 organizations including pro-choice groups, doctors, service providers, and trade unions, such as the Child Poverty Action Group, the Co-operative Women's Guild, the FPA, and Brook. In the following decade, several attempts were made to restrain access to abortions, but all failed in parliament. Brook repeatedly spread their message to the public by writing in newspapers and medical journals. For instance, in 1977, Caroline Woodroffe wrote a letter to the *BMJ* to rebut some of the arguments put forward in the Bynon Abortion Amendment bill of 1977, which aimed to 'remove the worst exploitation of women in the private sector'. Woodroffe carefully presented the benefit of a 'pregnancy advice service' such as that run by Brook in terms of increasing the likelihood of early abortions and filling the gap left by the inadequate provision of abortions under the NHS.[64] In 1984, a report published in the medical journal *The Lancet* by the Royal College of Obstetricians and Gynaecologists demonstrated

---

[62] On the history of the Abortion Act and its opposition see Sheldon, Davis, O'Neill, and Parker, *The Abortion Act 1967*.
[63] Ibid, 75.
[64] Caroline Woodroffe, 'Amendment of Abortion Act', *British Medical Journal* 1.6062 (1977): 711.

that many abortions were being unnecessarily delayed, particularly for young women. One way to tackle this, it was suggested, would be to open and advertise more youth advisory centres. Caroline Woodroffe and Fay Hutchinson took the opportunity, following this report, to publish a letter in *The Lancet* calling for family planning clinics to expand their working remit to encompass pregnancy diagnosis, counselling, and referral for abortions, as well as contraception aftercare, in order to reduce late abortions.[65]

In 1985, at their board meeting, Brook members discussed the tactics they should deploy in order to avoid a bill being debated in parliament about the upper time limit for abortion. Dilys Cossey led the discussion; it was agreed that Caroline Woodroffe would write to the minister asking what progress had been made in implementing the Department's policy of improving services to reduce late abortions.

In their 1987 annual report, Brook took a stance against David Alton's amendment bill, which suggested reducing the upper limit for abortion from 28 weeks to 18 weeks. Brook reminded its readers that in 1986, 38% of abortions performed at 18 weeks and over had been for teenagers. Drawing on its experience in pregnancy counselling, Brook argued that young women who presented late for a termination were 'often unaware of the signs of pregnancy and the significance of a missed period and frequently concealed their pregnancy in fear of rejection by family and friends. Anomalies and inefficiency in the abortion service further compound the problem by denying women early abortion referrals.'[66] In Brook's view, restrictive legislation would not help; instead, widespread implementation of sex education and more open discussion of the subject in society more generally was needed. Brook urged the government and health authorities to address the underlying causes of late abortion and provide an efficient and accessible abortion service.

In 1987, Alison Frater, the General Secretary of Brook, wrote to Tony Newton, Minister of State for Health. She stressed the necessity of maintaining access to late abortions, that is, abortions performed after 18 weeks. To support her position, she explained that 5,000 women per year needed access to abortion at this stage of pregnancy. One of the key reasons to abort in late pregnancy was foetal abnormality, she argued, and Brook opposed the implication in the Bill that women would be made to carry 'gravely handicapped babies to term'.[67] She also drew on her experience at Brook to illustrate the

---

[65] Caroline Woodroffe and Fay Hutchinson, 'Late abortions', *The Lancet*, 25 February 1984.
[66] 'Brook Annual Report, 1987', in SA/BRO/E/1/4, Wellcome Library, London.
[67] 'Letter from Alison Frater to Tony Newton, 5th November 1987', in SA/BRO/B/1/10, Wellcome Library, London.

need for late abortion: 10% of new clients who attended a clinic were already pregnant. For the majority, she explained, it was an unwanted pregnancy, causing severe distress and putting at risk 'their own mental health and the general well-being of their personal and family relationships'. A small proportion of these clients were pregnant because they were victims of rape, while for the majority their pregnancies resulted from lack of education in sex and personal relationships at school, 'an avoidance of discussion of sexuality in their family home and the general unavailability of accessible contraceptive services'. For clients who attended the clinic when they were already more than 15 or 18 weeks pregnant, the reasons for their delay in searching for help involved an inability to recognize pregnancy symptoms or fears that prevented them from seeking help. Tragically, Frater continued, some young women remained isolated until birth, as illustrated by newspaper headlines full of lurid stories of desperate teenagers 'abandoning their babies in bins, public toilets, telephone boxes and hospital lobbies'. The solution to these desperate situations was not restricting the availability of late abortion but instead improving access to sex education so that young people would recognize the signs of pregnancy, as well as creating accessible, efficient birth control and abortion counselling services that would help make early termination feasible. Frater also urged Newton to achieve a consensus in the House of Commons that the 'issue of abortion be raised only once if at all during any parliamentary session', in order to limit the stress caused for many hundreds of thousands of women and their families by constant attempts to undermine the Abortion Act.

In 1990, an amendment for a decision on the time limit for abortion was put forward under the Human Fertilization and Embryology Bill. Debate took place in Parliament regarding whether the time limit for abortion should be increased or decreased. Until that point, abortions up to 28 weeks had been legal provided that the conditions of the 1967 Abortion Act were met, although terminations were very rarely carried out beyond 24 weeks, except in the case of foetal abnormalities. Aware that this upper limit could be reduced and concerned about their young clients who tended to seek help later in pregnancy, Brook wrote to the members of Parliament. In their letter, they stressed the extent of the problem by providing statistics: in 1987, Brook argued, just under 40% of all late abortions (more than 20 weeks) were carried out on women under the age of 20. They set out three explanations for this: failure to recognize the signs of pregnancy due to ignorance; fear of being rejected and therefore concealing pregnancy; and lack of accessible contraceptive services for young people. To humanize their message and to provide unique evidence to Parliament, Brook utilized their experiential knowledge as a form of expertise and described five case studies of clients that illustrated the effects that a change in the current legislation would have on young people. One of these case studies was Sandra, whose outcome might have been different. Sandra, 16, presented at a Brook clinic when she was 22 weeks pregnant, accompanied by her older sister, 19. Sandra had refused to believe she was pregnant. Both sisters affirmed that their father would kick Sandra out of the home if the pregnancy was to be discovered. Since late terminations were unavailable on the NHS, Sandra had to find the money to pay for a private abortion. If the upper time limit were reduced to 24 weeks, it was very unlikely, Brook argued, that Sandra would have obtained her termination, and thus she and her baby would probably be homeless.[68] This kind of resort to case studies where emotions were put centre stage was not unusual for Brook, who would sometimes publish similar accounts in their annual report to create sympathy and shed light on the human misery behind unwanted pregnancy and the urgency of providing adequate contraceptive services. In addition, this resort to experiential expertise also relates to changing nature of activism in the 1980s and 1990s—as argued by historian Jennifer Crane who has shown how experiential expertise was used during these decades—which became increasingly emotional not only because of the nature of the issue and its sensitivity, but also because of changing activist styles.[69]

Campaigning against Gillick, 1980–1986

One of the many common attacks on Brook was a result of their work with under-16s. From the end of the 1970s, 'moral traditionalists',[70] to borrow Jane Lewis and James Hampshire's expression, targeted Brook because they saw it as encouraging a decline in moral values, especially among the young, by providing contraceptive advice and sex education. 'Moral traditionalists' considered marriage and the family as the 'twin foundations of a civilized society'[71] and condemned premarital sex. The Responsible Society was particularly active in accusing Brook of encouraging promiscuity. In their view, one category of young people was in particular need of protection from 'sex lobbies': the under-16s. For these 'moral traditionalists', under-16s were

---

[68] 'Letter from Dr John McEwan, chair, and Dr Margaret Jones, general secretary, to members of Parliament, 18th April 1990', in SA/BRO/B/1/10, Wellcome Library, London.
[69] Crane, *Child Protection in England*.
[70] Hampshire and Lewis, 'The ravages of permissiveness', 292.　　[71] Ibid., 298.

'children', and as such, parents' rights and control took precedence over their children's agency and doctors' confidentiality.[72] Brook defended itself from the charge of seeing children by arguing that 'the use of the term "children" is emotive—we are not seeing prepubertal children but adolescents who are sexually mature and are trying to cope with their feelings in a society which artificially prolongs their dependence and tries to deny the reality of their sexuality.'[73] Brook referred to the under-16s as girls and not children.

In 1974, the DHSS guidance on family planning services had made it clear that it was legal for a doctor to advise a patient under 16 on contraception in a confidential matter. Moreover, the British Medical Association also strongly supported confidential services for under-16s. In 1979, the Minister of Health, Gerard Vaughan, declared that 'provision must be made for the occasional possibility of counselling, and if necessary contraception being provided to young people without the knowledge of their parents'.[74] However, in 1980, a new pressure group, Responsibility in Welfare, was created; this group, led by the Catholic doctor Adrian Rogers, explicitly targeted the provision of contraceptive advice to the under-16s. In November, Rogers, as a medical officer of Devon County Council Home, publicly announced that he would refuse to prescribe contraception to any under-16 girls. His position was supported by the County Council, who declared that no girl under 16 in its care would be allowed contraceptives.

Following this controversy, the DHSS issued a memorandum underlining that 'special care was needed not to undermine parental responsibility and the stability of the family'.[75] However, the memorandum told doctors that it would be 'most unusual' to provide 'contraceptive advice without parental consent' to under-16s. The memorandum stated that doctors should always seek to persuade an under-16 to inform their parents, adding nevertheless that 'it is, however, widely accepted that consultations between doctors and patients are confidential; and the Department recognises the importance which doctors and patients attach to this principle'. To abandon confidentiality might prevent some 'girls' from seeking professional advice, exposing them to 'the immediate risks of pregnancy and of sexually-transmitted diseases, as well as other long-term physical, psychological and emotional consequences which are equally a threat to stable family life'. In sum, doctors

---

[72] On this history, see Pilcher, 'Gillick and after'.
[73] Answer to the Responsible Society, 'Sexual pressure on children', *British Medical Journal* 2.6135 (1978): 499.
[74] 'BAC Annual Report, 1979', in SA/BRO/E/1/4 in SA/BRO/B/1/10, Wellcome Library, London.
[75] Department of Health and Social Security, Circular, HN (80) 46, December 1980.

could in exceptional circumstances prescribe contraception to under-16s without parental knowledge and consent but that ideally parents should be informed, the final decision resting with the clinical judgement of the doctors.[76] In June 1981, the *British Medical Association* issued a handbook on medical ethics and confirmed their position regarding confidentiality if a doctor failed to persuade a girl to involve her parents. If a girl under 16 had the maturity to understand the possible consequences of her actions, her own informed consent could be valid.[77]

Brook, aware of the challenges posed by 'moral traditionalists' in their attempts to prevent under-16s from attending the service, published an information sheet presenting the position of the government and medical authorities on prescribing contraception for under-16s in order to inform its clients and more generally other voluntary bodies and GPs.[78]

These attacks against Brook culminated in the 1984 Gillick case, where Victoria Gillick went to court to fight her Area Health Authority's refusal to promise not to give contraception to her daughters under the age of 16 without her consent. Her case was unsuccessful, but she continued to appeal to the court. Gillick took up Brook as her target, accusing them of 'ignoring the DHSS guideline that 'it would be most unusual to provide advice about contraception without parental consent'.[79] In December 1984, the latter ruled in her favour, stating that the DHSS guideline was unlawful and that parents' consent prevailed over that of children. This decision was reversed in October 1985 by the law. However, Gillick's victory, albeit short-lived, had drastic consequences for young people under 16 attending Brook clinics, in that they could no longer be prescribed contraception.

Brook members were deeply worried about the potential of the Gillick victory; they mobilized in order to block and then overturn the decision. They multiplied their strategies to make their opposition known to politicians and the wider public. They intervened in the public debate, gathering media coverage and highlighting the damage Gillick could do and had done to young people. These public statements came from Brook members in various locations. For instance, Brook members were vocal in the mass media prior to Gillick's victory, pinpointing the many individual circumstances that might lead a girl to conceal from her parents that she was using contraception. In addition, Brook repeatedly stressed that they always tried to encourage a

---

[76] Ibid.   [77] British Medical Association, *The Handbook of Medical Ethics* (London, 1980).
[78] Brook Advisory Centre, *Under Sixteens*, in SA/BRO/E/7, Wellcome Library, London.
[79] 'Mother of 10 fights sex for under-16s', *The Times*, 19 November 1984.

client to involve her parents. Dr Fay Hutchinson from London explained, in an article covering Gillick's campaign and responding to Gillick's accusation towards Brook, that Brook always tried to persuade young girls to tell their parents they wanted birth control, but that there were some 'problems'. Hutchinson explained that 'some mothers don't want to seem to be encouraging their daughter to have sex. Some girls don't want their mother to be involved. About a third of the under-16s said their mothers knew they were coming to the clinic.'[80] Similarly, in an article for *The Guardian*, Brook used statistics to highlight the significance of their work and to counter accusations that they were encouraging promiscuity. They argued that in the last eight years, the number of pregnancies (abortions and births) among 15-year-olds had remained constant. Brook counsellors believed that this stability was due to the DHSS guideline, which made it clear that under-16s would be treated in confidence. As a result, the number who sought contraception had doubled, Brook explained, but 'the total number of pregnancies to teenagers had dropped' sharply in the last ten years, and so had the number of births, with nearly half of them accounted for by 19-year-olds. Brook expressed their concern that these 'relatively good figures for very young girls would change drastically if Gillick were to win her case':

> we see girls who have been frightened away by their GPs, or other clinics, often unintentionally. It hasn't prevented them from having sex, only from getting contraception. By the time they get to us they are all too often already pregnant. The younger they are, the easier they are to frighten away. There is no doubt in our mind that the number of pregnancies among the under-16s would rise sharply indeed if these girls thought we'd tell their parents if they came to us for help.[81]

In Edinburgh, Dr Judy Bury further underlined that under-16s were encouraged by the Brook centre to inform their parents and that 'two-thirds had informed their mother within three months of the first visit'.[82] However, attempts to suppress confidentiality would mean that the under-16s would never approached a centre.

---

[80] Dr Fay Hutchinson, quoted in 'Mother of 10 fights sex for under-16s', *The Times*, 19 November 1984.
[81] Brook, quoted in Polly Toynbee, '"It's hard work bringing up children. It takes time, and effort and love", says Victoria Gillick, "Now someone is saying to us that all that counts for nothing, nothing! We don't have to be consulted"', *The Guardian*, 19 November 1984.
[82] Dr Judy Bury, quoted in 'Doctor's plea for pill confidentiality', *Times Educational Supplement*, 23 March 1984.

In addition to mass media, Brook voiced their concerns in medical journals. Fay Hutchinson tried to gain the support of GPs regarding advising under-16s in a confidential manner by writing an article, 'How to handle teenage birth control', for the magazine *GP*. This article offered an insight into the counselling needed by under-16s in terms of confidentiality and the best attitude to adopt towards young people. Hutchinson wrote that doctors should be aware of their own 'ethical position' and beliefs but should avoid imposing these on their patients. She reiterated the importance of confidentiality, 'except in very rare and extreme circumstances where evidence of exploitation or abuse is apparent'. In these cases, Hutchinson argued, girls usually agreed to the involvement of family and professionals for their own protection.[83] This article set out the benefits of confidentiality in counselling and stressed that mandatory requirement for parents to be informed would be a deterrent against young people seeking medical advice when they were at risk of pregnancy. Similarly, in January 1984, the Brook chair Caroline Woodroffe was interviewed in *GP*, defending Brook's policy of prescribing contraception to adolescents in order to prevent unwanted pregnancies. She countered the criticism that the centre sought to diminish parents' authority by stressing that Brook always tried to involve the family: 'what amazes me is that anybody could ever think we did not try to involve the family. We think that the family is very important to these girls, and it is obvious to me that, if possible, they should be involved.'[84] She also tackled the claim that sexual activity had increased among teenagers due to the availability of contraceptives: 'I think this is absolute rubbish. Anybody with an ounce of common sense knows that is not the case because teenagers do not wait to have sex only when they have contraception—if only they were so rational!'

Alongside denouncing the potential effects the Gillick victory would have on young people, Brook also raised concerns about the practical effects of the subsequent victory. Alison Frater, the Brook general secretary, explained in an article for *The Times* about the mounting resistance to Gillick's appeal that attendance of under-16s had dropped by half since December 1984. She added that: 'Many of the girls not keeping appointments have been to us before and are on contraceptives. They do not dare return in case we tell their parents, but I don't for one minute believe they have stopped having sex, so what will the consequences be?'[85] Moreover, some Brook members also publicly promised

---

[83] Fay Hutchinson, 'How to handle teenage birth control', *GP*, 16 November 1984.
[84] 'Parental privilege: a minor concern?', *GP*, 6 January 1984.
[85] Alison Frater, quoted in Angela Neustatter, 'Gillick: The anxiety and opposition grow', *The Times*, 19 June 1985, 11.

they would continue to maintain confidentiality. For instance, Dr Sheila Abdullah of the Liverpool Brook centre stated in the *Liverpool Echo*, just after Gillick's victory, that her centre would 'still give fully confidential treatment to girls under 16 fearing pregnancy'.[86] She also faced Victoria Gillick in a public debate on TV in June 1985 and was subsequently interviewed by the *Liverpool Daily Post*. In a one-page article she shared her concerns about the damage done by Gillick to young people: 'When you are working in the field and see the awful traumas of unplanned pregnancy, the guilt and fear it produces which can blight human relationships, it is obvious that to outlaw help would be going back to the dark ages.'[87] Moreover, she emphasized the irony of the situation, in that young people 'show maturity in coming for advice and yet they are the ones we are now turning away'. However, she added that Brook were still counselling under-16s in a completely confidential way, despite being unable to prescribe contraception.

In addition to voicing their opposition through the mass media, Brook also campaigned alongside other organizations; they convened the Under Sixteen Group of organizations affected by the court appeal judgment, including members of the British Medical Association, the FPA, the Children's Legal Centre, the Royal College of Nursing, and the National Association of Family Planning Doctors, among others. This group aimed to disseminate information on the consequences of the ruling for young people and to lobby politicians to change the ruling. They organized a protest against the Gillick ruling in London in June 1985.

Brook also wrote lengthy reports on the ruling's dramatic consequences for their clients. In their annual report, they shared the anonymized stories of affected young people; Jane was an example of a client badly affected by the new ruling. The first time she attended the centre to obtain contraception, she was 15 and had already had an abortion. Prior to December 1984, Jane received counselling and contraceptive help at Brook. After December, however, the centre could not give her contraceptives without her mother's consent, which put Jane in an impossible situation. A committed Catholic, her mother refused to give Jane permission to use contraception despite knowing about the abortion. The mother stated that she would rather not have been asked. When Jane returned to the centre in 1985, she was pregnant again and desperate for a second abortion.[88] Adolescent girls were not the only

---

[86] 'Minister to appeal new move on the pill verdict', *Liverpool Echo*, 21 December 1984.
[87] 'A doctor who fears the worst', *Liverpool Daily Post*, 19 June 1985.
[88] 'Alarm and confusion prevent under 16s from seeking help', 17 May 1985, in SA/FPA/C/E16/5/8, Wellcome Library, London.

ones affected; young boys' agency was also limited, as shown by the example of John. A regular at Brook, John had started attending the clinic during his first sexual relationship when he was 14. Following a counselling session, he was given sheaths and thereafter attended regularly for more supplies. On one occasion, he brought his girlfriend along to discuss different contraceptive options. After December 1984, John only visited Brook once, to explain that he could not face asking his mother for permission to be given contraceptives. After that, Brook staff never saw him again.[89] These two examples show how dramatic the ruling was for young people and the detrimental consequences it had for some of them.

Brook also tried to provide practical information to young people about the change in the law. For instance, Suzie Hayman wrote an article in the teenage magazine *Just Seventeen* about the legal implication of Gillick's victory for the under-16s.[90] In so doing Brook participated in constructing and addressing this new audience.

Following the overturning of Gillick's victory, Caroline Woodroffe and Fay Hutchinson met with DHSS officers and stressed that the law should be clearly stated in a new guideline on family planning. In addition, they asked the DHSS to encourage health authorities to gear their services towards young people's needs and formulated a checklist to help them do so (see Chapter 4 for the checklist).[91] Brook members signed open letters published in newspapers, calling for the government to 'introduce legislation to ensure the right of all teenagers—boys and girls—to receive advice and help in confidence from an informed, professional source'.[92] They also wrote to the Minister of Health to state their dismay regarding the General Medical Council's statement on confidentiality. Indeed, following the Gillick victory, the GMC issued new guidance to doctors on the confidentiality of personal health information. This guideline, due to its poor framing, conveyed a misunderstanding about the rights of doctors to break confidentiality with patients they did not consider mature enough to consent to treatment. Brook, alongside other bodies such as the FPA and the Children's Legal Centre, called for a change in order to guarantee the confidentiality of the service.[93] Several Brook members voiced their commitment to providing confidential treatment to under-16s in the

---

[89] Ibid.   [90] Suzie Hayman, 'The effects of the Gillick case', *Just Seventeen*, 20 March 1985, 61.
[91] 'Minutes of the Meeting of the Board of Directors, 13th November 1985', in SA/BRO/B/1/10, Wellcome Library, London. See also 'Need for improved birth control services for young people', *British Medical Journal* 292.6518 (1986): 495.
[92] 'Mothers united', *The Times*, 8 October 1985, 14.
[93] 'Letter from Caroline Woodroffe to Barney Hayhoe MP, Minister for Health, DHSS, 14th February 1986', in SA/BRO/1/10, Wellcome Library, London.

press. For instance, Darrell Thorpe, administrative officer for Birmingham Brook, condemned the GMC decision, arguing that 'it will prevent youngsters from seeking doctors' help and that will lead to an increase in pregnancies'.[94] As seen in these different examples, Brook used diverse terms to qualify their clients and the under-sixteens, such as teenagers, youngster, boys and girls but never referred to them as children.

Brook members also published articles that provided an overview of the effects of the short-lived victory. Caroline Woodroffe and S. McClinton penned a letter to the *British Medical Journal* to evaluate the effect of the change in the law via the data collected by Brook. They argued that doctors had been 'severely restricted in their ability to protect sexually active 15 year olds from pregnancy because fewer 15 year olds at risk have sought advice and because fewer of those who have sought advice have obtained contraception'.[95] According to their data, in the first six months of 1985, Brook recorded a drop of 46% in the number of new clients under 16. Brook also undertook a retrospective study of all their new female clients under 16 at Walworth, London in the first six months of 1984 and 1985. There were 83 clients in the first period and 40 in the second, a decrease of 52%. Most of these clients were aged 15 and sexually active. However, in the 1985 group, following the change in the law, there were proportionally more pregnant clients: 30% in 1985 compared to 16.5% in 1984. Moreover, fewer under-16s were prescribed contraception in 1985. These data show the detrimental effects the law had on under-16s. Dr Judy Bury from Edinburgh Brook also stressed that the number of under-16s visiting the centre declined in 1985; while a greater proportion of them were pregnant, 'they only came along when it was too late'.[96]

Dr Sheila Abdullah from Liverpool and Dr Caroline Bailey from London both reflected on the damage Gillick had done in an article in *The Times*. Abdullah stated that: 'If what you're trying to do is protect teenagers from pregnancy, you don't do it by stopping them getting help. It's pernicious. It has driven into worse corners the people who are *really* needy',[97] while Bailey emphasized the power situation in which young girls found themselves: 'the Gillick ruling has meant reverting back to the jungle, with power as usual going to the strong. It's already terrible being 15, an age of powerlessness. Girls need more help, not less.'[98]

---

[94] 'Pill decision rapped by counsellors', *Birmingham Mail*, 12 February 1986.
[95] C. Woodroffe and S. McClinton, 'Contraceptives and the under 16s', *British Medical Journal* 291.6504 (1985): 1280.
[96] Ian Swanson, 'Ruling on the pill too late', 18 October 1985.
[97] Caroline Moorehead, 'Anguish of the teenage mothers', *The Times*, 18 October 1985.
[98] Ibid.

Alison Frater also published a piece in *The Times* in January 1986, explaining why young girls still needed help after the overturn of Gillick. She provided the example of Jocelyn, a pregnant 17-year-old who had phoned Brook after finding their number in a teenage magazine. Jocelyn, crying on the phone, explained that she could not tell her mum—'she would kill me'—and could not go to her GP since he had known her since 'she was a baby'. The family planning clinic was in the same building as her doctor and only opened in the afternoon when Jocelyn was in school. Jocelyn embodied many of the shortcomings of the health system, Fraser argued; the overturn of the Gillick appeal did not solve the problems with providing advice to teenagers about sex and contraception. The DHSS, Frater stated, should issue a statement clarifying its position and encouraging the development of youth advisory services across the country, as the provision of services was desperately lacking. These services should be open in the evenings and on Saturdays, provide counselling, fast on-the-spot pregnancy diagnosis, abortion referral and counselling, and be confidential and open to men as well. Fraser then presented statistics to show the inadequacy of the current provision: one in ten teenagers turning 15 in 1986 would have an abortion before the age of 20. However, only an equal proportion of teenagers were currently attending family planning compared to ten years previously. She concluded by saying: 'it's not the motivation of teenagers that is responsible for this disappointing trend, it is a lack of appropriate services'.[99] Jane Fraser, Education and Publication Unit officer also faced Victoria Gillick in a debate at Keele University organized by the Student Christian Movement.[100] In March, the DHSS finally updated its guideline. As in 1980, the DHSS stressed the need to take 'special care not to undermine parental responsibility and family stability'. However, it put forward some key principles to allow doctors to provide treatment to under-16s without parental knowledge: the doctor should be satisfied that the 'young person was mature enough to understand what was involved; sexual intercourse would begin with or without contraception; without contraception the young person's physical or mental health was likely to suffer; the young person's best interests required the doctor to give contraceptive advice or treatment without parental consent.'[101]

As shown by these examples, Brook played a significant role as a leader in teenage sexuality and as such was visible in the mass media through sharing

---

[99] Alison Frater, 'After Gillick, why girls still need help', *The Times*, 22 January 1986, 16.
[100] 'Gillick to speak at University', *Birmingham Post*, 8 April 1986.
[101] John Illman, 'New advice on the under-age Pill', *Daily Mail*, 7 March 1986, 2.

expertise. It also campaigned against Gillick by joining forces with other associations, denouncing the terrible effects the change in the law could have and had already had on young people, and lobbying politicians.

The Health of the Nation

While expanding access to contraception was central to Brook's work, another key area was to implement different strategies and solutions in order to remedy the high level of teenage pregnancies. Indeed, the conception rate for women under 16, as shown in Table 3.1, had increased from 6.8 in 1969 to 9.4 in 1988. What is interesting about this table is the impact of the NHS Reorganization Act; from that point onwards the trend declined steadily until 1981, when it reached 7.2. However, in the context of the subsequent

Table 3.1 Teenage pregnancy among under-16s in England and Wales, trends in conception among girls under 16 (the rate is per 1,000 girls 13–15)

years	conception leading to maternity		conception terminated by abortions		total conception	
	number	rate	number	rate	number	rate
1969	4,900	5.1	1,700	1.7	6,500	6.8
1970	5,200	5.4	2,500	2.5	7,700	7.9
1971	5,500	5.5	3,200	3.2	8,700	8.7
1972	5,700	5.5	3,900	3.8	9,600	9.3
1973	5,400	5.1	4,400	4.1	9,800	9.2
1974	4,800	4.4	4,500	4.1	9,300	8.5
1975	4,400	3.9	4,800	4.2	9,200	8.1
1976	4,300	3.7	4,900	4.2	9,200	7.9
1977	4,200	3.6	4,800	4	9,000	7.6
1978	4,400	3.7	4,700	3.9	9,100	7.6
1979	4,100	3.4	5,000	4.2	9,100	7.5
1980	3,900	3.3	4,600	3.9	8,500	7.2
1981	3,700	3.1	4,900	4.1	8,600	7.3
1982	3,900	3.4	5,100	4.4	9,000	7.8
1983	4,000	3.6	5,300	4.7	9,300	8.3
1984	4,300	3.8	5,400	4.8	9,700	8.6
1985	4,200	3.8	5,200	4.8	9,400	8.6
1986	4,200	4	5,000	4.7	9,200	8.7
1987	4,200	4.2	5,000	5	9,200	9.3
1988	4,100	4.4	4,700	5	8,800	9.4
1989	4,000	4.5	4,400	4.9	8,400	9.4
1990		5		5.1	8,600	10.1

Source: OPCS.

debate about the confidentiality of contraceptive service for under-16s, the conception rate increased again, reaching 9.4 in 1988. In addition, this rise in teenage pregnancies had been matched by a decline in the number of family planning sessions.

This issue came to the fore of the political agenda in the 1990s with the report *The Health of the Nation*. While political recognition was a key milestone for Brook in expanding access to their services, it was also the culmination of decades of activism during which they had fought to raise awareness of the issue of teenage pregnancy. Indeed, Brook repeatedly published statements in their annual reports and in interviews with the media where they referred to statistics and sociological studies that had shown the higher risks of mortality and morbidity for pregnant teenagers and that teenage mothers were more likely to suffer depression, poor housing, and poverty.[102] Moreover, as shown in the previous sections, Brook had campaigned to make contraceptive services for young people widely available and open at convenient times in order to encourage young people to use contraception. Specific health campaigns were also designed, as will be shown in Chapter 7, to encourage young people to visit Brook services. One key reason put forward by Brook for the high level of teenage pregnancy was a lack of knowledge about sex, in general, and about contraceptive services for young people, in particular, as well as a stark lack of facilities. In articulating these arguments, Brook helped to entrench new understandings of teenage pregnancy as a fundamental failure of public health services to reach out to young people and provide them with adequate information and methods. This argument seems to have eventually prevailed and achieved strong political backup with the report *The Health of the Nation*, published in 1992.

A first draft of *The Health of the Nation* was published as a green paper in 1991, stimulating wide debate. More than 2,000 individuals and organizations expressed their views on the paper. From the material found in the archives about Brook's contribution to the debate, it seems that some of their key concerns were taken on board in the elaboration of the official report. In correspondence sent to the Minister of Health, Brook highlighted the need for young people to be a focus of the strategy as well as the fact that sexual health and HIV should be a key priority: 'Brook believes that sexual health is an area worthy of occupying key status in the health strategy of the nation.'[103] Brook

---

[102] See, for example, 'Risks of teenage motherhood', in Brook Annual report, 1987, SA/BRO/E/1/3, Wellcome Library, London.

[103] 'The Health of the Nation, BAC's response to the consultative document for health in England, 23rd October 1991', in SA/BRO/B/1/14, Wellcome Library, London.

collaborated with other groups such as the FPA, National AIDS Trust, the Birth Control Trust, and the Sex Education Forum to present a joint briefing paper to MPs for the debate around *The Health of the Nation*. Their main key argument was to emphasize the need for sex education for young people.

As a result, the final report defined sexual health and HIV as a key area for action. The report singled out young people's sexuality in particular due to the high level of teenage pregnancies in Britain. It recognized the 'particular needs of young people' and emphasized that 'there should be special provision for family planning and counselling services for young people which emphasises the importance of loving, stable personal relationships'.[104] In addition to identifying the key areas for action, *The Health of the Nation* 'set national objectives and targets in these key areas, indicated the action needed to achieve the targets, outlined initiatives to help implement strategy and the framework for monitoring, development and review'. One of the key targets was to reduce the rate of conception among under-16s by at least 50% by the year 2000. Additionally, a paragraph was dedicated to sex education, but there were no clear guidelines on tackling the issue in the classroom. The report stated that pupils aged 11–14 must study the 'ways in which the healthy functioning of the human body may be affected by HIV',[105] but it reiterated that school governing bodies were responsible for deciding whether any further sex education should be included in the school curriculum.

Following the release of the report, Brook came to be considered a 'role model' for establishing contraceptive services geared towards young people in particular, as well as a key expert in the field of teenage sexuality. As a result of increasing demand from local authorities, Brook published the leaflet *A Service for Young People* in 1993, a step-by-step guide to assist health authorities in the development and purchase of young people's services.

Conclusion

Over a period of 30 years, Brook evolved from a small voluntary organization, with limited influence, to holding a position of predominance within the field of sexual health services at both the national and local level. This shift occurred due to the activism of Brook members, who formed alliances with other organizations, via their involvement in different sexual health charities, to

---

[104] Department of Health, *The Health of the Nation: A Strategy for Health in England* (1992): 100.
[105] Ibid., 99.

lobby politicians. By providing a service to young people, Brook participated in constructing their clients as teenagers, using terms such as 'young people', 'girls' and 'boys', and 'under-16s' but never or very rarely 'children'. This terminology contributed to carving out a distinct space within this broader landscape of birth control activism and Brook positioned itself as the main leader of birth control services for young people.

This chapter has revealed the reasons why individuals joined the charity and has identified a wider network of sexual and reproductive health activism, in which Brook was the key leader with regards to young people. The first generation of Brook members were drawn to the charity because they had previous experience working for the FPA. However, Brook activists departed from the original aim of the FPA in that they believed in providing information on contraception regardless of social class or marital status. Of course, some of the first generation of FPA activists such as Helena Wright and Joan Malleson did fit unmarried women in their private practice but not in FPA clinics as they had to adhere to the politics of respectability. Many were convinced feminists and believed that equality could only be achieved if young women were given the means to protect themselves against unwanted pregnancies.

Brook members also developed close connections with other voluntary organizations campaigning for better access to contraceptive facilities, such as the Birth Control Trust. These social connections meant that there was a sense of belonging and a common feeling of fighting alongside each other that drove the movement to increase the provision of contraception and abortion. These alliances proved successful, and Brook exerted influence on some legislative changes, especially the free provision of family planning services under the new NHS Reorganization Act, the safeguarding of the Abortion Act, and the fight against the prohibition of contraceptives and advice to under-16s. Brook also convinced the Minister of Health to increase the provision of contraceptive services. Yet, progressive and conservative activist causes clashed in this period, because of the nature of the issue, that is, young people's sexuality. As this chapter has revealed, progressive voluntary groups tried to expand birth control services while conservative groups sought to limit access to contraceptive advice and options for young people. Brook fought to maintain contraceptive information for the under-16s and portrayed them as young people who sought to act responsibly, while conservative activists constructed the under-16s as children in need of protection. The argument put forward by both sides increasingly relied on emotions and lived-experiences.

Brook's activist work and the potential success the charity had in changing the law was limited by its lack of funding. Brook members grew increasingly frustrated over time with the lack of financial commitment by Area Health Authorities and the Department of Health and Social Security, which meant that the centre had to spend a great deal of energy and time seeking funding from elsewhere. Furthermore, the constant threat of funding cuts meant that Brook found itself unable to expand its services despite growing demand. The financial situation did improve in the 1990s following the release of the report *The Health of the Nation*, which prompted Area Health Authorities to tackle the issue of teenage pregnancy, positioning Brook as the key player in this domain and as a sound voice of information on the best way to set up services dedicated to the young.

Three decades of activism had positioned Brook as the main leader of birth control services for young people. Its work was paramount in recognizing young people's right to contraceptive information and services and, consequently, Brook was able to influence the drafting of *Health of the Nation* in the 1990s.

4
The Centres
Location, Materiality, and Sensory Aspects

In 1973, journalist Vicki Mackenzie paid a visit to Brook in Tottenham Court Road in London. She shared her impression in an article published in the youth magazine *Look Now*:

> I went along to the main London centre in Tottenham Court Road and found a huge, homely building with trendy magazines strewn over the tables, flowers in the window boxes and astrological posters all over the walls. It was all very unclinical—in fact it struck me as being rather relaxing.[1]

The location of the centre, its layout, its ambience and atmosphere, as well as its interior décoration were all given careful attention by Brook members, as these elements conveyed a particular image of Brook. Recent scholarship has increasingly focused on the sensory and material aspect of the medical setting. Work by Victoria Bates has offered new understandings of the way that paying close attention to colours in hospital settings can challenge the political periodization of postwar Britain, offering an 'alternative model'[2] for understanding change over time. Martin Moore has shown the importance of the waiting room within the history of the NHS and GP practices, paying particular attention to its furniture as a marker of class. While this scholarship offers exciting new avenues of research, it has mainly focused on design and architecture, and little has been done on centres created in existing buildings. Through a focus on the clinical setting of Brook, this chapter contributes to this recent scholarship on material culture by showing the growing importance of space, materiality, and senses in the history of the health service in

---

[1] Vicki Mackenzie, 'What everyone should know about birth control', *Look Now*, 23 February 1973.
[2] Victoria Bates, 'Cold white of day: White, colour, and materiality in the twentieth-century British hospital', *Twentieth Century British History* 34.1 (2023): 1–37; Martin D. Moore, '"Bright-While-You-Wait"? Waiting Rooms and the National Health Service, c.1948–1958', in Jennifer Crane and Jane Hand (eds), *Posters, Protests and Prescriptions: Cultural Histories of the National Health Service in Britain* (Manchester University Press, 2022): 199–228.

postwar Britain. It argues that materiality and sensory aspects were crucial in creating an informal environment, conducive to encouraging feelings of trust and reducing the stress experienced by clients. It stressed the challenges Brook faced when existing premises had to be turned into something new on a limited budget. The chapter first explores the key conditions that made a centre a Brook centre. It goes on to analyse the locations of the clinics and what these locations reveal about the young people who were understood to be the beneficiaries of the Brook centres in terms of class and 'race'. It then focuses on the material and sensory aspects of the layout of the centres through descriptions gathered from newspapers, clients' testimonies, and historical pictures.

The checklist for creating a centre

Brook centres were set up in different locations and a wide range of freedom was given to local and regional centres. The organization policy was left to the discretion of the local and regional board. While each centre that wanted to be affiliated with Brook, or to bear its name, had to comply with a specific set of goals, the running of the centre as such was not centralized. This meant that in practice, services could differ and local centres had some leeway to develop work in domains that they felt were necessary.

In 1973, Brook published a checklist for birth control centres for young people, based on their experience.[3] They recommended a list of key principles that each Brook centre should adopt in order to ensure the smooth running and quality of Brook services. As the following principles illustrate, client expectations and comfort were central in this guideline. First, the opening times of the centre were defined in order to accommodate young people's lifestyles. Since young people worked or studied during the day, it was easier for them to attend the clinic at lunchtime or during the evenings. As a result, Brook recommended that: 'Centres had to be opened full time, including lunch time, evenings and Saturday morning, with full time information and advice available by a manned telephone.' The second key principle was that 'boyfriends should be positively welcome and included in the consultation with the doctor'. This principle arose from the fact that many young girls attended the centre with their boyfriends. In addition, Brook's main aim was to instil in young people a sense of sexual responsibility and this would be best

---

[3] 'Brook Annual Report 1973', in SA/BRO/E/1/1, Welcome Library, London.

achieved if boyfriends shared the burden of contraception. The third principle was that music and refreshment should be offered on site. This was meant to create an 'unclinical' atmosphere where young people would feel at ease. The fourth principle related to the waiting time for new clients, which should not exceed a day or two, and clients should not have to wait in the centre. In addition, the centre should be able to provide a walk-in clinic for those who attended without appointments. It was recommended that new clients be given the opportunity for a private talk with a counsellor or social worker and an unhurried consultation with the doctor and nurse, allowing for enough time to discuss any issues and to raise questions if needed. This measure was made in recognition of the fact that many young people had anxieties about their sexual lives that needed to be taken seriously. The charity also recommended that on-the-spot pregnancy testing, with immediate results, and pregnancy and abortion counselling with social workers and doctors should be an integrated part of the service. Moreover, the centre should be able to arrange speedy referrals for abortion. In addition, contraception should be decided upon before abortion referral and clients should be informed about the availability of follow-up and support from the doctor and social worker after the procedure. Besides contraceptives, the checklist urged doctors to prescribe other substances such as antibiotics and antifungal agents. The contraceptive methods available should be prescribed in line with scientific best practice and following the recommendation of the medical advisory board. For instance, new versions of IUDs and the post-coital oestrogen pill as an emergency measure to prevent conception became widely available in centres. Finally, the checklist recommended confidentiality and emphasized that it was crucial to encourage young clients to attend the centre. These guidelines testified to the deep concern Brook had for the well-being of their clients and their standards for high-quality and efficient clinical services.

Their expertise in setting up centres was recognized by Area Health Authorities, which asked Brook for information and help with setting up similar centres. As a result, Dilys Cossey published *Safe Sex for Teenagers* in 1978, a report that covered the need for such services and explained how to implement them.[4] In 1985, Caroline Woodroffe wrote to the DHSS to encourage AHA to open more clinics for young people. In the same document, she suggested a checklist for services geared to the needs of young people. She reiterated some key points made in 1973, notably the need for convenient opening times, counselling, on-the-spot pregnancy tests, pregnancy counselling

[4] Dilys Cossey, 'Safe sex for teenagers, 1978', in SA/BRO/E/7, Wellcome Library, London.

and abortion referrals, walk-in appointments, and making clients' partners feel welcome. These new guidelines also emphasized the need to employ some sympathetic staff so that young people would want 'to communicate'. There was also a mention, seemingly added due to the Gillick case, that younger clients—not just those under 16—should be encouraged to invite a parent or relative to come with them where appropriate. Two new recommendations that were absent in the first checklist were the need to liaise with other professional workers, and to publicize the services in places where young people would see and hear about them.[5]

Location and clientele

The location of the centres reflected concerns about the clientele they targeted; this seemed to be consistent across cities. At first, university students and students in higher education were the main target clientele. As explained in chapter 2, it was the concern about middle-class girls becoming pregnant and missing out on education opportunities that had driven Helen Brook's commitment to set up the centres. University students were a key demographic for London Brook. A similar rationale underpinned the creation of the centres in Birmingham, Liverpool, and Edinburgh. In the memorandum setting out the need to open a Birmingham Brook centre, the authors outlined the ideal location of the centre, providing insights into the clientele that Cole and Lafitte were targeting. The centre, they wrote, should be opened in a central location with easy access for students from Birmingham's two universities, its college of commerce, and its training colleges, as well as for hospital nurses and other young groups.[6] This reflected the type of clientele targeted by Helen Brook in London, indicating a shared ambition to ensure that young people in higher education were not jeopardizing their professional opportunities through unwanted pregnancies. Located in Edgbaston, home of the University of Birmingham, Birmingham Brook was specifically opened to provide advice to this demographic. In 1973 in Birmingham, the Health Centre at the University of Aston asked Brook to hold a session on their premises. More telling was the fact that a meeting preceding the opening of Brook in Birmingham took place at Aston University. Similarly, in Edinburgh

---

[5] 'Suggestions made by Caroline Woodroffe 6th November 1985 to DHSS', in SA/BRO/B1/10, Wellcome Library, London.
[6] 'A Birmingham Centre for Family Planning Advice for the unmarried, preliminary suggestions by Prof Lafitte and Dr Martin Cole, April 1964', in COLE 55, Bishopsgate Institute, London.

and Liverpool, the centres were located close to the universities and a significant proportion of the clients were students.

The opening of these centres in university cities occurred at the same time as student protests were taking place across the country, demanding that universities give students more say in their studies and welfare. In Edinburgh, for instance, the opening of Brook went hand-in-hand with a scandal where students were protesting against the rector and demanding to be more involved in the decisions taken. Moreover, students were also campaigning for the provision of contraception; at the University of Glasgow and the University of Sussex, students voted in favour of birth control centres. At Durham University, students also campaigned for a birth control clinic at the health centre.[7] Student health centres would issue the pill to female students if there were no health contraindications. The emphasis that Brook placed on responsible clients in their initial targeted demographic was part of a broader movement where young people were themselves asking to be taken seriously as responsible young adults and to be prescribed contraception, in particular the pill. In 1968, following the scandal at the University of Edinburgh, several articles were published in the mass media, presenting the results of journalists' investigation into the subject of birth control and students. One of these journalists was Wendy Cooper, who published a series on contraception and the unmarried at the time of the opening of Birmingham Brook. She wrote a lengthy article on students and the pill, reminding readers that one in ten unmarried female students would become pregnant at university and that one-third of these pregnancies would end in abortion. These numbers were in line with young women of similar age in the general population, she explained, but the implication of pregnancy for unmarried students was dramatic, as it signified an end to education and to a potential career. Moreover, pregnancies also pushed students to get married earlier; however, the university system, with its grants and accommodation policies, did not cater for married students. Cooper called for widespread prescription of the pill by student health centres, under medical supervision; she stated that young women were not promiscuous but had sexual intercourse because they were in 'loving, responsible relationship[s]'. They displayed responsible sexual behaviours and as such deserved to be given the means to protect themselves. Cooper listed the university health centres that already issued the pill (universities in Sheffield, London, Sussex, and Birmingham) and reported that Cambridge and Oxford

---

[7] Bruce Kemble, 'Hogg swipes at the pill student', *Daily Express*, 16 January 1968, 8.

would soon be offering a similar service.⁸ This focus on students highlighted concerns about jeopardizing the careers of young unmarried women.

In addition to students, Brook centres also increasingly sought to attract other groups of clients who were perceived to need contraception. One of these groups was women who had just had an abortion or a baby. Ensuring that these women were protected against unwanted pregnancies required the centre to see them immediately after the abortion or delivery. In 1969, at the invitation of Consultant Gynaecologist Brudenell at King's College Hospitals, a Brook evening birth control consultation for the unmarried was set up at the antenatal department; Dr J. R. Newton was appointed as the medical officer in charge.⁹ A similar evening session also started at Lewisham Hospital, as the result of an invitation from the senior consultant Mr Buckle, and in 1970 at Bartholomew's Hospital; all these sessions took place in London. In a similar fashion, in order to prevent young women who had undergone a termination of pregnancy from finding themselves pregnant again, a Brook session started at the Calthorpe nursing home in Birmingham, an abortion clinic that had been opened by Martin Cole.

Another way of assessing the need for contraceptive advice was through the lens of social class. In London, the centre on Tottenham Court Road which opened in 1968 was not only aimed at university students, since it was close to Bloomsbury, but also at working girls. In Bristol too, a centre opened in the city centre in 1970 as well as in Birmingham in 1973. The latter was aimed at 'busy working girls who otherwise would find it difficult to get advice'.¹⁰ The centre was open twice during weekdays on lunchbreaks in order to provide 'office girls and shop assistants' with birth control information. However, it was soon recognized that the main demographic of these centres was middle-class young people working in offices, those with professional appointments, and students. They were described as 'the more literate, more verbally able, and more self-assured members of the age group'.¹¹ Efforts were therefore made to attract a wider social base, especially among young people from deprived areas. In London, Brook had a clinic in Walworth, a socially diverse neighbourhood with stark inequalities.

In Liverpool, a drop-in clinic was organized in partnership with the FPA to provide a 'wide range of help and counselling' to young people, as expressed by the secretary Sheila Fleetwood. The drop-in was characterized by its informal

---

[8] Wendy Cooper, 'Students and the pill', *The Guardian*, 12 February 1968, 7.
[9] 'Brook Annual Report, 1968', in SA/BRO/E/1/1, Wellcome Library, London.
[10] 'Lunchbreak advice for girls', *Birmingham Evening Mail*, 9 January 1973.
[11] 'Brook Wessex Branch, Annual Report, 1971', in SA/BRO/D/1/1/1, Wellcome Library, London.

nature; young people could show up without an appointment and more time was given to counselling on non-medical issues. This service was designed to reach out to those who would 'slip through the net of formal services'.[12]

In London, a Brook centre opened in 1991 to help homeless young people. The same year, a centre opened in Craigmillar, a deprived area of Edinburgh that had seen riots in the 1980s and had a high number of teenage pregnancies. Edinburgh Brook teamed up with Womanzone, a health project for women in Craigmillar, to offer a Brook session on Tuesday evenings. Both organizations were concerned about the number of young mothers under the age of 20 living in the area. As explained by Cathie Wright, education project leader for Brook and organizer of the Brook session in Craigmillar, the rationale behind the session was that many young women had become mothers because 'of a lack of other options, of self esteem and knowledge'.[13] In addition, this high number of pregnancies indicated a high level of unprotected sex in an area with a high HIV prevalence. The centre formed a planning group to offer a forum for discussion and challenge about teenage sexuality and in particular teenage mothers. In June 1991, they organized the workshop 'Teenage pregnancy—what choice?' It was run at Castlebrae High School, with three teenage mothers sharing their experiences and the challenges they faced. Following this workshop, a study was undertaken by a community education student to assess the need for a clinic service among young women from the area. The results showed that young women would welcome a service where they 'could express themselves openly in a confidential and safe environment'.[14] Following the report, a Brook session was opened at the Womanzone centre, funded by a grant from the KC Trust and Lothian Region Education Department.

Alongside class, 'race' also became a key concern for Brook. Multiracial neighbourhoods, with their poor housing and high levels of poverty, unemployment, and teenage pregnancies, were deemed crucial areas for the provision of contraceptive information. In Bristol, Brook worked with other organizations to set up this provision at the Social Services Centre in St Paul's, 'an area of poor and inadequate housing in a multi-racial setting'.[15] The aim was to provide a place where people 'could bring their problems and obtain both a

---

[12] 'Brook Advisory Centre Merseyside, Annual Report 1979', in SA/BRO/D/12/1/1, Wellcome Library, London.
[13] 'Edinburgh Brook, 23rd Annual Report, 1991/92', in SA/BRO/D/7/1/1, Wellcome Library, London.
[14] 'Edinburgh Brook 25th Annual Report, 1993/94', in SA/BRO/D/7/1/1, Wellcome Library, London.
[15] 'Brook Wessex Branch, Annual Report, 1972', in SA/BRO/D/1/1/1, Wellcome Library, London.

sympathetic hearing and factual advice'.[16] The success of this endeavour was not as expected and a community engagement person was hired to spread awareness of Brook's offerings in the community, funded by a grant from the Home Office under its Urban Programme. Launched in 1968 by Harold Wilson, this programme was a package of grants from the Home Office, awarded to local authorities and voluntary organizations in order to 'establish projects to alleviate inner city stress'. The programme was the result of concerns around inner city life, similar to the American Poverty Programme, and aimed to confront the fierce attacks on immigration and immigrant communities, notably Enoch Powell's infamous Rivers of Blood speech. Its purpose was to provide rapid aid to inner city areas that were deemed to be under 'urban stress' and were displaying signs of 'multiple deprivation' and 'additional social need',[17] often containing higher proportions of Black and minority ethnic residents.[18] Another aim of the programme was to arrest the social and economic decline of inner cities. As Paul Gilroy has argued, 'Britain's "race" politics are quite inconceivable away from the context of the inner-city.'[19] Sociologists James Rhodes and Lawrence Brown have explained that 'the "inner city" has offered a framing device through which the minority ethnic presence and its purported 'problems' have been articulated and understood'.[20] The inner city came to represent a racialized space within a city, giving rise to assumptions about the 'deviant' behaviours of its inhabitants and contributing to the pathologized imaginary of the 'inner city'. It was in this context, and under the Urban Programme, that Birmingham received a grant to open a centre in the multiracial neighbourhood of Handsworth in July 1973, in an old bank. The centre had a coffee bar, a reception area where non-medical contraceptives were sold, shops, and a clinic. It was open daily and staffed by two doctors, two nurses, and a social worker. The local newspaper that covered the opening stressed that the centre

---

[16] Ibid.

[17] Richard Batley and John Edwards, 'The urban programme: A report on some programme funded projects', *British Journal of Social Work* 4.3 (1974): 305-31. On the Urban Programme and urban regeneration, see Andrew Tallon, *Urban Regeneration in the UK*, 3rd Edition (Routledge, 2021); Michael Pacione, *Geographies of Division in Urban Britain* (Routledge, 1997).

[18] Alan Harding and Brendan Nevin, *Cities and Public Policy: A Review Paper* (Government Office for Science, 2015); Gareth Rees and John Lambert, *Cities in Crisis: The Political Economy of Urban Development in Postwar Britain* (Edward Arnold, 1985): 128. See also Otto Saumarez Smith, 'The inner city crisis and the end of urban modernism in 1970s Britain', *Twentieth Century British History* 27.4 (2016): 578-98.

[19] Paul Gilroy, *There Ain't No Black in the Union Jack* (Routledge, 1987): 311.

[20] James Rhodes and Laurence Brown, 'The rise and fall of the "inner city": Race, space and urban policy in postwar England', *Journal of Ethnic and Migration Studies* 45.17 (2019): 3243-59.

was 'expected to largely cater for coloured clients'.[21] Some two years earlier, in their annual report, Birmingham Brook had stated their ambition of opening a new branch for 'those lacking motivation to seek advice and to be placed in [a] deprived area'.[22] This reference to a lack of motivation to seek advice tapped into the racialized stereotypes of Black sexuality, whereby young Black boys were thought to display excessive sexual drives while refusing to protect themselves, and young Black girls were depicted as promiscuous, hyperfertile, and irresponsible regarding birth control.[23]

In 1978, the Inner Urban Areas Act established city partnerships between local authorities and diverse stakeholders, among them charities and community services. Brook took up this opportunity and applied for funding. As a result, Hackney and Islington Inner City Partnership provided funding to open a centre in Islington, a multiracial and mixed-class neighbourhood. The first report on the work of the centre underlined the importance of its services; many clients had come to Brook because they had grave 'social problems', making the counselling work of the centre all the more crucial. The complexity of race in the context of the Brook is apparent in the way that counsellor Pauline Crabbe, who was the first Black woman magistrate and who worked on race relations, captured the socio-economic difficulties of young Black people and the impact of these difficulties on their sexual behaviours. She also highlighted the high rate of unemployment experienced by young Black men. In this context, young Black women, who were more likely to be in employment, were understood to be particularly at risk of teenage pregnancy. Indeed, Crabbe argued that young Black men were often 'envious or jealous' of their girlfriends' success and consequently put pressure on them to have a baby so that they would have to stay at home. Brook's role was to counsel these young people and provide them with adequate contraception. 'Race', therefore, was considered a key factor of vulnerability. A Brook centre in Brixton, home to a large Caribbean community, was funded by Lambeth Inner City Partnership. Finding premises

---

[21] 'Coffee bar centre for sex advice', *Birmingham Evening Mail*, 5 June 1973.

[22] 'Birmingham BAC Annual Report, 1971', in SA/BRO/E/1/1, Wellcome Library, London.

[23] On these racialized stereotypes and prejudices, see Anne Hanley, 'Migration, racism and sexual health in postwar Britain', *History Workshop Journal* 94 (2022): 202–22; Chris Waters, '"Dark strangers" in our midst: Discourses of race and nation in Britain, 1947–1963', *Twentieth-Century British Studies* 36.2 (1997): 207–38; Marcus Collins, 'Pride and prejudice: West Indian men in mid-twentieth-century Britain', *Journal of British Studies* 40.3 (2001): 391–418; Jones, 'Human weeds, not fit to breed?' On the idea of promiscuity and sexual irresponsibility among immigrants and especially West Indians, see Sheila Patterson, *Immigrants in London: Report of a Study Group set up by the London Council of Social Service* (National Council of Social Service, 1963).

proved difficult, but the Brixton centre opened in 1980 due to the work of Guyana-born counsellor Dorothy van Heeswyk. Prior to joining Brook, van Heeswyk had worked as a counsellor at Melting Pot, an organization for young Black people who were part of the care system. This had given her experience in working with young people from minoritized backgrounds and therefore she could better understand how a centre in a neighbourhood with a strong community of young black people should operate in order to meet their needs. As these examples illustrate, the location of the clinic was a strategic choice, reflecting views on the groups who were most likely to be the main clients of Brook.

Apart from the neighbourhood in which the centres operated, another key consideration for making sure that young people would visit the centres was their accessibility. Dorothy van Heeswyk, who opened the first Brook centre in Brixton, remembered that it took her a while to find a 'good venue'.[24] The criteria that she was using was: 'it needed to be accessible but not visible by passing buses and be anonymous enough looking so that young women, and it was primarily young women, could come without friends of their parents identifying where they would go'. The venue she found was on the top floor of a building used for something else; it was on a very accessible street, but as she explained, 'you wouldn't know that Brook was there, there was just a small notice'. In Edinburgh, as remembered by ex-client Lesley, the centre was located in 'a street off the main street and in a small building'. Similarly in London, Jenny, who visited Brook in London in the early 1970s, remembered that the centre was discreetly located in East Street, next to the market. She walked through the market, 'pretended to buy a few vegetables and then just slipped in the door to find this very nice professional, not clinical but not unfriendly but professional feel about the place and masses of other women in the waiting room who'd come from all corners of the country, from Ireland, from Scotland, I was astonished that people had to travel so far to get any advice.'[25] Similarly, in an article published in the teenage magazine *Just Seventeen* discussing the Brook Advisory Centre, the journalist Kathryn Brown, who visited Birmingham Brook, explained that 'the entrance is very unobtrusive, so no one can tell immediately where you're going'.[26]

---

[24] Private interview via Zoom with Dorothy van Heeswyk, October 2022.
[25] 'Interview with Jenny, transcripts of BBC interviews on Brook for *Everyman*, 1994', in PP/MEW/C/4/4, Wellcome Library, London.
[26] Kathryn Brown, 'A day in the life of a Brook Advisory Centre', *Just Seventeen*, 22 April 1989.

Layout of the centres

The Brook centres paid particular attention to their design and atmosphere. Indeed, they wanted to be different from the FPA clinics and to appear less formal in order to fit with young people's expectations. As explained by Pauline Crabbe in an article covering the work of Brook in 1973, 'We're trying to get away from the image of the doctor in a white coat with a steriliser in the background and a couch in the corner. We will be in our normal clothes and have pop music in the background.'[27] Creating a non-clinical atmosphere was therefore paramount in their strategy to attract young people. This section analyses the ways through which Brook created a nice and welcoming environment in existing buildings and the constraints imposed by this existing architecture.

A common narrative found in the testimonies of Brook members and clients, as well as journalists covering the work of Brook, was that there existed a stark contrast between the outside appearance of the building in which the Brook centre was located—usually described as an old, austere, or non-engaging building—and the warm atmosphere one felt when entering the premises. For instance, in a 1986 article covering the work done at Walworth Brook in London, journalist Rosalind Sharpe explained that on a hot July lunch break she had 'battled her way along the East Street market in South London'[28] and suddenly found what she was looking for, a 'doorway in an otherwise blank wall, with an unpretentious sign saying Brook Advisory Centre in orange letters'. Sharpe then shared her first impression: 'And inside what a contrast with the hot hubbub of the market! And what a surprise after the rather unwelcoming exterior.' She went on to describe her feelings about and assessment of the premises, stressing that everything was very informal and very 'common-sensical'. She noted that in spite of Brook not having much money to spare on furniture, the place was welcoming and 'somehow reassuring'—a crucial element, she reckoned, since many young people who attended the centre were very anxious and confused. It was therefore critical that the first impression was one of 'helpful sympathy'. In the picture accompanying the article, a nurse, talking to a client, was shown wearing plain normal clothes, sitting at her desk while the client sat next to her at the edge of the desk rather than in front of her. This spatial arrangement conveyed a sense of closeness and intimacy that broke with the usual formal

---

[27] Vicki Mackenzie, 'What everyone should know about birth control', *Look Now*, 23 February 1973.
[28] Rosalind Sharpe, 'Happy birthday Brook!', *Family Circle*, November 1986.

and hierarchical layout of GP practices, where the patient sat in front of the GP. The caption read: 'a nurse advises a client in informal surroundings at a Brook clinic'.[29] While the journalist and clients felt welcome within Brook centre, the staff who worked there remembered the difficult conditions. Wendy Thomas, chief executive of London Brook between 1988 and 1994, explained that 'it was a pretty dilapidated building and those stairs were always scary'.[30]

Similarly, Dorothy Keeping, who worked at Bristol Brook, remembered in an interview that the overall ambience of the place differed from the outside look of the building:

> Brook [Avon] was then situated in Clifton, Bristol, near the university. It was on the third floor of an old house and one had to climb a narrow winding staircase to reach the top floor. But on arrival at the clinic one immediately felt an air of welcome. The doctors did not wear white coats; the staff both medical and administrative were relaxed and particularly welcoming.[31]

To convey this feeling of a relaxed and safe environment, the layout of the centre and its furniture was chosen with a great deal of thought, even in a context where Brook members did not have much to spend on decorating their premises. A close look at pictures of the Brook Centres available in their archives at the Wellcome Library shows the sort of furniture and spatial arrangement that characterized some Brook centres. Van Heeswyk, who was in charge of opening a Brook in Brixton, mentioned that she had visited the Birmingham Brook and retained one key idea, the fact that 'they had a very clear space for reception and handing out the pill and that needed to be very easy to access'.[32] As a result, the reception desk in Brixton was right at the top of the stairs when clients entered the centre. The waiting area was usually situated next to the reception but separate, and was decorated. Plants and flowers were usually on display. In Edinburgh, for instance, ex-client Lesley recalled noticing a lot of plants when she entered the waiting area.

Similarly, pictures taken in Tottenham Court Centre in London in the late 1960s and early 1970s show the entry room of the Brook clinic as shown in

---

[29] Ibid.
[30] Wendy Thomas, transcript of 'Wellcome Witness Seminar: 50 Years of Brook', Friday 6 February 2015.
[31] Dorothy Keeping, written testimony, transcript of 'Wellcome Witness Seminar: 50 Years of Brook', Friday 6 February 2015.
[32] Private interview via Zoom with Dorothy van Heeswyk, October 2022.

118 RESPONSIBLE PLEASURE

Figure 4.1 Tottenham Court Road Centre late 1960s
SA/BRO/K/3/5/4/1, Wellcome Library, London

Figure 4.1. Clients climbed the stairs in a narrow building and then arrived in a long and narrow corridor that served as a waiting room, with chairs aligned against the wall. Halfway along this corridor was the reception area, a sort of white concrete cubicle with a door on the side and a square opening. Since this layout was imposed by the design of building, Brook had to find ways of making this austere design look welcoming. Hanging from the ceiling and placed on the floor next to the cubicle were two plants; it can be seen that the receptionist was in plain clothes.

In Liverpool, due to financial constraints Brook operated within the premises of the Family Planning Association building. The pictures taken in Liverpool Brook in the mid-1980s reflected the slightly different atmosphere. As shown in Figure 4.2, plants were equally on display in a bright waiting room. The reception was adjacent to the large waiting room with a small office and some more flowers on the office desk.

Similarly, pictures taken in Walworth clinic in London in 1985 show the reception desk with plants and two receptionists wearing normal clothes. The use of plants and flowers helped to create a warm environment and provided touches of colour in buildings that otherwise would have been rather monochrome and sometimes lacked natural light.

Besides the plants, the furniture was crucial in providing a welcoming feeling. This attention to décor was part of a broader movement in healthcare. Indeed, as Martin Moore has argued, in postwar Britain GP surgeries were redesigned with 'bright, cheerful and comfortable décor' in an attempt to alleviate patients' anxieties. Providing a comfortable and cheerful environment was thought to help patients waiting in GP practices to 'contain and divert their feelings'.[33] Similar concerns seem to have been shared by the Brook centres.

Regarding Brixton Brook, Dorothy van Heeswyk stated that she wanted the place to be beautiful and 'where people feel comfortable'. She had worked with an architect and later explained that 'it was extraordinarily beautiful, really, beautiful. And when I launched it, I think people were a bit taken aback because it was Brixton and I realised they expected red, yellow and green and what I created was something that was merely beautiful. On the basis that everybody should have something that is aesthetically beautiful.'[34] Heeswyk referred to the colour scheme of Rastafari and Jamaica since the centre was located in Brixton, heart of a vibrant Caribbean community. Figure 4.3, taken in the Brixton centre in 1985, shows a warm waiting room with what appears to have been a low sitting sofa made up of a small single bed standing against the wall, with the mattress covered in a striped, colourful blanket. Various patterned cushions in different colours formed the back of the sofa. Leaning against the wall were also a set of chairs. On the right-hand side of the sofa-bed, a side table can be seen, on which stood a radio cassette player and some magazines. Music usually played in the background in Brook centres, as it was found that it helped make young people feel at ease. In addition, music covered

---

[33] Moore, 'Bright-while-you-wait'?
[34] Private interview via Zoom with Dorothy van Heeswyk, October 2022.

120 RESPONSIBLE PLEASURE

Figure 4.2 Liverpool in the mid-1980s
SA/BRO/K/3/4/1, Wellcome Library, London

Figure 4.3 Brixton Centre 1984
SA/BRO/K/3/5/2/1, Wellcome Library, London

private conversation. In some centres, a TV could be found in the waiting room, such as in Edinburgh and Birmingham.[35]

In front of the sofa in Brixton, a low white table was covered with youth magazines, leaflets, and a box of tissues. Youth magazines were usually on display in every centre. In Liverpool, where BAC operated within the premises of the FPA, a small coffee table with four piles of different youth, women's, and fashion magazines stood in the middle of the bright and airy waiting room. The magazines chosen, in this case, *Country Life*, *Options*, and *Vogue* reflected a different readership than a regular Brook centre since married women also attended this centre but at different times. Generally, magazines not only served the purpose of creating an informal atmosphere, but also helped young people to pass the time while waiting to see the nurse or doctor.

In addition to the youth magazines, leaflets on sexual and reproductive health were also given for free and openly displayed. As was the case with GP

---

[35] Jennifer F. Robertson, 'Edinburgh Brook 21st Birthday. Preaching responsible sex', in GC/39/7, Wellcome Library, London; Kathryn Brown, 'A day in the life of a Brook Advisory Centre', *Just Seventeen*, 22 April 1987.

practices in postwar Britain—where the waiting room was used to 'cultivate health citizenship', to borrow from Martin D. Moore's expression—waiting rooms in Brook also served the purpose of educating young people on matters of sexual health. In Brixton, on the wall and hanging over the side table, was a shelf displaying sexual health leaflets that clients could consult and take home.

Similarly, at the bottom of the reception desk, located within a sort of cubicle with an alcove opposite the sofa at the end of the waiting room, there was another shelf displaying a wide range of leaflets about sexual health. A variety of posters décorated the walls of the waiting room and reception desk, informing clients about sexual health and also other community services such as a Clapham community project, a young women's group, and 'maternity rights for women at work'. A similar layout was used in Tottenham Court Road in the 1980s. Over the years, the décor had changed in Tottenham Court Road. While at first the stair wall was white and immaculate, by the 1980s, as shown in Figure 4.4 it had a shelf displaying a variety of leaflets on contraceptive methods such as *Straight Facts about Sex and Birth Control*, *Intrauterine Devices*, *Morning after Birth Control*, and *The Pill*. General information on sexual and reproductive health was also conveyed in leaflets such as *Cystitis* and *Everyone is Doing the Breast Test*. The shelf was

Figure 4.4 Tottenham Court Road Centre 1980s
SA/BRO/K/3/5/4/2, Wellcome Library, London

also used to display samples of different contraceptive methods and brands, such as condoms, pills, and contraceptive jelly. In 1994, at the reception desk, the space under the alcove displayed a giant poster of two rows of washing lines on which different sizes and types of condoms were hung against a black background.

This furniture and décor created a cosy and relaxed atmosphere, similar to that of a living room. This atmosphere was meant to put the client at ease and to encourage them to share and discuss their stories, as well as diminishing the anxieties some of them might have felt in visiting a place they did not know due to a pressing issue around a very intimate aspect of their lives. Client anxieties were basically designed into the materiality of the waiting room. The impact that the furniture and lay out had on clients was made explicit in an article published in *City Gen* in 1972. The 'city girl reporter' Vanessa visited Birmingham Brook centre. She mentioned butterflies in her stomach while walking up the stairs to the centre. She took a deep breath and then entered a 'friendly and modern reception area'.[36] The smiling receptionist led her to the waiting room. Vanessa went on to explain that '[waiting room] is hardly the description for it. More like being in the groovy sitting-room of someone's flat, with its modern tube-chairs, low coffee tables overspilling with trendy magazines and relaxing background music. This friendly "coffee-bar" atmosphere works wonders in calming your nerves and you soon strike up a conversation with the girl sitting next to you.' In spite of all these efforts, some buildings were more difficult to maintain in functioning order, while some premises became inappropriate, and Brook had to change location. This was the case in Edinburgh where the centre was at first established in a flat. The front room served as the waiting room, the two bedrooms were surgeries, and the kitchen was transformed into the nurse station/coffee room/telephone reception. Edinburgh Brook expanded twice because of lack of space. In 1975, Brook bought the little shop next door; it housed the secretarial staff, the clinics notes, and telephone. In 1978, another shop was bought to provide another office. Finally, in 1982, Brook acquired the adjacent 'dilapidated-looking shop' premises.[37] Edinburg Brook worked with an architect and turned the premises into a modern centre with easy access for disabled clients.[38] The new centre offered three surgeries, two interview rooms, a roomy waiting room, and a toilet suitable for accommodating a

---

[36] 'Mainly personal, Vanessa visits one of those clinics', *City Gen*, 19 October 1972.
[37] 'Edinburgh Brook Annual report, 1982', in SA/BRO/D/7/1/1, Wellcome Library, London.
[38] 'Edinburgh Brook Annual report, 1983', in SA/BRO/D/7/1/1, Wellcome Library, London.

wheelchair. But these changes, while improving the running of the centre, were sometimes bittersweet for some Brook members. Dr Jennifer Robertson remembered with nostalgia the old premises of Brook, where she had fond memories:

> The late 1970s hold my warmest memories of Brook. I worked a Thursday night with Dr Crispin [...] The waiting room reverberated with the groans of an ancient white and black TV, and a steamy coffee machine which, frequently, frustratingly broke down. The toy box in the corner was vital for the amusement of toddlers, and many of the boyfriends! The poor counsellor mingled with the clients and rendered assistance behind a curtain in the nurse room or in the broom cupboard.[39]

She then described the new premises: 'We had sparkling white formica, new comfy seats, a reliable coffee machine and a noisy radio.' But she nevertheless missed the old building: 'in 1984, the secretary moved back to the old flat—I must admit I envied them. I missed the old TV and the frenzy in the corridor.'[40] This reveals that the overcrowded centre had its charm and sometimes felt slightly more welcoming than the brand new modern centre.

Alongside the attention to décor, some dedicated areas were also delineated for children. In Brixton, van Heeswyk remembered that she ensured that there was an 'area for children to play so that people would come' in the waiting room. This concern arose from the fact that many young women had to bring their children with them to the clinic; dedicated space was therefore created to make them feel comfortable. Ex-client Jenny recollected that BAC's waiting room in East Street was meant to accommodate families. 'I phoned and booked an appointment and then was accompanied by a friend, a platonic friend, and we sat rather disconcertingly surrounded by toys because I think it doubled up as, not a playgroup but certainly people expected to be with children in the afternoon.'[41] Similarly, as recalled by medical officer Jennifer F. Robertson from Edinburgh Brook, 'the toy box in the corner was vital for the amusement of toddlers'.[42]

---

[39] Jennifer F. Robertson, 'Edinburgh Brook, 21st birthday: Preaching responsible sex', *Edinburgh Medicine* 54 (1989).
[40] Ibid.
[41] 'Interview with Jenny, transcripts of BBC interviews on Brook for *Everyman*, 1994', in PP/MEW/C/4/4, Wellcome Library, London.
[42] Jennifer F. Robertson, 'Edinburgh Brook 21st Birthday: Preaching responsible sex', in GC/39/7, Wellcome Library, London.

Finally, tea, coffee, and biscuits were all available in the waiting room. The use of tea in care settings has been analysed by Sophie Duckworth, who argues that the ritual of tea helps patients to feel cared for and feel 'at home'.[43] Drinking tea 'is experienced as a comfort', she explains, and offering tea is understood as 'a gesture of hospitality and sociality'. Individuals who have been offered tea 'associate feelings of interpersonal warmth such as "kindness" and "trust"'. The same argument could be made about Brook. The tea, coffee, and biscuits were meant to show kindness to clients, as well as a feeling of cosiness, not far from the feeling of spending time in one's living room. In addition, tea, coffee, and biscuits conveyed a sense of comfort and contributed to reducing clients' stress levels. Indeed, some young people, as will be shown in Chapter 5, visited the centre at moments of crisis when they feared they might be pregnant or when they were anxious about finding a birth control method. Time and again, the BAC annual reports referred to the clients' feelings of anxiety. In this context, tea, coffee, and biscuits undoubtedly provided a gentle way of easing these feelings.

The *Daily Mail*, known to be critical of the work of Brook, published an article in 1986 on the Brook in south London. The article was actually very positive and conveyed a vivid description of the centre's atmosphere, capturing the feeling one had when waiting in a Brook centre.

> This clinic doesn't feel like a clinic. It's not all gleaming white and sanitised. Instead, the staff are called by their first names, the young women doctors wear casual trousers and the secretary jeans. The waiting room was filling up with chattering girls, pleased to be where their secret could be out in the open. There was no one here to scold them. They could smoke a cigarette and relax—something a lot of them could not do in their own homes. Pop music blared from a transistor in another room. And every so often Anna the secretary wheeled in a trolley load of cups of instant coffee. I was surprised. There was nothing shame-making about the clinic. Furtive maybe. But apart from that almost as sophisticated as an airport lounge.[44]

In 1993, several of these different elements were formalized in the leaflet *A Service for Young People: Information for Those Concerned with Providing Birth Control Services for Young People*, under the heading 'informality'.

---

[43] Sophie Duckworth, '"Time for Tea": Tea Practices and Care in a British Hospice', in Aaron Parkhurst and Timothy Carroll (eds), *Medical Materialities: Toward a Material Culture of Medical Anthropology* (Routledge, 2019).

[44] Judy Graham, 'My evening at the clinic where schoolgirls get the pill', *Daily Mail*, 21 May 1986, 12.

Indeed, it was explained that 'simple measures can help to convey an atmosphere of informality.' Amongst these measures were: smiling staff, no uniforms or white coats to be worn; to arrange seating in groups in the waiting room; to display attractive posters; and to play youth music in the waiting room.[45] In addition, this information pack contained a model layout for a Brook Advisory Centre, which graphically depicted the spatial arrangement of the centre. The plan included an entrance into a corridor with a waiting room (15 × 15 ft) on the left with seating for twelve, a coffee corner, a TV, and a display board. On the right side of the corridor was the reception (20 × 20 ft), containing space for client records, a computer desk, index files, office files, a small fridge, a coffee machine, and a small sink. The rest of the centre was made up of one doctor's consultation room (7 × 7 ft) with a desk and a chair, one examination room (11.5 × 8 ft) with a couch, a sterilizing area and a washbasin, one interview room (7 × 10 ft) with a desk and two armchairs, a supply room (8 × 7 ft) with a book and leaflet display shelf and storage, a WC suitable for disabled access, and a room (8 × 7 ft) for flexible usage containing a couch/bed, a desk, and two chairs.

The waiting room of Brook centres offered a welcoming and relaxing atmosphere; however, there was a tension between this environment and the sensory discomfort that clients experienced during internal examinations, smear tests, and contraceptive insertions. In order to obtain contraception, clients were required to undergo internal examinations, which were recognized by Brook doctors as uncomfortable procedures. Some doctors developed techniques to make the process more comfortable for the clients. They provided information to the client about what to expect during the procedure, and they offered support and resources such as counselling if they spotted any anxieties. Moreover, Dr Hutchinson in London gave her clients the speculum to hold and insert themselves into their vagina. Despite these efforts, these procedures remained uncomfortable experiences for many clients. This tension was sometimes implicitly recognized by Brook staff when they discussed the lay out of the centre. When Edinburgh changed premises, the nurses explained that additional space meant an additional consulting room for them to best serve clients who underwent contraceptive insertion, a procedure that required 'privacy and time'.

In all, these similar layouts and the informal atmosphere of the centres contributed to creating a national common identity across centres in different

---

[45] Brook Advisory Centre, *A Service for Young People: Information for Those Concerned with Providing Birth Control Services for Young People* (Education and Publication Unit, 1993).

cities. Lauren Pikó has demonstrated how sensory experience in malls and cinema in Milton Keynes helped to unit different part of the city.[46] A similar argument could be made about sensory uniformity in Brook centres. It helped to foster a sense of cohesion on the national level. Moreover, sharing a similar sensory environment further united diverging experiences amongst different actors, such as clinical and medical staff, administrative staff, and clients, providing a shared sense of belonging.

Conclusion

This chapter has shown the different ways in which Brook tried to make its services accessible to young people. They devised some guidelines about the key elements that should be considered when opening and running a centre dedicated to providing contraceptive advice and methods to young people, covering issues ranging from opening times to services provided. In addition, they set up centres in specific locations. Over the years, there was an increasing recognition that Brook centres were catering mainly for middle-class people and students. As a result, new centres were opened in deprived areas, where class and 'race' intersected as key markers of vulnerability. Finally, Brook members wanted to make the centres attractive to young people. To do so, they offered a welcoming and informal environment: low seating; children's play areas; coffee, tea, and biscuits; plants; youth magazines; and leaflets about sexual health designed especially for young people. These all contributed to creating a relaxing and warm ambience where clients could feel comfortable and at ease. Yet this positive sensory experience could have been counterbalanced by the sensory discomfort of the consultation. Moreover, in providing a similar environment across centres in different cities, Brook created a cohesive national project of offering sexual and reproductive health services in an informal and welcoming atmosphere. This focus on the materiality of the centre shows the increasing importance of feelings and emotions in the broader history of welfare services in postwar Britain.

---

[46] Lauren Pikó, '"You've never seen anything like it": Multiplexes, shopping malls and sensory overwhelm in Milton Keynes, 1979–1986', *The Senses and Society* 12.2 (2017): 147–61.

5
'It's an excellent service for a lot of young people and a place of trust for them'

The Clients and the Shaping of Brook Centres

In an episode of the BBC television documentary series *Everyman*, marking the 30th anniversary of the Brook in 1994, Liza recalled her experience as a teenage Brook client in 1982. She was in her late teens and lived with her parents. She had started what she felt was a long-term relationship and 'wanted to sort her contraceptives out'.[1] She went to Brook because many of her friends from the art school where she studied went there and she did not want to go to her family doctor 'for obvious reasons really'. Liza's refusal to visit her family doctor might have been connected to embarrassment at talking to an adult in authority who had known her throughout her childhood and knew her family. It could also indicate the mistrust Liza had of GPs, who she felt were potentially susceptible to breaches of confidentiality. In addition, she remembered feeling very embarrassed when she entered the centre: 'Sadly it was embarrassing, because I was embarrassed that I was taking control of my sexuality. It was so casual to everyone but I was thinking, yes but I've never done this before.' This unease (Liza used 'embarrassing' and 'embarrassed' in the same sentence) is testimony to the fact that even in the 1980s, sexual intercourse among young people was still considered somewhat taboo.

Despite her unease, Liza stressed that there was a 'nice calm feeling'. She considered that the Brook staff knew what they were talking about:

> it was very specifically contraception and my insides and how it works and what was right for me and I felt that the one to one was very special. There was no moralising, there was no judging, it was refreshing and that was something that did not occur [to me] till two days after I came out, thinking 'Christ, I've just been treated as a woman in there'.

---

[1] 'Liza, interview for the Everyman broadcast in 1994', in PP/MEW/C/4/4, Wellcome Library, London.

Liza's example is typical of clients' experience with the Brook service and points to the key elements addressed by this chapter: clients turned to Brook because they felt uncomfortable visiting their family doctor, a long-known figure of authority, or they mistrusted their family doctors; friends' experience proved crucial in motivating individuals to attend the centre; clients valued a service that allegedly did not moralize at them. This chapter therefore focuses on clients' reasons for attending Brook and their experience with the service. In so doing, it adds to the growing literature on youth sexuality in the so-called sexual revolution and its aftermath. Recent work by Hannah Charnock has shown the importance of integrating the sexual lived experiences of young people when reassessing the sexual revolution in order to understand why premarital sex became more common in the 1960s and 1970s. Using oral history and Mass Observation Archives, she has highlighted the importance of peer influence and friendship in the way young women thought about and lived their sexuality. Sexual experience was seen as a gradual process that would lead to maturity and a sense of being an adult. It was at once condemned through the trope of the 'nice girl' and valued among girls as a form of social currency.[2] Similarly, Jane O'Neill has demonstrated that among Scottish female students there was a rising incidence of sexual experience alongside significant evidence of 'traditional beliefs and scepticism regarding casual sex'.[3] For young women, a steady relationship 'remained an important context to justify sexual behaviour and safeguard one's reputation'.[4] This chapter takes this body of research further by focusing on an understudied aspect, namely the use of sexual health services, young people's reasons for visiting these services, and their personal experiences.

Drawing on oral history interviews, case histories, statistics gathered in social surveys, and media coverage of these centres, this chapter explores young people's experiences of Brook and offers fresh insights into the relationship between sexual experiences, methods of birth control, and sexual knowledge. Of course, using a small sample of existing and new oral history interviews do not allow me to make bold generalizations. Moreover, given the nature of the sources, there could be a certain selection bias, particularly in relation to the portrayal of GPs and the positive experience Brook clients had in the centre. Indeed, young people turned to Brook because they did not want to visit their GPs. Yet, this does not mean that all GPs were patronizing or

[2] Charnock, 'Teenage girls'.
[3] Jane O'Neill, '"Education Not Fornication?": Sexual Morality among Students in Scotland, 1955–1975', in Jodi Burkett (ed.), *Students in Twentieth-Century Britain and Ireland* (London, 2018): 91.
[4] Ibid.

displayed negative attitudes towards the provision of contraception to young people. Some might have been supportive and therefore young people did not feel the need to attend a Brook clinic.

In all, this chapter argues that finding a friendly, non-judgmental, and confidential service—a place where anxieties, fears, and emotions could be expressed—was central for young people. They valued self-determination and praised the service for taking them seriously. Some even went on to work for Brook. However, not all the experiences were positive; this chapter also highlights gaps in the services and instances where clients felt judged. In so doing, the chapter also contributes to the scholarship on the key role played by charities in filling the gap left by state services by highlighting the extent to which Brook was perceived as essential for young people.

The chapter first provides an overview of the demographics of the clients and the way they changed over time, placing these demographics in the broader context of the sexual changes that occurred between 1964 and 1998. It then explores the absence of data on ethnicity and its related implications for addressing the needs of specific communities; the chapter then moves on to explore young people's lived experiences with the centres and the impact their visits had on their lives. Finally, the chapter explores the impact that clients had on the development of BAC services.

Demographics over time

Brook centres were aimed at young, unmarried people in particular. The number of clients seen in Brook centres increased from 1,056 in the year of its first centre in 1964 to 91,632 by 1998 when there were 18 centres in operation.[5] Up until the end of the 1970s, Brook annual reports used the terms 'girls', 'young women', 'boys', and 'young men' interchangeably to refer to clients aged between 16 and 25. The age of majority was 21 until 1970, when it was lowered to 18. However, the age of consent was 16 for heterosexual young people and 21 for homosexual men. Brook initially only saw clients aged between 16 and 25 in order to stay within the remit of the law. The upper age limit was not a consistent rule across Brook centres; clients were welcome to use the service for as long as they wanted, provided there were enough sessions to cater for them. However, the common practice was to refer clients to FPA clinics once they were married. From 1969, Helen Brook decided to

---

[5] 'Annual Reports of BAC, 1980', in SA/ALR/F.1, Wellcome Library, London.

allow under-16s to be seen in the clinics and to be prescribed contraception.[6] She recalled having taken the decision without informing her committee at an FPA meeting; the press was present and pushed the FPA to clarify its position on the subject. Helen Brook stood up and said, 'Well, Brook will see the under-16s from now on.'[7] Helen Brook was the founder of Brook and therefore her opinion was followed as a source of authority. In the annual reports, under-16s were always referred to as 'girls' and 'boys', never as 'children'. As Brook put it in an article in 1978, 'the use of the term "children" is emotive—we are not seeing prepubertal children but adolescents who are sexually mature and are trying to cope with their feelings in a society which artificially prolongs their dependence and tries to deny the reality of their sexuality'.[8]

During the period under study, sociological surveys revealed dramatic changes in young people's sexual behaviours. Young people were having heterosexual intercourse at younger ages than the previous generation; puberty was also occurring at a younger age. Two sociological surveys by Michael Schofield and Christine Farrell[9] carried out at ten-year intervals between 1964 and 1974 showed that in 1964, 16% of 15–19 year olds said they had experienced sexual intercourse at least once; this number increased to 51% by 1975.[10] Table 5.1 shows how sexual experience differed according to gender. In 1964, about 26% of boys said they had experienced sexual intercourse by the age of 17, compared to 10% of girls. By 1975, these numbers had increased to 50% and 37% respectively. Farrell's survey also picked up an issue regarding sexual experience for girls under 16. The data suggested that one girl out of eight was likely to have sexual intercourse before 16. Considering these statistics, Farrell wondered whether the age of consent (16) should be lowered. She underlined the experience of experts working with young people, such as the Brook member Fay Hutchinson, who explained that girls did not present themselves for help until they were 16, even though they were having intercourse. Therefore, the author stressed the paradoxical effect of the law: while

---

[6] 'On the pill by 16 starts row', *Daily Express*, 2 October 1969.
[7] 'Helen Brook, interviewed by Rebecca Abrams', C408/014, National Life Stories, British Library, London.
[8] 'In Answer to the Responsible Society, "Sexual Pressure on children"', *British Medical Journal* 2.6135 (1978): 499.
[9] Christine Farrell carried out a study on 0'how young people in the 1970s remembered learning about sex' and on the sexual behaviours of adolescents. Her team interviewed 1,905 people: 1,556 teenagers, 186 mothers and 163 fathers. Among the teenagers, 50.3% were boys and 49.7% girls. See Christine Farrell, *My Mother Said...: The Way Young People Learn About Sex and Birth Control* (Routledge & Kegan Paul, 1978).
[10] Michael George Schofield, *The Sexual Behaviour of Young People* (Little, Brown, 1965); Farrell, *My Mother Said.*

Table 5.1 Teenage sexual experience, 1964 and 1974–1975

Percentage of single teenage males with experience of sexual intercourse			Percentage of single teenage females with experience of sexual intercourse		
Age	1964	1974–1975	Age	1964	1974–1975
16	14	32	16	5	21
17	26	50	17	10	37
18	34	65	18	17	47

Source: Judith Bury, *Teenage Pregnancy in Britain* (Birth Control Trust, 1984), 33.

aimed at protecting girls, the law nevertheless prevented them from seeking help to protect themselves against unwanted pregnancies.

Similarly, recent research has shown a reduction of the gap between men and women, in terms of time of first sexual intercourse, between the 1950s and 2010s. According to the three National Surveys of Sexual Attitude and Lifestyle (NATSAL) conducted approximately decennially between 1990 and 2012, involving interviews with 45,199 people born between the 1930s and the 1990s, the median age at first sexual intercourse has declined from 21 for women and 19 for men born in the late 1930s to 16 for both men and women born in the early 1990s.[11] In 1995, it was found that most young people were having their first sexual intercourse at 17.[12]

The NATSAL surveys further revealed that the proportion of young people having heterosexual intercourse before 16 increased from 15.4% for those born in the late 1930s to 30.9% for those born in 1990 to 1996. This increase was also noted by teenage magazines in the 1980s. Indeed, in 1980, *19* magazine, a young women's magazine created in 1968 and aimed at 16–19-year-olds, carried out a survey of its readers to find out about girls' experiences in the 1980s. Around 10,000 readers answered questions about sex, relationship, marriage, sex equality, politics, and parents: 39% of the 10,000 readers surveyed had experienced sexual intercourse before 16.[13] In 1982, *19* magazine replicated this experience with another survey of its readers about sex: 6,000 readers answered the questionnaire; 27% of girls said they had experienced their first sexual intercourse before 16.[14] These numbers were slightly higher

[11] Ruth Lewis, Clare Tanton, Catherine H. et al., 'Heterosexual practices among young people in Britain: Evidence from three national surveys of sexual attitudes and lifestyles', *Journal of Adolescent Health* 61.6 (2017): 694–702.
[12] Ibid.
[13] 'Sex has no regrets for the 1980s girl', *19* (April 1980): 37 in SA/FPA/BRO/F1/14, Wellcome Library, London.
[14] 'Results of our nationwide sex survey', *19* (April 1982), in SA/FPA/BRO/F1/16, Wellcome Library, London.

than the percentages in the NATSAL surveys and plausibly reflects the fact that *19* readers who decided to answer the questions were those who had more sexual experience. Therefore, the sample might not be representative of young people's sexual behaviours. These surveys, while potentially biased, nevertheless indicated that young people were more ready to share their sexual experiences.

In the first NATSAL survey carried out in 1990, data were broken down by social class.[15] The survey pointed to the persistence of social class difference in age at first sexual intercourse. In the 1970s, young people from working-class backgrounds had their first sexual intercourse earlier than those from middle-class backgrounds; this was still the case in 1994.[16] The average age at first sexual intercourse for young people aged 16–24 years old in 1990 was 18 for men and women from social class 1, 17 for social classes II and III, and 16 for social classes IV and V. However, oral history studies have nuanced these statistics. While focusing on the period before the sexual revolution, the study of Szreter and Fisher shed light on class differences in premarital sexuality amongst individuals in the mid-twentieth century. Middle class respondents were more likely to have a wide range of premarital physical sexual behaviours with their future spouse and were likely to be very careful to avoid penetrative sex before marriage. Working-class girls policed boy's attempts to show their respectability. Once, this test was passed 'consent to sex was then construed as mutual consent to get married and was much more likely to result in full sexual intercourse before marriage than was typical among the middle classes'.[17] The influence of ethnicity was also assessed in the 1990 NATSAL. The median age at first sexual intercourse, not broken down by birth cohort, was 18 for both white men and white women, 17 for Black men and 18 for Black women, and 20 for Asian men and 21 for Asian women.

In addition to age and class, several studies have focused on the use of birth control methods by teenagers. In Farrell's study, of the sexually experienced teenagers, only 8% said they never used any methods of birth control and only one-third reported having done so constantly. Young people tended to use less reliable forms of contraception for their first experiences but then changed to more reliable methods. The sheath was the most common method used; 52% mentioned using the sheath as their first method of contraception, while 11% used the pill. However, 39% mentioned the pill as their most recent method

---

[15] Kaye Wellings, Julia Field, Anne M. Johnson, and Jane Wadsworth, *Sexual Behaviour in Britain: The National Survey of Sexual Attitudes and Lifestyles* (Penguin, 1994).
[16] Karen Dunnell, *Family Formation: 1976* (HM Stationery Office, 1979); Farrell, *My Mother Said*.
[17] Szreter and Fisher, *Sex Before the Sexual Revolution*, 56.

used compared to 37% for the sheath. The sheath was used by 74% of teenagers, 48% used the pill, and 40% mentioned that they had used the withdrawal method.[18] Those who said they had always used birth control were more likely to be middle-class girls from older age groups: 53% of sexually experienced middle-class girls had always used birth control, compared with 32% of working-class girls; the proportions were 43% for middle-class boys and 25% for working-class boys.[19] The majority of teenagers admitted to relying mainly on their peers for sources of information.

Similarly, recent studies have shown that incidence of birth control used at first sexual intercourse by teenagers has increased over the years. As shown in Table 5.2 based on the 3rd NATSAL, 77% of men and 83% of women who were teenagers in the 1990s used a reliable form of contraception (condom, pill, or emergency contraception) at first sexual intercourse, compared to 52% of men and 56% of women who were teenagers in the late 1970s and early 1980s. The proportion of people who used no contraception at first sexual intercourse decreased from 39% of men and 34% of women born from 1948 to 1957 to 21% of men and 15% of women born from 1978 to 1987. In addition, these statistics show the increasing popularity of the condom over the years and the success of the safer sex message spread by Health Authority

Table 5.2 Contraception used on occasion of first heterosexual intercourse, by date of birth

Born in	1988–1996	1978–1987	1968–1977	1958–1967	1948–1957	1938–1947
Men						
used condom	81	68	56	39	38	35
used another reliable method	7	9	11	20	14	9
used unreliable method	2	2	5	6	9	3
no contraception	10	21	28	35	39	21
Women						
used condom	82	73	59	45	39	39
used another reliable method	8	10	17	24	18	8
used unreliable method	1	2	4	3	10	11
no contraception	10	15	19	27	34	42

Source: 3rd Natsal.

[18] Farrell, *My Mother Said*, 26. [19] Ibid., 32.

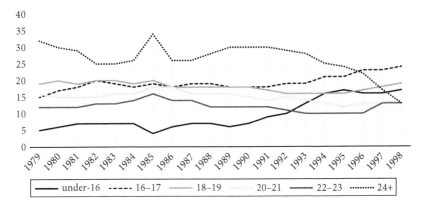

Figure 5.1 Age of new clients

Campaign, Brook (see Chapter 7), and other charities working in the sector such as the FPA.

These trends were somewhat reflected in the statistics generated by Brook. Not all centres recorded data on age at first sexual intercourse, but those that did showed that the majority of clients who came to Brook were already sexually active. In 1971, 7.5% of all Brook clients had had sexual intercourse before the age of 16.[20] In addition, all the centres took note of the age at which clients attended the clinics. Over the years, as shown in Figure 5.1 there was a definite trend towards younger clients than in the first years of the centre's activity. For instance, the clinics saw an increasing proportion of under-16s visiting the centres, from 0.5% of all new clients in 1972 to around 6% in the 1980s, with a drop to 4% in 1985 due to the short-lived Gillick case when providing contraception to under-16s without parental consent was temporarily made illegal, and up to 17% by 1998. The proportion of 16–17-year-olds also increased slightly over the years, while the proportion of 18–19-year-olds remained relatively stable. The proportion of 24+ dropped dramatically in the mid 1990s, in line with new guidelines that asked Brook to catered manly for clients aged 25 and under. This shows that an increasing proportion of young people were turning to Brook for help and advice.

The first Brook reports also contained information about the socio-economic status of young people, though this information was no longer recorded after 1974. Between 1971 and 1974, the majority of Brook clients belonged to social class III (skilled non-manual and manual, about 40%) and II

---

[20] 'Brook Annual Report, 1971', in SA/BRO/E/1, Wellcome Library, London.

(intermediate, about 20%), while 30% were students. This shows that middle-class teenagers were the main client base of Brook.[21] The first report of the Brook Centre following its official opening in 1964 provided a glimpse into the clients' demographics and reasons for attending. Out of the 1,056 clients in 1965, the majority were young women; one-third were students, one-third were secretaries, and the remaining one-third were professionals.[22] In 1972, based on the statistics published by the centre, the 'typical' Brook client was a 'girl aged nineteen or twenty, a student, receptionist or secretary, who had come because a friend recommended the Brook. She had a steady boyfriend, her first sexual partner, who had been using condoms and she was prescribed the pill for greater safety.'[23] In 1984, the typical client was a girl aged 16–19 years who had come to Brook for contraception and was prescribed the pill.[24] In 1998, the typical client was a little younger, aged 16–18 years.[25] The main difference from previous decades was that the main method of contraception was no longer the pill but instead the condom.

The reasons for attending the centre were recorded in the statistics but unfortunately not broken down by age. The majority of the clients attended for birth control methods and advice. Up until 1975, the centres also collected data on methods of birth control used before attending the centre. In 1971, for instance, 35% of new clients had used the sheath, 18% the contraceptive pill, and 13.5% had not used anything.[26] In 1974, 28% of new clients had used the sheath, 36% the contraceptive pill, and 10% no method.[27] These data were indicative of the methods used prior to visiting Brook, but this did not mean that clients used these methods consistently.

As shown in Table 5.3, the pill was at first the favourite method of birth control,[28] followed by the cap in the early days of Brook, and then the Intra-Uterine Device (IUD). Over the years, the condom gained in popularity and became the main method used by first-time clients. This take-up in condom use was due to several factors: the AIDS crisis and the public health campaign that accompanied it and stressed the importance of having protected sex; the effort made by Brook to encourage young men to take responsibility for

---

[21] 'Brook Annual Report, 1971', in SA/ALR/F.1, Wellcome Library, London.
[22] 'Annual Report of the Brook Advisory Centre', *Family Planning* 15 (1966): 47–50.
[23] 'Brook Annual Report, 1972', in SA/ALR/F.1, Wellcome Library, London.
[24] 'Brook Annual Report, 1984', in SA/BRO/E/1/2, Wellcome Library, London.
[25] 'Brook Annual Report, 1998', in SA/BRO/E/1/4, Wellcome Library, London.
[26] 'Brook Annual Report, 1971', in SA/ALR/F.1, Wellcome Library, London.
[27] 'Brook Annual Report, 1974', in SA/ALR/F.1, Wellcome Library, London.
[28] There was a drop between 1972 and 1973 in the proportion of women who were prescribed the pill. This was due to media coverage of its adverse effects.

Table 5.3 Methods of contraception for new clients by percentage

	1971	1973	1979	1982	1985	1988	1991	1995	1998
Oral contraception	83	70	80	86	73	66	43	31	20
Cap	7	3	3	4	6	4	1	0	0
IUD	1	5	9	5	4	2	1	1	0
Other contraception	1	2	8	5	3	3	1	1	5
Sheath				4	14	25	32	49	48
Postcoital contraception				2	6	11	18	30	39
No method used				28	26	27	22	17	16

Source: Brook Annual Reports.

contraception; Brook's free provision of condoms; the lifting of the ban on advertising condoms on TV in 1986; and concerns around the side-effects of the pill. Combined, these elements worked to make the condom more accessible, legitimate, and attractive.

The percentage of new clients that came seeking pregnancy tests also increased, from 2.3% in 1971 to 15% in 1982, 21% in 1990, and 24% in 1998.[29] Some came for a pregnancy test or were referred for a termination, while an increasing number of clients wanted to discuss their sexual and emotional problems, showing that anxieties about sex were common in young people. Young men also visited the centre. 'Boys' accompanied their girlfriends at their first appointment; in 1972 for instance, a quarter of girls visited the centre with their boyfriends. But boys on their own only represented a small percentage of clients attending the centre, amounting to 4.3% of clients in 1993 and 10% in 1995, in spite of Brook's effort to attract more male clients (see Chapter 7). These statistics suggest that birth control was still seen as a woman's responsibility.

Race and ethnicity

The statistics collected by the centres therefore reflected the concerns of Brook members; age of clients, birth control methods chosen, and number of pregnancy tests carried out were key policy issues for Brook. While at first Brook members collected information on the socio-economic profile of their clients,

---

[29] 'Brook Annual Report, 1971', in SA/BRO/E/1/1; 'Brook Annual Report, 1982', in SA/BRO/E/1/2; 'Brook Annual Report, 1990', in SA/BRO/E/1/3; 'Brook Annual Report, 1998', in SA/BRO/E/1/4, Wellcome Library, London.

showing that class was considered a key interest, this information was abandoned in the mid-1970s. One category that was not recorded until 1995 was ethnicity. This omission aligned with the politics around the census in Britain; it was only in 1991 that questions about ethnic identity appeared on the decennial census.[30] Attempts at including ethnicity in the census went back to the late 1960s, in the context of the first Race Relations Acts, but had previously met with reluctance because of the sensitivity of the question, which was deemed potentially divisive. Collecting information on ethnicity, it was believed, could be a double-edged sword. On the one hand, it could form a critical basis of knowledge used to monitor and combat racial disadvantage and racial discrimination and could be used to provide true evidence against false and 'wild estimates of the future of [the] coloured population'.[31] On the other hand, it could be perceived as offensive to both people of colour and white respondents and utilized to campaign for more restrictive immigration policies, as historian Debra Thompson has argued. In lieu of a direct question on ethnicity, the 1971 census asked for the birthplace of each individual in a household and for that of his or her parents. In the mid-1970s, a growing number of organizations asked for racial statistics to be collected, including the Race Relations Board, the Community Relations Commission, the Parliamentary Select Committee on Race Relations and Immigration, and the Office of Population Censuses and Surveys. However, the 1981 census did not include data on ethnicity, for two reasons. First, the Office of Population Censuses and Surveys struggled to define a question that would generate the data they needed: four pilot studies revealed that Afro-Caribbean parents objected to being asked to identify their British-born children as West Indian. Second, Black activists became increasingly vocal against the suggestion, fearing that this data would be used to develop discriminatory immigration policies, especially around nationality law, or to make a case for the wholesale repatriation of Black people.[32] It was only in 1991 that the census integrated questions about ethnicity as a response to mounting pressure from different bodies, among them the Home Affairs Committee on Racial Disadvantage, Lord Scarman's 1982 Report on the Brixton riots, and the

---

[30] Jacqueline Nassy Brown, 'The racial state of the everyday and the making of ethnic statistics in Britain', *Social Text* 27.1 (2009): 11–36.

[31] PRO HO 376/175, memo by Miss M. Hornsby, 11 November 1966, quoted in Debra Thomson, 'The Ethnic Question: Census Politics in Great Britain', in Patrick Simon, Victor Piché, and Amélie A. Gagnon (eds), *Social Statistics and Ethnic Diversity: Cross-national Perspectives in Classifications and Identity Politics* (Springer, 2015): 111–39.

[32] Thomson, 'The ethnic question: Census politics in Great Britain'. See also Nassy Brown, 'The racial state of the everyday'.

Sub-Committee on Race Relations and Immigration, 'counting to justify positive action'. Therefore, it is highly plausible that Brook did not collect statistics on ethnicity because it feared the data might be misused by anti-immigrationists and racial hate groups who alleged that migrants were 'hyper fertile'.

Yet, this lack of statistics had further implications for the well-being of minoritized individuals, since it did not allow the centres to highlight and identify their potential specific sexual and reproductive health needs or to ascertain the proportion of minoritized clients attending specific centres. There were some punctual recognitions that clients from multiracial neighbourhoods were key targets of Brook services. Indeed, as shown in Chapter 4, several centres opened in multiracial and deprived neighbourhoods such as St Pauls in Bristol and Handsworth in Birmingham in 1973. Similarly, Chapter 7 analyses the outreach and educational activities that Brook developed for clients from ethnic minority communities. Moreover, many annual reports stressed the multicultural aspect of Brook clients. For instance, in 1980, London Brook stated in an 'othering' vocabulary that 'our clients are as varied and colourful as one would expect from the cosmopolitan city we serve';[33] the following year, another said 'Our clients come from all walks of life, ethnic groups and the styles of dress and hair are varied and fascinating.'[34] In Islington, the annual report mentioned that there were clients from most ethnic minority groups resident in the district, including West Indian, Cypriot, and Asian people.[35]

However, the lack of statistics on the subject prevented an accurate picture of the take-up of the service by young people from ethnic minorities. This issue was thematized by Brook members as early as 1979. Indeed, Islington Health District in London published its operational plan in October 1979, underscoring the need to make health services attractive to members of ethnic minorities. To meet this demand, secretary Jacky Warren wrote to Caroline Woodroffe to suggest recording the number of clients from ethnic minorities who were attending Islington. She based her request on the fact that: 'The days when it was considered racist to record ethnic minorities are gone, and people in the race relations fields now advocate it as a useful tool in social policy reforms.'[36] This suggestion was not taken up, but the subject came up again

---

[33] 'London Brook annual report, 1979', in SA/BRO/D10/1/1, Wellcome Library, London.
[34] 'London Brook annual report, 1980', in SA/BRI/D10/1/2, Wellcome Library, London.
[35] 'London Brook annual report, 1980', in SA/BRI/D10/1/2, Wellcome Library, London.
[36] 'Letter from Jacky Warren to Caroline Woodroffe, 12 November 1979', in SA/BRO/D/10/6/4/1, Wellcome Library, London.

two years later. In a 1981 letter from Caroline Woodroffe to Mike Coffey, district nursing officer, she explained that a second survey of the Area Health Authority highlighted the need to improve the take-up of NHS services by ethnic minority groups. In this regard, she explained that while Brook did not keep figures on ethnic minorities, a substantial proportion of Brook's young clients were '[b]lack, including young [b]lack men'.[37] In Islington, at that time, about half of the clients who had attended the most recent session of the clinic were of 'West Indian or African origin'. She stressed the difficulties Brook faced in being trusted by 'these young people' but was proud that Brook was usually able to 'help them go on to seek other treatment they may need, or to register with a GP if they have not'. Despite the call from the Islington Area Health Authority to assess the take-up of services by minority ethnic communities, Brook still did not collect statistics on the subject.

This situation persisted in the 1990s even in the context of Brook's implementation of its equal opportunity policy. In 1990, the centre devised a list of recommendations regarding this policy. In the list, Brook acknowledged the need to obtain an overall client profile by recording information about the personal characteristics of Brook clients in a form that could be aggregated for statistical purposes. Brook mentioned relevant characteristics such as ethnicity, gender, employment status, disability, clients' preferred language for written and spoken communication, and sexual orientation.[38] However, the collection of these data does not seem to have been made compulsory. Some centres punctually started recording the ethnicity of their clients. For instance, in 1990, over a month between November and December, Tottentham Court Road asked each of its new clients about their ethnicity. The results showed that 59% of their clients were white British, 18% were Black British, 7% were Indian/Bangladeshi/Pakistani, 2% were West Indian, 5% were Irish, 2% were European, 0% were Turkish/Greek/Cypriot, and 75 were recorded under 'Other'. In 1991, ethnic statistics were compiled across all London Brook centres between March and August. The categories expanded to include African and Chinese/Vietnamese clients. As shown in Table 5.4, Brook catered for a diverse group of young people.

---

[37] 'Letter from Caroline Woodroffe to Mike Coffey, District Nursing Officer, 4 December 1981', in SA/BRO/D/10/6/4/1, Wellcome Library, London.
[38] 'Equal opportunities—applied to clients' services, Brook 20 November 1990', in SA/BRO/C7/1, Wellcome Library, London.

Table 5.4 Ethnic description of clients of London Brook (10 centres) by percentage

Ethnic origin	1991	1992	1993	1994
Irish	4.35	4.1	3.1	3.25
Black British	14.98	15.6	14	14.84
White British	58.58	55.7	54.7	53.97
West Indian	3.18	3.2	3.1	2.97
African	3.77	3.9	4.1	4.31
Indian/Pakistani/Bangladeshi	2.33	3.2	4.6	4.64
Chinese/Vietnamese	0.62	< 1	1.1	1.04
Turkish/Greek/Cypriot	1.28	1	1.3	1.12
Other European	4.31	4.4	2.9	2.3
Other	6.6	8.2	5.8	22.72
Mixed race			5.3	5.26

Sources: London Brook Annual Reports.

After the release of these statistics, it was decided that more outreach work was needed to attract a more diverse range of young people to Brook.[39] The statistics were therefore used to find out whether the services were reaching all groups in the community. However, apart from this statement, there was nothing else that explained how these statistics informed the policy of the services. Even by 1995, only London and Birmingham Brook had procedures in place to monitor ethnicity.

The initial lack of monitoring of ethnicity and its later restriction to London and Birmingham created a real missed opportunity for Brook, as it would have helped the charity better identify the sexual and reproductive health needs of young clients from ethnic minorities and thus assess the quality of its own services. Indeed, being able to identify the types of birth control methods recommended to clients according to ethnicity would have been a key element in ensuring that no unconscious or conscious racial/ethnic bias informed the provision of specific methods of contraception.

Clients' lived experiences with the centre

These trends towards early age at first sexual intercourse can potentially explain why an increasing number of young people were turning to Brook for help and advice. Young people sought help because they had specific needs and demands.

[39] 'Minutes of the Executive Committee, 22 June 1992', in SA/BRO/D/10/2/2/8, Wellcome Library, London.

Lack of sex education

Young people were actively trying to gain access to contraceptives despite the barriers they faced; there was a common narrative in the majority of the testimonies collected where clients were turning to Brook for help because Brook was providing information on a subject that could not be discussed at home. Young people displayed agency and strong will in trying to manage their sexual lives in a climate where discussing sex remained taboo in their domestic contexts and where the main source of information on contraception was friends. While growing up, interviewees received little information on sex and contraception, even those who were teenagers in the 1990s. Sex education was very limited (see Chapter 7 for the historical context and Brook's role in producing sex education materials). The majority of the interviewees underlined the lack of sex education at home and at school and the fact that they could not or did not want to discuss the topic with their parents. This lack of information and communication made Brook particularly attractive as a place for discussing and providing answers to young people's questions. For instance, Lucy, born in Plymouth in 1973, explained that her school did not offer anything useful:

> And we didn't have anything at school. I went to a Catholic school. Um, except, um, I remember when I was about 15 or 16, one of the girls in our class had her mother come in, who was the mother, I think, of five children. And she came in to teach us about the rhythm method. <laugh>, that's what I say. [...] We didn't have, um, what I would think of now as being, you know, a sort of medically informed up-to-date set of guidance about all the different options. We just had the kind of Catholic ideology given to us.[40]

She underlined the few options she had for discussing anything related to sex and explained why she had gone to Brook for advice:

> because I've become sexually active when I was about 14, which was obviously, um, quite young, legally speaking, and um, because I came from this background where I could not have discussed my sex life or my, um, you know, my sort of contraceptive choices at home, at least not with my parents. I would've discussed it with my sisters. Um, and definitely did discuss it with

[40] Private interview with Lucy, 15 May 2020.

my sisters later. Um, I was sort of, you know, I had to seek advice from externally and I couldn't have gone to my doctors.[41]

In the course of the interview, she returned to her lack of support in terms of obtaining information on birth control, especially from her parents. 'So my parents, I should say were really strict Catholics. [...] so my, I never had any education at home about, um, sexual education, let alone anything to do with contraception.'

Similarly, Jenny, interviewed for the *Everyman* TV show on Brook, recalled that her sexual knowledge was patchy in the 1960s. She did not have sex education at school and did not discuss the subject with her parents; the main information she had was from her friends, but it was unreliable. As she put it: 'it was rather King's suit of clothes, we all presumed that or tried to make out that we knew more than we did, so what we did learn along the lines was very hit and miss and whether at the end of it we cobbled anything together like the truth or any framework was pretty accidental'.[42] The absence or limited content of sex education at school was invoked as a key reason for young people's attendance of Brook by Sally Price, secretary of the Birmingham Brook. In an article on sex education in Birmingham, she explained that 'dozens of young people who come to our clinic with sex problems tell us they have virtually no information given to them at school whatsoever. And what bits they did receive if any, were so devoid of the realities of life as to be almost meaningless.'[43]

Alison, who grew up in Liverpool and attended a Brook clinic in the late 1980s, also went to a Catholic school and deplored the information she had received; 'it was laughable',[44] she reflected, adding that 'we never had any sex education until about two or three weeks before we were due to leave. And we were approaching 16 by then.' This sex education consisted of information about periods and childbirth, but nothing related to the sexual act or contraception. This lack of information was all the more dramatic given that some of the girls in her school were having 'unprotected sex and were taking chances' at 15.

---

[41] Ibid.
[42] 'Jenny, interview for the Everyman broadcast in 1994', in PP/MEW/C/4/4, Wellcome Library, London.
[43] Peter Seeds, 'The divided city', *Sunday Mirror*, 9 May 1971, 23.
[44] 'Alison, interview for the Everyman broadcast in 1994', in PP/MEW/C/4/4, Wellcome Library, London.

The taboo endured and the lack of sexual education at home remained something mentioned even for teenagers in the 1990s. Tracey, who visited a Brook centre in the late 1990s, explained her lack of knowledge around contraception. 'My mum had never, ever spoke to me about anything like that. Um, and obviously when you're young, you're a little bit stupid. Aren't you <laugh>, yeah.'[45]

However, not all parents were reluctant or opposed to discussing sexuality with their offspring. Indeed, some parents brought their teenagers to the clinic. In a 1967 article covering the first year of activity of Birmingham Brook, the journalist interviewed a married couple; the wife had accompanied the couple's daughter to Brook. The journalist took great care to stress that this example was rather exceptional. Highly educated, with a 'background of liberal thought and experience', and exceptionally close to their 17-year-old daughter, these parents 'could discuss sex naturally and openly with their children'.[46] The daughter had told her parents about her sexual experience from the start, and the family decided it would be better for her to use contraception. The girl was nevertheless rather anxious about going to the centre on her own, and the mother told the journalist that her daughter 'was glad (she) had gone along with her'. Both mother and daughter were 'tremendously impressed with the happy atmosphere there among the girls as well as staff'—so much so, explained the mother, that she took leaflets advertising the centre home with her and gave them to her friends. Both parents stressed how important these centres were for 'avoid[ing the] futile anxiety which so filled the life of their generation'. This example suggests that some parents wanted to provide their children with a different upbringing from that of their own youth, where sex had been shrouded in secrecy. In so doing, they supported their daughters' greater freedom.

Another example of parental gratitude towards Brook could be found in a letter discussed in the Annual Report of 1981. Of course, Brook only published positive letters supporting its work and stressing the quality of its services. Nevertheless, this letter revealed that some parents were supportive of their teenagers' experiences. A mother wrote to Brook, thanking them 'for the marvellous way doctors and counsellors at Brook helped my daughter recently'.[47] Aged 17, the girl 'was distraught' to find she was pregnant, and the mother booked her an appointment at Brook, 'to receive help and advice'.

---

[45] Private interview with Tracey, 12 May 2020.
[46] 'One mother's view', *Birmingham Post*, 5 September 1967, 8.
[47] '"Letter from a Mother", quoted in Brook Annual Report 1981', in SA/ALR/F.1, Wellcome Library, London.

The letter explained that communication existed between the mother and the daughter but help was nevertheless needed at this 'difficult time'. The mother, who was also writing on behalf of her daughter, stressed how grateful they were for the quality of the service: 'Everyone was so kind and helpful, and after talking it over and giving it much thought she had an abortion. It was such a difficult time for her but it would have been much worse without the understanding of people like Dr [redacted] and [redacted].'

Liza also mentioned one important facet regarding sexual information: the fact that although her parents were very open, especially her mother, she still preferred not to approach the subject of sex with them. 'I think it was more my decision not to talk to my parents about sex.'[48] This suggests that for some Brook clients, finding contraceptive information on their own might have been perceived as an independent quest and even as empowering.

In 1987, Isobel Allen published the *Education in Sex and Personal Relationship Policy Report*. The report was based on 209 interviews with teenagers aged 14–16, 99 boys and 110 girls, and 212 parents, 149 mothers, and 63 fathers in three different cities in England, one in the North-East, one in the Midlands, and one in the South-East.[49] The results revealed that young people would first turn to their mother (41%) or a friend (32%) if they had any questions about sex, contraception, and relationships.[50] There were striking differences between boys and girls, with 54% of girls saying they would turn first to their mother with a question about sex and 55% with a question about contraception, compared with only 27% and 22% for boys respectively. These numbers therefore nuanced the findings of this section and show that for girls talking to their mother was a legitimate option.

Resistance from other services

Although young people tended to have patchy sexual knowledge due to lack of information, they nevertheless found ways of filling their knowledge gaps and obtaining contraceptives. However, their quest for contraceptive information was not easy. In 1970, Margaret Bone, on behalf of the Department of Health and Social Security, carried out a survey on family planning services in England and Wales in order to assess the adequacy of existing services and

---

[48] 'Liza, interview for the Everyman broadcast in 1994', in PP/MEW/C/4/4, Wellcome Library, London.
[49] Isobel Allen, *Education in Sex and Personal Relationship* (Policy Studies Institute, 1987).
[50] Ibid., 138–9.

to suggest ways to develop them. She interviewed 2,500 married women and 1,000 single women; among the latter, 59% were under 20. The survey revealed that only 10% of 16–35-year-old single women had ever used these family planning services (GPs and clinics). A higher proportion of women aged 20 and over had used the services compared to younger girls (16% and 8% respectively).[51] The findings also illuminated that although single women who used the services were more likely to visit their GPs, they preferred the idea of using clinics catering especially for the unmarried.[52] Those who never used family planning services said that they expected the clinics to offer more sympathetic advice than GPs. In addition, they said they would feel embarrassed to visit their GP because the doctor knew them. Oral history testimonies collected by Kirstin Hay with Scottish women about their experiences in obtaining the pill as unmarried women in the 1960s to 1980s also reflected this reluctance to turn to GPs.[53] Indeed, Hay demonstrates that many young women were afraid of visiting their family doctor due to potential lack of confidentiality and lack of anonymity, that is, the fact of being seen entering their doctor's practice. In addition, several of her respondents shared negative experience with their GPs who proved judgmental and refused to prescribe the pill.[54]

In 1994, a survey was carried with 4,481 teenagers aged 15–16 (51.6% male and 48.4% female) from 30 schools in rural, semi-urban, and urban areas of England outside of major conurbations (61.0% lived in a town or city) to discover their attitude to the GP consultation and contraceptive services.[55] This study reveals the reluctance of young people to seek contraceptive help at their GP practice because of a lack of trust in confidentiality, lack of staff friendliness, and delays in appointments.

Time and again, in Brook Annual Reports, the resistance of other services to provide contraceptive information was mentioned. For instance, in 1976, Brook Merseyside's annual report stressed that many clients had first been refused information by other services:

---

[51] Margaret Bone, *Family Planning Services in England and Wales: Office of Population Censuses and Surveys* (Her Majesty's Stationery Office, 1973), 53.

[52] Ibid., 54.

[53] Kristin Hay, *An Oral History of Birth Control Practices in Scotland: Gender, Sexuality and Scottish Society c.1965–1980* (unpublished PhD dissertation, University of Strathclyde, 2022).

[54] Kristin Hay, '"He made clear his utter contempt of me and I can remember it still"': Unmarried women's experiences of accessing the pill in Scotland c.1968–1980', article under review.

[55] Chris Donovan et al., 'Teenagers' views on the general practice consultation and provision of contraception: The Adolescent Working Group', *British Journal of General Practice* 47.424 (1997): 715–18.

Throughout 1976, we have repeated instances of responsible young people having been refused birth control even though they were at risk of unwanted pregnancy. While some in this group were far-sighted and persistent enough to seek our help and receive the advice they sorely needed, we had reason to ponder on the fact that no doubt many others less persistent inevitably must have been discouraged from pursuing a responsible course of action.[56]

These results were somewhat reflected in the testimonies of Brook users. Among those who had visited the centre in the late 1960s and early 1970s, many reflected on their bad experiences with the FPA. Indeed, some young people first sought help at a FPA clinic but were turned down or had a bad experience and subsequently went to Brook. This was the case for Sarah, born in 1947. She visited the Brook clinic in Edinburgh in 1968 just after its opening. A student at the university, Sarah went to Brook with a friend because they wanted to start taking the pill.[57] At the time when Sarah attended the centre, she had already had sex, aged 17, before going to university. She stressed how difficult it was to obtain the pill or any reliable contraception for unmarried young women. She described the ambience of the time regarding sex as being 'oh my god I must not get pregnant, because that was the last thing we wanted'. She recalled that she had first tried a FPA clinic in 1967, but had needed to lie about her marital status in order to obtain the contraceptive pill. She stated that lying was not easy and reflected on the whole atmosphere of the FPA clinic as being for married women and children. When she learnt about the opening of Brook, she 'was over the moon, you know, because it was intended [for] young people. It was bloody marvellous'. Sarah could not remember exactly where she learnt of the existence of Brook, but suspected it was in the local press. When asked whether she discussed the subject with her parents, she replied that she had wanted to protect them from 'what she was up to'. There was also the possibility of seeing a GP, Sarah explained, but she did not trust the one in her neighbourhood, as some of her friends had reported bad experiences with him. In comparison, in Brook the wide majority of the doctors were female doctors. Male doctors who worked in the centre usually worked at the sessions opened in hospitals, such as Kings College in London. Her friends' experience proved essential in Sarah's assessment of her options. Sarah emphasized several times during the interview that she thought the Brook clinic was a 'marvellous place' and that it meant a lot for her and

[56] 'Merseyside Annual Report, 1976', in SA/BRO/D/12/1/1, Wellcome Library, London.
[57] Private phone interview with Sarah, February 2020.

other young women of her age in the late 1960s to have a service especially created for them. Interestingly, Sarah explained that she did not use the sheath because it was not under her control; she wanted to be 'in control and be certain and safe' when having sex, hence the pill was her best option. This shows that for Sarah, taking responsibility for birth control was essential in ensuring she was not at risk of pregnancy. Sarah used the pill for at least a year before she started to become worried about its side effects. Sarah did not remember if she went back to Brook for her pill supply but assumed that she did. She underscored that she had no memory of what happened inside the Brook clinic, whereas she had a clear memory of her experience at the FPA clinic; in the latter, she felt judged and had to lie and the whole experience was, as she put it, very 'unsettling'. Further analysing this lack of memory, Sarah suggested it was testimony to the fact that everything went 'smoothly and was easy at Brook'.

In a similar fashion, Janet, interviewed for the BBC *Everyman* TV programme broadcast in 1994, emphasized that she visited the FPA before visiting Brook, after having started a relationship with her boyfriend in the 1960s. She explained that they took 'a conscious decision to use contraceptives'.[58] At the FPA clinic, she was refused contraceptives as she was not married. Having read about BAC in the magazine *Nova*, an outspoken feminist fashion magazine (launched in 1960) that covered political social and sexual issues, the couple decided it was a place that could help them. In addition, Janet explained that she had read what she referred to as 'the Sunday Times bible, living with the pill' and knew exactly what she wanted. She remembered entering the BAC and finding:

> it was just like a breath of fresh air, here were people who weren't going to ask about my marital status or my morals although I had no conscience at all and I went in and I suppose I was counselled by somebody who talked to me about why I was there and then I went and saw the doctor and it was just wonderful, they gave me the advice and the help that I needed in a thoroughly sensible and unquestioning way.

She later added, 'it was wonderful because the doctors treated me as I was somebody intelligent'.

---

[58] 'Janet, interview for the Everyman broadcast in 1994', in PP/MEW/C/4/4, Wellcome Library, London.

Lorna also reflected on the different providers she had tried in order to obtain contraceptives. As a teenager in the 1960s, she had become sexually active 'quite young', as she explained.[59] At 16, she was in a 'steady relationship'; her boyfriend's flat was once raided by the police because a neighbour complained about some noise. She was undressed and the policemen were, she recalled, 'very unpleasant and very racist', because her boyfriend was a Black man, six years older than her. She was frightened of the policemen, who made comments about her 'wrong' behaviour and argued that she was 'in need of care and protection', even though her relationship with her boyfriend was consensual and based on deep feelings of love. Once the policemen left, she ran to her sister, who, on learning that she was having unprotected sex, took her to the FPA clinic for contraception. Lorna remembered that she had to lie about her marital status in order to be fitted with a cap in the 1960s. She later attended a Brook centre.

Similarly, Claire attended Brook for contraception in the late 1960s. She justified going to Brook because the FPA would not necessarily provide for the unmarried and GPs were often untrained in the matter:

> I wasn't in a, a steady relationship at the time. Okay. Um, I just thought it would be a desirable thing to do. Yes. It was at the point where you couldn't really rely on a GP to know much about it necessarily. It was before the inclusion of birth control as a, you know, a contraception in the NHS generally. So, you had to either go to the FPA and at that point, the FPA wasn't necessarily seeing unmarried people, so you were really kind of, it was Brook or nothing. Really.[60]

Alison also found the FPA very judgmental, even in the 1980s. Alison had her first sexual experience aged 17 and protected herself by using a condom. A few months later, she consulted her GP because she had painful periods and was put on the pill. At age 19, Alison went back to her GP to complain about migraines; the GP decided the pill was the culprit, refused to renew the prescription, and did not offer alternative methods. Alison then decided to go to the FPA clinic, attending for a year. She stated: 'I really didn't like that place either, it was really really clinical, it was like a hospital, it stank of antiseptic, whitewashed walls and the nurses were really judgemental, really

---

[59] Lorna, interview for the Everyman broadcast in 1994', in PP/MEW/C/4/4, Wellcome Library, London.
[60] Private interview on the phone with Claire, May 2021.

overstarched uniforms, they were horrible and had a very judgemental attitude.'[61] Alison explained that she found Brook by chance by walking through Liverpool town centre and thought, 'brilliant, I found it'.

Likewise, Karen, a client at Brook in the mid-1980s, sent a thank-you letter to Brook for making her 'experience such a positive one'.[62] This letter was one of the only letters I found in the archive. While she did not explain the circumstances under which she visited Brook, she stated that 'in the past I had some fairly negative experiences of the health services and the particular circumstances which led up to my visit to the Brook made me feel especially anxious'. However, she was positively surprised and emphasized the good care she received: 'it wasn't just that both the nurse and doctor who I actually consulted with were kind, concerned and free of judgements, but that everyone who I dealt with, from the person I initially spoke to on the phone to the reception staff who I actually saw when I arrived seemed to go out their way to make me feel comfortable and relaxed'.

Apart from the FPA, GPs also proved to be a barrier for young clients trying to obtain contraception. Indeed, clients often turned to Brook because they trusted the charity more than their male GP, who was generally their family doctor and from an older generation, and had proven to be judgmental or patronizing in the past; others simply did not try going to their GP because of their friends' bad experiences. In all the testimonies, Brook clients mentioned their experience with male GPs. This could reflect two things. First, the underrepresentation of female GPs in Britain. For instance, in 1988 the number of female GPs was 6,505 against 20,915 for male GPs. The number of female doctors rose sharply over the years to reach 20,435 in 2013.[63] Second, this could also reflect that fact that female GPs might have been more open to provide contraceptive advice to young people.

For instance, Wendy Thomas, who was chief executive of London Brook from 1988 to 1994, first visited Brook as a client in the late 1960s. She underlined how difficult it was for young people to obtain contraception at that time:

And it's very interesting, the '60s, I think, because everyone that wasn't around in the '60s thinks it was a wonderfully trendy time and everybody

---

[61] 'Alison, interview for the Everyman broadcast in 1994', in PP/MEW/C/4/4, Wellcome Library, London.
[62] 'Letter from Karen, 14 November 1986', in SA/BRO/D/10/4/2/1, Wellcome Library, London.
[63] Laura Jefferson, Karen Bloor, and Alan Maynard, 'Women in medicine: Historical perspectives and recent trends', *British Medical Bulletin* 114.1 (2015): 7.

was having lots of sex. Well, actually, as I was always pointing out to people, it was rather difficult to get contraception if you weren't married. But I was a student from 1967 to 1970 in London University and I pitched up to my GP in Bournemouth when I wanted the pill and he said I was too young to be having sex, and I said, well, I was too young to be pregnant. I thought they were rather different things and he was very scared of me, I had very long hair and very short skirt, and he didn't quite know where to look [*laughter*]. Anyway, his embarrassment got the better of him and he did actually write me a prescription, though I subsequently went to Brook after that.[64]

Another example is Lucy, born in 1953, who visited a Brook centre in Birmingham in the early 1970s. She came to Birmingham to study at the Elizabeth School of Nursing. During the first year of her studies she lived in the nursing home, but in her second year, she moved into a rented property in Edgbaston with seven friends. Lucy remembered this period as being a lot of 'fun, party and what was going on in the early '70s and I think a lot of us were a little bit adventurous but what happened in my situation is one of the girls, whom I lived with, got pregnant'.[65] This pregnancy acted as a wake-up call for Lucy and her friends. She recalled that the situation 'prompted discussions in the house about "oh jeez this is real and what could happen" and the thought to go the Brook Advisory Service'. Lucy explained that there was a Brook centre in her local neighbourhood. She stressed that for

> a lot of us too, going to the GP then, it was difficult, or discussion around precautions and stuff like that. I would certainly not have gone to a GP in my hometown, small country town, no way. And, also, you know, in the early '70s, I think we still thought [a] GP was a little bit of a guard. So, I think that [was] what prompted some of us, six in the house who were sexually active, to go to the Brook.

This testimony revealed that Lucy would have felt embarrassed to discuss contraception with her GP and that she expected her GP to display a moral judgement.

Other clients turned to Brook because the doctors were mainly female doctors. In an article covering the work of the Brook Liverpool, a 16 year-old girl explained her reason to visit Brook. She attended the centre with her

---

[64] Wendy Thomas, in transcript of *Wellcome Witness Seminar: 50 Years of Brook*, 6 February 2015.
[65] Private interview on the phone with Lucy, 20 May 2020.

boyfriend to ask about going on the pill. She turned to Brook because she disliked her own male doctor: 'I didn't like my own doctor—they've got female doctors here and I prefer that. Male doctors just aren't very gentle.'[66]

The non-judgemental nature of Brook was noted repeatedly by interviewees and stood in sharp contrast with their assessment of GPs' attitudes. Jenny, who attended a Brook centre in the 1960s in London, explained that she would have never gone to her GP because her GP was her local family doctor, who knew her personally; 'it would have been insupportable, the idea of going to him'.[67] Jenny recalled that she expected a form of judgement from Brook but instead found 'these professional people telling us that we were being adult and treating us like adults and you were able, very easily, to talk to them'. Moreover, Jenny valued the fact that she could attend the centre and be honest about her situation: 'you did not have to pretend, weave a story that you were immediately marrying or engaged'. This implicitly referred to the FPA's policy, where contraception was only prescribed to married or about-to-be married women.

In a similar way, Emily, who visited Brook as a client in 1980 at age 21, remembered that at age 17 she went to the FPA clinic in Sheffield, as there was no Brook in Sheffield at the time, and was fitted with an IUD.[68] She then moved to Birmingham for university. Due to bad bleeding from the IUD, she was put on the pill by the university service. After leaving university, needing another prescription, she attended Brook. Emily explained that another option would have been her GP, but she had rejected this option as he was very conservative. Once, she had been to see him for a cold and had been asked about her marital status and whether she was on the pill; the GP also encouraged her to see the nurse about the natural method of birth control. Emily could not remember where she had learnt about Brook but said 'everyone knew about it'. During her visit, she discussed the methods that suited her best and asked to be fitted with another IUD. Thinking that the bleeding might have been coincidental, the Brook doctor agreed to give it another try. Since Birmingham Brook did not have an age limit, Emily continued to use them until she was sterilized at age 37. Emily's example shows determination on her part, a strong desire to attain her favoured contraceptive method and the trust she placed in Brook's services. Emily's

---

[66] 'When sex tempts the teenagers', in *Liverpool Echo*, 21 February 1979, 8.
[67] 'Jenny, interview for the Everyman broadcast in 1994', in PP/MEW/C/4/4, Wellcome Library, London.
[68] Private phone interview with Emily, 24 February 2020.

needs and opinions were respected, which was why she used the Brook service until the end of her reproductive life.

As these testimonies illustrate, some clients did not want to turn to their GPs because it was very often their male family doctor who knew them and their family. GPs were deemed untrustworthy and perceived to be judgemental; in contrast, Brook acquired the reputation of offering a trusted and confidential service mainly by female doctors, which explained the popularity of the latter.

Transformative experience

The majority of young clients went to Brook to ask for contraception. They visited the centre to obtain the pill after starting a sexual relationship. This means that many of them took some risks before seeking protection. Lesley, interviewed in 1994 for the *Everyman* BBC broadcast, recalled that she went to Brook in the early 1970s in Edinburgh with a friend. On learning that Lesley was having sex with her steady boyfriend, without using any methods of contraception other than 'being careful', the friend booked her an appointment. Interestingly, Lesley underlined that she was in a long-term and steady relationship. This mirrored one of the key arguments put forward by Brook to counter criticism that they were encouraging promiscuity, namely the fact that the majority of their clients were having sex within a steady relationship. Once they entered the clinic, Lesley recalled her embarrassment when her friend announced to a full waiting room 'to [her] absolute horror'[69] that 'my friend is not using anything and she needs help'. Lesley's testimony highlights two issues that seem to have been recurrent among Brook service users. First, young people tended to seek help from Brook once they were in a relationship and had already engaged in sexual intercourse. Second, friends were paramount in young people's experience with the service, serving as a channel of information. According to Brook statistics, in 1973, 53% of new Brook clients explained that they were visiting the centre because a friend had recommended it to them. Word of mouth proved successful in transmitting information about the service among young people.

When young people turned to Brook, they tended to know in advance what sort of contraception they wanted. For example, Florence, born in 1968, who visited the centre when she was 17 to attain the pill, explained: 'I went knowing

---

[69] 'Lesley, interview for the Everyman broadcast', in PP/MEW/C/4/4, Wellcome Library, London.

what I wanted. I knew exactly what I wanted.'[70] Florence's mother worked at Birmingham Brook and Florence remembered going to the centre regularly when she was a child and loving the friendly atmosphere. It was therefore natural for her to turn to Brook once she became sexually active.

In addition to contraceptive methods, some clients visited Brook because they feared that they were pregnant and needed pregnancy testing, counselling, and abortion referrals. For instance, Lucy, who attended a Brook centre in Birmingham in the mid-1970s, recalled that her roommate first visited the centre because she feared she was pregnant. Her fears were well-founded, and Brook helped her to obtain an abortion.[71] Similarly, Marnie, an African-Caribbean client, attended the Brook clinic in London in the 1970s because she suspected she was pregnant. She remembered having learnt about Brook from a friend in college. She was using an IUD but nevertheless felt she might be pregnant. She went to Brook for a pregnancy test, which turned out to be positive. She explained that it was 'a dreadful shock to her' because she thought that she had taken all the necessary precautions against getting pregnant. However, she explained that after the initial shock, it went 'fairly smoothly'; she recalled that 'I knew I didn't want to go through with the pregnancy and the people at Brook were very helpful and I had a fair amount of counselling and they arranged the termination for me.'[72]

In a similar fashion, Mel, interviewed for the *Everyman* broadcast, remembered her recent abortion. Mel asked that the camera did not show her face because of what she referred to as the 'stigma of abortion'. In 1992, Mel was on the pill and had a chest infection. She was prescribed antibiotics and 'wasn't told by the doctor that it could affect her pill'.[73] She found herself pregnant and went to see a local doctor on an 'emergency ticket'. Upon the confirmation of the positive pregnancy test, the doctor asked Mel what she wanted to do about it and Mel decided on an abortion. The doctor refused to perform one based on religious beliefs. Mel remembered that the doctor kept using the word 'baby', which was upsetting for her. Mel asked the doctor to refer her to a colleague who would arrange an interruption of pregnancy. The doctor sent her to the FPA clinic. Mel remembered the kindness of the staff when she arrived but stated that their behaviour changed when she explained she wanted an abortion: 'gone were the smiles'. The doctor explained to her that the first appointment with Local Health Authorities would be at 14 weeks of

---

[70] Private phone interview with Florence, 24 February 2020.
[71] Private interview on the phone with Lucy, 20 May 2020.
[72] 'Marnie, interview for the Everyman broadcast', in PP/MEW/C/4/4, Wellcome Library, London.
[73] 'Mel, interview for the Everyman broadcast', in PP/MEW/C/4/4, Wellcome Library, London.

pregnancy, which was beyond the time limit allowed by that Health Authority for a termination. Mel explained that upon learning this, 'I was very upset, hysterical, sobbing, just needed someone to give me a hug basically but there she was, just sat arms crossed on the other side of the desk, just looking at me, very disinterested.' Mel left the appointment, desperate. A friend told her about Brook. Mel came from a city that was not too far from Liverpool so she decided to go to Liverpool to attend Brook. 'The atmosphere was completely different in the Brook, they were really relaxed, very non-judgemental, whatever I wanted to do was fine by them and within two weeks of going in to see them, I'd had the operation and it was all over with, a huge weight had been lifted from my shoulders.' This testimony shows how difficult it was to obtain an abortion in the early 1990s. Brook were quick to react, and displayed a non-judgemental attitude in the context of a deeply upsetting decision. Mel was later asked in the interview why she did not want to show her face. She explained that she was proud of what she did and could say 'I've had an abortion, I am alright, I haven't grown another head and God hasn't struck me down on the pavement for doing so. But on the other hand there is still the stigma attached to abortion, people think they're disgusting things that nasty women have done and it is not like that.' This reflection on the stigma attached to abortion illustrates the difficult process young women had to go through; they not only found the process upsetting but also found themselves the object of condemnation.

Another reason for clients to attend Brook was that they simply wanted to discuss their fears and emotions relating to their sexual relationships; a minority had psychosexual problems. Marnie returned to Brook in the 1980s for counselling because 'she didn't feel like making love at that time'[74] and thought that Brook was a 'good place to go'. She recalled having counselling with Fay Hutchinson and explained that she was very 'sympathetic, she didn't advise and she didn't offer opinions'. Marnie stressed that she was able to discuss how 'she was feeling' and to uncover 'layers of herself that had become hidden'.

There was a common narrative, found in the majority of the testimonies, that clients were treated as adults by professional, non-judgemental staff and that this experience was deemed empowering. These elements can be seen in a written testimony published in 1983 in the *Daily Mail*. A married woman wrote a letter to the *Daily Mail* to 'put the record straight' in view of the bad publicity given to Brook by the newspaper. She shared her experience and

[74] 'Marnie, interview for the Everyman broadcast', in PP/MEW/C/4/4, Wellcome Library, London.

stressed the positive influence that Brook had provided in her life when she was 19 with 'a lot of family and personal problems' and was 'desperate'.[75] Before turning to Brook, she went to her GP, but did not receive the help she expected. She visited Brook for more than two years and received 'expert counselling' free of charge. Now happily married with a loving husband, two children and a beautiful home, she stated that she 'owed' the centre her current situation and praised 'the help and encouragement' she had received. 'It's an excellent service for a lot of young people and a place of trust for them', she concluded. The centre had a long-lasting positive impact on this woman, and she presented the help she received as transformative.

Lucy, the nursing student who visited a Brook clinic in Birmingham, emphasized the smoothness of her experience. She booked an appointment over the phone before attending the centre. While feeling a 'bit intimidated' because of the slight age difference between her and the doctor, she nevertheless found the process easy and appreciated that she was given information and treated with respect: 'You didn't feel judged, um, you felt it was open and that you could talk and that part of it was very easy, it was an open and honest discussion. My recollection too is that it wasn't only about the pill, it was about all sorts of precautions that you could take and were available and for a lot of us we went on the contraceptive pill.'[76]

Some ex-clients underlined the transformative nature of their experience at Brook. For instance, in 2020 on the *Mumsnet* forum, an anonymous poster in her mid-fifties shared her experience with the service on a thread about feminism and gynaecology:

> When I was (much) younger I went to Brook clinics for sexual health gubbins and they were fantastic, even told me to ask for a particular speculum for a more comfortable smear. It was a very woman-positive atmosphere and there were people there who changed the way I thought about my own autonomy, like my genitals didn't just exist relative to penetrative sex and pregnancy.[77]

This testimony is revealing of the way Brook tried to empower young women; the centre ensured their gynaecological experience was smooth and comfortable and provided them with knowledge about their body. Another long

---

[75] 'Brook Bond', *Daily Mail*, 17 November 1983, 27.
[76] Private phone interview with Lucy, 20 May 2020.
[77] https://www.mumsnet.com/talk/womens_rights/3909214-Feminism-and-gynaecology, visited 7 November 2022.

testimony on *Mumsnet* also emphasized the impact Brook had on a client at two different moments in her reproductive journey.

> I used Brook twice. I used them once in my teens (late '80s). It felt like my whole year at school (it wasn't, just felt like it) [I] went up to Brook on Tottenham Ct Rd to get the pill... It was my first foray into an adult world of looking after myself really. I didn't want to go to the GP, I'd had a disastrous discussion with my mum about my sex life. I was nearly 16, it was love, I was with him until I was 19, we were both virgin but she did not approve at all, which I now understand. I felt like my mum and I went from being 'best friends (in retrospect I'm not sure how healthy that was) to child and disapproving authority figure overnight. I'm not sure our relationship has ever recovered. I digress as I am wont to. However, her extreme reaction to my burgeoning sexuality was if anything, entrenching me in my decision: I needed contraception. Brook were kind, friendly, extremely respectful of me and of my wish for confidentiality. They didn't just hand me over the pill as I think my GP might have (and subsequently has!). They took time, asked me how I felt in my relationship, talked to me about the bigger picture in terms of starting to have sex. I felt listened to, and valued.
>
> Fast forward to my early 20s and an unwanted pregnancy, he told me (in great, sociopathic in retrospect, detail) how he was infertile due to chicken pox in childhood (impossible). I bought it and was stupid enough (STIs anyone?) not to use contraception. We split up and then I discovered I was pregnant. Weirdly, the week before, my mother and I had had a conversation in which she had turned to me and said, 'If you ever got pregnant, you'd keep it wouldn't you? I'd help you look after the baby.' I felt I had no one I could talk to, I knew absolutely that I didn't want the pregnancy to continue and once again I turned to Brook. I had some amazing counselling through Brook, really looking at my options (including to keep the baby). I don't feel whoopidoo about the abortion that I had, but I know to this day that it was absolutely the right decision.[78]

This long excerpt, written in entertaining prose, uncovers several interesting elements. The first is that taking responsibility for birth control was perceived

---

[78] This testimony is from a *Mumsnet* thread that answered a call for testimonies to celebrate the 50th anniversary of Brook. Of course, testimonies published on an open platform to celebrate a charity are more likely to be positive (though some negative recollections were also published): https://www.mumsnet.com/talk/site_stuff/1895087-Ever-used-a-Brook-clinic-or-service-Are-you-willing-to-share-your-stories-to-celebrate-Brooks-fiftieth-birthday.

as a first step into adulthood by this anonymous Brook user. Second, as an under-16, she justified her first sexual experience through the prism of love. Moreover, her quest for contraception impacted her relationship with her mother. In spite of her mother's disapproval, she persisted in her search for contraception, showing her determination. In this context, Brook was presented as a life-saving service where confidentiality and empathy were guaranteed. The poster felt 'listened to and valued'; the trust she placed in Brook services was again underlined in her subsequent visit to Brook for an abortion. Once again, her visit to Brook was framed within the context of difficult communication with her mother, showing that Brook services were key in meeting the needs of teenagers who could not talk to their parents. The poster praised Brook's counselling service; in both instances she was able to discuss her feelings and options.

Not all clients visited the clinics in person; thousands of letters were sent each year to Brook local branches asking for advice. Excerpts from several of these letters were included in the Annual Reports. It is striking how young clients framed their narrative around the values of responsibility and committed relationships so cherished by Brook. This way of presenting themselves was arguably a strategy for aligning with the Brook public narrative of what constituted good sexuality, namely protected intercourse in a steady relationship. However, the choice of letters containing these elements also reflected Brook's concern about its public image. In 1971, a letter from a 17-year-old emphasized that she had been 'involved in a real and steady relationship for over a year'. Still a virgin, she was nevertheless considering a sexual relationship, since 'we both realise the extent of our feelings for one another and know that our relationship is deep and meaningful [enough] for sexual intercourse to form a natural part of it'.[79] She had rejected the idea of turning to her family doctor for help, fearing he would tell her parents. This fear might have been triggered by the 1970 case of Dr Browne, who broke his patient's confidentiality as shown in the previous chapter. These letters attest to the trust the young writers placed in Brook as a resource that preserved confidentiality and offered advice. Here, again, this letter shows that GPs were not perceived as a reliable source of help.

Similarly in 1971, another girl wrote a letter to ask where to obtain the pill, since she was planning to spend a weekend with her boyfriend. Although she felt the need to emphasize her morality, stating that she did not 'believe in sex

---

[79] 'Request for help in Brook Advisory Centre, Annual Report, 1971', in SA/ALR/F.1, Wellcome Library, London.

before marriage', she nevertheless wanted to take precautions in case she 'should forget herself'.[80]

Negative experiences

However, not all experiences were positive, and some clients felt judged while others complained that the general non-judgemental attitude meant they did not receive enough emotional support. For instance, some clients felt that Brook failed to meet their needs. A testimony of a former client found on a *Mumsnet* forum thread is indicative of the way agency was restricted. This anonymous poster answered a call for testimonies from Brook to celebrate its 50th birthday. Writing in 2013, she described her bad experience in the 1980s when she refused to undergo an internal examination:

> I went to the Tottenham Court Road Brook clinic in the '80s. I was told I 'had to have' an internal exam and a smear test before I could get the Pill. I declined and I was offered counselling to help me 'get over my fear of being touched'. I had no fear of being touched! I was having lots of sex with my BF! I didn't appreciate my birth control being held hostage until I had an exam and so I went to my GP who gave me a 12 month supply after taking my blood pressure.[81]

Although this testimony was made retrospectively, on an open web platform, and few details were given about the Brook user, it nevertheless shows there was resistance from Brook's users when they were met with demands they considered inappropriate. In this case, the user was not a passive client but instead resisted the power of the doctor and found an alternative way of acquiring what she wanted.

Similarly, in the BBC *Everyman* broadcast, an ex-client of Brook reflected on the different providers she had tried in order to obtain contraceptives. Lorna, already mentioned above, explained that she was refused the pill because she was not in a steady relationship. She had attended a FPA clinic to obtain the pill and had to lie about her marital status. Lorna had then attended Brook after going to the FPA. She explained that she had been

---

[80] Ibid.
[81] Testimony posted on 30 October 2013: https://www.mumsnet.com/Talk/site_stuff/1895087-Ever-used-a-Brook-clinic-or-service-Are-you-willing-to-share-your-stories-to-celebrate-Brooks-fiftieth-birthday, visited 25 April 2020.

hopeful: 'I knew that was a place where people unmarried could go and I thought that would be wonderful, not to have to tell lies.'[82] However, she was disappointed. It was 1967 and she wanted the pill. The doctors asked her many questions about her relationship, concluded that the relationship would not survive university and refused to give her the pill. Lorna left and found herself pregnant the following year; 'it was just dreadful', as she put it. 'This was 1968 by this time and although the Abortion Act that was passed in 1967 had been passed, it still really wasn't in operation at all and I didn't know what to do, I was absolutely panic stricken really and for about four months I just thought about nothing else except with dealing with this pregnancy which I didn't want.' She attempted three illegal abortions, but none of them worked. Finally, her sister found a GP willing to help her and she was booked for a private abortion. After she had the abortion, she was told she had to go on the pill. She wrote to Brook to express her disappointment. A week later, she received a phone call from a member of Brook who apologized and asked her to come back. Lorna saw another Brook doctor this time, who gave her the pill. This testimony illuminates Lorna's ordeal and her determination to deal with her unwanted pregnancy. It shows that Brook adopted a judgemental attitude, refusing Lorna access to the pill based on a moral judgement of her relationship. However, it is also apparent that this moralizing attitude might have been linked to a specific doctor; once Lorna complained about it, she did receive the help she needed.

Tracey's testimony also indicates that she did not receive enough support. Tracey attended Brook aged 15 to access contraception (condoms) in 1998. She then fell pregnant and Brook helped to arrange an abortion. While Brook facilitated the abortion referral process, Tracey felt she did not receive enough emotional support. When she fell pregnant again at 17, she decided to keep the baby, traumatized by her previous experience of abortion. Reflecting on her experience, she said, 'Looking back now I did not like the fact that it was so private. I was only 15. So I had this huge procedure done and no one from my family knew. After I had it done, I didn't receive any support whatsoever.'[83] This indicates that there was some downside to the confidential and non-judgemental approach where clients were treated as responsible adults. Tracey felt she lacked emotional support after the abortion procedure.

Finally, another negative experience was connected to a past traumatic event and the uncaring attitude of a Brook doctor. Laura attended Brook in

---

[82] 'Lorna, interview for the Everyman broadcast in 1994', in PP/MEW/C/4/4, Wellcome Library, London.
[83] Private phone interview with Tracey, 12 May 2020.

CLIENTS AND THE SHAPING OF BROOK CENTRES 161

Birmingham in the 1980s after starting a relationship. She went for a smear test because she knew 'that it was something [she] should do to look after [her] sexual health'. She remembered learning about Brook's existence through stickers in public toilets. Reflecting on her experience, she concluded that 'it was quite traumatic actually'. It was the first time she had undergone a smear test and 'didn't understand a speculum would be involved or what a speculum was'. She described the process as traumatic:

> And, um, the doctor or the, the person that gave me the smear test, he was very sort of, went for it with a speculum and, and I felt very, um, vulnerable. Um, I think I kind of like, didn't wanna like open my legs right up. And I wasn't like physically, um, I was, uh, I was, um, sort of, uh, you know, like clamped up inside, just didn't, was like, what was this? What that, that's a horrible big metal thing you're gonna put in me. And I was trying to, I, I, you know, I did it and I tried to be brave, but then, then he, he said before he, I think, maybe, can't remember, before or after he'd done it. He said to me, are you sure you are not a virgin? And I said yes. He was very dismissive. He had sort of showed no care for the fact that I was freaked out. I remember coming out of there, like really shaken and feeling like he hadn't taken my fear into consideration.[84]

The traumatic nature of this experience and the violence she felt, she later explained, had been reinforced because Laura had been raped and was still traumatized by it. Therefore, the speculum felt intrusive and the lack of care from the doctor added another layer to an already upsetting experience.

These testimonies show evidence that in spite of Brook's reputation as non-judgemental, kind, and welcoming, some clients nevertheless had more difficult experiences at the centre. These negative encounters might have been due to the work of particular doctors or nurses. Nevertheless, they show that sexual health services for young people still had room for improvement.

Clients' influence on the services

Brook was the main sexual and reproductive health charity catering specifically for young people. As such, they tried to stay alert to young people's evolving sexual and reproductive health needs. Several strategies were implemented by

---

[84] Private interview on the phone with Laura, 23 May 2020.

Brook to assess the quality of their services and evaluate the satisfaction and needs of its clients. In so doing, they empowered their teenage clients by putting their needs at the centre of their policy.

There were some indicators that clients were generally happy about the services they received. Return visits were recorded in the statistics and consistently accounted for about 50% of all visits to the centre. For instance, in 1979, while the charity saw 23,413 new clients, the number of returning clients was 34,627. Second, word of mouth proved an effective way of making Brook services known, testifying to the satisfaction of the clients who recommended the service to their friends. Finally, some clients went on to work for Brook due to their positive experiences at the centre. For instance, Wendy Thomas started as a client at Brook and became Brook's policy officer. Emily's experience with Brook, mentioned above, was so positive that she ended up working for them. This was also the case for Sarah, who attended Edinburgh Brook in 1968; she went on to work for Brook London in 1973. After university, she had left Edinburgh for a 'boring' job in Brighton. There, she was part of the Women's Liberation Movement and as such very supportive of women's access to reliable contraception. She saw an advertisement for a job as personal assistant to the general secretary of Brook. Having had 'a good experience at Brook' and sharing their views on enabling access to contraception for young women, she applied and was offered the job. She worked there for a year, doing administrative work as well as outreach work with schools.[85]

In addition, Brook took active measures to evaluate their services and react to emerging needs and requests from clients. First, they asked for feedback on their services. As early as 1969, Joan Woodward from Birmingham Brook carried out a survey with a sample of Brook's clients (117 of the 846 female clients who attended the centre in 1967) in order to assess their needs and the extent to which they thought Brook services were meeting their expectations.[86] Clients were generally happy about the care they received; they enjoyed coming to the centre due to the friendly atmosphere and because it 'was so nice to be treated as a responsible adult', as a client put it. Criticisms were nevertheless voiced about the overcrowding of the clinics and the subsequent feeling of embarrassment. In addition, clients expressed the desire to be seen by the same doctor at each appointment in order to develop a more trusting relationship. Trust in Brook services was crucial for clients, who needed a safe

---

[85] Private phone interview with Sarah, 19 February 2020.
[86] 'Joan Woodward, Survey of Birmingham Brook Clients, 1969', in SA/BRO/SJ, Wellcome Library, London.

space where they could freely discuss their fears and anxieties. Finally, the survey revealed the need to develop counselling; young people generally needed more time to express their reasons for coming to the centre and required counselling that was specifically aimed at understanding the anxieties they felt. Birmingham Brook, receptive to its clients' feedback, took measures to address these concerns; new clients were assigned a specific doctor, while a multidisciplinary team of counsellors, doctors, and nurses was set up, with additional time being reserved for longer counselling sessions.

In 1973, 'talkabout' sessions were also started in London. They were presented as an experiment to help Brook members 'consider how to improve the quality of their services'.[87] New clients were invited as a group 'to discuss birth control methods, their feelings and anxieties relating to a possible pregnancy and their motivation towards contraception' in an informal setting with music playing in the background, creating a relaxed atmosphere. While discussions were taking place among the group, each client had the opportunity to see the doctor individually and in private. These sessions were conceived as a place where young people could talk about their problems freely and where staff could gain a sense of clients' needs. What transpired from this experiment was that an informal atmosphere helped to create a trusted environment where young people could open up. Accordingly, music became a part of the daily routine of the clinic. More importantly, clients explained that they valued having time to discuss their emotions with the staff. Consequently, an additional counsellor was hired to allow more time for each appointment.[88]

In 1979 in Edinburgh, Judy Bury carried out a survey with 50 new, unmarried, non-pregnant clients aged under 25 regarding their opinion of Brook. One way of improving the services, suggested young clients, would be for new clients to be given information on arrival at the clinic about who they would see and what they should expect during the visit. This suggestion was taken on board in Edinburgh Brook and new guidelines were implemented.[89]

In the 1980s, patients became increasingly perceived as consumers, whose needs and views were to be taken seriously in a market-orientated public service field. This shift in Brook's agenda can be seen through the rhetoric it used, emphasising 'users' views', as many of its members were keen to improve its services based on clients' feedback. From 1987, a box was installed in each Brook centre to receive feedback from clients. Following this, in 1989, Brook carried out a telephone survey with clients under 16 in order to gain a better

---

[87] 'Brook Advisory Centre, London, 1973', in SA/BRO/D10/1/1, Wellcome Library, London.
[88] Ibid. [89] 'Brook Annual Report, 1980', in SA/BRO/E/1/2, Wellcome Library, London.

understanding of the gaps in the service.[90] What transpired from the survey was that the majority of young clients did not trust their GPs to maintain confidentiality and asked Brook not to disclose any information to them.

The minutes from the 1992 members' meeting committee, chaired by Gill Lenderyou, show reflections on the work done by London Brook. She mentioned the new targets set by the 'Health of the Nation' report to reduce the rate of conception among under-16s by at least 50% by 2000 (see Chapter 3). She explained that these were 'huge targets' but should be considered as aims for Brook while continuing to prioritize young people's needs. She added, 'I urge you to keep working, keep thinking, evaluate what you do and always remember to ask your clients what is right for them, what they want, what works for them and make their needs your targets.'[91]

In addition, Brook members were starting to look abroad in order to study what other countries were doing to keep their teenage pregnancy rates low in comparison to Britain. The Netherlands was a powerful example from which to draw inspiration. Alison Hadley, chief policy officer, remembered Brook's tour to the Netherlands in the 1990s. There, they met with young people and discussed their views on sex education, contraception, and sexual and reproductive health services. She explained:

> And it was a fascinating trip, but we were there about two hours when we realised, actually, that we couldn't import the cultural backdrop that makes so many things so different there, but the one thing that was tangible and we could import was the young people's trust in confidentiality. So interestingly, even though things were much more liberal and people talked much more openly about sex and the Dutch expected young people to be sexually active during their teenage years when they were ready, confidentiality was still really important to Dutch young people. And one girl said to us, you know, 'My doctor wouldn't tell anyone, we trust our doctors.' And we thought: blimey, now we're a long way from that.[92]

As a result, and as will be seen in Chapter 7, Hadley developed a new campaign advertising the confidentiality of Brook services. This excerpt also showed the cultural difference between Britain and the Netherlands and is suggestive of

---

[90] 'Brook, the minutes of the members' meeting, 1987', in SA/BRO/D/10/2/2/8, Wellcome Library, London.
[91] 'Brook, the minutes of the members' meeting, 15 July 1992', in SA/BRO/D/10/2/2/8, Wellcome Library, London.
[92] Private interview in person with Alison Hadley, 24 February 2020.

the way in which Britain's classist, gendered, and hierarchical society intersected and produced the control of young people's sexuality as an intergenerational authority issue.

In addition to seeking young people's feedback, Brook also reacted to what they perceived as growing trends within their services. For instance, in 1970, due to the high number of clients attending the clinic in distress, fearing that they were pregnant, Bristol BAC created a special pregnancy advisory session. These clients did not yet know whether they wanted to pursue the pregnancy or undergo a termination. The majority of clients' parents were ignorant about what was happening in their children's lives. Counselling was therefore set up as a way of helping these clients go through their options and work out what they wanted. Emotional support, advice, and help were provided.[93]

Eventually, another key method of empowering clients was to give them a say in the running of the services. To this effect, a steering committee was created in 1996; advertisements were displayed in each branch, requesting young people to volunteer as members of this steering committee.[94] This shows that Brook not only tried to empower its clients at a provision level, but also at a political level. This emphasis on clients' opinions and needs culminated in the 1997 New Strategic Plan adopted by the Brook council. Under the leadership of Margaret Jones, its main aim was to answer clients' needs in a better way. Brook stated its commitment to put 'young people first'[95] by pledging to incorporate 'the views of the current and future users of Brook' into its service development. As a result, Brook commissioned a market research company to inform its new service standard, which had to be based 'firmly on users' views'. The rhetoric of market and service users testifies to the new orientation taken by many public services and charities in the 1990s.[96]

Conclusion

Young people's sexual behaviour changed quite considerably over the period studied in this book. Age at first sexual intercourse declined over this period, and an increasing number of young people turned to Brook for information

---

[93] 'Brook Advisory Centre, Annual Report, 1972', in SA/ALR/F.1, Wellcome Library, London.
[94] 'Minutes of the meeting of the Board of Directors, 25 September 1996', in SA/BRO/B/1/15, Wellcome Library, London.
[95] '"Free confidential sex advice and contraception for young people", Brook Annual Reports 1997/1998', SA/BRO/E/1/4, Wellcome Library, London.
[96] Mold, *Making the Patient-Consumer*.

166 RESPONSIBLE PLEASURE

and contraception. Brook's recorded statistics provide fascinating insights into the demographic of the clinic, reflecting the general trend towards earlier age at first sexual intercourse as well as the success of certain contraceptive methods. However, the statistics do show some gaps, especially regarding the ethnicity of clients. This lack of information might have been caused by a fear that data on ethnicity would be used for political purposes by anti-immigrationists. However, as I have argued, it also prevented the charity from obtaining a reliable picture of the take-up of their services and identifying potential gaps.

Through a resort to oral history, this chapter has shed light on clients' experiences with the service and illuminated young people's agency. Due to a lack of sex education, information on contraception was desperately needed by young people, but it was not merely imposed upon them; young people were not passive users of these services. They moved between different providers with contradictory policies and ideologies. Before turning to Brook, some consulted their GPs, FPA clinics, friends, and magazines, thereby actively trying to find information and gain access to contraception. Friendship was a major source of information for young people and word of mouth proved crucial in advertising the Brook service. This reveals the intricate network of sexual health knowledge and services navigated by young people, sometimes confidently and at other times in despair.

In addition, this chapter demonstrates that the building of a trusted relationship between Brook and its clients was crucial not only for the successful running of the clinics, but also for the young people who attended the service. Indeed, some young people used Brook services at turning points in their life when making decisions that had long-lasting implications for their well-being. Finding a friendly, non-judgemental, and confidential service, a place where they could express their anxieties, fears, and emotions, was central for them. Young people valued self-determination and praised the service for taking them seriously. Some even went on to work for Brook.

From the start, Brook valued clients' experiences at the centre. However, with the advent of the idea of the patient as a consumer in the 1980s, the client experience became paramount in the way Brook envisaged their work. They devised several ways to assess the quality of their services and set the standard for a client-centred approach to sexual health services in the 1990.

6
Counselling Young People Towards Sexual Maturity

In a private interview conducted in 2019, Dilys Cossey, OBE, a Brook board member from 1984 to 2001 and chair from 1995 to 2001, reflected on the uniqueness of the Brook.

> They were not judgmental. They were there to help and it didn't matter what happened and they would help you and find out what you really wanted. And of course that was, that's what I always felt about Brook that they, they had this immensely sympathetic and tolerant, not tolerant, but understanding attitude towards young people. And of course at the beginning young women.[1]

One of the defining characteristics of the Brook was its concern with emotional and sexual problems and its focus on counselling. From its inception to the present day, Brook has been at the forefront of providing contraceptive advice and emotional and sexual counselling. It was the first organization to adopt a holistic approach to young people's sexual needs. Since there was no other charity that focused on young people, Brook had to innovate and create its own standards for good practices in sexual and contraceptive counselling. Brook targeted a new generation who wished to be considered adults, and perfected a new vision of the teenage sexual subject where information on contraception had a central position in young people's sexual behaviour and choices. In so doing, Brook contributed to forming the model of the responsible young sexual subject who had protected sex and made informed decisions about the best sexual outcome.

This chapter explores what Brook members defined as the key components and values underpinning their counselling. It argues that Brook pioneered a new form of counselling where trust, confidentiality, and a non-judgmental attitude (at least in front of the client) were paramount elements. It then

---

[1] Private interview with Dilys Cossey, April 2019.

moves on to analyse in detail the three types of counselling offered in the centres. In so doing, the chapter shows that some tensions were present in the work of the centres in the first two decades of their running. Conservative and radical visions coexisted. The disjuncture between the supposedly groundbreaking, progressive radicalism of the centre in advising younger and unmarried women and its racial and moral conservatism created tensions. Indeed, this chapter argues that in the first two decades of Brook's counselling work, doctors, counsellors, and social workers while praising a non-judgmental attitude towards youth sexuality nevertheless unconsciously imposed a model of 'good' sexual behaviour. This model was class-based and racialized. In this way, the chapter shows that moral management remained, at first, a crucial element of the services provided by Brook. While this moral management might have been partially a rhetoric strategy, allowing Brook to affirm its respectability, it nevertheless left a concrete impact in some areas of counselling. As time passed, as the first generation of counsellors and doctors were replaced by younger ones and as teenage sexuality became more publicly debated and therefore more socially accepted, non-judgmental attitudes and non-directive counselling took precedent over more traditional visions of counselling. Clear guidelines were gradually implemented that tried to foster a non-judgmental and culturally diverse environment.

Good counselling practices

The early, stated aims of Brook were 'the prevention and the mitigation of the suffering caused by unwanted pregnancy and illegal abortion by educating young persons in matter[s] of sex and contraception and developing among them a sense of responsibility in regard to sexual behaviours'.[2] From the start, the centre put to the fore education through counselling by doctors, nurses, and counsellors, and the idea that young people should become responsible for the choices they made vis-à-vis their sex lives. Consequently, by foregrounding the work of the centre within the framework of counselling and responsibility, Brook members anticipated criticisms of promiscuity and therefore presented a more conservative model where responsible behaviours, namely steady relationships that could potentially lead to marriage, appeared as the cornerstone of their work. While never affirming it explicitly, this norm was based on

[2] 'Brook Advisory Centre, Aims and Principles, July 1964', in SA/FPA/A13/13, Wellcome Library, London.

the white/middle-class value of committed intimacy. This model did not fundamentally reshape or undermine the principles that informed the FPA, as explained in Chapter 1. Indeed, by emphasizing commitment and heteronormative relationships, the provision of advice to the unmarried was not a break in practice but should rather be considered a reconfiguration with a continuation in general principles and prejudices around class and race.

In a similar vein, Dr Faith Spicer, the first doctor working in Brook in London, defined her work as follows: 'If we can show, and I believe we can, that we are helping adolescents to understand themselves, their feelings and their needs, then we are doing [a] valuable job [...] by setting up advice centres of this sort we can help more people towards maturity [...]'.[3] This idea of helping individuals to understand themselves and to reach maturity resonates with Nikolas Rose's argument that in the second half of the twentieth century, experts played a pivotal role in creating a choosing, willing, and self-governing self.[4] Indeed, Brook recognized the ability of teenagers and young people to make informed decisions, subject to them receiving the 'right' type of support and 'correct' information. Counselling was therefore perceived by Brook workers as a way of enabling young people to take responsibility for their action and decide for themselves what would be the best sexual behaviours. And clients seemed to have absorbed Brook's message; as one put it in a survey study carried out in Birmingham in 1968, 'it was so nice to be treated as a responsible adult'.[5]

Paradoxically, this aim contains in itself a sort of refutation of the argument of autonomy, since young people were still deemed as a vulnerable category of the population that needed help, and, as such, were in need of advice. Brook doctors and counsellors acted as guides and gatekeepers through young people's journey towards sexual maturity. Brook doctors and counsellors saw young clients in steady relationships as mature enough to make their own decisions. White young middle-class women were usually viewed as responsible young adults who attended the clinic because they were in steady relationships and wanted to protect themselves against unwanted pregnancy. Their behaviour was construed as the 'norm' from which other groups deviated. In the first annual report of Brook published in the *Family Planning Journal*, Faith Spicer explained that 'the greatest proportion of people coming to the centre are young women, quite sure at the time that they have a steady

---

[3] Faith Spicer, 'The Marie Stopes advice for young people', *Family Planning* 13.2 (1964): 31.
[4] Rose, *Inventing Our Selves*.
[5] Joan Woodward, 'Birmingham Brook', *Family Planning* 19.3 (1970): 88.

relationship who wish to discuss, often in great detail and sometimes together with their young men, methods of birth control'.[6] These young people were depicted as 'responsible'. However, any deviation from this model was deemed problematic. Promiscuity, in particular, was pathologized as illustrated by the following quote from the founder of the centre, Helen Brook: 'If a girl is promiscuous, you have got to ask why. Promiscuity is a sign of some sort of disturbance. They are the ones who need the most love and the most help.'[7] Promiscuity was usually associated with sexual knowingness on the part of white working-class girls and perceived to be the result of socially deprived backgrounds. For Brook members in the first decade of Brook's work, maturity and responsibility in sexuality equated committed and loving intimacy and this was their definition of 'good' sexuality.

To guide young people towards sexual maturity, Brook counsellors, social workers, and doctors defined three essential components of what they perceived as 'good' counselling practice: the ability to listen to the client; a non-judgmental attitude; and a guarantee of the confidentiality of the services.

Listening to the client

In many reports and committee minutes, listening to the client retained a central place. Liz Elking, who joined the London Walworth centre as a counsellor in 1974, said that the Brook method was to 'listen hard, put all the alternatives and try to help the youngsters to reach their own decisions'.[8] Listening also meant that the client would talk and express his/her emotions.

Brook staff resorted to an emotion-based counselling where clients were encouraged to express their feelings and needs. This emphasis on emotions was not new. From the interwar years onwards, in the field of sexual counselling and marriage relationships, the expression of emotions held a significant role in the understanding of the fragility of relationships, sexual development, and sexual dysfunctions. The idea that emotions and authenticity were key to successful relationships were spread by marriage and sexual reformers, the Marriage Guidance Movement, church organizations, the Family Planning Association, and agony aunts and advice columns in magazines and newspapers,

---

[6] 'Annual Report of the Brook Advisory Centre', *Family Planning* 15.3 (1966): 47–50.
[7] 'The woman behind a revolutionary idea talks to the Mercury', *Birmingham Sunday Mercury*, 18 September 1966, 11.
[8] Liz Elking, 'A full-time friend for Walworth, 10th February 1974', in SA/BRO/J3/1, Wellcome Library, London.

among others.⁹ Brook's work also drew on this tradition but also represented a departure from it, since Brook applied it to advising young people, a clear break from the interwar focus on married people. In addition, the resort to emotional counselling was also a used as a rhetorical device in Brook's public discourse. Indeed, Brook based its respectability on providing counselling for emotional problems and relationships, alongside contraception. This emphasis was meant to counter potential criticisms of Brook acting as a 'contraceptive shop'. In using emotions in this way, Brook staff were trying to find a balance between the progressive radicalism of the clinic in advising young and unmarried women and a form of racial and moral conservatism via the teaching of 'good' sexual behaviours.

Giving the opportunity to young people to express their feelings and to identify and discuss their emotions was central to Brook's work. In 1982, Dr Fay Hutchinson wrote:

> I realise I don't actually talk to young people very much; most of my effort is directed to trying to get them [to] talk, about themselves, why they've come to see me, what they want to do, what's causing them concern and what they can do to cope with it. Though I may not [be] talking much I am busy observing the patients, trying to assess them, responding to their needs, asking appropriate open-ended questions and giving them time to try and express themselves.¹⁰

Similarly, in an oral history interview I carried out in 2020 with Joan Woodward, a social worker who worked at Birmingham Brook from 1967 to the mid-1980s, she recalled what made Brook so distinctive: 'they wanted to offer contraception to young people who would have a chance to come and have a chat, to talk very informally and in a very friendly way with a social worker'.¹¹ Brook workers, then, encouraged informal and friendly discussions

---

⁹ Teri Chettiar, 'The Psychiatric Family: Citizenship, Private Life, and Emotional Health in Welfare State Britain, 1945–79', PhD dissertation, University of Evanston, 2013; Marcus Collins, *Modern Love: Personal Relationships in Twentieth-Century Britain* (University of Delaware Press, 2006); Alana Harris, 'Love Divine and Love Sublime: The Catholic Marriage Advisory Council, the Marriage Guidance Movement and the State', in her *Love and Romance in Britain, 1918–1970* (Palgrave Macmillan, 2015): 188–224; Claire Langhamer, 'Love, selfhood and authenticity in post-war Britain', *Cultural and Social History* 9.2 (2012): 277–97; Langhamer, *The English in Love*; Lewis, Clark, and Morgan, *Whom God Hath Joined Together*; Rusterholz, 'You can't dismiss that as being less happy, you see it is different'.

¹⁰ Fay Hutchinson, 'Young Advisory Work: What Can You Say to Young People Today?', in Katharine Draper (ed.), *Practice of Psychosexual Medicine: Selected Papers from the First International Conference on Psychosexual Medicine* (John Libbey, 1983): 172.

¹¹ Private interview on the phone with Joan Woodward, 18 May 2020.

and expressing one's own emotions, a practice that contributed to stabilizing a new form of sexual subjectivity for young people.

Non-judgmental attitude

Another paramount element of the way Brook members understood their work was the perceived absence of moral judgment. Indeed, in 1969, the task of Brook was not only defined in terms of education and responsibility but also referred to the attitude that individuals working in the centre should adopt: 'to help young people between the ages of 16 (age of consent) [and] 25 to accept responsibility for their emotional lives without attempting to impose external moral standards'.[12] The founder Helen Brook would compare the doctors' work in Brook centres to that of 'non-moralising mother-figure doctors'.[13] This non-judgmental attitude was particularly well perceived and valued by clients. In a 1967 article published in the *Birmingham Post*, the local newspaper that extensively covered the heated debate preceding the opening of Birmingham Brook, a young white couple shared their experience at Brook.[14] The 'girl' 21, engaged, explained that she had been sleeping with her fiancé since she was 16. She mentioned that she had had 'a major scare' and phoned a FPA clinic for help. She was told they could see her, provided that she was getting married in the coming three months. Since she was not, they directed her to Brook. The girl explained that she was 'apprehensive' before phoning Brook but was amazed by the reaction on the other side of the line; the receptionist asked her about the urgency of her needs. The client thought 'that was marvellous: they were concerned with your needs, your real needs, and not to sit in judgement on your morals'.[15]

The 'motherly figure' mentioned above by Helen Brook was a recurrent trope deployed by Brook workers when they described their role towards their clients. Time and again, Brook referred to the mother figure: 'for a young woman the security of a mother figure with the expertise of highly qualified doctors is of untold value when things go wrong, as they so often do, when one

---

[12] Betty Hunter, 'Brook Advisory Centre, some general information, February 1969', in SA/BRO/J/3/1, Wellcome Library, London.
[13] Helen Brook, in SA/BRO/J1/7, Wellcome Library, London.
[14] On this debate see Caroline Rusterholz, 'Youth sexuality, responsibility, and the opening of the Brook advisory centres in London and Birmingham in the 1960s', *Journal of British Studies* 61.2 (2022): 315–342.
[15] 'Cases and Circumstances', *The Birmingham Post*, 5 September 1967, 8.

is young and experimenting and exploring';[16] 'we are providing a sort of mothering service'.[17] Dr Fay Hutchinson, in a paper presenting her work at a conference on psychosexual medicine in 1982, would also make this analogy. Referring to a case of a 16-year-old client she said: 'When she undressed for examination, you could see the frightened little girl she was, who needed mothering and tenderness. Studying the doctor–patient relationship I realise that "mothering" is not the only role I have, though it is one I feel comfortable with.'[18]

This emphasis on mothering and tenderness also hints to the emotional labour that the work of counselling entailed. Counsellors and social workers had to display the right mix and degree of emotions, finding the right balance between being empathetic and caring enough while maintaining a certain emotional distance and refraining from using emotive language to discuss client's situation and needs. This non-judgmental attitude was paramount in Brook, as remembered by one of the London Brook counsellors in an interview I carried out in 2020. Joanna Brien started working at Brook after spending a couple of years working for the British Pregnancy Advisory Service—a charity created after the passing of the Abortion Act in 1967 to provide safe, affordable abortions—where she undertook a short period of training in counselling. She then joined London Brook as a counsellor in the early 1980s. Reflecting on her role and on the uniqueness of Brook services, Brien highlighted that Brook offered young people the opportunity 'to talk to someone in a non-judgmental space'.[19] She referred to the role of the counsellor as 'an ally', and explained that she joined Brook 'to provide young people with a level of understanding, and respect that young people did not have' since the majority could not talk with their parents or their friends about their sexual life: 'Brook wasn't moralistic, it was sort of saying, yes, this is enjoyable activity, but you need to do it as safely as you can'. Similarly, Dr Gillian Vanhegan, a doctor and later the medical director at London Brook explained that she had joined Brook in the early 1980s. The centre had appealed to her because 'it was very open-minded, flexible, not rigid, very welcoming to young people, non-judgemental as compared to other sexual health organizations'.[20]

But the repetition of the mother trope in the narrative of Brook's workers was also strategic. A mother is associated with care and with the well-being of

---

[16] 'The Work of Brook Advisory Centres, undated', SA/BRO/J1/7, Wellcome Library, London.
[17] Helen Brook, 'In the club', in GC/105/4, Wellcome Library, London, 16.
[18] Hutchinson, 'Young Advisory Work', 172.
[19] Joanna Brien, private interview on the phone, 29 March 2020.
[20] Gillian Vanhegan, private interview on the phone, 20 February 2020.

her children; by resorting to this comparison, members underlined their commitment to their clients, and showed that they had their best interests at heart. In addition, a mother would protect her children from the dangers of life, hence the work of Brook was one of protection and prevention. Moreover, by drawing on the mother trope, Brook workers also implicitly denounced the disinvestment of parents who should be responsible for educating their children and adolescents on sexual matters. Nevertheless, this emphasis on the mother figure also had the potential to undermine the autonomy of young people: doctors should be understood as another form of authority and sometimes as judges of 'good sexual behaviour', as the next sections will show, no matter how caring and respectful the relationship between the client and the doctor.

In 1990, the newly created Counselling Advisory Committee (CAC), which was created in 1988 to harmonize counselling practices across the different local branches of Brook, reaffirmed the centrality of the non-judgmental attitude in a report defining the role of the Brook counsellor. It stressed the necessity to 'provide a safe environment where there is trust and respect so that clients can feel they are being heard non-judgmentally'.[21] In addition, CAC implemented an equal opportunities policy that emphasized that all clients should be treated equally and that there should be no discrimination on the grounds of 'sex, sexual orientation, disability, marital status, domestic circumstances, class, religion, national or ethnic origins'.[22]

Confidentiality of the services

The last foundational cornerstone of Brook was the confidentiality of the counselling service. At first, Brook clinics only saw clients between 16 and 25 to stay within the remit of the law; the age of consent being 16, while the age of maturity was 21 until 1970 when it was lowered to 18. For clients over 16 years old, confidentiality was straightforward, since under the Family Law reform act of 1968, a person of 16 years old was medically an adult and able to consent to her own treatment. However, the under-16s posed a problem. In 1969, in response to the increase in the teenage pregnancy rate and the fact that many girls under 16 were coming to the centre desperate for help, Helen

---

[21] Counselling Advisory Committee, 'Counselling at Brook Centres, 20 November 1990', in S/BRO/C7/1, Wellcome Library, London.
[22] Ibid.

Brook decided to allow under-16s to be seen in Brook centres.²³ As a result, Brook members tried to gain clients' permission to inform their GPs when they were put on the pill. When the client agreed, the GP was notified.²⁴

In 1970, a young white 16-year-old girl attended Birmingham Brook with her boyfriend to obtain the pill. The couple were in a steady relationship, having gone out together for the previous five years, and hoped to marry after finishing their studies. They had already had intercourse using a sheath, but feared this method was not reliable and the girl wanted to go on the pill. The young couple had obviously discussed the matter together and made up their minds on the most sensible method for them. The girl was hesitant to let Brook inform her GP, Dr Browne, since her father had a close relationship with him. The counsellor reassured her by emphasizing that the letter would be written in confidence.²⁵ However, Dr Browne broke his patient's confidentiality and informed her parents without telling her first, because, as he later explained, 'every attempt had to be made to point out to her the error of her ways'.²⁶ Brook members, distressed about the situation, reported Dr Browne to the General Medical Council for his failure to honour the confidence placed in him by his patient and by the Brook doctors.

Birmingham Brook took a strong stance by expressing publicly 'its determination to continue to assist the unmarried of any age who show a responsible attitude in choosing to consult its professional experts in order to avoid the risks of unwanted pregnancy and abortion'.²⁷ The centre guaranteed the 'strictest confidence to all its clients'. National and local newspapers extensively covered the case, amounting to more than 400 articles on the subject, with people supporting Browne and parents' right to know about their children's sex lives pitted against partisans for confidentiality. Dr Browne was found 'not guilty' of professional misconduct. Following this incident, the British Medical Association reaffirmed the supremacy of confidentiality by stating that a doctor could not ethically second-guess a patient's judgement of his or her best interest and must respect their refusal to allow information to be given to a third party.²⁸ Following the Browne case, Brook reported an increase in young people seeking contraceptive advice, especially those aged 16 and under.

---

²³ 'Committed to the young people upstairs', *The Guardian*, 15 December 1978, 7.

²⁴ There was a famous case of breach of confidentiality by Dr Browne in 1971. See Caroline Rusterholz, 'Teenagers, Sex, and the Brook Advisory Centres, 1964–1985', in Siân Pooley and Jono Taylor (eds), *Children's Experiences of Welfare in Modern Britain* (Institute of Historical Research, 2021): 492–540.

²⁵ 'Doctor and the error of girls' ways', *Evening Mail*, 5 March 1971.   ²⁶ Ibid.   ²⁷ Ibid.

²⁸ 'Secret stayed sacred—BMA', *The Guardian*, 22 July 1971.

In 1974, the provision of contraception became free under the NHS. The 1974 Department of Health memorandum of guidance on family planning services specifically retained a role for Brook as a service provider and advised that a doctor who provided contraceptives for a girl under 16 even when he 'was unable to obtain a parent's permission was not acting unlawfully',[29] provided that he acted 'in good faith' to protect the girl against the 'potentially harmful effects of intercourse'.[30]

In the 1980s, with the Gillick case, confidentiality and the availability of contraception for under-16s would again be put into question as shown in Chapter 3. The Gillick's victory was short-lived and reversed in October 1985 by the law. However, this brief interlude did jeopardize the confidentiality of Brook services, and doctors, counsellors, and social workers were extremely worried about the situation, fearing young people would lose confidence in their services.[31]

In 1991, Brook defined their counselling as a confidential service geared particularly towards young people, many of whom did not have experience of their feelings and needs being taken seriously and who may not have expected to be treated as adults. Counsellors worked within a multidisciplinary team in a client-centred philosophy and practice. The skills of the counsellors were shared with other staff members, who took a counselling skills approach to their medical, nursing, and reception tasks.[32] The role of the Brook counsellor was to counsel and register all new clients. The counsellor took the client's basic details, explained the services available, explored the reason for the visit, encouraged the client to talk 'honestly and without embarrassment about himself or herself', discussed the client's relationship and prepared them for consultation with doctors. If the counsellor identified any indication of emotional, sexual, or social problems, he or she assessed, with the client, the need for long-term counselling. In 1993, Brook became an organizational member of the British Association for Counselling, and as such, Brook members had to abide by the Code of Ethics and Practice. One of the key definitions of counselling articulated by the British Association of Counselling and used by Brook was that 'the aim of counselling is to provide an opportunity for a client to work towards living in a more satisfying and resourceful way'.[33]

---

[29] '1974 DHSS Guidance', in SA/FPA/C/E16/5/8, Wellcome Library, London.   [30] Ibid.
[31] On the effects of Gillick on BAC's clients see Chapter 3.
[32] 'Counselling at Brook, 8 May 1991', in SA/BRO/C7/1, Wellcome Library, London.
[33] 'Basic Principles of Counselling, 11 November 1990', in SA/BRO/C7/1, Wellcome Library, London. The same definition was found in the Code of Ethics and Practice for Counsellors, British Association for Counselling, 1989.

Counselling in practice

Brook centres were first staffed by doctors and nurses trained in family planning practice provided that their attitude and personality to the young was 'satisfactory'.[34] The doctors usually had had added experience in child development and/or psychiatry.[35] Some had additional training in counselling in psychosexual problems, usually acquired through the seminar method devised by Michael Balint offered in FPA clinics, and since 1974, by the Institute for Psychosexual Medicine.

Balint was a Hungarian psychoanalyst who worked at the Tavistock Institute of Human Relations in London, one of the key British institutes in psychoanalysis.[36] He devised a method to help general practitioners answer the needs of their patients via training in psychotherapy. Balint was interested in the way that a patient presents his/her illness to the doctor and the latter listens, reassures, and suggests treatment. Balint highlighted the dynamic of the relationship between the patient and the doctor, since the way in which the doctor answers the patient in turn shapes the patient's expectations and manner of articulating his or her needs. As such, the doctor should also be an object of study, since her training, personality and norms and mores within the medical profession impact her work. Balint believed that a doctor should therefore undergo training to free herself from prejudices.[37] The training devised by Balint saw doctors exchanging experiences of ongoing cases in small groups and describing their difficulties as frankly as possible, under the supervision of a leader. The dynamic of the group enabled doctors to identify mistakes, blind spots, and limitations, allowing a better understanding of their problems.

At the London Brook, a consultant psychotherapist attached to the centre held a seminar fortnightly with the doctors. In this seminar, doctors discussed their cases and shared their experiences and difficulties, based, again, on Balint's technique. The aim of this supervision seminar, explained counsellor Brien, was to work on the assumptions that one held regarding young people's sexuality and to know what they were, so as to 'be able to stand back from them'.[38] In Brien's view, one of the key elements of a successful counselling

---

[34] 'Report of a meeting between Lord Brain, Mrs Robin Brook, Dr Spice and Mrs Parker, 7th December 1964', in SA/BRO/C1/1, Wellcome Library, London.
[35] Ibid.   [36] Chettiar, *The Psychiatric Family*.
[37] Michael Balint, 'Psychotherapy and the general practitioner: I', *British Medical Journal* 1.5011 (1957): 157.
[38] Joanna Brien, private interview on the phone, 29 March 2020.

session was the counsellor's 'ability to not impose her own views'. This was perfectly in line with Balint's training. In 1988, the need to harmonize counselling practices across centres led to the creation of a Counselling Advisory Committee (CAC). Made up of counsellors and social workers from the different Brook branches, its aim was to offer guidance to the Brook board on the policies and practices of counselling offered by the organization.[39] The CAC underlined the need for ongoing training in counselling, and for the supervision of counsellors during working hours. The CAC also set out a minimum qualification for counsellors. In 1994, a suitable counsellor needed to be an accredited counsellor with the British Association for Counselling or to have a relevant qualification in social work, youth and community work, psychology, psychotherapy, or counselling. In addition, the counsellor was expected to have 300 hours of counselling experience.[40]

However, the allocation of responsibilities among the staff differed between regional centres. In Birmingham, from the start, social workers worked alongside doctors and nurses. Indeed, at his or her first appointment, every client in Birmingham was interviewed by a social worker trained in interviewing techniques, whereas in London they were interviewed by a nurse, who ascertained the reason for the client's visit and completed the particulars of registration. In addition, this interview covered the anxieties of the patient and the potential need for referral to further counselling service and therapy. In so doing, social workers were believed to implement a sort of triage service and to save time for the doctor. A consultation with the doctor followed this first in-depth interview.[41] In London, at first, social workers had limited power in the centre. But soon tensions arose in London around the allocation of responsibility. Helen Brook believed that social worker had to play a key role in the Brook Centres. In her opinion, social workers would help give the clinic an unclinical atmosphere, to get away from the 'doctor patient–relationship'. However, doctors in London, particularly Faith Spicer, who was the doctor in charge since Brook's creation, opposed this approach and were hostile to working with social workers or allowing nurses to have additional power and prescribe contraception. Helen Brook was nevertheless convinced that social workers were essential for developing a trusted relationship with the patients. In 1967, Dr Faith Spicer resigned following the reorganization of the

---

[39] 'Minutes of the meeting of the counselling advisory committee, 27 April 1988', in SA/BRO/C7/1, Wellcome Library, London.
[40] 'Brook Advisory Centres counselling advisor committee subgroup, 6 October 1994', in SA/BRO/C7/1, Wellcome Library, London.
[41] 'Birmingham Annual Reports, 1967', SA/BRO/D3/1/1, Wellcome Library, London.

Brook in London when the centre, owing to the long waiting list, decided to hire lay workers to provide advice for emotional problems. Spicer strongly opposed the involvement of lay people; she wanted to keep the work of the centre under strict medical supervision.[42] Since then, social workers had extended responsibility in London clinics. In 1975, Dr Ruth MacGillivray, who was the doctor in charge of the London Brook, announced in the magazine *GP* that counselling was not the exclusive territory of doctors. In her view, nurses and social workers could also be good counsellors provided they met the essential criteria, namely 'emphatic listening and the ability to talk simply about anatomy, physiology, sociology and to draw analogies which can be easily understood.'[43]

Brook staff were predominantly white in the early days. As remembered by Dr Vanhegan when she joined London Brook in the early 1980s, the majority of the staff were white. There were some Asian doctors, as well as the Black counsellors Pauline Crabbe, a Jamaican-born English woman who had worked at Tottenham Court Road. Pauline Crabbe remembered that when she first started at Brook there:

> were very few black girls and black boys coming and one of the thing that I was instrumental in doing was getting our first black receptionist, because I felt that that was going to be a way in which if one black girl came in and saw a black girl on the counter she would say to her friends, it's all right—and if they saw me oh that's ok they've got a black counsellor.[44]

In Brixton too, the main counsellor was 'Black'. Dorothy van Heeswyk was born in Guyana. The latter recalled that she was hired to succeed to Pauline Crabbe. She explained that she fitted perfectly with the organization: 'light skin, middle class, very presentable'.[45] Van Heeswyk hired Janet Hibbert, a receptionist with Jamaican origin and with an African heritage and explained how important the receptionist was in a Brook centre; 'the receptionist is the heart, it is the first person people see'.[46] The fact that the receptionist had Jamaican roots and could therefore connect with the local demographics of Brixton was an important factor in van Heeswyk's selection, 'it was vital, we

---

[42] 'Lay workers supplanted doctor who quit', *Daily Telegraph*, 1967, in SA/FPA/A17/113, Wellcome Library, London.
[43] Ruth MacGillivray, 'Sex problems: Counselling', *GP*, 21 November 1975.
[44] Pauline Crabbe, 'In the Club', GC/105/3, Wellcome Library, London.
[45] Private interview with Dorothy van Heeswyk over Zoom, 11 November 2022. [46] Ibid.

needed someone with a connection to the community'.[47] Heeswyk further reflected on the issue of race and class. She explained that having grown up in Guyana made her particularly aware of these issues; 'she had a deep sense of race and class, before having the words' and gave her a commitment to political activism and an understanding of the various privileges one owns based on class and race. Van Heeswyk was part of the Black women's group in Brixton. Being light skinned, she explained, was an advantage. Asked whether she tried to hire people from different ethnic backgrounds in Brook, she replied that what mattered was to hire people who 'could relate well to young people'. Staff members had to share the value of 'respect and capacity to listen'. Similarly, Alison Frater who was chief officer at Brook from the mid-1980s explained that attention was being given to connect Brook centres with their local community; 'the staff team were from the local community. Reception staff counsellors and nurses especially included women from the Black Caribbean, Black African or South Asian communities.'[48]

However, despite informal attempts at increasing the ethnic diversity of the staff, it was only in the mid-1990s that diversity started to be taken seriously. Reception staff were by that time chosen to reflect the diversity of the clientele and in the 2000s, a period which is outside the focus of this study, Brook also started to employ transgender staff in order to make young transgender people feel welcome. The diversification of Brook staffs was nevertheless slow, as hinted by a remark made by Rachel Thompson in 1995 when she joined the newly formed Education Advisory Committee in 1995, whose purpose was to discuss overall policy for education, outreach, and development workers and draw up guidelines for the work, generate and identify new areas of work, and set overall education strategy. She complained at 'the lack of representation on the groups from ethnic and lesbian and gay communities. It did not seem such a good start that the EAC was exclusively white and female.'[49]

In 1993, counsellor Val Hill attended a conference on Issues of Race and Culture. Following this she argues that Brook needed to reflect on its practice at Branch level—that counsellors should not make assumptions about cultural background and this had implications for the training of counsellors. Val urged Brook to join the Race and Cultural Education in Counselling division of the British Association for Counselling, which Brook did.

---

[47] Ibid.   [48] Private interview with Alison Frater, 7 February 2020.
[49] 'Education Advisory Committee, Notes of the meeting held on 4 December 1995', in SA/BRO/B1/14, Wellcome Library, London.

The organization in each centre across the country may have varied, but there existed three common types of counselling: counselling for contraception; counselling for pregnancy and its outcome; and counselling for psychosexual problems. Counselling work at Brook was often crisis orientated. The majority came for birth control advice and supplies, with about 10–15% attending for pregnancy and sexual counselling. The vast majority, about 95%, were already sexually active.[50] In the practice of counselling, as the following sections show, tensions were present between the values that Brook cherished—namely listening to clients, a non-judgmental attitude, and confidentiality—and the model of good sexuality that the centre was trying to convey.

Counselling for contraception

The main goal of the centre was to avoid unwanted pregnancy through the provision of contraception. This work was supported by the Medical Advisory committee, a committee made up of medical professionals who held key positions in universities and hospitals and who had a deep knowledge of contraceptive research. This committee provided information on new contraceptive technologies, their risks and benefits, discussed potential clinical trials, and provided guidance on contraceptive information.

The majority of the clients were girls and young women who came for birth control advice and supply which were given via a consultation with a doctor. Female clients who requested contraception were asked for a general medical history; the doctor undertook a pelvic, vaginal, and breast examination, and their blood pressure was taken in order to spot any potential conditions and assess their suitability for the pill. Cervical smears and tests for vaginal infections were routine procedure before a contraceptive was prescribed. These procedures were considered best practice, were followed in FPA clinics by general practitioners, and had been recommended by the World Health Organization since 1966.[51] During the internal examination, girls were encouraged to hold the speculum and insert it themselves, to gain a better understanding of their own body through self-exploration, which was thought to be empowering. Clients were presented with varied methods of birth control, and the doctors talked the clients through the pros and cons of each method.

---

[50] 'Statistics based on the Annual Reports, 1972–1980', in SA/ALR/F.1, Wellcome Library, London.
[51] Lara Marks, *Sexual Chemistry: A History of the Contraceptive Pill* (Yale University Press, 2010): 124.

The pill

The majority of clients came to the centre to ask for the pill. The pill became available on the British market in 1961 on prescription for medical reasons, and at first mainly for married women through private agencies such as FPA clinics. At Brook, at first, doctors seemed to be very reluctant to prescribe the pill for those who did not conform to their moral standard of 'good sexual behaviour', namely intercourse occurring in a committed relationship. This attitude contradicted Brook's emphasis on a non-judgmental approach to young people's sexual needs and indicates that tensions existed within the service between Brook's progressive credentials and its conservative inclinations. For instance, at a conference in 1966 aimed at social workers, founder Helen Brook presented several examples of young clients attending the centre; one was refused the pill. The white 'girl of nearly 18' came to the centre to ask for the pill. The doctor undertook a long counselling session to find out the reasons why the 'girl' wanted the pill. The latter was having an affair with a married man and wanted to be protected against unwanted pregnancy. The doctor refused to prescribe her the pill on the basis that her immaturity was 'appalling'. The doctor acted as a gatekeeper of morality and judged the girl 'unsuitable to have the pill' since she was not in a committed, stable relationship.[52] At Bristol Brook, Dr Betty Orton, the doctor in charge of the sessions, refused to prescribe the pill to those under 18. This provoked a disagreement within Bristol Brook members, and London Brook intervened to reaffirm their policy that doctors would provide the pill to any girl over 16 'if they feel this is the right method in her particular case, and if it is what the girl herself wants'.[53] After the Family Planning Act of 1967, the pill became available to all women regardless of their marital status, on prescription in FPA clinics and Brook, and through general practitioners.[54]

In the first years of prescribing the pill, Brook presented it as a form of commitment for young people and as an indication of a stable relationship; this was a way of contradicting the criticism that Brook was encouraging promiscuity. In several articles, Brook doctors and members affirmed that the young people who came to the centre to ask for the pill were, for the most part, in steady relationships. For instance, the *Sunday Times* published the

---

[52] Helen Brook, 'Address to Westminster social workers, 5 September 1966', in SA/BRO/J1/7, Wellcome Library, London.
[53] 'Letter from Betty Hunter to Helen King, BAC Bristol secretary, 3rd July 1968', in SA/BRO/D1/2/1, Wellcome Library, London.
[54] Rusterholz, 'Teenagers.'

results of social worker Joan Woodward's 1969 study of girls attending Birmingham Brook, whereby she had found that 84% of girls had known their partner for six months or more and that the majority of the girls who came to ask for the pill were in already-established sexual relationships. This suggested that the pill acted as a link 'between particular sexual partners, and not as a preparation for general sexual experiment'. In the words of Sally Price, the secretary of Birmingham Brook, 'the very fact of a couple coming to us and saying they are sleeping together is a minor announcement that the relationship is serious. The vast majority have already made the decision to go on the pill before they arrive; it is a bond between them.'⁵⁵ This emphasis on heterosexual monogamy reflected both a rhetorical device to counter potential criticisms and, to some extent, a moral conservatism. This moral conservatism indicates that though Brook operated within a new climate, they did not provide a break with the interwar tradition of contraceptive advice that explicitly aimed to safeguard the marriage relationship. This position would evolve over the years in line with Brook's growing legitimacy. Indeed, from the mid-1970s the pill would be prescribed to any young woman over 16 who asked for it, no matters the status of her personal relationship.

The pill was the favourite method of birth control for both clients and doctors due to its efficacy. Yet, the demand for the pill fluctuated. By 1977, London Brook doctors were noticing that fears around side-effects and risks associated with the long-term use of oral contraceptives, fuelled by articles in the popular press, drove clients to seek better information and longer and fuller discussion about other contraceptive methods and their reliability and risks. They also noticed that while new clients tended to choose the pill, particularly early in their sexual experience when protection from pregnancy was paramount, established clients, who were more confident in themselves and their sexuality, were considering changing from the pill to IUDs or barrier methods such as the cap.⁵⁶

Dr Hutchinson made it clear in a talk in 1978 at a national conference on 'Accepting adolescent sexuality' that, for young girls, the pill was not necessarily the better choice if their periods were irregular. In addition, young people needed to be made aware that the pill provided no protection against sexually transmitted diseases. In this regard, condoms were presented as the safest method.

⁵⁵ 'After ten years of the pill: its unexpected role in the life of the young', *Sunday Times*, 27 February 1972, 29.
⁵⁶ 'London Centres Annual report, 1977–78, p. 6', in SA/ARL/F.4, Wellcome Library, London.

Another advantage of contraceptive counselling was to determine whether girls felt pressured to use the pill. As Joan Woodward, a social worker, remembered in a private phone interview: when she joined Birmingham Brook in 1967, the pill had become available for all women regardless of marital status. Woodward explained that young girls felt more and more pressurized into having sex with their partner because the partner would say, 'get on the pill and we can have sex and you won't become pregnant'.[57] Woodward stressed the difference in attitude between young men and women, since the girls 'wanted a relationship with somebody, [not just] safe sex with them'. Woodward argued that this situation created tensions and anxieties for young women, revealing the need for counselling. This quotation illustrates the tensions brought about by the availability of safer contraception; this new freedom also functioned as a new form of control for men.

IUDS, post-coital contraception, and Depo-Provera

Alongside the pill, other new methods of birth control were offered to young people. IUDs were presented as an option, but for under-16s who were under the age of consent, this method required parental permission—without it, fitting the IUD might lead to a charge of assault. IUDs were particularly recommended for clients who had had a termination, indicating that these clients were not perceived as 'responsible' enough to take the pill regularly. In 1977–1978, the prevalence of IUDs increased as that of the pill decreased; IUD use increased from 2% in 1974 in all centres to 9% in 1979. London Brook doctors again noticed increased anxieties about the potential risks of the pill and IUDs. As a result, contraceptive counselling required 'more discussion both when a method was chosen and when the client returned for check ups, to put the risks in perspective and consider alternative methods'.[58] In addition, many clients who were nulliparous (did not have a child) and had asked for an IUD were now reconsidering their choice due to the potential risk of pelvic infection; as a result, the number of IUD fittings decreased by 24% during 1979. In 1990 in Birmingham, only 2.3% of new clients were fitted with an IUD.

From 1973, Brook clinics also supplied clients with the post-coital pill as an emergency measure in case of rape and when there was no other alternative.

---

[57] Joan Woodward, private interview on the phone, 18 May 2020.
[58] 'London Centres Annual report, 1979–80, p. 5', in SA/ARL/F.4, Wellcome Library, London.

Few patients asked for it, since the majority did not know it was available. Due to the high doses of hormones, many clients had side-effects such as vomiting, headache, bleeding, and irregular cycles. However, in Brook's view, the benefits of avoiding an unwanted pregnancy and therefore a potential termination outweighed these side-effects. As a mitigation risk, it was recommended that this method should be prescribed as a one-off and that the client be put on 'adequate contraception'.[59] The decision to prescribe this method was backed up by the publication of an article in the *International Planned Parenthood Federation Medical Bulletin*, which stressed the efficiency of this method in preventing unwanted pregnancy.[60] If it was too late for a client to use emergency contraception, Brook doctors would recommend that the client consider termination of pregnancy. From 1982, post-coital contraception was advertised in Brook centres and in the Brook leaflets presenting the different methods of birth control available to young people (see Chapter 7). In 1976, long-acting injectable progestogens, such as Depo-Provera, while not yet officially approved by the Medicine Commission for routine use as contraceptives, was beginning to be prescribed by Brook doctors in situations where other contraceptive methods were not acceptable. This meant situations where clients preferred this solution, or where a doctor feared that the client would not take the pill on a regular basis or use other forms of contraception, but the doctor perceived that pregnancy had to be avoided. In late 1976, Depo-Provera was approved for use on a short-term basis, providing that women gave their consent and were informed about its side-effects. Moreover, this method was only prescribed in two circumstances: namely, if a woman had received the rubella vaccine, or if her partner had just undergone a vasectomy.

Depo-Provera was a contraceptive injection that had potential adverse effects including sterility, irregular menstruation, and cancer. Although this contraceptive was banned by the United States Food and Drug Agency (USFDA), its parent company launched the method in the UK. In 1977, the Brook Medical Advisory Committee reported in a meeting that members of the Women's Movement were concerned about the use of Depo-Provera on immigrant women.[61] Indeed, in the 1970s in Britain and the USA, women's health activists denounced the use of Depo-Provera on Black and Asian

---

[59] 'Brook Medical Advisory Committee: The use of post coital oestrogen, 1973', in SA/BRO/C1/1, Wellcome Library, London.

[60] 'Post coital oestrogen in large dose', *International Planned Parenthood Federation Medical Bulletin* 6.2 (1973): 3–4.

[61] 'Minute of the Medical Advisory Committee, 9 December 1977', in SA/BRO/C1/1, Wellcome Library, London.

women and women from working-class backgrounds. Evidence gathered by these activist groups showed that the drug was prescribed mainly to Black, Asian, and working-class women and very often without their formal consent.[62]

The meeting of the Medical Advisory Committee emphasized the responsibility of doctors to make sure that potential clients understood the treatment and had given their consent. In addition, the committee stressed that this method was meant to be used on a short-term basis. In this context, Dr Fay Hutchinson mentioned that a small number of West Indian girls at the London Brook had chosen Depo-Provera. She did not provide any information on the reasons for these girls' birth control choices and the criteria on which doctors based their decisions to suggest this method to the girls in question. No mention was made of white clients using this method. This raises the question of the extent to which assumptions about race were a key factor when assessing whether to offer this method to clients. Indeed, it may have been the case that young West Indian girls were deemed to be at higher risk of unwanted pregnancy due to their alleged 'irresponsibility' in failing to protect themselves. In addition, Birmingham Brook wrote to the Medical Advisory Committee to nuance the issue of consent, arguing that young people aged 12 to 16 years with learning difficulties might not understand or be adequately informed about the effectiveness, duration, and side-effects of Depo-Provera, but that the method might still be used when it was considered in the best interests of the client by those responsible for her care. This statement shows the limits of the idea of consent and raises the question of whether some coerced application might have been taking place in some Brook centres based on potential racial and ableist prejudices. This practice undermines the non-judgmental attitude cherished by Brook and also shows that the centre tried to enforce the white-middle class norm of protected intercourse in steady relationships.

Risks and vulnerability

In 1978, in the aforementioned conference on accepting adolescent sexuality, Dr Fay Hutchinson, speaking on behalf of Brook, recognized that young people did have knowledge about birth control, but had difficulty in applying this knowledge to themselves. The continuous use of birth control seemed to be the major issue; the majority of the female clients would only feel it was

---

[62] Lambert, 'The objectionable injectable'; Dadzie, Bryan, and Scafe, *The Heart of the Race*.

morally acceptable to use a contraceptive method if they had a regular partner. Due to this double standard, they did not want to appear prepared for having intercourse, fearing that carrying contraceptives or taking the pill would make them look as though they 'were asking for it'. The role of the counsellor and doctor was therefore to encourage them to depart from this idea, prioritize the safety of intercourse over any moral considerations and disentangle these anxieties.[63] This emphasis on safety over the stability of the relationship, once again, illustrates that Brook's stance on responsibility evolved over time. If at first, commitment was essential, by 1978 safety came first. In addition, this also shows that conflicts existed between the different values that Brook were trying to spread. Similarly, Hutchinson argued that some clients' behaviour, such as being reluctant to talk or appearing distressed, betrayed anxiety, guilt, and conflict that needed to be picked up and explored during the counselling session. From the 1980s onwards, Dr Gillian Vanhegan, in her contraceptive sessions, also talked about sex, sexuality, and consent. She endeavoured to find out with whom the client was having sex and why: 'all the questions that you need to know exactly what was happening to the young women',[64] in order to provide the best information about contraception.

Besides dealing with emotions, counsellors also focused their attention on the notion of risks in sexual behaviour and vulnerability. They qualified unprotected sexual intercourse as risky behaviour. Counsellors and doctors explained that its prevalence was due to several factors: young people lived 'in the present and did not plan ahead';[65] they favoured 'spontaneous behaviour'; there was a lack of acceptance of their sexuality on their own part and on the part of others, especially their parents; their sex education was lacking; and they encountered practical difficulties with contraceptive methods.[66] Brook counsellors and doctors' role was therefore to mitigate these different aspects by recognizing young people as sexual beings when they visited the clinics; they tried to instil in these clients a sense of sexual responsibility through the idea that safe sex was paramount, and explained the practicalities of contraceptive methods. In addition, class and race also influence counsellors' view about risks in sexual behaviour. For white working-class young women, contraception was described as a means of control; their lack of control over

---

[63] Fay Hutchinson, 'A doctor's view in accepting adolescent sexuality, July 1978', in SA/BRO/E11, Wellcome Library, London.
[64] Gillian Vanhegan, private interview on the phone, 20 February 2020.
[65] Joanna Brien, private interview on the phone, 29 March 2020.
[66] Ruth Coles, 'Acceptability and use-effectiveness of contraception for teenagers', *Journal of Biosociological Science Supplement* 5 (1978): 159.

their reproductive bodies condemned them to unwanted pregnancies and abortions. White young working-class women were usually described as having more sexual experience than white young middle-class women, taking more risks, and as such needed more counselling in order to avoid the risks of unprotected intercourse. Indeed, those of lower socio-economic status, who belonged to classes 4 and 5, were deemed to be at higher risk of unprotected sex since they were 'socially and emotionally deprived'. These white girls were said to be used by boys as 'sexual conveniences'.[67]

Assumptions around 'race' also permeated the work of counsellors, in particular the 'view' of the alleged apathy of young Black women who 'got themselves pregnant'. Writing in a 1978 special issue on fertility in adolescence, counsellor Pauline Crabbe flagged up the difficulties faced by young Black girls who became pregnant: 'black girls who have babies in their early teens are especially vulnerable. They are less likely than white girls to fight their way back into education or training for a job and they tend to sink into apathy more quickly and accept a second child because they feel already permanently enslaved by the first birth.'[68] In drawing on this vocabulary, Crabbe referred to Black girls as slaves of their men's desire. This was a strong wording that distanced their attitudes by sending them back to the time of slavery, and in so doing stressed their differences, therefore othering their behaviours from those of white girls. Crabbe suggested that one of the means to tackle this issue was contraceptive education, in which Black adolescent girls would be taught to 'value their freedom and to show their men the benefits of partnership before they accept responsibility for parenthood'.[69] While recognizing the specific needs of young Black girls, these remarks draw on some negative stereotypes about the alleged 'apathy' of Black girls who became pregnant and the reluctance of Black boys to form committed relationships. However, Crabbe also considered Black girls to be the ones that made the decisions within the relationship, since they were said to be influenced by the 'old matriarchal tradition of the West Indies'. Counselling was therefore perceived as a way of teaching white middle-class 'British' values around 'sexual responsibility' and committed relationship to these young women, so that they could 'rebel against the prison sentence of early maternity'.

[67] Pauline Crabbe, 'The Brook Client, the social worker's viewpoint, in accepting adolescent sexuality, Conference 1978', SA/BRO/E11, Wellcome Library, London.
[68] Pauline Crabbe, 'Social and emotional aspects of pregnancy in teenagers', *Journal of Biosocial Science* 5 (1978): 173.
[69] Ibid.

At the same conference, Pauline Crabbe explained that young Black boys, usually from African-Caribbean backgrounds, shared many common problems with socially deprived white teenagers: 'lack of incentive, lack of opportunity, poor housing, an educational system that failed them, limited job prospects and poor communication within the home'. This led them to place more importance on sexuality. However, Black boys were presented as opposing contraception and encouraging parenthood, while at the same time deemed 'unprepared to accept the continuing responsibility of fatherhood'.

To some extent, Brook members tried to address what they perceived as sociostructural inequalities, since they recognized the additional social challenge that Black girls, Black boys, and white working-class girls faced and devoted energy to finding ways of reaching out to these 'vulnerable' young people. Nevertheless, in so doing, they eased the process of assimilation into British norms by conveying standards of good sexual behaviour based on middle-class values, namely protected intercourse in a steady relationship. They thus acted as potential levellers of culturally perceived different sexual behaviours.

HIV and AIDS also became a concern for Brook, who qualified unprotected penetrative sex as risky behaviours in the context of the spread of the virus. In 1989, the counselling Advisory Committee wrote a guideline for introducing the subject of HIV/AIDs to clients attending the centres. In the minutes debating the guideline it was said, that, according to Brook staff, young people did not ask for information about HIV. As a result, staff did not feel an obligation to initiate discussion. Staff felt slightly reluctance to approach the subject and this was linked, it was believed, with the tradition in Brook to concentrate on the 'positive and enjoyable aspects of sexuality to balance the punitive and disabling attitudes so often encountered by young people'.[70] In addition, staff explained that young people did not perceive that they could be at risk of infection. The staff was conscious of approaching the subject sensitively in order to avoid creating unnecessary alarm or hostility.[71] As such, they endeavoured to recommend the use of the sheath alongside any other form of contraception. It was decided that a leaflet would be useful as a basis for discussion with clients. This proved successful, as the take-up of the sheath dramatically increased. This was not Brook's first attempt at encouraging the use of the sheath. In 1979 Dylis Cossey wrote a little pamphlet called *Teenage*

---

[70] 'Minute of the Counselling Advisory Committee meeting, 25 April 1989', in SA/BRO/C/7/1, Wellcome Library, London.
[71] 'How the introduce the subject of HIV/AIDS to clients attending Brook Centres so that information and advice will be effective in helping to reduce the spread of HIV, 6 April 1989', in SA/BRO/C7/1, Wellcome Library, London.

Birth Control: The Case for the Condom, where she presented the advantage of the method in terms or reliability, protection against sexual transmitted disease, and the sharing of birth control responsibility.[72] She encouraged local health authorities to provide condoms for free and plead for its wide publicity. The take up of condoms with clients rapidly increased due to the AIDS crisis. For instance, in 1987 in Birmingham, 40.7% of new clients decided to use the pill while 17.5% went for the sheath, and 32.9% chose no method of birth control.[73] In 1990, 32.2% of new Birmingham clients decided to use the sheath.[74] By 1994, this number had increased to 46.9%.[75] This increase in sheath users testifies to two key elements: the success of campaigns aimed at raising awareness about the dangers of sexually transmitted diseases, such as the widely publicized leaflet created by Brook, *Love Carefully: Use a Condom*, in 1987 (see Chapter 7); and the fact that young men seemed to be becoming more involved in contraceptive responsibility.

Under-16s

There was also a consensus that under-16s needed longer counselling contraceptive sessions, as they needed to understand the legal implications of a sexual relationship before the age of consent; they saw the counsellor in addition to the doctor. Under the Family Law Reform Act of 1969, a person over 16 was medically an adult and able to consent to her own treatment, and thus had a right to professional confidentiality. In addition, doctors, counsellors, and nurses took great care to explain 'the possible health risks of early sexual activity'.[76] Second, to prescribe contraception to under-16s, doctors were generally required to gain the parents' authorization, and they did try to convince their clients to inform their parents. However, if they could not, Brook considered it the doctor's responsibility to make the right decision and to 'assess whether the young person was mature enough to understand what she was doing'.[77] Care was also taken to ensure the client was not pressurized and that she entered freely into the relationship. From 1971, when social

---

[72] Dilys Cossey, *Teenage Birth Control: The Case for the Condom* (Brook Advisory Centre, 1979).
[73] 'Birmingham Centre annual report, 1987', in SA/BRO/D3/1/2, Wellcome Library, London.
[74] 'Birmingham Centre Annual Report 1990', in SA/BRO/D3/1/2, Wellcome Library, London.
[75] 'Birmingham Centre Annual Report 1994', in SA/BRO/D3/1/3, Wellcome Library, London.
[76] 'Know your organisation: The Brook Advisory Centre', in SA/BRO/J3/1, Wellcome Library, London.
[77] Ruth Skrine, *Growing into Medicine: The Life and Loves of a Psychosexual Doctor* (Book Guild, 2014): 132. In her memoirs, Dr Ruth Skrine reflected on the occasional sessions she held for Brook centres in the late 1960s.

worker Pauline Crabbe joined the London team, counselling by social workers for under-16s became common practice. 'We started by offering counselling to the under-16s because there's the legal side and the emotional side and the getting permission from parents side, all of that had to be gone into.'[78] In an article published in 1980 in *Modern Medicine*, Dr Fay Hutchinson discussed the counselling work of Brook. She explained that 'immature youngsters going through emotional difficulties and having early sexual relationships need protection'.[79] She considered contraception as a way of 'buying time' so that, with maturity, a young person could form a 'more suitable relationship' without the damage of pregnancy. In 1984, chairman Caroline Woodroffe explained the purpose of counselling the under-16s:

> What we are aiming at is that they can go away and feel they are in control of their own lives and that they are the ones making the decisions. We aim to help them stop feeling it is merely happening to them but that they are doing it—that is the way one grows up! We try to encourage self-determination and self-esteem and respect for themselves, their boyfriends and their family.[80]

Therefore, the counselling for under-16 was delivered in an empowering fashion, encouraging young people to assert themselves.

The counselling for contraception provided by Brook therefore functioned as a way of presenting methods of contraception to young people, helping them understand their emotions, teaching safe-sex practices, and raising awareness about risky sexual behaviours. The pill was the most prescribed method of contraception. As a confidential service, Brook became increasingly popular as a place where young people could obtain the pill. In addition, in encouraging young people to express their needs and helping them choose a birth control method, Brook helped to stabilize a new form of sexual subjectivity where emotions and self-reflection were paramount.

Counselling for pregnancy

Pregnancy testing, abortion counselling and referral, prenatal referrals, and contraceptive aftercare were available in the majority of the centres. At first,

---

[78] 'Interview with Pauline Crabbe', *In the Club*, GC/15/43, Wellcome Library, London.
[79] Fay Hutchinson, 'Counselling: When the pill buys time', *Modern Medicine*, February 1980, 49.
[80] Toni Turner, 'Parental privilege: A minor concern?', *GP*, 6 January 1984.

counselling was principally thought of in conjunction with birth control, but soon many young girls came to the clinics pregnant, and counselling for pregnancy became an important, distinct, aspect of the clinical work. Some young women turned to the centre because they suspected they were pregnant, and in that case, first, Brook workers sought to confirm the pregnancy with a pregnancy test. If the test turned out to be negative, the centre offered the girl a contraceptive counselling session to determine the best method of contraception, so that she did not find herself in a similar position again.

A potential unwanted pregnancy was (and is, still) a source of many contradictory emotions, and doctors and counsellors were very concerned with helping the client to disentangle them and identify what would be the best outcome for her, given her own particular circumstances. Listening to the clients was essential. Strikingly, counsellors avoided emotive language in order to allow a client to make her own decision without being influenced. In an article published in *Youth Counselling Bulletin* in 1976, Dr Ruth Coles, the medical director of Avon Brook, explained that counselling must be non-directive. Each client should be allowed to 'tell her story, and her feelings and wishes must be listened to and interpreted within a neutral atmosphere'.[81] Similarly, Pauline Crabbe, the former welfare secretary for the National Council for the Unmarried Mother and Her Child, first Black woman magistrate and counsellor for the London Brook, remembered in an interview in 1987, 'I used to school myself by, for instance, not using emotive terms, talking about a pregnancy and not a baby, because that keeps the sort of distance from it. [...] If you press somebody to make a decision by either using emotive terms or anything else it's not a valid decision.'[82]

While Brook advisors recommended that time was needed to think about the best decision, time was also a sensitive issue, especially for young women, who would sometimes present themselves for help at Brook in an advanced stage of pregnancy. They needed to make a fast decision. As a result, Brook members established a list of sympathetic doctors who would perform an abortion when the waiting time at the NHS was too long. Dr Ruth Cole, in 1971, explained that she had learnt 'how long the NHS pipeline took and the psychological trauma this caused the patient (and me because they were constantly on the phone expecting me to know when this would be done)'. As shown by this quotation, the long process of state-supported abortion created additional anxieties for the client, who had to deal with uncertainty,

---

[81] Ruth Coles, 'Pregnancy counselling for young people', *Youth Counselling Bulletin*, 1976.
[82] Pauline Crabbe, '*In the Club*', in GC/105/43, Wellcome Library, London.

and the doctor, who was trying to reassure the client while at the same time dealing with the bureaucracy of the NHS. The role of the counsellor in pregnancy counselling did not change much over the years. In 1994, the Counselling Advisory Committee published a document presenting the services offered by Brook and reaffirmed that pregnancy testing and pregnancy counselling were essential. In the case of a positive test, the counsellor discussed all the options available to the client and their implications, including the relative risks of pregnancy and termination. The document also explained that a counsellor would take a non-directive approach in order to help the client to clarify the best outcome for herself.[83]

In addition, Brook counselling also entailed seeking a way to persuade and help under-16 clients to inform their parents in order to gain abortion approval. Following the 1967 Abortion Act, termination was a possibility, but required the approval of two doctors and, for a minor, a parent. Brook members acted as facilitators for communication between young girls and their parents. The mediated case of 'Rosie' (cited in the Brook annual report in 1980) illustrates this point. Rosie, 15-years-old, came to the centre because she feared she was pregnant, and had a pregnancy test that turned out to be positive. The counsellor first needed to identify Rosie's feelings about the baby. Doctors and counsellors had a common understanding that if a girl had delayed her visit to the centre, this might point to the 'woman's instinctive wish to have a child'. She might not be in the right circumstances to welcome a child, but her emotions told her otherwise, and a delay in seeking help was used as a way to keep the child. However, in the case of Rosie, her main emotion was fear that the responsibility that having a child entailed. Since she was under the age of consent and legally a minor in medical terms, the main issue was the necessity of parental permission to have an abortion; as such, she was paralysed by the idea of announcing her pregnancy. The counsellor had to explain carefully to Rosie that it would soon be too late for an abortion. With the help of the counsellor, Rosie found the courage to tell her mother.[84] In this scenario, then, the role of the counsellor was therefore to provide emotional support for the client as the latter made her decision and faced its consequences by informing her parents. This supportive role was apparently highly valued by clients, as illustrated by a letter sent by a mother of a 17-year-old teenager to Brook, thanking them 'for the marvellous way doctors and

---

[83] 'Aims of the Services, 1994', in SA/BRO/C7/1, Wellcome Library, London.
[84] 'Caroline Woodroffe Brook, Annual Report, 1979–1980', in SA/BRO/B1/7, Wellcome Library, London.

counsellors at Brook helped my distraught daughter recently. Everyone was so kind and helpful, and after talking it over and giving it much thought she had an abortion.'[85] This letter was published in the Brook annual report and was clearly selected for its positive assessment of Brook's services; nevertheless, it provides an insight into the way counsellors acted as another form of help, even when young people had secured the support of a parent. The letter offers insight into the kinds of experiences it hoped its clients to have. It is testimony to the emotional struggles clients faced and the essential work of Brook counsellors in helping clients.

Counselling for psychosexual problems

The third type of counselling available in the clinic was psychosexual counselling. In this counselling, emotional labour played a central role. Sexual counselling had been a focus since the interwar years, but gained in popularity after the Second World War, when the emotional stability that depended on the sexual harmony of British citizens was deemed fundamental to the rebuilding of society.[86] Moreover, the development of sexology, with the success of the Kinsey report and its 'Little Kinsey' British counterpart, put the search for sexual pleasure at the centre of postwar Britain and the stability of relationships.[87] In order to help couples reach sexual satisfaction, many Family Planning Clinics turned to psychosexual training, which was heavily influenced by psychoanalysis; FPA members were trained by Michael Balint and later the Institute for Psychosexual Medicine.[88]

This counselling developed in different ways in the centres, since there were no clear guidelines and treatments. While psychosexual counselling did help young people in some ways, with its emphasis on past events and trauma, it nevertheless also contributed to pathologizing young people's sexual behaviours. Psychosexual counselling dealt mainly with anxiety, and as clinic doctor Fay Hutchinson noted, 'the younger the client the more areas of anxiety she is likely to have'.[89] According to Hutchinson, the clients presented with a wide range of psychosexual problems, including lack of orgasm, fear of intercourse,

---

[85] 'Letter from a Mother, 1981', in SA/ALR/F.1, Wellcome Library, London.
[86] Teri Chettiar, 'Treating marriage as "the sick entity": Gender, emotional life, and the psychology of marriage improvement in postwar Britain', *History of Psychology* 18.3 (2015): 270–82.
[87] Bingham, 'The "K-Bomb"'. [88] On training see Rusterholz, *Women's Medicine*, chapter 2.
[89] 'Fay Hutchinson, The Brook Clinic, the doctor's viewpoint', in SA/BRO/E11, Wellcome Library, London.

impotence, anxieties related to the body, sexual abuse, same-sex attraction, and difficulty with parental relations. Counselling for the under-16s was presented by clinic authorities as a way of 'buying time' for the girls 'to continue developing and maturing so that she may make [a] good relationship in the future'.[90] In psychosexual counselling emotional labour was central and helped to ease the tensions between non-judgmental attitudes and conservative views on sexual relationship.

The counselling treatment offered depended on the counsellors' personality and training. In 1967 in Birmingham, social worker Joan Woodward carried out a survey of clients' experiences and needs, which revealed a need for the development of counselling. The survey identified a gap in the service in terms of the fact that young people generally needed more time to express the reason why they had come and needed counselling that was specifically aimed at understanding the anxieties they felt. As a result, a multidisciplinary team of counsellors, doctors, psychologists, and nurses was set up, and additional counselling sessions were organized.

The same year, in London, Margaret Christie Brown was hired as a clinical doctor; she started a weekly session for what the clinic called 'girls with special problems'. The sessions lasted 50 minutes in order to allow the clients to discuss their anxieties at length. Clients were seen as many times as was necessary to make a diagnosis, or were referred to other bodies for help.[91] Christie Brown explained that many unmarried girls needed help with emotional difficulties because they had not fully come to terms with the lives they were living. She stressed again that contradictory attitudes made for a difficult decision for these young people: 'In a society where parents are likely to regard this action as sinful, conflict is inevitable. These young people have usually seriously thought out the terms of their relationship.'[92] From 1970, this openness towards youth sexuality extended beyond the notion of safe sex. Dr Christie Brown counselled young women in the London Brook Centre. She underlined the fact that Brook's focus was not only on safe sex and avoiding the negative consequences of unprotected intercourse; the centre also sought to 'help some of them enjoy their sexuality'. Thus, for the first time, the notion of enjoyment and pleasure was finally connected to that of young people. Indeed, while sexual pleasure became increasingly discussed and central to the sexual life of married couples from the interwar years onwards, and thus

---

[90] Ibid. [91] 'Brook Advisory Centre', *Family Planning* 17.2 (1968): 40.
[92] Margaret Christie Brown, quoted in '9000 use centre for unmarried', *Daily Telegraph*, 31 July 1967.

became a new field of practice in FPA clinics, associating sexual pleasure with young people was still highly controversial since it was feared it would encourage promiscuity.[93] Sex education in school, when not simply absent, focused mainly on combating venereal diseases; sexual pleasure was never addressed. While the mass media started to address the issue of sexual pleasure for women in the late 1960s and early 1970s, teenage magazines at that time remained fairly conventional, and did not venture into sexual pleasure.[94] Brook was the first charity to take on the challenge of offering practical help with the issue of sexual pleasure for young people. This work might have been potentially influenced by the second-wave feminist focus on women's sexual pleasure, but this influence was never explicitly acknowledged. However, here again, this progressive idea was undermined by conservative views on the 'right' type of relationship and gendered sexual roles. Clients were expected to display maturity, and this was assessed based on their adherence to the white-middle class idea of monogamous, heterosexual, committed relationships. Girls who had multiple partners were described as having troubled personalities, either needing attention or rebelling against their parents.[95] Boys, as a rule, were never described as being promiscuous. This was largely due to a gendered understanding of sexual development where boys were thought of as having a sexual urge difficult to harness, whereas girls were looking for emotional attachment.

Doctors and social workers, when presenting study cases in diverse publications, invariably applied a gendered framework whereby ideas about femininity, masculinity, and gendered sexual behaviours were predominant. These ideas pathologized behaviours that did not fit the model. For instance, Dr Margaret Christie Brown from the London centre applied what she called 'the Freudian theory of psychosexual development' to help clients enjoy their sexuality. She considered that past events and childhood relationships could act as an unconscious blockage to sexual life. For instance, she explained that a proportion of girls were sexually unresponsive because they partially rejected their female role and 'had identified with their father instead of their mother'.[96] She explained that these girls had a history

---

[93] On sexual disorders as a new field of practice see Rusterholz, *Women's Medicine*, chapter 2. On the development of sexual counselling see also Caroline Rusterholz, 'You can't dismiss that as being less happy, you see it is different'.

[94] See Adrian Bingham, 'Newspaper problem pages and British sexual culture since 1918', *Media History* 18.1 (2012): 51–63; McRobbie, *Feminism and Youth Culture*, 81–134.

[95] 'Annual Report of the Brook Advisory Centre', *Family Planning* 15.2 (1966): 47–50.

[96] Dr Margaret Christie Brown, 'Psycho-sexual counselling: The method followed in the London Brook Advisory Centres', *British Journal of Sexual Medicine*, 1974, in SA/BRO/J/3/1, Wellcome Library, London.

of 'tomboyishness and were ambivalent in appearance and frequently wore boys' clothes'. They had a dominant personality and were usually ambitious. Helping them to identify these elements by themselves was thought to be a first step towards sexual adjustment and would offer a way out of pathologized behaviours. Similarly, clinic doctor Ruth MacGillivray had a gendered understanding of young people's sexual behaviours where 'boys have tremendous sexual drive' and girls 'are more interested in attracting the opposite sex for reasons of prestige and companionship. While enjoying mutual caresses, most do not have the same urge for coitus.'[97] This gendered view on sexuality presented male sexuality as inherently animal, uncontrolled, and driven by impulse. This implies that girls should be responsible for marshalling young boys' sexual drives. MacGillivray also encouraged girls to consider orgasm as 'the excitement felt of seeing a pop idol in concert' and as an 'unexpected bonus'. She however enjoined them to find a sexual position where their clitoris could be stimulated since it is the locus of pleasure. She nevertheless reaffirmed that penetration was essential in that it allowed for a more satisfactory coit.

The counsellor Joan Woodward from Birmingham used the method of 'combining an intellectual understanding of the problem, with where necessary, an increased awareness of the emotional and fantasy aspects through the use of dream material, plus a chance to gain practical experiences free of anxiety through the sensate focus techniques'. For instance, she counselled Jane, who needed help because she had lost 'her libido'. She presented the case by first emphasizing the strict upbringing of Jane, daughter of a vicar, where sex was never mentioned. Jane unconsciously blocked her sexual desire in order to 'remain the non-sexual child her parents have unwittingly made her'. She talked with Jane about her childhood experience and guided her to recognize 'conflicted emotions'. At that point, Joan Woodward recommended the programme of 'sensate focus', used by the sexologists Masters and Johnson, a series of touching without intercourse in order to arouse pleasurable feelings that lead gradually to genital stimulation and eventually sexual intercourse.[98] This diversity of techniques points to the fragmented and volatile nature of sexual counselling, where gendered understandings of sexuality cohabited with more feminist notions of female sexual pleasure. This emphasis on teenagers and young women's sexual pleasure was radical in the

---

[97] MacGillivray, 'Sex Problems, Counselling'.
[98] Joan Woodward, 'The role of the social worker in psychosexual counselling', *Social Work Today*, 11 January 1977.

context of British society in the 1970s, where young people's sexuality was usually discussed in moralizing terms. But it also constituted a continuity with the work done in FPA clinics to encourage sexual pleasure. From the late 1980s, Dr Gillian Vanhegan also ran a separate psychosexual counselling session at London Brook. In the 1970s, she followed the training of the Institute of Psychosexual Medicine and qualified as a psychosexual counsellor. She explained that she mostly saw young men who had erectile problems due to 'anxieties of various sorts, because of experience, because of bullying, because of teasing about things'. She also sometimes counselled young women who had vaginismus and could not consummate their relationship. Their problem, she argued, was a result of abuse from their cultural background; the clients were fighting in their own minds between their (for example) Muslim, Catholic, or Orthodox backgrounds and the life they were trying to live in twentieth-century London where sex was more acceptable. She also counselled other girls about their lack of enjoyment of sex. She attributed this situation to a dilemma whereby young people felt that they have to have sex to be part of a group but did not enjoy the sexual act. There was a lot of counselling around pleasure, the expectation of pleasure, and what should be done.[99] She underlined that her counselling method resulted from her own training and experience and that there were no formal guides or textbooks recommended by Brook that psychosexual counsellors had to follow.

In Birmingham in 1983, a self-help group for pre-orgasmic women, that is, women who had never experienced an orgasm, was instituted as part of the counselling service and led by a counsellor.[100] The resort to self-help showed the clear influence of feminist ideas about the need for women to support themselves and know their own bodies. The success of the group was such that four new groups were run in 1984. The participants evaluated the groups as successful in meeting their needs and subsequently decided to continue to meet as unfacilitated self-help groups in premises of their own choosing.

Sexual abuse

Over the years, an increasing number of young clients came to the centre because they had been sexually abused. Brook members began to recognize

---

[99] Gillian Vanhegan, private interview on the phone, 20 February 2020.
[100] 'Birmingham BAC, Annual report 1983', in SA/BRO/D3/1/2, Wellcome Library, London.

this as an urgent issue that needed to be addressed, and in the early 1990s they devised a harmonized policy. Until then, the policy had been that Brook should be aware of the problem and provide appropriate help by referring clients to appropriate local resources, such as social services. In addition, while every effort was made to guarantee the client's confidentiality, it was argued that Brook could not be expected to 'always maintain confidentiality in cases of child sex abuse'. When a victim of sexual abuse refused referral to another agency, Brook considered it important to offer ongoing help as appropriate. In addition, counsellors were advised to try to help the client consider disclosure to the appropriate statutory agency 'in view of the danger to the client of continuing abuse and the possibility of siblings being or becoming involved'.[101] Indeed, there was a potential conflict between the wishes of the client to maintain confidentiality and the responsibility that the counsellor felt for that client and for any siblings involved. Brook considered it good practice to explain the need to breach confidentiality to the client, and the policy was that the client's agreement should be sought whenever possible.

In 1994, a common framework was devised for branch practice. Branches were reminded that client confidentiality was at the centre of professional codes of practice, but that this confidentiality might be broken in exceptional circumstances, when the health, safety, or welfare of a person was at serious risk. First, it was advised that any member of staff who heard a disclosure of sexual abuse from a client must confer with the senior counsellor. The client should be referred to the senior counsellor, and every effort should be made to maintain the client's confidentiality, but a guarantee of this confidentiality should not be given. If a client wished to remain anonymous, it was recommended that the counsellor make detailed and extensive notes on the case in the client's file. If the sexual abuse occurred in the past and no other person was at risk, it was up to the client whether or not to inform an appropriate agency. If the client reported ongoing sexual abuse, the counsellor should help and encourage the client to disclose the situation to an appropriate statutory agency. If a Brook counsellor considered that the client lacked the maturity to consent to disclosure and that it was in the client's best interest to disclose to an appropriate agency because of the risk of serious harm, the client's confidentiality could be broken, but the client should be informed first. If there was a danger to others, for example siblings, the Brook counsellor should consider the probability of serious harm ensuing and the information should be passed on to an appropriate agency after the client was informed that this action

---

[101] 'Child Sex Abuse, 1986', in SA/BRO/C7/1, Wellcome Library, London.

would be taken. In cases where the client was the perpetrator of child sexual abuse, counsellors were advised to help the client understand the seriousness of this situation and the need for the abuse to stop. Confidentiality could be broken to protect young people from serious harm, but here again, the client should be informed first. This framework also recognized the emotional toll that sexual abuse could have upon staff members, and therefore it was recommended that staff hold regular meetings and seminars to debrief their cases and discuss their emotions.

Conclusion

The counselling offered by Brook was meant to educate young people towards sexual maturity and encourage them to take responsibility for their sexual lives. At first, the work mainly conveyed the white middle-class norm of protected intercourse in a steady, loving heterosexual relationship. Counselling was therefore developed as a way of helping a 'better management of the self'. In so doing, Brook did not represent a departure from the values favoured by the interwar tradition of contraceptive advice as exemplified by the Family Planning Association, but instead readapted these values for young people. The counselling practices provided by Brook were required to follow the ideal of a non-judgmental listening approach to young people's sexual needs. However, this ideal was at first undermined by a moral conservatism that favoured heteronormative sexual behaviours based on the white middle-class model of protected intercourse in a steady, loving heterosexual relationship. In addition, race and class had a powerful impact on the perception of who belonged to vulnerable categories in need of counselling. Indeed, prejudices were not always conscious, and though attention paid to one particular group might have emerged from empathetic considerations for the reproductive outcomes of individuals from that group, it nevertheless remained the case that stereotypes and generalizations underpinned these considerations. Counselling might therefore have been used as a way of teaching the white middle-class value of commitment through the ideas of love and sexual responsibility. In spite of these limitations, counselling nevertheless helped to stabilize a new form of sexual subjectivity where young people were encouraged to express their feelings and views about their sexuality. But these norms became less prevalent over time and an increasing emphasis was put on ensuring young people protected themselves against unwanted pregnancies and sexually transmitted disease while enjoying their sexuality.

In providing their services, Brook offered three different types of counselling. Contraceptive counselling was mainly aimed at identifying the best method of birth control according to the medical history and emotional maturity of the client. For under-16s, doctors, nurses, and counsellors all worked to ascertain that the client was mature enough, in their own view, to engage in sexual intercourse. The types of methods recommended evolved over the years. From the mid-1980s, sheaths gained in popularity in the context of the AIDS crisis and Brook's focus on getting young men involved in contraceptive responsibility. Counselling for pregnancy required several sessions, as this was a highly emotional subject where counsellors had to find the right balance between being caring and not using language that was too emotive, in order to allow the client to identify her emotions and reach the best decisions given her particular circumstances. The third type of counselling concerned sexual anxieties. The fact that young people were recognized as sexual agents who could enjoy their sexuality was radical. Indeed, until this point, helping married couples to achieve sexual pleasure had been gaining momentum in FPA clinics, but the idea had never been applied to young people due to fears that it would encourage promiscuity. However, while sexual pleasure was addressed, providing a novel element, the idea of promiscuity limited the sexual freedom allowed to young girls. In addition, sexual counselling drew on a gendered understanding of sexual behaviours, where young men were thought of having greater sexual drive and young women were in search of emotional attachment; this framework, to a certain extent, pathologized young people's sexual behaviours when they deviated from these gendered sexual roles. Brook members helped to establish a new vision of the teenage sexual self, where responsibility, commitment, and protection functioned together. This emphasis on emotionally committed relationships was part of a broader trend in counselling work, where emotional maturity was perceived as the cornerstone of British society.

But Brook's aims evolved over time and a greater emphasis was increasingly placed on helping young people to enjoy their sexuality. This emphasis became explicit within Brook's work from the 1980s, when for instance staff expressed unease to approach the subject of AIDS fearing that would jeopardize the positive view on sex they were trying to share where pleasure was paramount. In the mid-1990s, Brook recognized the need to find a new statement of purpose to better align their aim with the work they were already doing. In 1996, a debate took place between board members to articulate this new purpose. Ex-press officer and board member Suzie Hayman explained that the original statement of Brook's aims 'felt as though it had been set by adults with the intention of controlling young people's behaviours, which was why the new statement emphasized enjoyment'.[102] The new statement adopted in 1997 put enjoyment at the centre of its mission: 'Brook exists to enable all young people to make informed choices about their personal and sexual relationships so that they can enjoy their sexuality without harm.'[103]

---

[102] 'Minutes of the meeting of the Board of Directors, 16 February 1996', in SA/BRO/B/1/14, Wellcome Library, London.
[103] Ibid.

7
Education and Information on Contraception

In a 1978 Brook annual report, the organizing secretary of Edinburgh Brook, Jean Malcolm, wrote: 'it is not always realised that an integral part of the function of a Brook Centre is education [...] The education done by workers from Brook takes place both outside the centres, in schools, youth club and community projects, and in the clinic session.'[1] Part of what made Brook services distinctive was the variety of the tactics used to educate young people. Over time, Brook developed several public health and education campaigns and educational resources, with the aim of informing young people about their services and promoting awareness about contraception and sexual and reproductive health.

The history of British public health campaigns around sex education has recently received increased attention from scholars, especially with regards to sex education and the AIDS crisis.[2] However, apart from the work of Hannah J. Elizabeth, no one has addressed Brook's contribution to these topics. Based on archival materials, leaflets, posters, and oral history interviews, this chapter asserts that Brook played a pioneering role in providing birth control information to young people and organizing sex education campaigns, while simultaneously responding to emerging political and public issues, especially

---

[1] 'Jean Malcolm in BAC Annual Report, 1978/1979', in SA/BRO/E/1/1, Wellcome Library, London. Some materials in this chapter, albeit in an altered form, have been published previously: Rusterholz, 'A mechanical view of sex outside the context of love and the family'; Caroline Rusterholz, 'A Private Matter? The Brook Advisory Centre and Young People's Everyday Sexual and Reproductive Health in the 1960s–1990s', in Hannah Froom, Tracey Loughran, Kate Mahoney, and Daisy Payling (eds),*'Everyday Health', Embodiment, and Selfhood since 1950* (Manchester University Press, forthcoming 2024). Many thanks to the editors for their work and in particular to Tracey Loughran for her support and constructive feedback.

[2] On sex education, see Lesley Hall, 'In Ignorance and in Knowledge: Reflections on the History of Sex Education in Britain', in Roger Davidson and Lutz Sauerteig (eds), *Shaping Sexual Knowledge: A Cultural History of Sex Education in Twentieth Century Europe* (Routledge, 2009): 31–48; Rachel Thomson, 'Prevention, promotion and adolescent sexuality: The politics of school sex education in England and Wales', *Sexual and Marital Therapy* 9.2 (1994): 115–26; Hampshire and Lewis, 'The ravages of permissiveness'. On the AIDS crisis, see Berridge, *AIDS in the UK*; Hannah J. Elizabeth, 'Love carefully and without "over-bearing fears": The persuasive power of authenticity in late 1980s British AIDS education material for adolescents', *Social History of Medicine* 34.4 (2021): 131–42.

those relating to under-16s as discussed in Chapter 3. The chapter takes a chronological approach, examining various campaigns that highlight broader contemporary concerns. First, it examines the work that Brook undertook in order to publicize their services and the opposition it faced, which exemplifies the controversial nature of providing contraceptive information to young people. The chapter then delves into the sex education materials produced by Brook, followed by their attempts to become more inclusive. In the 1970s, following the enactment of the Chronically Sick and Disabled Persons Act of 1970, Brook introduced a new initiative aimed at improving access to sexual health information and services for young people with disabilities. In the 1980s, Brook collaborated with the FPA to encourage boys to share responsibility for birth control and sought to encourage young people from minoritized backgrounds to attend Brook. Brook also developed visual and creative materials for educating young people about AIDS from the 1980s to the 1990s. In the 1990s, confidentiality became a critical issue when advertising sexual health services and Brook played a pivotal role in informing public health policy on this topic. This chapter argues that Brook paved the way for a new generation of inclusive, positive, and appealing sex education materials that catered to the needs of young people.

Information on services

As Jean Malcolm's quotation at the opening of this chapter suggests, sex education was a critical area of focus for Brook. The primary aim of sex education was to address the issue of unwanted pregnancies and abortions through information on contraception. Initially, this education was provided through contraceptive services and counselling at Brook centres, as discussed in Chapter 6. However, in order for young people to utilize these services, they needed to be aware of their existence. Therefore, Brook put significant effort into publicizing their services and consistently worked to expand their client base in order to reach out to young people who may not have known about them. These potential clients were deemed to be at higher risk of engaging in sexual activities without using contraception, or of using it inconsistently. Hence, it was crucial to educate them about 'responsible sex', which meant using contraception every time they engaged in penetrative sexual intercourse. To connect with these young people, Brook had to be visible in public spaces frequently used by the young. Right at their inception, Brook designed an informative leaflet detailing their services. The leaflet featured a picture of two hands held together, along with information on the location of the centre. The image was chosen to underscore the idea of committed heterosexual young people in steady relationships, consistent with Brook's initial rhetorical strategy for gaining legitimacy.[3]

In 1972, an advertising agency created a cinema advert promoting Brook services, which was screened in various London cinemas. The advert is not very explicit. It depicts a young heterosexual white couple walking along a path in a forest; they stop to share a kiss against a tree. The young man then puts his arm around his girlfriend's shoulders, and they continue their walk. Meanwhile, a male voice in the background explains the benefits of Brook services in euphemistic terms to the viewer: 'When you care a lot and want to show each other how you feel, it's natural to worry about what might happen if you are not careful. Don't keep your questions to yourself—talk to each other, then talk to somebody at the Brook Advisory Centre.'[4] The clip ended with the slogan 'Brook Advisory Centre—helpful people who have helpful answers.'

This enigmatic advertisement did not explicitly mention the services offered by Brook due to fears of censorship. The cryptic message caught the attention of the press, who speculated whether it was an advertisement for cigarettes or contraception.[5] As the first official advertisement for Brook, it was indicative of the broader climate of the time: discussing contraception for young people was still considered taboo. Following this screening, a leaflet was produced featuring the same young couple: the young man holding the young woman against his torso, with his head leaning towards hers, eyes shut, in a caring and protective embrace. The young woman holds her arms around his back and looks ahead with soft eyes, her head resting against his chest. Above the picture, the slogan reads: 'How the Brook help teenagers needing advice about sex', and below the image: 'Brook Advisory Centre, helpful people with helpful answers.'[6]

Between 1974 and 1983, Brook published several versions of an explanatory leaflet, *What is the Brook*, that advertised and described their services. The content of the leaflet evolved slightly over the years; it was divided into several sections with subheadings. In the 1974 version, the leaflet contained five subheadings. *What is Brook*? explained that Helen Brook had set up the first

---

[3] 'Brook Advisory Centre for young people', in SA/BRO/E/2, Wellcome Library, London.
[4] Available online: https://wellcomelibrary.org/item/b20292727#?c=0&m=0&s=0&cv=0, accessed 23 July 2020.
[5] 'Wendy Smith, Brook Advisory Centre Cinema Campaign', in SA/BRO/H1/1/3, Wellcome Library, London.
[6] 'How the Brook helps teenagers needing advice about sex', in SA/BRO/E/2, Wellcome Library, London.

centre to meet 'the needs of young people for advice and practical help with birth control and emotional and sexual problems'.[7] *Would you like advice about birth control?* used the script of the 1972 cinema advert about being involved in a steady relationship, emphasizing that the services were mainly for young people in committed relationships. It encouraged young people to come as a couple or on their own, explained that supplies of birth control were available in the centre, and underlined the confidentiality of the services as well as the friendly staff and welcoming atmosphere. In the 1978 version, under the same subheading, the reference to a steady relationship was abandoned, and instead the focus was placed on the risks of 'making love' without precautions. As explained in Chapters 1 and 2, this shows that the idea of the committed relationship was a tool used to gain legitimacy; it would be abandoned over time in favour of spreading a message about risks and safe sex. Yet the reference to love was still present, limiting sexual intercourse to loving partners.

The third subheading in 1974 was *Are you having any problems with a relationship?*; this section stressed that people at Brook were ready to listen to young people's problems. The fourth subheading, *Are you worried about being pregnant?* explained that Brook offered pregnancy testing and counselling, while the final subheading approached the issue of cost by emphasizing that the services were either free or available for a minimal fee.

Over time, other subheadings were added to the leaflet. *Do you have to be 16 before you can get advice?* appeared in 1978 to reassure under-16s that they were welcome at the centre, in the context of increasing opposition to Brook services (see Chapter 3). *Do you need educational information?* was added in 1981 to provide information about the educational materials produced by Brook. In 1983, the leaflet added two new sections: *Are you worried about infection?* emphasized Brook's work around sexual and transmitted diseases, while *Do you know about morning after contraception?* informed clients about the possibility of obtaining emergency contraception through the morning after pill or the fitting of a coil. These new additions illuminated the holistic approach taken by Brook, which offered a wide range of services on sexual health.

In addition to these informative leaflets and the cinema advert, there were some attempts to define Brook services more clearly, but these were met with opposition. Brook tried to put up posters advertising their services on public transport such as buses and trains, but this proved difficult and generated

---

[7] 'What is the Brook, 1974', in SA/BRO/E/4, Wellcome Library, London.

controversy, as I have shown elsewhere.⁸ Indeed, censorship operated on various fronts. In 1967, the British Code of Advertising Practice sanctioned the widespread advertising of contraceptives as long as 'they did not contain anything deemed offensive to decency'.⁹ However, posters in buses in Birmingham in 1972, as well as in a railway station in Bristol in 1973, were censored by the West Midlands Transport Board and British Transport Advertising respectively. Both objected to contraceptive advertisement, asserting that they were 'controversial and liable to upset some passengers'.¹⁰

Brook also wanted to advertise their services more widely in newspapers and on TV. In 1969, the Independent Broadcasting Authority, the regulatory body for commercial television and radio, changed its code of advertising standards to allow the advertising of 'official or officially sponsored family planning services' but not of specific contraceptive products or brands.¹¹ In 1986, after much controversy and in the context of the AIDS epidemic, the advertisement of condoms on British TV channels was eventually allowed. The Newspaper Publishers' Association, for its part, did not take a stance on the subject and individual editors oversaw the decision of whether or not to publish advertisements for contraceptives.¹² In spite of these legal changes, Brook faced constant opposition from diverse bodies such as the IBA, London Transport, and some newspapers who refused to publicize the centre's services. To protest this situation, Brook press officer and agony aunt Suzie Hayman published a booklet entitled 'Sex and Advertisement', which received wide coverage in the mass media.¹³ Hayman decried the ways that censorship operated in Britain and the hypocrisy that underpinned its application, as she saw it.¹⁴ References to sexuality and even underage sex, as well as pictures of naked female bodies, she argued, were widely used to sell different types of products and advertise services. Yet 'honest' and 'clear statements of [Brook's] services', especially the use of the terms 'unmarried' and 'birth control' in the

---

⁸ Rusterholz, 'A mechanical view of sex outside the context of love and the family'.

⁹ Quoted in Paul Jobling, 'Playing safe: The politics of pleasure and Gender in the promotion of condoms in Britain, 1970-1982', *Journal of Design History* 10.1 (1997): 53-70.

¹⁰ Julia Langdon, 'The Brook Advisory Centre', *Labour Weekly*, 18 August 1972. See also 'Buses ban on birth control advice', *Daily Mail*, 13 February 1973.

¹¹ 'IBA, "The Control of Advertising, Annual Report 1972-1973"', in SA/BRO/H1/1/1, Wellcome Library, London.

¹² 'Letter from N. C. Sanderson, Home Office to Ms Yvonne Millwood, Independent Broadcasting Authority, 17 August 1987', HO256/1160, National Archives, London.

¹³ Suzie Hayman, *Advertising and Contraceptives* (Birth Control Trust, 1977).

¹⁴ Regarding censorship more generally, by 1970, as Travis has shown, the police and the Home Office did not necessarily agree on which works should be censored. The Home Office had a more tolerant attitude to obscenity than the police. See Alan Travis, *Bound and Gagged: A Secret History of Obscenity in Britain* (Profile Books, 2000): 166-215.

same sentence, was deemed offensive.[15] This shows that contraception for young people was still perceived as damaging their morality, that is, encouraging promiscuity and unmarried sexual activity.

In the 1990s, several publicity campaigns were undertaken in order to advertise Brook services more widely. For instance, Birmingham Brook designed four posters with striking black and white images of young people, which were displayed on billboards and buses. The posters highlighted four key themes: choosing contraception, emergency contraception, pregnancy testing and counselling, and counselling for young men and women. Smaller posters and postcards were also designed and displayed.[16] Additionally, in 1996, Brook was commissioned by the Health Education Authority to work with Southampton University's Centre for Sexual Health Research in order to gain insight into young people's opinions regarding the promotion of sexual health services for their age group.[17] Eighteen single-sex focus groups were organized in urban, semi-urban, and rural areas across England. Participants were selected to represent a diverse range of socio-economic backgrounds and experiences with the services. The results of the study were particularly illuminating with regard to appropriate language, poster design, and sites of posters and leaflets. Young people wanted to see the words 'sex advice', 'free', 'confidential', 'private', 'approachable', and 'friendly', but recommended avoiding terms such as 'family planning', 'clinic', 'GUM', and 'VD'. They also stressed that colourful, bold, and glossy materials should be used. Following these recommendations, Brook produced a new poster advertising their services.

Alongside this publicity, Brook also used mass media as a channel of communication. From their inception, Brook had recognized that coverage of their work in newspapers and magazines was essential for making their services widely known. As we will see in the last section of this chapter, Brook services were widely recommended in problem pages in teenage and women's magazines. However, the psychological weight of the cultural association of teenage sexuality with promiscuity and illegitimacy needed to be challenged in order to allow Brook to publicize its services and provide contraception on a large scale. Brook used mass media as a powerful tool, undertaking an intense campaign aimed at tackling false claims around increasing promiscuity. To do so, and as explained in Chapters 1 and 2, they put forward a narrative that

---

[15] Hayman, *Advertising and Contraceptives*.
[16] 'Brook Annual Report, 1995', SA/FPA/BRO/E/4, Wellcome Library, London.
[17] 'Board Minute, 28 June 1996', SA/FPA/BRO/B/14, Wellcome Library, London.
Stephen Peckham, Roger Ingham, and Ian Diamond, *Teenage Pregnancy: Prevention and Programmes* (University of Southampton, 1996).

encouraged responsible sexual behaviours in the young in order to counter accusations of encouraging promiscuity. In addition, Brook recurrently maintained a public stance affirming that young people who turned to Brook centres for help were displaying responsible behaviours. Furthermore, they argued that the majority of their clients were not promiscuous but in steady and committed relationships. To spread this message, Brook relied on clinical statistics, transmitted to the press through their annual reports and press releases, which described their work and their clientele. For instance, in 1971, the charity issued a press release following the visit of Lord Aberdere, minister of state for the DHSS. This release highlighted the profile of clients and showed that Brook was responding to clients' demand for responsibility. A subsection of the press release was purposely entitled 'Brook's girls not "promiscuous"'. This section provided statistics to back up the claim that these young women were in steady relationships. 'Despite generalisations now common about promiscuity among teenagers, in a two-year follow up of some 600 patients at Kings College Hospital BAC it was found that only 6% had changed partner.'[18]

In addition, Brook invited journalists to visit their clinics and report on their work. Several such visits covered the opening of various Brook centres.[19] In 1970, the agony aunt Evelyn Home of *Woman* visited Brook in London.[20] In addition, Brook hired a public relations officer in 1969. Valerie Gilbert (1969–1974) and press and information officer Suzie Hayman (1975–1984) encouraged magazines to mention BAC to their readers.[21] This job involved making Brook services widely known in the media as well as reacting to articles written on young people's sexuality. In a private interview, Suzie Hayman reflected on this work:

> What I was mainly doing was press, so my first sort of task was to send a letter to all the papers saying, I'm Suzie Hayman and I'm now Brook advisor you know, if you want any information or any questions you've got on any of these subjects, please do come, call me. Mainly what I was doing was trying to raise the profile. Okay. Um, I would do letters to press from, you know, on behalf of Caroline, which you would sign, I'd write the letter and she, you know, reacting to some reactive or raising issues. Okay. Probably, in the beginning, only reactive. And a lot of it is reactive. A lot of what this sort of

---

[18] 'Press release, 7 June 1971', in SA/BRO/D/3/3/3, Wellcome Library, London.
[19] See, for instance, 'Cases and circumstances', *Birmingham Post*, 5 September 1967, 8.
[20] 'BAC Annual Report 1970', in SA/ALR/F1, Wellcome Library, London.
[21] 'BAC Annual Report 1974', in SA/ALR/F1, Wellcome Library, London.

work is, had, necessarily is reactive, but we were trying to react to everything that was relevant to Brook. Yeah. So it would be sex education, young people, contraceptive [for] young people, um, and pregnancy, all those sorts of things. Um, but more and more, it got to the point. This is, what I was very proud of was that certainly towards the latter time, by being there, the press would come to me for a quote on any of those subjects. So there, there was a story about pregnancy, young people, blah, blah, blah. They would come to us for a quote because they knew I would be able to instantly react and give our little quote with myself or from Caroline as the, um, as the head or from Faye Hutchinson as the chief medical officer.[22]

Brook made use of different mediums to inform young people about their services, publishing informative leaflets, creating cinema advertisements, and trying to put posters and advertisements in public spaces. However, the latter proved controversial and during the first two decade of Brook's work, publicity materials were censored, showing that providing contraceptive information to young people was still deemed unacceptable. To counter these setbacks, Brook also used the mass media to make their services widely known by becoming the main expert in teenage sexuality.

Sex education materials

From their inception, Brook had not only promoted their services but also provided teaching resources and speakers for sex education in schools. Brook was not the sole organization producing sex education material; the Health Education Authority and the Family Planning Association were also active in this domain. However, Brook had the advantage of being in constant contact with young people and using their knowledge of teenage sexuality to inform their educational materials. This work reflected Brook's commitment to 'educate young people in matters of sex and contraception'. However, they realized that only a small number of young people, mostly girls, were seeking their services. Therefore, Brook understood the importance of broadening the scope of their work, which included sex education in schools and training for individuals who worked with young people.

In the first half of the twentieth century, sex education in school was virtually absent, since it was believed that it was parents' responsibility to

---

[22] Suzie Hayman, private interview, 19 September 2018.

teach their children about the facts of life. From the Second World War onwards, attitudes started to shift in line with growing concerns about the moral and physical health of the nation and the increasing incidence of venereal diseases. This prompted the Board of Education to publish an advisory pamphlet on sex education in 1943.[23] However, sex education remained non-compulsory, and it was left up to individual schools to design their sex education programmes. Up until the 1960s, there was an unofficial consensus on the benefit of sex education as a public health measure to combat the spread of venereal diseases and as a tool to ingrain traditional moral sexual roles.[24] The responsibility for sex education was shared between the Departments of Health and Education. While the Department of Health was in favour of developing policy on the subject, the Department of Education, fearing controversy, resisted the idea. The two Departments subcontracted the responsibility to the Central Council for Health Education, which became the Health Education Council in 1968. The latter worked with independent voluntary agencies such as the National Marriage Guidance Council, the FPA, and later Brook in order to train and provide resources for teachers. By the 1970s, many schools offered sex education classes with content on relationships instead of a narrow focus on the facts of life. However, as Hannah Charnock's work on teenagers and sexual knowledge between 1950 and 1980 has illustrated, the sort of sex education that was increasingly provided at school was nevertheless deemed inadequate by young people.[25]

During the 1980s, conservative groups strongly opposed sex education in schools, resulting in a shift of decision-making power from the government to parents regarding the content of sex education. With this vilification of sex education, the government lost its decisional power to parents regarding sex education in the classroom. The Education Bill of 1986 gave school governing bodies the responsibility to determine the content of sex education with 'due regard to moral considerations and the value of family life'. This abolition of Local Education Authorities and the consequent devolution of power to school governors meant that the latter were more susceptible

---

[23] Board of Education, *Sex Education in Schools and Youth Organisations* (His Majesty's Stationary Office, 1943).
[24] Lesley Hall, 'Birds, Bees and General Embarrassment: Sex Education in Britain from Social Purity to Section 2', in Richard Aldrich (ed.), *Public or Private Education?: Lessons from History* (Woburn Press, 2004): 93–112; Hall, 'In Ignorance and in Knowledge: Reflections on the History of Sex Education in Britain'; Rachel Thomson, 'Moral rhetoric and public health pragmatism: The recent politics of sex education', *Feminist Review* 48.1 (1994): 40–60; Thomson, 'Prevention, Promotion and Adolescent Sexuality'; Hampshire and Lewis, 'The ravages of permissiveness'.
[25] Hannah Charnock, *Girlhood, Sexuality and Identity in England, 1950–1980* (University of Exeter, 2017); Charnock, 'Teenage Girls'.

to parental pressures. The bill also enabled parents to opt their children out of sex education classes.[26] In 1988, with the introduction of the national curriculum, some aspects of sex education became compulsory; 'biological' aspects of sex education had to be taught within the curriculum for science. The same year, the Local Government Act introduced Section 28, which stated that local authorities should not promote 'the teaching in any maintained school of the acceptability of homosexuality as a pretended family relationship'.[27] This clause created confusion and anxiety among those teaching sex education. It was the direct result of the 1986 media panic and controversy over the use in schools of the children's book *Jenny Lives with Eric and Martin*, the story of a little girl who lived with a homosexual couple.[28] In the wake of this debate, the Sex Education Forum was created, comprised of eight members: the Health Visitors Association, the Catholic Marriage Advisory Council (Marriage Care), the Health Education Authority, the National Marriage Guidance Council (RELATE), SPOD (a sexual health charity for people with disability), the Family Planning Association, Brook Advisory Centre, and the National Children's Bureau. Its aim was to develop 'a common set of values for sex education that all members could sign up to'.[29]

In 1991, the secretary of state for education, Kenneth Baker, introduced the study of HIV/AIDS to the science curriculum. However, this move sparked a significant political debate, which ultimately resulted in the Education Act 1993. This act made biological reproduction a compulsory part of the curriculum, but removed all 'non-biological' topics, including discussion about sexually transmitted diseases and HIV/AIDS. The Education Act of 1993 also granted parents the right to withdraw their children from sex education lessons that were outside of the national curriculum. This meant that some children may not have received comprehensive information about sexually transmitted diseases or HIV/AIDS if their parents opted them out of these lessons.

Brook's work in sex education took place in this changing and hostile climate. It started in Birmingham Brook, which set up a 'talks and sex

---

[26] Joe Moran, 'Childhood sexuality and education: The case of Section 28', *Sexualities* 4.1 (2001): 73–89.

[27] 2A(1) Local Government Act 1986, created by S.28 Local Government Act 1988. See Jeffrey Weeks, 'CLAUSE 28', *Marriage, Domestic Life, and Social Change: Writings for Jacqueline Burgoyne, 1944–88* (1991): 178.

[28] Adam Mars-Jones, 'The book that launched clause 28', *Index on Censorship* 17.8 (1988): 37–40.

[29] *Our history, 30 years of campaigning*. Available online: https://www.sexeducationforum.org.uk/about/our-history-30-years-campaigning

education group' in 1969.³⁰ Nine evening lectures on sex education for teachers were given in the autumn of 1969, followed by a similar course in 1970.³¹ Meanwhile, in Bristol, Brook members were increasingly called upon to provide 'factual information on birth control and talks on personal relations'.³² As a result, a seminar was organized in 1970 entitled 'Sex Education and the role of Brook'. The seminar took place at Bristol University and was attended by Brook workers from London, Birmingham, Edinburgh, and Coventry, as well as many social workers, teachers, and individuals involved in education.³³ In each Brook branch, requests were regularly made for Brook members to give talks in schools or to train teachers to do so. For instance, in 1974, Brook members had undertaken more than 150 speaking engagements to over 10,000 people, from small groups in schools and youth clubs to large public meetings of women's organizations.³⁴ In 1982, again, more than 150 talks were given in schools and to youth groups.³⁵ As remembered by counsellor Dorothy van Heeswyk, who visited local schools in Brixton, 'it was important to set up time after the lecture with only young people for them to come and speak privately'.³⁶

The provision of sex education in a variety of educational settings was enhanced by the development of teaching materials. This work was pioneered by Birmingham Brook, who in 1969 recognized the need to assess the available materials and visual aids and subsequently created their own educational resources to meet the demand from teachers. They produced taped interviews as teaching resources that would aid in the discussion of sexual knowledge. For instance, the *Hello Gorgeous* series consisted of seven interviews with young girls and mothers about sexual relationships and sex education. Similarly, *Boys Talking* was a series of interviews with boys between the ages of 14 and 18, which aimed to promote group discussion on topics such as 'they are all after the same thing', 'boys talk about it more than girls', 'who makes the first move', and 'I suppose I was really a bit of a fool'.³⁷ By placing the lived sexual experiences of young people at the centre of the narrative, these tapes were able to connect with the young audience on an emotional level, creating a sense of community. Furthermore, by integrating the voices of young men, Brook subtly conveyed the message that contraception was not solely the

---

[30] 'Birmingham BAC, Annual Report, 1969', in SA/ALR/F1, Wellcome Library, London.
[31] 'BAC Annual Report, 1969', in SA/ALR/F1, Wellcome Library, London.
[32] 'Wessex Branch BAC, Annual Report, 1971', in SA/BRO/D/1/1/1, Wellcome Library, London.
[33] Ibid.   [34] 'BAC Annual Report, 1974', in SA/ALR/F1, Wellcome Library, London.
[35] 'BAC Annual Report, 1982', in SA/BRO/E/1/2, Wellcome Library, London.
[36] Dorothy van Heeswyk, private interview, 11 November 2022.
[37] 'BAC Annual Report 1974', in SA/ALR/F1, Wellcome Library, London.

responsibility of girls; boys too had a role to play. By highlighting the emotional struggles and anxieties associated with sexual relations, Brook recognized that these issues were shared by both sexes.

In addition to this material produced for teachers by Birmingham Brook, counsellor Pauline Crabbe and Dr Ruth MacGillivray, from London Brook, worked in partnership with the Medical Recording Service Foundation in 1974 to produce two tapes, *Abortion counselling* and *Counselling for young people*, for medical professionals.[38] The Medical Recording Service Foundation, which later became the Graves Medical Audiovisual Library, was an educational charity whose goal was to use audio-visual materials for medical and paramedical education. Started by the doctors John and Valerie Graves in 1957 as an offshoot of the College of General Practitioners, it became the leading supplier of audio-visual materials for medical education.[39] Unfortunately, I was unable to find the tapes; however, their description in the 1974 annual report offers some insights into their content. *Abortion counselling* was described as a discussion between Crabbe and MacGillivray on how they handled the problem of abortion counselling, including topics such as confirmation of pregnancy; discussion with clients regarding what they needed to know about abortion; those who needed advice and why they came; and future actions of referral to gynaecologists, ante-natal clinics, and contraception. *Counselling for young people* was described as a discussion on the problems of teenagers aged 15 to 18 who lived in the period defined as the sexual revolution. It covered issues such as 'young people's outward composure may cover a lot of fears; the inarticulate youngster who may find it difficult to communicate and have inaccurate information; the serious emotional problems; the medical approach; the interview; the confidence of the consultation'.[40]

Alongside these audio and video materials, Brook produced a comprehensive range of educational materials, including leaflets and teaching packs aimed at teachers, schoolchildren, and clients. Through these materials, Brook developed a recognizable style that employed simple vocabulary and graphically explicit materials to approach discussion of sex and contraception in a down-to-earth, direct manner. This approach is exemplified in the 1973 eight-page leaflet *Safe Sex, contraception,* as shown in Figure 7.1 which Birmingham Brook created in order to address the questions most frequently asked by their clients. The leaflet presented all the available methods of birth

---

[38] Ibid.   [39] Available online: https://wellcomecollection.org/works/ptawt3ap
[40] 'BAC Annual Report 1974', in SA/ALR/F1, Wellcome Library, London.

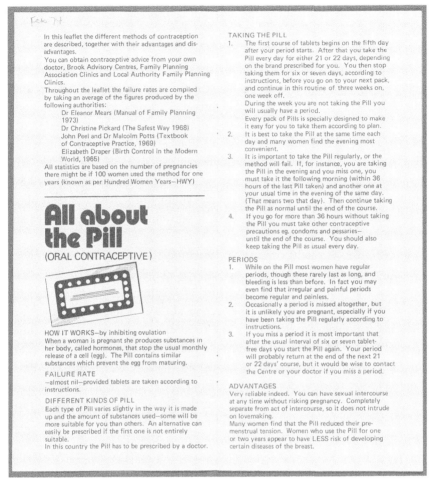

Figure 7.1 Safe sex contraception
SA/BRO/E/5, Wellcome Library, London

control at that time, along with the advantages and effectiveness of each method, using drawings to illustrate the different options.[41] Moreover, the leaflet listed the brand names of contraceptives that did not need a doctor's prescription. The purpose was to enable young people 'to go to a chemist and ask for exactly what they want[ed]'.[42]

In 1976, Brook produced the *Safe Sex* kit, a teaching tool designed to provide factual contraceptive information by showing a young couple's visit

---

[41] 'Safe Sex, contraception', in SA/BRO/E/5, Wellcome Library, London.
[42] 'Safe Sex, Press Release', 1973, in SA/BRO/B1/3, Wellcome Library, London.

to a doctor. The kit included the *Safe Sex, contraception* leaflet and a set of contraceptive samples, such as a pill packet, IUDs, sheaths, caps, cream foams, and pessaries.[43]

Overall, Brook's educational materials were instrumental in promoting a better understanding of sexual health and contraception by providing accurate information in a clear and accessible format. This production of educational material was formalized through the opening of the Publication and Education Unit in 1978, funded partly through an annual grant from the Department of Health and Social Security. The unit created new materials for teachers and responded to demands for information. In 1981, the unit replied to 1,800 written letters authored by young people, youth workers, and parents about information on contraception; in 1982, it sent out more than 30,000 educational materials.[44]

In 1980, Brook produced four new teaching aids aimed at promoting sex education and contraception. The first aid was a booklet titled *Abortion*, which provided information on the procedure of obtaining an abortion and the different ways to go about it. The second aid was a discussion tape titled *Girls talking about sex education*. The third aid was a set of slides entitled *Gyneacological Examination,* featuring a naked female model and a doctor; this showcased the examination procedure. Finally, the fourth aid was a *Contraception teaching pack*, which offered advice and material for teachers to use when introducing the topic of contraception.[45] The pack covered three main themes: biology of sex; methods of contraception; and use of contraception. Each was arranged around resource materials that featured visual graphics, typical of Brook's style. For instance, the leaflet *A Look at your body* combined a frontal depiction of the male and female genitals with an identification of the different anatomical parts and cut-side views of the same genitals. These visual illustrations allowed students to grasp the concept of male and female sexual anatomy more easily.[46] In addition to these aids, the teaching pack also contained more sophisticated materials, such as roleplay activities and fictional letters to agony aunts. These materials were designed to foster group discussion on a wide variety of topics, including sexual experimentation, relationships, consent, and intergenerational discussion. By providing students with a safe space to discuss these topics, the materials helped raise awareness about safe sex practices and sexual responsibility.

[43] 'BAC Annual Report 1976', in SA/ALR/F1, Wellcome Library, London.
[44] 'BAC Annual Report, 1981 and 1983', in SA/BRO/E/1/2, Wellcome Library, London.
[45] 'Education and Publication Unit Catalogue, 1981', in SA/BRO/E/6, Wellcome Library, London.
[46] 'Teaching pack', in SA/BRO/J4/1, Wellcome Library, London.

This teaching pack proved controversial and was attacked by conservative lobbies, such as the Responsible Society and Conservative MPs, who accused Brook of offering 'a mechanical view of sex outside the context of love and the family'.[47] Indeed, Valerie Riches, general secretary of the Responsible Society, wrote an article published in the *Daily Telegraph* on 13 March 1980 entitled 'The sex industry versus the parents'. In it, she claimed that Brook educational materials reflected a specific philosophy whereby children should be liberated from the repressive attitudes of parents and teachers and that sex should be dissociated from emotions.[48] This debate also reached the political arena; in 1981, Tory MP James Pawsey used a late-night debate in the Commons to qualify the pack's content as pornographic, stating that it 'contained some of the most pornographic material I have ever seen'.[49] This was picked up by the *Daily Telegraph*.[50] Pawsey denounced the leaflet's graphic illustrations, arguing that it contained 'full frontals and goes into considerable details about sexual intercourse'. The chairman of Brook, Caroline Woodroffe, replied to Pawsey's comment in a brief letter published in *The Guardian* entitled 'Body talk for honesty'.[51] She asked, '[Do you] really think you can illustrate how to use a condom or cap with drawings of fully dressed people?', pinpointing the ridiculousness of teaching young people about contraception without using images of naked bodies. Suzie Hayman also differentiated the visual materials used by the leaflet from obscene materials by stressing that the drawings were 'artistic[,] very gentle and not crude and they could be seen any day in the National Gallery'.[52] She also drew a clear line between pornography, which was meant 'to titillate and excite',[53] and Brook material, which was used to educate and inform. However, the conservative lobby was powerful and put pressure on the Department of Health and Social Security, who made its funding of Brook conditional on the removal of teaching aid materials such as the *Look at safe sex* leaflet (see Figure 7.2), a wordsearch puzzle about contraception that was said to present contraception as a game, and a tape recording of girls talking about choosing safe sex. These items were censored because they provided factual information on contraception without reference to marriage and offered visual depictions of naked bodies. This censorship

---

[47] Sandra Hempel, 'Health minister intervenes after material is criticised: Sex study pack toned down', *Times Education Supplement*, 30 July 1981.
[48] Valerie Riches, 'The sex industry, versus the parents', *Daily Telegraph*, 13 March 1980.
[49] 'Pregnancy advice pack puts grant at risk', *The Guardian*, 12 June 1981.
[50] 'Sex teaching aid pornographic claims Tory MP', *Daily Telegraph*, 3 June 1981.
[51] Caroline Woodroffe, 'Body talk for honesty', *The Guardian*, 6 June 1981.
[52] 'Sex teaching aid pornographic claims Tory MP', *Daily Telegraph*, 3 June 1981.
[53] 'Sex guide is pornographic', *Pulse*, 13 June 1981.

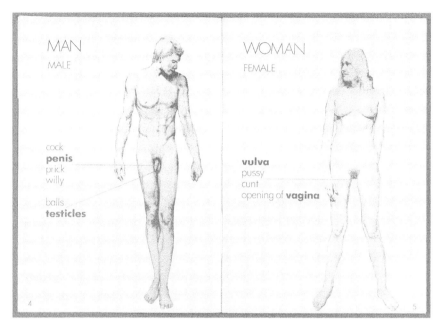

Figure 7.2 A look at safe sex: Contraception, birth control, family planning, 1978
SA/BRO/E/5, Wellcome Library, London

shows the boundaries of what was considered acceptable in a climate where conservative moralists were gaining increasing power over the Department of Health and Social Security.

In addition, and as a result of the controversy around the contraception teaching pack, tight control by the Department of Education and Science (DES) was implemented through the setting up of the School Publication Advisory panel to advise Brook on the educational material they produced specifically for use in schools.[54] This panel was made up of Brook members and experts in the field of education and was guided by the DES representative Jasper Ungoed Thomas. However, the influence of the DES was contained to education materials aimed at schools. As a result, another unit was created in BAC—the 'Out of school' publication unit—which was free from the oversight of the DES, and consequently enjoyed greater freedom.

The education and publication unit officer Reverend Jane Fraser was in charge of creating educational materials. In subsequent years, a revision of the contraceptive teaching pack was undertaken, and the visual representation

---

[54] On the role BAC played in creating sex education material during the AIDS crises, see Elizabeth, 'Love carefully and without "over-bearing fears"'.

of naked bodies was adapted with a transversal view and the removal of colloquial language. In 1989, Brook launched *Taught not Caught. Strategies for sex education*, a resource book for use in the school setting aimed at 9- to 16-year-olds, followed in 1990 by another resource book aimed at 5- to 11-year-olds, *Knowing me, Knowing you, Strategies for sex education in the primary school*. This book contained active cross-curriculum lesson plans, workshops for parents, governors, and teachers, and activities for pupils. The materials produced in the book were trialled and tested in the classroom.[55] In 1998, Brook's educational materials for school were collected in booklet guides with information on each resource, such as target age, aims, and knowledge acquisition.[56] Through this multilayered work, Brook played a key role in shaping school pupils' sexual knowledge and fostering discussion on sexual relationships.

HIV and AIDS

In the late 1980s, Brook also started to produce some information leaflets through its out-of-school publication unit in the context of AIDS, adopting a new stylistic approach that borrowed from comic books and teenage magazines. Recent works have paid increasing attention to public health campaigns during the AIDS crisis. By the end of 1981, self-help voluntary communities of homosexual men started to emerge, campaigning for raised awareness about AIDS, providing emotional and practical support for those affected by the disease and their partners and family, and collecting money for research.[57] In 1983, the Terrence Higgins Trust was established, followed by self-help groups such as Body Positive in 1984. Rooted in community experience, these organizations provided safe-sex education that 'help[ed] to minimise risky behaviours among gay men'. In the following decade, a growing body of voluntary organizations became involved in providing information and support about AIDS to affected communities.[58] These voluntary groups and service providers became professionalized and the government relied on them to provide a wide range of services. Brook was one of these voluntary service providers. They reacted to the AIDS crisis rapidly but in an uncoordinated manner. Indeed,

---

[55] Brook, *Making Sex Education Easier: A Guide to Sex Education and Sex Education Resources from Brook Publication* (Brook Education and Publication, 1998).
[56] Ibid.   [57] Berridge, *AIDS in the UK*.
[58] Jeffrey Weeks et al., 'Community and contracts: Tensions and dilemmas in the voluntary sector response to HIV and AIDS', *Policy Studies* 17 (1996): 108–10.

Brook local staff started to undertake some preventative work on the subject within their centres, such as offering free condoms to all clients as they left the building, as well as making them available to take in the waiting area. In addition, some doctors, nurses, and social workers started to approach the subject of HIV prevention in their consultations; consequently, Brook designed a dedicated set of guidelines (see Chapter 6). Brook also received funding to carry out outreach work in order to raise awareness about HIV. This was the case in Edinburgh; in 1988, HIV infection was estimated to affect 1 out of 100 men in the city. As a consequence, Brook received funding from the Lothian Regional Council Social Work Committee to work on three different Lothian drug projects. It was hoped that the expertise of Brook would be helpful in devising strategies to combat the spread of HIV.[59] In partnership with the Lothian Health Board AIDS team, Brook also offered training for professionals who worked with people in high-risk situations.

In addition to their work within the centres, Brook also developed educational materials for schools and for a broader audience through their out-of-school publication group. Drawing inspiration from the comic format and the vignettes of life stories typically found in teenage magazines, Brook capitalized on the success of this format to spread messages about safer sex. In 1987, the first leaflet using this new style was published under the title *Love Carefully, use a condom*. A comic book leaflet produced in tandem with the FPA, in consultation with the Terrence Higgins Trust, and funded by the DHSS, its aim was 'to specifically address the problems young heterosexual people' faced when seeking 'to protect each other from AIDS'.[60] The Brook 1987 annual report presented the leaflet, explaining that while young people were becoming more aware of AIDS and thus more fearful and worried about the disease, Brook's experience with their clients suggested that many were refusing to accept that they themselves might be at risk. Brook drew parallels with behaviour regarding unwanted pregnancy. Caroline Bailey, counsellor at a London Brook clinic, was quoted as saying: 'In the same way that some may still perceive the risk of pregnancy they say it can't happen to me.' The leaflet was said to encourage young couples to discuss the risks of AIDS, more specifically to help 'young women develop the assertion skills they need to protect themselves from AIDS',[61] and to promote the use of condoms in addition to the chosen method of contraception.

---

[59] 'BAC Annual Report, 1988', SA/BRO/E/1/2, Wellcome Library, London.

[60] Alison Hadley, *Press Release: Love Carefully—Use a Condom: Top-Ten Starts Endorse Brook Advisory Centres Leaflet for Young People* (Brook Press and Information Office, 9 April 1987).

[61] 'BAC Annual Report, 1987', in SA/BRO/E/1/3, Wellcome Library, London.

Historian Hannah Elizabeth conducted a meticulous analysis of the debates between the FPA and Brook regarding the production of this leaflet. This analysis reveals some tensions between the two institutions regarding the key message to be spread.[62] The leaflet received endorsement from three top ten pop stars through short statements, which was a tactic that Brook had already adopted for other promotional and educational materials (see the following section on Brook and young men, as well as Chapter 3 on activism). Additionally, agony aunt Melanie McFadyean from *Just Seventeen* provided basic information on AIDS and the way HIV was transmitted between individuals. The cartoon strip depicted Sylvia's difficult negotiation with her boyfriend Jim about using a condom. Two other teenagers were also present; they provided examples of good sex practices by using a condom on top of another contraceptive method. Therefore, the cartoon offered information on AIDS, 'dispelled common myths',[63] enumerated sources of information and help, and urged young people to visit a Brook or FPA clinic for free condoms.

This leaflet was followed by others that used the same cartoon strip format to encourage safer sex practices. In 1989, Brook collaborated with the Health Education Authority to publish an educational comic that would 'address the difficulties young people faced when negotiating sexual encounters, safer sex and saying "no"'. The comic also discussed the need for both sexes to understand each other's perception of sex and sexual intercourse. As part of the collaboration, a market research company was commissioned to conduct qualitative research among young people to assess the feasibility of 'using a comic format to educate them on safer sex'.[64] The research revealed that a comic format with bright colours and short dialogue would be suitable for young people aged 14–17. Titled *Say yes? Say no? Say maybe?*, the 16-page booklet was written by agony aunt Suzie Hayman and spread the message about HIV prevention and contraception with 'everyday scenarios familiar to young people'. This booklet consisted of nine headings. *How do you start?* explored the issue of making the first move and recognizing signs of interest and attraction. This section tackled gendered stereotypes, prejudices, and myths, such as girls who wear 'a tight T-shirt or a short skirt [are] asking for it' or girls who asked a boy out are 'slag' or boys who tell girls they liked them are 'fool', or girls 'shouldn't be too knowing'. The leaflets provided alternative models where boys expressed their feelings, asked girls what they wanted, and

---

[62] Elizabeth, 'Love carefully and without "over-bearing fears"'.   [63] Hadley, *Press Release*.
[64] Burns Research Partner, *Safer sex and young people: A report on a qualitative study looking at the feasibility of using a comic format to educate young people about safer sex* (1988).

asked permission before touching any part of their body. Girls were encouraged to assert themselves by making their 'feelings and wants known clearly and directly' and saying no when they did not want to do something. *When will it happen?* addressed the circumstances under which sexual relations might occur. It challenged the idea that sex 'just happened' and encouraged young people to recognize that they thought about it before it happened and therefore should be ready for it. It also challenged the belief that 'nice girls don't have sex' and argued that 'nice girls feel sexy and nice girls make love'. This section also emphasized that not 'everyone is having sex'. *The Good Grope Guide* provided information on what happens to the body during sexual arousal and penetrative intercourse. It explained that girls might take more time to reach climax and stressed the importance of taking time and stimulating the clitoris during penetrative intercourse. This section also challenged the idea that once penetrative sex occurred 'foreplay' should be abandoned. On the contrary, the leaflet emphasized the importance of foreplay and sexplay and of communicating with each other about pleasure. The next section examined HIV and AIDS and gave information on how the virus spreads. It challenged the idea that the virus only affected gay men and drug users and offered ways to protect oneself against HIV, such as using a condom at every penetrative intercourse or having sex without letting 'his semen get into her unprotected sex passage' by keeping outside. The following four sections, *Birth control blues*, *Using it*, *Getting it on*, and *Getting it* focused on the necessity of using birth control methods to be protected against unwanted pregnancies, sexual infections, and HIV. It recommended the condom as the safest method of birth control and provided information on how to put it on while maintaining sexual arousal, and also where to obtain it. The leaflet therefore presented different love practices while emphasizing protection, as exemplifying by the quotation 'You can loveplay, foreplay, any kind of sexplay...but best of all, playsafe.'[65]

This booklet was created for health promotion units, HIV coordinators, and parents in order to promote sexual health education. According to testimony published in the Brook annual report, parents praised the usefulness of the booklet, especially in situations where discussing sex with their children was difficult. One parent stated:

> I realised when I saw love-bites on my eldest son's neck that he was becoming sexually active and I have no idea how much he knew. My children, like many of their friends, regard it as an invasion of privacy if

---

[65] Brook Advisory Centre, *Say yes? Say no? Say maybe?* (Brook Advisory Centre, 1991).

I talk sex to them. I thought of giving them text books but they seem so clinical. When I saw the Brook booklet it seemed the right approach. It says everything I would like to say. It's light but not trivial. I know several friends feel the same and have put it into their children's bedroom.[66]

The leaflet was launched at a press conference chaired by Clare Rayner, who was the agony aunt for *Woman's Own*, *Petticoat*, and the *Sun* in the 1970s.

From the same collaboration, Brook published the booklet *Love bytes*, aimed at young people in their mid-teens. It provided information and advice on sexual relationships and AIDS. Using cartoon format, problem pages, letters, charts, and an information sheet, the script delivered a positive message about the enjoyability and acceptability of non-penetrative sex. Additionally, it stressed the importance of using condoms during penetrative sex in order to prevent the transmission of sexually transmitted infections.[67]

In 1993, three leaflets were designed using the cartoon style with the goal of reinforcing messages about safer sex: *Cool it, Do you come here often?*, and *What turns you on?* Presented as a complement to *Love Carefully*, these leaflets were produced 'in response to a growing awareness of young people's lack of information about safer sex and the need to encourage non-penetrative sex practices'.[68] Their target audience was young people who had just started relationships or who were about to do so. The leaflets were designed to be used by health educators and youth workers as triggers for discussion. Each leaflet addressed similar topics, but in slightly different ways.

Cool it (see Figure 7.3) emphasized the benefits of delaying sexual intercourse to allow young people to get to know each other better and of trying to provide pleasure through means other than penetrative sex. It also reinforced the idea of using a condom during every instance of sexual intercourse. *Do you come here often?* (see Figure 7.4) stressed that not everyone was having sex or found sex pleasurable. It encouraged discussion about sexual practices, pleasure, and safer sex. *Whatever turns you on* (see Figure 7.5) focused on different means of providing pleasure, such as kissing, licking, sucking, and masturbating. The three leaflets also provided information on HIV and its transmission, as well as safer sex practices. Importantly, these leaflets conveyed a positive attitude to young people's sexuality, underlying pleasure and enjoyment while spreading the message about safer sex. They shifted the focus away from

---

[66] 'BAC Annual Report, 1991', in SA/BRO/E/1/3, Wellcome Library, London.
[67] 'Love Bytes, in Model Penis pack content', in SA/BRO/C/6/2, Wellcome Library, London.
[68] Brook Advisory Centre, *A new approach in education in safer sex* (1993). Available online: https://wellcomecollection.org/works/fjscvqng

Figure 7.3 Brook, *Cool it*, 1993
Wellcome Collection

Figure 7.4 Brook, *Do you come here often?* 1993
Wellcome Collection

Figure 7.5 Brook, *Whatever turns you on*, 1993
Wellcome Collection

penetrative sex as the only form of sexual intercourse, helping to 'queer' teenage sexuality by stating that the leaflets were meant to 'encourage young people to see giving and receiving sexual pleasure in terms other than penetrative sex'.[69] Indeed, Brook aimed to share information on pleasure-seeking activities with low risk of sexually transmitted disease and pregnancy. By emphasizing the importance of self-masturbation to get to know one's body in order to learn what felt pleasurable, Brook contributed to creating new meanings of sexual relations with pleasure at the centre of the argument. This was radical and queered the heteronormative vision of pleasurable sex by offering alternative models to sex other than 'penis and vagina', and fully integrated young women's sexual pleasure as essential in sexual relations. They wrote: 'There is a lot of things you can try. There is kissing, cuddling, tickling, stroking, massages, fondling and you can finger and rub each other to climax.' While Brook tapped into gendered representations of teenage behaviour such as the fact that young men tended to boast about their sexual prowess and that same-gender friends discussed their sexual experiences together while mixed-gender friends did not, the leaflets also challenged these narratives by emphasizing young boys' fear of sexual performance and inadequacy. In *Cool it*, a young boy is seen at a party boasting about his sex life to his friends by saying 'and it was so wild I thought the bed would go through the floor'. The boy is later seen confessing to one of his friends that it was in fact 'crap' and he felt so 'embarrassed' and 'could not go on with it'. The friend then shared his own sexual experience with his girlfriend Paula, which was limited to sex play, and emphasized that when they eventually felt ready to have sex, 'we know what make each other tick'.[70] Contrary to gender stereotypes, the discussion occurred between two boys rather than two girls and it was a male friend who recommended forms of sexual relations other than penetrative intercourse.

However, in *Do you come here often?*, gender stereotypes are depicted, with a young boy, Steve, pressuring his girlfriend Kerry to have penetrative sex and getting angry when she refuses. Kerry is then seen crying with her female best friend, who gently explains that she has a great time with her boyfriend but without going 'all the way', and shares different ways of providing and receiving pleasure through 'a good snog' or 'stroke each other all over'. While the leaflet provided information on non-penetrative sex, its teenage characters were nevertheless traditional in their gendered behaviours.

[69] 'Whatever turns you on', in PP/MEW/C/3/7, Wellcome Library, London.
[70] Brook, *Cool it* (1993). Available online: https://wellcomecollection.org/works/c5wp8mgh

Finally, in *Whatever turns you on*, a young couple is seen discussing the fact that one of their female friends feared she might be pregnant. The boyfriend first says 'you', then corrects his choice of word with 'we', must go to the doctor. The young couple is then seen in a Brook clinic discussing with a doctor or nurse about safer sex and different ways to provide pleasure without penetrative sex. The leaflet strongly emphasizes the shared responsibility of using contraception and engaging in sexual behaviour.

In 1995, on World AIDS Day, three more leaflets were published to stress the importance of using two methods of birth control—the pill and the condom—in order to protect against unwanted pregnancy and sexually transmitted diseases. *But that's the double dutch*, *Play safe on holiday* and *The cool lovers' guide to slick condom use* followed the recognizable style of Brook with a colourful comic format and were successfully trialled with young people.[71]

Over the years, sex education materials produced by Brook evolved in both style and content. Initially, the focus of Brook's sex education materials was to provide information about contraceptive methods and safer sex practice through the use of graphics, illustrations, roleplays, and various activities that promoted responsible sexual behaviour. However, as time passed, the materials increasingly emphasized the importance of enjoyable and safe sexual experiences, which included the use of condoms. The use of condoms became central in leaflets produced in the late 1980s and early 1990s, as a way of protecting oneself against HIV and sexual and transmitted diseases. To communicate this message effectively, Brook utilized cartoons as a format for engaging and educating young people. This approach was found to be particularly effective for capturing their attention and interest. Additionally, Brook also leveraged the endorsement of teen celebrities on occasion to increase the reach and impact of the message.

Inclusive sexual health information

Sex education and information on sex and contraception were key to Brook's aims to educate young people and instil in them a sense of responsibility through safer sex practices. The content of the information provided, as well as the target audience, demonstrates Brook's commitment to providing inclusive services. In fact, Brook pioneered a new initiative in improving access to sexual health information and services for 'physically handicapped and mentally

[71] 'BAC Annual Report, 1995', in SA/BRO/E/1/3, Wellcome Library, London.

subnormal young people', to use the terminology of the time. They also paid increasing attention to inclusion of young people from sexual minorities and minority ethnic backgrounds.

In the early 1970s, following the rediscovery of poverty and the subsequent push towards a reduction of inequality, disabled people finally became a new 'worthy target for state-funded provision'.[72] This was illustrated by the passing of the Chronically Sick and Disabled Person Act of 1970, which gave people with disabilities the right to equal access to recreational and educational facilities. In the context of growing recognition of the rights and needs of disabled people, Brook developed a new dimension to their work. This first occurred in Birmingham. From July 1970, a team of doctors, nurses, and social workers with a special grant from local authority made special visits to a hostel for 'young adult spastics'. According to the Brook Annual Report, 'the young people are relieved to have their sexual needs recognised and discussed and contraceptives prescribed when needed'.[73]

In 1974, Brook participated in a working group on the sexual needs of blind and/or deaf young people. In addition, Birmingham also utilized two films, *Touching*, part of a series of films designed to encourage children to explore ways to heighten sensory awareness, and *Just what can you do*, as teaching resources to use with young people with disabilities. In 1976, Birmingham Brook produced a tape talking about contraception for blind people. In 1978, Brook created the *Look at Safe Sex* leaflet for young people with learning and reading difficulties. It graphically depicted the different methods of birth control (and the ways to insert them) through the use of young women and men's naked bodies and the language used by young people to describe genitalia alongside their scientific homonyms.[74]

Brook felt that physically disabled young people's sexual needs were not being met and thus made a video entitled 'Why is it for them and not me?' in 1983. This video featured four young adults with 'congenital or derived disability', discussing their lack of sex education and their sexual needs. For the creation of the video, Brook worked in tandem with the Spastics Society and SPOD (Sexual and Personal Relationships and the Disabled). At the launch of the video, the secretary of the All-Party Disablement Group recognized the role played by Brook in enabling disabled young people to live

---

[72] Jameel Hampton, *Disability and the Welfare State in Britain* (Policy Press, 2016): 82.
[73] 'BAC Annual Report, 1972', in SA/ALR/F1, Wellcome Library London.
[74] The nature of the information, however, proved controversial and BAC was attacked by conservative lobbies such as the Responsible Society. On this issue, see Rusterholz, 'A mechanical view of sex outside the context of love and the family'.

fulfilling lives: 'In our efforts to integrate disabled people into the community and enable them to lead fuller lives, we have sadly neglected to give sufficient understanding and attention to their emotional and sexual needs. Attitudes run deep and there is a tremendous need for education. I welcome this film as a step forward in that direction.'[75] Easy access to Brook centres for people with mobility issues was also added to the agenda in 1983. Edinburgh Brook received a grant to accommodate wheelchair users.[76] However, adapting the centres' infrastructure was not the norm and this was due to the lack of funding that prevented Brook to find adequate premises for their centres. In London, for instance, the Tottenham Court Road centre was in an old building, on the third floor and without a lift. This meant that people with mobility issues could not access the Brook services.

Young people with learning disabilities also attracted Brook's attention. In 1983, sex education for this group expanded dramatically. The Sex Education Resources Centre in Avon, set up in 1978, worked with Avon Health Office to arrange three training days for carers and developed a syllabus for a twelve-session course with disabled young people aged 18 and over. In Edinburgh in 1983, counsellors met with a group of disabled women to discuss their needs and devised policy accordingly.[77]

In addition, social worker Dorothy Keeping created a felt cut-out doll mounted on stiff cardboard and dressed in removable clothes in order to explain sex education to young people with learning disabilities. This doll, named Daisy by the young people, was part of a broader social and sex education programme consisting of 13 units. In 1983, Dorothy Keeping was pictured in the annual Brook report using the Daisy doll, surrounded by disabled teenagers, who were listening attentively. She received a grant from the Health Education Council to evaluate this programme; over four years, the programme was extensively tested in various settings such as 'Adult Training Centres, mental handicap hospitals, residential units, as part of independent living schemes and with pupils in their final year at special school'. The programme was then amended by Reverend Jane Fraser based on the input received by participants.[78]

In 1987 the programme was officially launched under the title *Not a child anymore*; it included a wide range of materials and teaching aids. The

---

[75] Quoted in 'BAC Annual Report 1981', in SA/ALR/F1, Wellcome Library, London.
[76] 'Edinburgh annual report, 1983/84', in SA/BRO/D/7/1/1, Wellcome Library, London.
[77] Ibid.
[78] 'Brook Advisory Centre, A complete social and educational programme for young adults with mental handicap, *Not a child anymore*', in SA/BRO/B/1/10, Wellcome Library, London.

programme contained male and female clothed models, which could be assembled to demonstrate states of reproduction such as ovulation, pregnancy, and birth. In addition, the models could be used to train recognition of body parts, identify male and female differences, teach appropriate ways of touching, and explain sexual intercourse. The programme also provided guidance on how to tackle 'unwanted sexual advances and how to resist by both words and action'.[79] This was especially important as disabled young people might have encountered instances of abuses, and for some, they might have been unable to identify them, or oppose them.

The teaching aids offered a wealth of information that could be adapted to meet the unique needs of care workers. Their flexibility proved to be a key factor in the programme's success, with numerous articles in the mass media highlighting its quality. To promote the launch of the teaching aid pack, Jane Fraser, the Education and Publication Unit Project officer and author of the teaching aid notes, organized a series of workshops in London, Birmingham, and Edinburgh for care and social workers. These workshops offered valuable information about the pack's content and showed how it could be tailored to suit the varying developmental needs of young people with disabilities. The workshops were well received and helped to raise awareness about the programme among professionals in the field.

Brook's commitment to inclusion went beyond addressing the needs of young people with learning and physical disabilities; they also sought to include all sexual identities. Their educational materials were initially focused on young heterosexuals, particularly young women, as the centres had been established to address unwanted pregnancies and illegitimate births; however, over time, Brook began to include resources in their educational kit to help individuals come to terms with their sexuality and accept their sexual orientation. For instance, in 1985, the Education and Publication Unit designed discussion cards for use in classrooms to stimulate debates on a variety of topics. One card discussed violence against young men; it featured Duncan and Calum, two boys who took swimming lessons. Duncan's father was worried about an abduction in a nearby village and insisted on picking up the boys after practice. Embarrassed by the situation, Duncan suggested they leave the building through the backdoor. As they crossed some wasteland to reach a friend's house, a group of boys surrounded them, made derogatory comments about their short hair and swimming attire, and

---

[79] 'Jane Fraser, *Not a child anymore*, extension notes, 25 April 1989', in SA/BRO/B/1/10, Wellcome Library, London.

called them 'poofsters'.[80] The suggested discussion questions centred on whether appearance could indicate sexual orientation and the need to conform to a macho image.

Brook's commitment to inclusive sex education was further asserted during the controversy surrounding Section 28. The charity publicly expressed concern 'about the impact of the clause on sex education'.[81] They reiterated their belief that the purpose of sex education was 'to help young people come to terms with their sexuality and sexual orientation'. Brook argued that sex education should be free to initiate 'open and informed discussion' on a wide range of subjects, including homosexuality 'in a bid to overcome the widespread ignorance and misinformation'. Rather than being subject to restrictive legislation, homosexuality should be integrated into a comprehensive sex education programme. This was particularly urgent in light of the emergence of AIDS, as there was a pressing need to replace fear, ignorance, and prejudice with accurate information, confidence, and responsibility. Brook concluded that Section 28 was incompatible with these goals.

In the 1990s, there was an increasing focus on gay and lesbian communities; this was reflected in a report commissioned by Brook in 1998 on young people's views about good sex advice services. The report not only ensured a diverse sample in terms of sexual orientation but also repeatedly emphasized the needs and opinions of young gay men and lesbians.[82] The report identified confidentiality and homophobia among staff as the prime concerns for these individuals.[83] Brook took note of these findings and, in the following decade, developed new educational materials to make their services more inclusive.

Another area in which Brook aimed to produce inclusive educational and promotional materials was in their increasing sensitivity to and better representation of ethnic minorities. From 1983 onwards, the annual reports included pictures of young people from diverse ethnicities. For instance, the 1983 annual report cover featured a picture of a Black mother in a wheelchair holding her young daughter between her legs. In 1986, Brook collaborated with the FPA, Public Service Announcements, and London Weekend Television for a 30-second advertisement with the slogan 'contraception isn't a game of chance—think about it'. The advertisement featured two young

---

[80] 'Duncan and Calum discussion card', in SA/BRO/B/1/10, Wellcome Library, London.
[81] 'Letter from Fiona Fox to Board Member, BAC statement on clause 28, 21 April 1988', in SA/BRO/B/1/10, Wellcome Library, London.
[82] Egg Research and Consultancy, *Someone With a Smile Would be your Best Bet... What Young People Want from Sex Advice Services* (Brook Advisory Centre, 1998).
[83] Ibid.

women, one White and the other Black, discussing the importance of acting sexually responsible both for their own sake and for that of their family and friends. The three safer sex leaflets published in 1993 (see the previous section) also featured young people from different ethnicities. Similarly, a photoshoot organized for *Mizz* magazine in 1994 featured a young couple from diverse backgrounds visiting the Tottenham Court Road centre. The models were a young White girl and a boy from a mixed-race background.

During the discussion of various teaching packs, the issue of representing skin colour was brought up. For example, the clothes for the Daisy doll (as previously mentioned) were designed to offer a 'neutral alternative to flesh which would be racially indeterminate in colour'.[84] Similarly, in 1990, Brook produced a penis model pack where the penis was white because 'this would be nondiscriminatory and therefore not as realistic as flesh coloured model'.[85]

In addition to visually diverse representations, educational materials also acknowledged the unique needs of young people from ethnic minority backgrounds. For example, the 1987 revised version of the contraceptive teaching pack, renamed the Contraception and Relationship Resource Pack, included notes for teachers that emphasized the importance of exposing young people to a wide range of attitudes, beliefs, and practices in a multicultural and multi-ethnic society. This highlighted the need to develop awareness and understanding among young people of different cultural backgrounds.[86]

In 1989, Brook sought to replace its gynaecological examination slides with the video 'The gynaecological examination, what happened?' To aid in the production of the video, Brook commissioned a research report to obtain women's opinions on the slide set. The research aimed to explore women's knowledge and feelings about gynaecological examinations, determine their reaction to the slide set, and find ways to improve it in order to make it acceptable to women of different ethnic groups.[87] Six group discussions about the slides were conducted among women of different ethnic backgrounds: Bengali, Chinese, Hindu, Turkish, Greek-Cypriot, and Caucasian and Afro-Caribbean women. Participants were aged between 18 and 30 years, with

---

[84] 'Minutes of the Out of School Publication Group, 10 October 1986', in SA/BRO/C/6, Wellcome Library, London.
[85] 'Minutes of the sixth meeting of the out of School Publication Unit, 27 June 1990', in SA/BRO/C/6, Wellcome Library, London.
[86] 'Note to teachers, Contraception resources pack, 1987', in SA/BRO/C/6, Wellcome Library, London.
[87] MaS Research, *A study of the gynaecological examination slide set-summary report* (September 1989).

different marital statuses and sexual experiences. An interpreter was present during the 90-minute discussion.

The main findings revealed that most women were frightened about having a gynaecological examination and were shocked by the nakedness of the model, who appeared uncomfortable and nervous. Therefore, the video should instead be reassuring and sensitive, showing a model who was modestly dressed, happy, and relaxed. The report recommended that the video should include women from different ethnicities, discussing their experiences and fears of gynaecological examination. Based on these recommendations, Brook produced a video and a leaflet introducing teachers to the material. The leaflet emphasized that the video featured soundtracks in different languages: Cantonese, Greek, Turkish, Hindi, and Bengali. The leaflet also stated: 'It is recognised that particular ethnic minorities in the UK may find gynaecological examination problematic. Women in these groups appeared in the video, talking about their experience and expectation.'[88]

It is challenging to determine the effectiveness of Brook's educational materials in helping young people navigate their sexuality, since no impact study has been conducted to assess their reception. However, Brook increasingly tested their educational materials with young people and made the necessary amendments before their official release. Although the extent of the impact on young people's lives is uncertain, it is well established by sociological studies that inclusive and open sex education, as repeatedly advocated by Brook, helps create a safe environment that promote safer sex practices. Moreover, Brook argued that following the example of the Netherlands, such education could lead to fewer teenage pregnancies and delayed age at first intercourse.

Young men and contraception

While Brook was initially established to prevent unwanted pregnancies and provide counselling for young women, the centres were open to both sexes from the start. Young women were actively encouraged to bring their partners. In fact, many appointments were booked by boys over the phone; in 1973, 12% of female clients were accompanied by their boyfriends. It was not uncommon for boys to visit the centre in groups, sometimes as part of a dare, knowing that

---

[88] 'The gynaecological examination, What happened? The presenter's notes', in SA/FPA/C/G/4/6/18, Wellcome Library, London.

free condoms were available. This behaviour is indicative of a masculine culture in which boys teased each other and boasted about contraception. By 1981 in London, male clients represented 2% of all new clients in London; this increased to 3% in 1982. These numbers did not include the many boys who accompanied their girlfriends.[89]

During the 1970s and 1980s, Brook and the Family Planning Association sought to shift the responsibility for contraceptive use away from women by encouraging boys to become more involved in contraceptive decision-making.[90] The promotion of condoms was a central part of this effort. However, there were significant obstacles to increasing the legitimacy and widespread use of condoms. Medical authorities did not endorse their use strongly enough and doctors were at first resistant of being a source for condoms, considering young boys requesting condoms as 'lads on the pull' rather than a sign of caring responsibility.[91] In addition, there was little public awareness or support for condoms, so publicity was hindered. To address these issues, Dilys Cossey, a member of the Birth Control Trust, authored a booklet titled *Teenage birth control, the case for the condom*, which called for a more concerted effort to promote condoms. Cossey suggested that a comprehensive advertising campaign utilizing humour and featuring popular public figures should be implemented across multiple media platforms, including TV, cinema, mass media, and teenage magazines. This use of celebrities would become routine in the following decade. Cossey also recommended that GPs provide condoms to patients and that the NHS make them available for free. By removing financial barriers to access, she hoped to increase uptake and normalize the use of condoms as a form of contraception.

In 1981, Brook produced a leaflet aimed at boys entitled *What you need to know about the sheath*, a clear refocus on the need to include boys in contraceptive decisions; this provided a clear and graphic depiction of the correct way to put on a sheath. In 1983, a TV advert jointly produced by Brook, the FPA, and the ITV television channel attracted the wrath of the IBA because they believed that the film condoned premarital sexuality. Aimed at teenage boys—more specifically urban and lower-class boys, in order to encourage them to take contraceptive precautions—the 30-second film featured the actor and singer Adam Faith, a well-known figure among teenagers.

---

[89] 'London Annual Reports 1980–1989', in SA/BRO/D10/1/2, Wellcome Library, London.
[90] Katherine Jones, '"Men too": Masculinities and contraceptive politics in late twentieth century Britain', *Contemporary British History* 34 (2020): 44–70.
[91] See press cuttings preserved in the archives of the Birth Control Campaign at the Wellcome Library, London, SA/BCC.

Taking place in a burger bar, two boys discuss the fact that their friend has got a girl pregnant. One of them says that this behaviour is not clever—that 'getting caught at 16' is nothing to be proud of and that a 'trip to the chemist' might have saved them 'a lot of grief'. Adam Faith then joins the discussion, saying, 'Any idiot can get a girl into trouble. If you want to know more about contraception, we send you a list of clinics where young people are welcome.' Then follows the main central message: 'If you're not man enough to use birth control, you're not old enough to make love.'[92] This campaign aimed to change the gender dynamic that since the commercialization of the pill, had placed the responsibility for birth control on young women. It was part of a broader and longer strategy developed by the FPA to raise awareness among young men about their role in negotiating birth control responsibly.[93] Indeed, Brook explained in their annual report and to different newspapers that the most at-risk group was sexually active teenage girls and the group least likely to receive information was the teenage boys who put them at risk. Therefore, they opted for 'an attack on the traditional macho image which leads some sexually active young men to refuse contraception and see a pregnancy as something on which to boast'. Due to censorship, Brook had to change the take-home message into 'Any idiot can get a girl into trouble, don't let it be you.'[94] This message was implicit. It was only with the AIDS crisis that more straightforward information on condoms would be allowed on TV, and only after 9 p.m.

In 1985, press officer Alison Frater published a report on the work done by Brook with young men.[95] In it, she explained that young men were likely to drop in between sessions and tended to visit the centre in small groups. When boys began to use the centres in London, Frater explained, their behaviour was loud and aggressive and disrupted the normal running of the sessions. As a result, a special session reserved for boys was set up in Walworth Brook, London, in 1982, to cater for boys' needs; the London annual reports specifically mentioned 'boys' as a subcategory.[96] In addition, as mentioned in the previous section, Brook also produced materials on AIDs that targeted young boys specifically. In June 1990, London Brook decided to make 'saving the male' the theme of their year in order 'to encourage more young men to view

---

[92] 'IBA aborts birth control film', *The Guardian*, 23 February 1983.
[93] On encouraging men to be involved in birth control, see Jones, '"Men too": Masculinities and contraceptive politics in late twentieth century Britain'.
[94] 'Faith in contraception news clip', *City Limit*, 29 December 1983.
[95] Alison Frater, *Young Men at the Brook Advisory Centre* (Family Planning Association, 1985).
[96] 'London Annual reports 1980–1989', in SA/BRO/D10/1/2, Wellcome Library, London.

relationships responsibly. We have never deliberately excluded them but it is so easy to see contraception as mainly a woman's issue',[97] said Wendy Thomas, London Brook's general manager. Finally, centres aimed solely at young men were opened. In 1994, London Brook opened one of these centres, staffed exclusively by male doctors. In Birmingham Brook in 1995, a series of five beer mats were created and distributed in pubs with a message aimed especially at young boys.

In addition to targeting young men as clients, educational materials were also created specifically for them. In response to the AIDS crisis, Brook developed resource materials that emphasized the importance of using condoms. In 1991, they published the penis model pack, see Figure 7.6 which consisted of a leaflet and a penis model that allowed condoms to be fitted on it.

The goal of the kit was to promote the correct use of condoms among young people. It was used in clinics to teach clients how to put on a condom correctly. Interestingly, in their 1991 annual report, Brook noted that young people 'often complain[ed] that condoms [were] either too small or slip[ped] off but when clients have been asked to demonstrate on the model penis how they put on a condom, Brook staff have found that many put them on inside out, finding it impossible to roll the condom down on the length of the penis.'[98] Moreover, in 1993, all branches adopted the c-card, a card that provided free

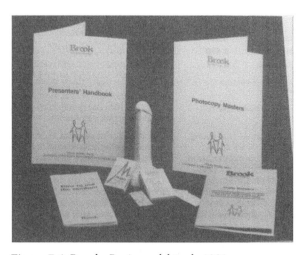

Figure 7.6 Brook, *Penis model pack*, 1991
Wellcome Collection

---

[97] 'Press release, Save the Male, 27 June 1990', in SA/FPA/C/G/4/6/18, Wellcome Library, London.
[98] 'Sexual Health, BAC Annual Report, 1990–1991', SA/BRO/E/1/3, Wellcome Library, London.

access to condoms. This was seen as a way of encouraging young boys to visit the centre and take advantage of the resources available to them.

Confidentiality

Finally, the last key concern of Brook was ensuring confidentiality when advising young people about contraception. As explained in Chapter 3, Brook fought the Gillick attempt to block the provision of contraceptive information to young people under 16 without parental approval. In the decade that followed, confidentiality became a key concern of Brook. The charity fought to change the General Medical Council's guidance to doctors regarding confidentiality and patients under the age of 16 (see Chapter 3). In 1990, with the approval of the Board, Dr Fay Hutchinson wrote to the president of the General Medical Council to share the findings of a survey conducted by Brook, which indicated that between 50% and 80% of new clients under the age of 16 did not give consent for their GP to be informed due to the fear of the GP breaching confidentiality. Brook believed that it would be in the best interest of their clients to inform their GPs, but they were unable to do so because there were no strict guidelines in place to ensure that GPs would not inform the client's parent without the client's consent.[99] Following the receipt of the letter, the GMC requested that Brook provide additional evidence on the matter.[100] In 1992, the GMC strengthened their ruling on confidentiality, stating that if a doctor breached confidentiality they must be able to prove that it was in the best interest of their patient. Although this was a positive step towards more confidential treatment, the ruling still fell short of guaranteeing confidentiality for individuals under the age of 16.[101]

In addition to lobbying the GMC, Brook published several booklets about confidentiality, not only in relation to their own services but also to other health services and for teachers. In 1989, the Education and Publication unit released a booklet entitled *Confidentiality in Secondary Schools: Ethical and Legal Issues* (England and Wales), written by Jane Fraser. This booklet examined both the theoretical and practical aspects of confidentiality in schools. It explored 'the effect of breaking a pupil's confidence, the legal framework within which teachers work and the integration of guidelines

---

[99] 'Fay Hutchinson, Letter to Sir Robert, 17 January 1990', in SA/BRO/B1/12, Wellcome Library, London.
[100] 'Minutes of the board, 27 September 1990', in SA/BRO/B1/12, Wellcome Library, London.
[101] 'Minutes of the board, 2 December 1992', in SA/BRO/B1/12, Wellcome Library, London.

into school policy'.[102] The booklet offered case studies and trigger questions in order to encourage teachers to reflect on these issues and to consider different ways of approaching a variety of potentially difficult situations, such as unwanted pregnancy and sexual abuse. The report was positively reviewed in newspapers, with the *Times* featuring a one-page article on the topic.[103]

In the 1990s, the minutes of the board meeting frequently emphasized the importance of ensuring the confidentiality of sexual health services for young people. Furthermore, in 1991, Brook members visited the Netherlands to learn about the country's successful sexual health policies, which had resulted in one of the lowest rates of teenage pregnancy at that time. The Netherlands served as a compelling example that inspired Brook. Alison Hadley, the chief policy officer, remembered that during their visit, they toured the country, met with young people, and discussed their views on sex education, contraception, and sexual and reproductive health services. She then directed her efforts towards promoting the results of her visit to the Netherlands, stressing the importance of confidentiality in sexual health services for reducing teenage pregnancies. To achieve this, she participated in an interview in *GP* magazine, where she discussed her trip to the Netherlands and the importance of confidentiality.

In line with the *Health of the Nation* goal to reduce teenage pregnancies, Brook developed various methods to spread the message about the importance of confidentiality. Brook's chairman, John McEwan, and general secretary, Margaret Jones, wrote to the Royal College of General Practitioners, requesting them to publish a statement on the 'importance of confidentiality in the sexual health care of young people'.[104] Additionally, Brook partnered with the BMA, the General Medical Service Committee, the Royal College of General Practitioners, and the FPA. With funding from the Health Education Authority, they published a guidance note on confidentiality and the under-16s. The note was launched in November 1993 and received significant press coverage. It was sent to all GP practices and family planning clinics, with doctors being reminded that the consultation must remain confidential, regardless of whether they prescribed contraception to the under-16s.[105] Brook also collaborated with the same organizations to publish the leaflet *Private and Confidential, talking to doctors*, aiming to reassure young people about the confidentiality of their consultation with a doctor. The leaflet was

---

[102] *Press Release for Confidentiality in Secondary Schools: Ethical and Legal Issues* (England and Wales).
[103] 'Miss I've got a secret', *The Times*, 19 June 1989.
[104] 'Letter from John McEwan and Margaret Jones to Dr Coline Waine, 20 November 1992', in SA/BRO/B/1/13, Wellcome Library, London.
[105] 'Minutes of BAC board meeting, 8 December 1993', in SA/BRO/B/1/14, Wellcome Library, London.

distributed with the teenage magazine *Mizz*, which had a circulation of 240,000 copies.[106] Finally, a third booklet was produced on the same subject, but with the target audience of nurses, social workers, youth workers, and teachers.[107]

Teenage magazines

As the previous example illustrates, Brook collaborated with teenage magazines to spread information about confidentiality. Yet this collaboration was not limited to raising awareness about confidentiality; from its inception, Brook recognized the key role that teenage magazines could play in advertising their services. Indeed, due to a lack of sex education, many teenagers were actively trying to find help and advice about their sex lives through other means. In this context, teenage magazines represented an important source of information for teenagers, as historians Kaye Wellings and Hannah J. Elizabeth have demonstrated.[108] Recent historical work has further shown the importance of the problem page column as a way of shedding light on the everyday sexual problems of ordinary people.[109] Tracey Loughran has explored attitudes to sex and relationships in the problem pages of mainstream women's magazines, while Laura Kelly has illuminated the sexual problems and anxieties experienced by young people as disclosed in advice columns for young Irish people.[110] Moreover, Tracey Loughran has also argued that agony aunts had an authoritative voice when providing advice on sexual and reproductive health due to drawing on experiential expertise.[111] This section adds to these recent works by exploring the relationship between Brook and teenage magazines.

---

[106] 'Minutes of BAC board meeting, 14 December 1994', in SA/BRO/B/1/12, Wellcome Library, London.

[107] Ibid.

[108] Hannah J. Elizabeth, *[Re]inventing Childhood in the Age of AIDS: The Representation of HIV Positive Identities to Children and Adolescents in Britain, 1983-1997* (unpublished PhD thesis, University of Manchester, 2016): 111–49; Kaye Wellings, *The Role of Teenage Magazines in the Sexual Health of Young People* (London School of Hygiene & Tropical Medicine: Department of Public Health and Policy, November 1996).

[109] Bingham, 'Newspaper problem pages'; Claire Langhamer, 'Everyday advice on everyday love: Romantic expertise in mid-twentieth century Britain', *L' Homme: Zeitschrift Für Feministische Geschichtswissenschaft* 1 (2013): 35–52.

[110] Tracey Loughran, 'Sex, relationships, and "everyday psychology" on British magazine problem pages, c.1960–1990', *Medical Humanities*, first published online 22 December 2022; Laura Kelly, '"Please help me, I am so miserable!" Sexual health, emotions and counselling in teen and young adult problem pages in late 1980s Ireland', *Medical Humanities*, first published online 25 October 2022.

[111] Tracey Loughran, '"The Most Helpful Friends in the World": Letters Pages, Expertise and Emotion in British Women's Magazines, c.1960–80', in Laurel Foster and Joanne Hollows (eds), *Women's Periodicals and Print Culture in Britain, 1940s–2000s: The Postwar and Contemporary Period* (Edinburgh University Press, 2020): 133–49.

Time and again, women's and teenage magazines referred readers to Brook. These referrals reflected the efforts by Brook's public relations officer Valerie Gilbert (1969–1974) and later the press and information officer Suzie Hayman (1975–1984) to encourage magazines to mention Brook to their readers. In their 1972 annual report, Brook, for the first time, referred to the role of teenage magazines in publicizing their services and advising young people. They were glad to report that 19 mentions were made of Brook in *Petticoat*, a British weekly magazine for young women, which was published from 1966 until 1975. To Brook, the misery and suffering expressed by young people in letters sent to women's and teenage magazines suggested that they lacked people to turn to for personal advice. In particular, young people did not discuss sex in the private sphere of the home, underlying the need for Brook services.[112]

Magazines such as *Oh Boy* wrote lengthy articles about topics such as 'sex and the single girl', providing advice on what to do in the case of a suspected pregnancy. In this informative article, the journalist listed the different options available to young women and in particular recommended that young women who thought that they might be pregnant or who were pregnant should discuss the issue and think over the possibilities. In this instance, Brook was the 'best known' charity to help young women consider their options.[113] In their first edition, teenage magazine *Just Seventeen* provided Brook's details to their readers.[114] In 1981, it was estimated that an average of two advice columns a month recommended Brook to their readers.

The relationship between Brook and teenage magazines was reciprocal. Magazines would refer their clients to Brook and present the charity's work in special feature articles.[115] For instance, in 1987, the UK market-leading teenage magazine *Just Seventeen* provided vignettes of clients visiting the centre for different reasons; both male and female teenagers were represented, as well as clients of different ages.[116] Sixteen-year-old Jackie had engaged in unprotected sex and wanted the morning-after pill, 17-year-old Jane (accompanied by her boyfriend) was late having her period, and 18-year-old John had just started dating a new girl and wanted some information about AIDS.

---

[112] 'BAC Annual Report 1972', in SA/ALR/F1, Wellcome Library, London.
[113] 'Sex and the single girl: I think I am pregnant', *Oh Boy*, 24 November 1984.
[114] Gillian Martins, 'Facts of life: Couples', *Just Seventeen*, 15 December 1983; Melanie McFadyean, 'Just Seventeen advice', *Just Seventeen*, 1 December 1983.
[115] Tricia Kreitman, 'Body & soul: We are not able to make love', *Mizz*, 21 July 1985; Kate Charlesworth, 'New wives' tales', *Mizz*, 24 June 1985.
[116] 'A visit to Brook', *Just Seventeen*, 22 April 1987, 19.

This article and the stories were aimed at reassuring teenagers about the prospect of a visit to Brook.

Brook members, in turn, wrote informative pieces on teenage sexuality for teenage magazines and sometimes acted as agony aunts. For instance, Brook press officer Suzie Hayman penned several articles on sexual and reproductive health for *Just Seventeen* in the 1980s.[117] In 1985, she wrote in *Just Seventeen* about the Gillick ruling, which prevented under-16s from seeking contraceptives in centres without their parents' permission.[118] This experience led Hayman to publish 'It's more than sex! A survival guide to the teenage years', a book based on her articles for the magazine and aimed at a broader audience.[119] In addition to providing expert information for readers, Dr Fay Hutchinson also worked as an agony aunt, answering letters to *Nineteen* magazine from 1980 onwards. *Nineteen* had an estimated 175,000 readers a month in 1981.

This work was carried out because Brook acknowledged that in spite of all their efforts, the clinic could not fully meet young people's need for information. As Suzie Hayman reflected: 'I got [Hutchinson] the job of being the agony aunt of *Nineteen*. And of course, that was a tremendous link because the demographic of the magazine was actually 15, 16, 17. Yeah. Um, so we got a fair number of people, I think through that, you know, they'd read that.'[120]

The close relationship between Brook and teenage magazines was further reinforced by some agony aunts co-producing educational materials with BAC. For instance, *Just Seventeen*'s agony aunt Melanie McFadyean wrote the leaflet *Love Carefully* about AIDS in tandem with Brook and the FPA.[121] In 1991, McFadyean was also present at the opening of a Brook centre in Hackney, where she met young people and answered their questions. In addition, some agony aunts were involved with the charity; Anne Lovell was the administrative manager for Brook in the late 1960s and early 1970s before she became an agony aunt at *Bella*.[122] Tricia Kreitman, agony aunt for *Mizz* magazine, became a Brook board member in 1993 and later the chair in 2001.

---

[117] Suzie Hayman, '"What boys think" about love, sex and birth control', *Just Seventeen*, 6 March 1985; Suzie Hayman, 'Teenage mothers', *Just Seventeen*, 4 October 1984.
[118] Suzie Hayman, 'The effects of the Gillick case', *Just Seventeen*, 20 March 1985.
[119] Suzie Hayman, *It's More than Sex! A Survival Guide to the Teenage Years* (Wildwood House, 1986).
[120] Private interview with Suzie Hayman.
[121] Elizabeth, 'Love carefully and without "over-bearing fears": The persuasive power of authenticity in late 1980s British AIDS education material for adolescents'.
[122] Interview with Anne Lovell by Tracey Loughran, 24 September 2018. I would like to thank Tracey Loughran, who kindly shared the transcript of her interview with me.

Nick Fisher, agony uncle for *Just Seventeen*, turned to Brook for expert information on teenage sexual health, as he explained in a private interview:

> I wasn't a psychotherapist, I wasn't a doctor, I, you know, I was a journalist who wrote a lot of features about boyfriends (laughs) and this sort of thing, and so that made me do a lot of research and get involved with the Brook Advisory Service, and all sorts of, different, erm, charities and agencies that dealt with teenagers, to kind of get as much input and information and kind of right, er, right points of view that I could get.[123]

In 1991, Brook launched the first 24-hour telephone information service to offer young people practical information on contraception, pregnancy, abortion, sexually transmitted infections, emergency contraception, and other sex-related problems.[124] The launch of the helpline also shows that Brook kept up with new forms of media and technology to get the message across its users and to communicate with them. The recorded helpline, funded by the Department of Health, aimed to give young people easy access to essential information and to encourage them to seek medical help by referring them to appropriate services. Teenage magazines widely advertised this helpline. Between 1991 and 1992, the helpline received more than 9,000 calls.[125] In 1992, Brook teamed up with *Just Seventeen* and *More* to run four separate lines on four different topics: 'Missed a period?'; 'Emergency (after sex) contraception'; 'Information on abortion'; and 'Contraception: your questions answered'. The helpline aimed to give its large teenage audience quicker access to specific information.[126] Separate lines under specific headings appeared on the problem page of each issue of the two magazines. These helplines proved extremely popular and received more than 35,000 calls a year. Based on this success, Brook renewed its collaboration with *Just Seventeen* and opened two new lines in 1992. In 'Are you ready for sex?', agony aunt Anita Naik encouraged teenagers to resist pressure to have sex and only to do so when they felt ready. On the 'Condoms' line, agony uncle Nick Fisher underlined the importance of using condoms and discussed common fears about condom use. Young men were encouraged to practice putting on condoms on their own and to obtain free supplies by visiting a Brook centre. Again, these new helplines were extremely popular. As a result, the Brook central office noticed

---

[123] Interview with Nick Fisher by Tracey Loughran, 1 September 2018.
[124] 'The Brook Helpline, Annual Report, 1992', in SA/BRO/E/3, Wellcome Library, London.
[125] Ibid.   [126] Ibid.

an increase in calls from young people wanting to talk about starting a sexual relationship.[127]

This close collaboration between agony aunts and Brook ensured a wide advertisement of the centre to readers of teenage magazines while allowing Brook to lend its credentials and expertise to agony aunts.[128] Teenage magazines were therefore considered an ideal medium to reach out to the majority of sexually active young people who would not visit a Brook centre. This seemed to work, as some Brook clients later reported visiting a centre after having read about it. For instance, Jane, who attended a Brook clinic in 1970s London, vaguely remembered having learnt about it in a magazine: 'I think there was something about, it might have been in the papers, or it might have been in one of those magazines, like *Honey* or *Nova*, you know, it was kind of in the air.'[129]

Conclusion

Over the years, Brook deployed a wide range of strategies to inform and educate young people about contraception and safer sex. Despite their dedication to this cause, they faced many challenges and obstacles, with censorship being a major hurdle. Publicizing their services proved to be difficult, as various attempts to advertise Brook on public transport and television were censored. This censorship shows the resistance of various actors and organizations to the provision of contraceptive information to young people. However, Brook did not let this deter them. Instead, they invested their efforts into creating educational materials that could reach young people in other ways. By developing accessible and informative educational resources to be used in schools and by youth workers and social workers, they were able to reach out to young people effectively.

The analysis of the content of these materials shows an evolution in focus from responsible sexual behaviours in a committed heterosexual relationship to promoting enjoyable sexual relationships while prioritizing safer sex. This shift became especially obvious with the advent of the AIDs crisis, as Brook sought to encourage sexual practices other than penetrative sex and sexually transmitted diseases became prominent in the charity's educational materials. With this new orientation, Brook, to a certain extent, queered heteronormative sex by offering alternative sexual practices, as well as tackling some gendered

---

[127] Ibid. [128] Loughran, 'Sex, relationships, and "everyday psychology"'.
[129] Private phone interview with Jane, July 2021.

behaviour, such as a lack of male involvement in thinking about and using contraception.

Brook's educational materials also evolved in style, transitioning from informative leaflets with illustrations and straightforward descriptions of contraceptives to a comic format that borrowed from the imagery of teenage magazines. This shift occurred when Brook began to conduct surveys with teenagers to assess the acceptability of their materials, reflecting the growing influence of consumerism.

In addition, Brook pioneered inclusive sex education materials. As early as the 1970s, they developed materials for young people with learning and physical difficulties. They also slowly recognized the needs of sexual minorities while also paying increasing attention to the needs of ethnic minorities. In addition, Brook promoted more equal contraceptive responsibility by encouraging boys' attendance at the clinics and developing educational materials especially for them. This focus on boys took on a new meaning with the advent of AIDS, when it became imperative to address the issue of condom negotiation between young people.

Brook also focused on informing young people about the confidentiality of their services, drawing inspiration from international examples, such as the Netherlands, to advocate for doctor–patient confidentiality for young people under 16.

Finally, Brook continuously sought to improve and expand their strategies. They engaged with experts in the field to gather new research, feedback, and recommendations, which helped them develop more targeted and effective educational materials, such as the materials on confidentiality. Brook also collaborated with other organizations to share resources and expertise, ultimately allowing them to have a greater impact in promoting safe sex practices among young people.

Overall, the examination of Brook's sex education materials reveals both tensions and continuities in their strategies over time and emphasizes the importance of adapting to changing societal contexts and needs. On the one hand, the organization was at the forefront of creating innovative, educational resources that provided accurate, comprehensive, and inclusive information about sexuality and sexual health. On the other hand, they were also forced to respond to the public health crisis that was the AIDS epidemic. Brook's work was characterized by a commitment to both innovation and responsiveness. By creating new and effective educational resources and adapting to the evolving needs of young people, Brook played a vital role in promoting positive and enjoyable safer sex.

Conclusion

This book has explored the sexual lived-experiences of young people and the ways their sexual behaviours were publicly debated and institutionally handled. The history of Brook centres reveals the ascent of a notion of responsible sexual behaviour for young people. I argue that this notion of 'responsible sexuality' functions as a useful explanatory tool to understand the so-called 'sexual revolution' period and its aftermath. Rather than a narrative of progressive sexual liberation, the concept of 'responsible sexuality' allows us to trace instances of changes and resistances over time. It offers a narrative that illuminates the recurrent anxieties created by young people and sexuality over the three decades under study. By popularizing responsible sexual behaviour among young people and the broader public, Brook played an important role in the transition towards a more positive and empowering understanding of sexuality despite a backdrop of growing moral anxieties and resistances. Brook opened at a time of increasing public debate on the perceived loosening of moral standards and the emergence of a new sexual permissiveness. To these anxieties, I have argued that Brook opposed an obverse, powerful narrative of sexual responsibility, where protected sexual relationships in a loving and committed relationship became a cornerstone in the legitimization of contraception for young people. This narrative was not entirely new. Rooted in the interwar movement of sexual reformers, the notion of individual responsibility in the sexual realm was first aimed at married individuals. Brook members reconfigured and adapted it to the young in the 1960s.

This book's emphasis on the advent of responsible sexual behaviour nuances existing research on the history of teenage pregnancies. One established notion is that it was only from the end of the 1990s, under New Labour, that teenagers were finally considered responsible individuals, capable of making rational, informed, and responsible decisions.[1] I have demonstrated

---

[1] Daniel Monk, 'Teenage Pregnancies and Sex Eeducation: Constructing the Girl/Woman Subject', in Vanessa Munro and Carl Stychin (eds), *Sexuality and the Law: Feminist Engagements* (Routledge, 2007).

that this notion of responsibility was central in Brook's work and public discourse from its onset and throughout the period under study, although its emphasis varied with historical events and debates. The permanence of the notion of sexual responsibility adds to the scholarship that challenges the traditional periodization of postwar Britain by underlying a continuity between the prewar and postwar years, and shows that responsibility for young people became paramount as early as the 1960s. Young people did not live their sex lives liberated from traditional constraints. Indeed, the gap between their views on sex and those of contemporary commentators created tensions and anxieties that affected young people's ability to fully enjoy their sexuality. Brook was founded at the very moment when this generational tension became increasingly recognized and publicly discussed. I argue that Brook was an institutional response to that tension.

Brook's focus on responsible sexual behaviours was also a way of appeasing continuous moral anxieties around youth sexuality. These anxieties evolved over time and got channelled into focused concerns about particular 'problem' groups. I have argued that these concerns were highly class-based, gendered, and racialized. The sexual behaviours of young working-class and young 'New Commonwealth immigrants', and later 'Black British' young was presented as deeply problematic. From the late 1970s up until the creation of the Teenage Pregnancy Unit in 1998, teenage motherhood became an increasingly divisive political and cultural issue. Brook intervened in this debate by emphasizing the necessity to educate young people about responsible sexual behaviours. To do so, Brook opened centres in multicultural neighbourhoods such as Brixton in London and Handsworth in Birmingham and in deprived areas such as Craigmillar in Edinburgh. Moreover, sexual activity among young people under 16 attracted the ire of conservative traditionalists. In this context, Brook fought for the expansion of the provision of contraception to under-16s and the sex education of young people in schools.

Brook's emphasis on responsible sexuality helped to shape the public debate on young people's sexuality and sexual politics. Brook worked intensely with the media and positioned itself as a reliable authority on issues around what was first described as premarital sex before being labelled teenage sexuality. Public debate brought about new norms on sexual behaviours, shifting the boundaries for what was legitimate and permissible, and new ways of enforcing these norms. Brook used mass media as a channel of communication and undertook an intense campaign aimed at tackling false claims around increasing promiscuity. I demonstrate that mass media was at once an ally in inflecting public morality and an enemy in that it provided a tribune for the conservative lobbies that attacked Brook's work. Brook used the language of social science in presenting 'true' facts, that is, statistics and case studies, to counter the recurrent claims that it was encouraging promiscuity.

Brook's impact was not limited to inflecting the public debate: it also contributed to changing sexual politics nationally and locally. Brook members campaigned for expanding access to contraceptive services for young people in different cities. Alongside other organizations, they fought to maintain access to abortion as defined in the 1967 Abortion Act and denounced attempts at preventing under-16s to seek contraceptive services. They also actively contributed to ensuring the confidentiality of contraceptive services for young people. In line with other works on voluntary organizations, this book has shown that the nature of activism and campaigning styles changed over time and that Brook's activism became professionalized while the charity increasingly put experiential expertise with a focus on emotions at the centre of its campaigning strategies and used celebrities to endorse its work.[2]

Beyond Brook's impact on public debates and sexual politics, this book has also provided insight into Brook's impact on young people's sexual behaviours. Brook influenced the creation of a modern vocabulary of the self in relationship with sexuality and the possibility for teenagers to be autonomous subjects. Through its counselling services, its educational work in secondary schools, and its public health campaigns, Brook taught young people 'responsible' sexual behaviour and the importance of using contraception, and conveyed a model of good sexuality where safer sex practices were paramount. Over the years the emphasis changed from a focus on a committed relationship as the precondition for sexual intercourse to the recognition of sexual activities as enjoyable experience if accompanied with protection against unwanted pregnancies and sexual and transmitted diseases. In the 1990s, sexual responsibility was still encouraged by Brook but its meaning had shifted to signify safer sex with an emphasis on sexual pleasure. In addition, Brook also increasingly considered the diversity of sexual identities and developed materials for young gay and lesbians clients.

Moreover, Brook also challenged gendered birth control responsibility. While Brook was at first directed to young women, young men were encouraged to attend the clinics and from the 1980s public health campaigns were designed to encourage young men to share the responsibility of birth control. With the advent of the AIDS crisis, sexual health campaigns became increasingly important in educating young people about safe sex practices and Brook

[2] Hilton et al., *The Politics of Expertise*; Crane, *Child Protection in England*.

played a major role in designing these campaigns. In addition, contraceptive practices changed, along with preferences around methods of contraception. Throughout the period under study, the pill alongside condoms retained key positions in the methods recommended by Brook.

The charity was also deeply shaped by young people's experiences and needs. Teenagers used, resisted, or manipulated the norms around the 'conduct' of sexual behaviours and influenced the development of Brook services. This book's focus on the Brook clientele offers an alternative picture of young people from the 1960s to the 1990s that provides an obverse to the well-trodden narrative about ashamed unmarried mothers and the 'problem' young. The majority of young people attending the centres were young girls wanting to protect themselves from unwanted pregnancies and showing responsibility in looking for contraception. They were very often 'in love'. This element supports Langhamer's argument that love became paramount in postwar Britain.[3] In addition, some of these young people had faced barriers in trying to secure contraception: some sought help at other services and experienced moral judgement or were turned away. Moreover, young people influenced the running of the services; their demands and needs were taken seriously, and Brook adapted its policy accordingly. Over the years, Brook integrated clients' perspectives by experimenting with educational materials, surveying clients' satisfaction and needs in sexual and reproductive health, and hiring young people into a steering committee aimed at adjusting Brook policy. As a result, a strong emphasis was put on confidentiality and the non-judgmental nature of Brook services in their publicity materials.

This book has also shown that the notion of sexual responsibility was conceived differently according to who were deemed vulnerable and in need of contraceptive advice. At first, schoolgirls and university students were thought to be particularly in need of advice, since living away from home opened up space for sexual experimentation. Teaching them responsibility was conceived as a way of empowering them and of preventing young women jeopardizing their potential careers. But the category of those 'in need of help' was flexible. It comprised those with learning disabilities, the 'socially deprived'—working-class young women and young people from Black and Minority ethnic backgrounds—and young people aged under 16. Brook developed strategies to reach out to these young people. Brook produced educational materials for disabled young people and educational materials inclusive in terms of gender, age, and ethnicity. Brook showed sensitivity to their clients'

---

[3] Langhamer, 'Love, Selfhood, and Authenticity'.

diversity by trying to reach out to minoritized young people and in opening centres in deprived areas, hiring staff from ethnic minorities and translating their education materials into different languages. However, Brook's attempt at addressing the needs of minoritized clients was limited by a lack of statistics on these clients. The data gathered by the centre was broken down by age, class, and sex, but not by ethnicity. Until the 1980s, collecting data on ethnicity was perceived as racist. Brook also tried to address the needs of individuals with disabilities through the development of sex education materials. Moreover, young people who did not identify as heterosexual and were very anxious about their sexual orientation received support from Brook, which helped them to navigate their feelings and taught them that same-sex sexual feelings were completely natural.

However, Brook's work with socially deprived white working-class and ethnic minority young people was ambivalent and, at times, reflected a different, paternalistic vision of 'sexual responsibility' from that of the middle- and upper-class white girls. This vision tended to emphasize control over these groups' sexual behaviours instead of arguing for their legitimation. For working-class young women, Brook described contraception as a means of control; their lack of control over their bodies condemned them to unwanted pregnancies and abortions. Working-class girls were usually described as having more sexual activity than middle-class girls, and as such needed more control and education in order to avoid the risks of unprotected intercourse. Brook workers perceived non-white young people as having different sexual norms and behaviours. For young Black people, usually from African-Caribbean backgrounds, contraception was also considered a means of control but for a different reason. Assumptions of the over-fertility of young Black girls who 'got themselves pregnant' permeated the work of Brook members. Counselling was therefore perceived as a way of teaching white British 'middle-class' values around 'sexual responsibility'.

Finally, this book has also highlighted the local resistances and barriers Brook faced during the period under study. Establishing centres in certain areas, such as Liverpool or Birmingham, proved difficult due to local opposition by family planning members, church leaders, and local health authorities. Financial concerns and funding cuts impacted the running of Brook services, forcing some centres to shut down or to reduce their activities, while others were late to offer free services. Conservative lobbies were successful in limiting the provision of sex education in schools and in establishing the sort of sex educational materials that could be used in school, restricting Brook's freedom in devising these materials. Victoria Gillick jeopardized Brook's work with the under-16s and Brook's statistics showed a drop in attendance from this age group. Moreover, Brook had to redouble its effort to regain the trust of the under-16s and actively campaigned to emphasize the confidentiality of its services.

Today, contraception is more easily available to teenagers in Britain and Brook remains an active purveyor of sexual and reproductive health services. In recent years, the rate of teenage pregnancies in Britain has been declining; in 2020, the under-18 conception rate was the lowest on record. However, despite this positive trend, Britain still has one of the highest rates of teenage pregnancies in Western Europe. In addition, a report recently released stated 'the substantial variation in rates between local authorities, ranging from 2.1 to 30.4 conceptions per 1,000 15- to 17-year-olds, leaves no room for complacency'.[4] In addition, the provision of sex education remains inconsistent across different schools and regions, with some areas providing comprehensive education while others offer only minimal information. There are also ongoing debates around what should be included in sex education, with some arguing for a focus on abstinence and traditional family values, and others pushing for an inclusive and sex-positive approach. These debates reflect the ongoing struggle to provide young people with accurate and empowering information about their bodies and desires. Providing comprehensive information about sexual health is all the more important in an age where teenagers gather the majority of their information on social media platforms and where porn has become so prevalent in the life of young people.

I hope that the book provides a first step towards exploring the sexual lived-experiences of young people. There is still much scope for developing work to better understand the experiences of those who did not attend sexual health services, as well as the experiences of marginalized communities. I believe that by looking into the history of the development of Brook, we can better understand the resistances to establish accessible, confidential, and non-judgmental services for young people that offered a wide range of provisions, including contraception, emergency contraception, STS testing, abortion referrals, and sexual counselling.

---

[4] Local Government Association, *Breaking point: Securing the future of sexual health services*, 2022. Available online: https://www.local.gov.uk/publications/breaking-point-securing-future-sexual-health-services.

References

Oral history interviews with Brook staff

Joanna Brien, 29 March 2020
Dilys Cossey, 5 April 2019
Alison Frater, 7 February 2020
Alison Hadley, 24 February 2020
Suzie Hayman, 19 September 2018
Dorothy van Heeswyk, 11 November 2022
Gillian Vanhegan, 20 February 2020
Joan Woodward, 18 May 2020
Caroline Woodroffe, 21 September 2018

Oral history interviews with ex-Brook clients

Lucy, 15 May 2020
Laura, 23 May 2020
Tracey, 12 May 2020
Sarah, 19 February 2020
Florence, 24 February 2020
Emily, 24 February 2020
Claire, 22 May 2021
Jane, July 2021

Archived oral history interviews

Helen Brook, interviewed by Rebbeca Adams, in C408/014 British Library
Helen Brook, *In the Club*
Pauline Crabbe, *In the Club*, 1984, in GC/105/5, Wellcome Library, London
Dilys Cossey, *In the Club*, in GC/105/5, Wellcome Library, London
Dilys Cossey, in transcript of *Wellcome Witness Seminar: 50 Years of Brook*, 6 February 2015
Dorothy Keeping, written testimony, transcript of *Wellcome Witness Seminar: 50 Years of Brook*, Friday 6 February 2015
Faith Spicer, *In the Club*, GC/105/5, Wellcome Library, London
Interviews for *Everyman* TV broadcast on Brook Advisory Centre, PP/MEW/C/4/4, Wellcome Library, London
Wendy Thomas, in transcript of *Wellcome Witness Seminar: 50 Years of Brook*, 6 February 2015
Caroline Woodroffe, in transcript of *Wellcome Witness Seminar: 50 Years of Brook*, 6 February 2015

Wellcome Library, London

SA/BRO, Brook Advisory Centre
SA/FPA, Family Planning Association
PP/MEW, McEwan, John
SA/EUG/Eugenics Society
SA/ALR Abortion Law Reform

Bishopsgate Institute, London

COLE Martin Cole

National Archives, London

HO256/1160

Newspapers

Birmingham Post
Birmingham Sunday Mercury
Bristol Evening Post
Daily Express
Daily Mail
Daily Mirror
Daily Telegraph
Edinburgh Evening News
Evening Standard
Liverpool Echo
Observer
Sunday Mercury
Sunday Telegraph
The Guardian
The People
The Scotsman
The Times
Western Daily Press

Journals and magazines

British Medical Journal
The Lancet
Family Planning Journal
GP

Just Seventeen
Nineteen
Mizz
Oh Boy!
Petticoat

Archived websites

https://www.mumsnet.com/talk/womens_rights/3909214-Feminism-and-gynaecology, visited 7 November 2022

https://www.mumsnet.com/talk/site_stuff/1895087-Ever-used-a-Brook-clinic-or-service-Are-you-willing-to-share-your-stories-to-celebrate-Brooks-fiftieth-birthday

https://www.mumsnet.com/Talk/site_stuff/1895087-Ever-used-a-Brook-clinic-or-service-Are-you-willing-to-share-your-stories-to-celebrate-Brooks-fiftieth-birthday, visited 25 April 2020

Contemporary sources

Allen, Isobel, *Education in Sex and Personal Relationships* (Policy Studies Institute, 1987)

Board of Education, *Sex Education in Schools and Youth Organisations* (His Majesty's Stationary Office, 1943)

Bone, Margaret, *Family Planning Services in England and Wales: Office of Population Censuses and Surveys* (Her Majesty's Stationery Office, 1973)

British Medical Association, *The Handbook of Medical Ethics* (London, 1980)

Brook Advisory Centre, *Say Yes? Say No? Say Maybe?* (Brook Advisory Centre, 1991)

———, *Making Sex Education Easier: A Guide to Sex Education and Sex Education Resources from Brook Publication* (Brook Education and Publication, 1998)

Chesser, Eustace, *The Sexual, Marital and Family Relationship of the English Woman* (Hutchinson's Medical Publications, 1956)

Comfort, Alex, *Sex in Society* (Duckworth, 1963)

Cossey, Dilys, *Teenage Birth Control: The Case for the Condom* (Brook Advisory Centre, 1979)

Department of Health, *The Health of the Nation: A Strategy for Health in England*, 1992

Department of Health and Social Security, *Family Planning Services: Memorandum of Guidance.* Issued with HSC(IS)32. DHSS, 1974

———, Circular, HN (80) 46, December, 1980

Dunnell, Karen, *Family Formation: 1976* (HM Stationery Office, 1979)

Egg Research and Consultancy, *'Someone With a Smile Would be Your Best Bet...' What Young People Want from Sex Advice Services* (Brook Advisory Centre, 1998)

Fairbairn, Nicholas, *A Life is Too Short: Autobiography Volume 1* (Quartet Books, 1987)

Farrell, Christine, *My Mother Said... the Way Young People Learned about Sex and Birth Control* (Routledge & Kegan Paul, 1978)

Frater, Alison, *Young Men at the Brook Advisory Centre* (Family Planning Association, 1985)

Hadley, Alison, *Press Release: Love Carefully—Use a Condom: Top-Ten Starts Endorse Brook Advisory Centres Leaflet for Young People* (Brook Press and Information Office, 9 April 1987)

Hayman, Suzie, *Advertising and Contraceptives* (Birth Control Trust, 1977)
———, *It's More than Sex! A Survival Guide to the Teenage Years* (Wildwood House, 1986)
'James White', in *Hansard, HC*, 7 February 1975, vol. 885, col. 1758
Knight, Jill, 'Family planning group, 4th August 1980', *20th century House of Commons Hansard Sessional Papers*, Fifth Series, no. 990 (1980)
London Borough of Southwark, *Annual Report of the Medical Officer of Health and Principal School Medical Officer* (1967)
London Borough of Camden, *Annual Report of the Medical Officer of Health and Principal School Medical Officer* (1967)
London Borough of Hackney, *Annual Report on the Health of the Borough* (1970)
Morrison, Mr Charles, Answer to 'Family planning group' on 4th August 1980', *20th century House of Commons Hansard Sessional Papers,* Fifth Series, no. 990 (1980)
Paintin, David, *Abortion Law Reform in Britain (1964–2003): A Personal Account* (London, 2015)
Patterson, Sheila, *Immigrants in London: Report of a Study Group set up by the London Council of Social Service* (National Council of Social Service, 1963)
Pawsey, James, 'Family planning group, 4th August 1980', *20th century House of Commons Hansard Sessional Papers*, Fifth Series, no. 990 (1980)
Peckham, Stephen, Roger Ingham, and Ian Diamond, *Teenage Pregnancy: Prevention and Programmes* (University of Southampton, 1996)
Schofield, Michael, *The Sexual Behaviour of Young People* (Little, Brown, 1965)
Skrine, Ruth, *Growing into Medicine: The Life and Loves of a Psychosexual Doctor* (Book Guild Publishing, 2014)

Primary sources articles

'Annual Report of the Brook Advisory Centre', *Family Planning* 15 (1966): 47–50
Balint, Michael, 'Psychotherapy and the general practitioner: I', *British Medical Journal* 1.5011 (1957): 156
Bowman, Agnes, 'Family Planning for the unmarried?', *Family Planning* 12.4 (1964): 105
'Brook Advisory Centre', *Family Planning* 17.2 (1968): 40
Brook's answer to the Responsible Society, 'Sexual pressure on children', *British Medical Journal* 2.6135 (1978): 499
Christie Brown, Margaret, 'Psycho-sexual counselling: The method followed in the London Brook Advisory Centres', *British Journal of Sexual Medicine* 1.7 (1974): 41–44
Coles, Ruth, 'Pregnancy counselling for young people', *Youth Counselling Bulletin*, 1976
———, 'Acceptability and use-effectiveness of contraception for teenagers', *Journal of Biosociological Science Supplement* 5 (1978): 159
Crabbe, Pauline, 'Social and emotional aspects of pregnancy in teenagers', *Journal of Biosocial Science* 5 (1978): 173
Hague, Walter and Katherine, 'Sexual morality and the young', *Family Planning* 13.1 (1964): 20
Hayman, Suzie, 'The effects of the Gillick case', *Just Seventeen*, 20 March 1985, 61
'Hilda Lewis Memorial Fund', *British Medical Journal* 1 (1967): 701
Hutchinson, Fay, 'Counselling; When the pill buys time', *Modern Medicine* (February 1980): 49
———, 'Young Advisory Work: What Can You Say to Young People Today?', in Katharine Draper (ed.), *Practice of Psychosexual Medicine: Selected Papers from the First International Conference on Psychosexual Medicine* (John Libbey, 1983): 172

——, 'How to handle teenage birth control', *GP* (16 November 1984)
Lustig, Mrs B. L., 'Family planning for the unmarried?', *Family Planning* 13.1 (1964): 20
MacGillivray, Ruth, 'Sex problems: Counselling', *GP* (21 November 1975): 13–15
'Need for improved birth control services for young people', *British Medical Journal* 292.6518 (1986): 495
'Post coital oestrogen in large dose', *International Planned Parenthood Federation Medical Bulletin* 6.2 (1973): 3–4
Spicer, Faith, 'The Marie Stopes advice centre for young people', *Family Planning* 13 (1964): 31
Turner, Toni, 'Parental privilege: A minor concern?', *GP* (6 January 1984)
Woodroffe, Caroline, 'Amendment of Abortion Act', *British Medical Journal* 1.6062 (1977): 711
Woodroffe, Caroline, and Fay Hutchinson, 'Late abortions', *The Lancet* (25 February 1984)
Woodroffe, Caroline, and S. McClinton, 'Contraceptives and the under 16s', *British Medical Journal* 291.6504 (1985): 1280
Woodward, Joan, 'Birmingham Brook', *Family Planning* 19.3 (1970): 88
——, 'The role of the social worker in psychosexual counselling', *Social Work Today* (11 January 1977)

Secondary literature

Abrams, Lynn, 'Mothers and Daughters: Negotiating the Discourse on the "Good Woman" in 1950s and 1960s Britain', in N. Christie and M. Gauvreau (eds), *The Sixties and Beyond: Dechristianisation in North America and Western Europe, 1945–2000* (Toronto, 2013)
Aldgate, Anthony, *Censorship and the Permissive Society: British Cinema and Theatre, 1955–1965* (Oxford University Press, 1995)
Arai, Lisa, *Teenage Pregnancy: The Making and Unmaking of a Problem* (Policy Press, 2009)
Arnot, Madeleine, Miriam David, and Gaby Weiner, *Closing the Gender Gap: Post-war Education and Social Change* (Cambridge University Press, 1999)
Bailkin, Jordanna, *Afterlife of Empire* (University of California Press, 2012)
Bantigny, Ludovine, Christina Bard, and Claire Blandin (eds), 'L'expertise face aux enjeux biopolitiques. Genre, jeune, sexualité', special issue of *Histoire@Politique* 14.2 (2011)
Bates, Victoria, 'Cold white of day: White, colour, and materiality in the twentieth-century British hospital', *Twentieth Century British History* 34.1 (2023): 1–37
Batley, Richard, and John Edwards, 'The urban programme: A report on some programme funded projects', *British Journal of Social Work* 4.3 (1974): 305–31
Berridge, Virginia, *AIDS in the UK: The Making of Policy, 1981–1994* (Oxford University Press, 1996)
Bingham, Adrian, *Family Newspapers?: Sex, Private Life, and the British Popular Press 1918–1978* (Oxford University Press, 2009)
——, 'The "K-bomb": Social surveys, the popular press, and British sexual culture in the 1940s and 1950s', *Journal of British Studies* 50.1 (2011): 156–79
——, 'Newspaper problem pages and British sexual culture since 1918', *Media History* 18.1 (2012): 51–63
Bivins, Roberta, *Contagious Communities: Medicine, Migration, and the NHS in Post-war Britain* (Oxford University Press, 2015)
Black, Lawrence, 'There Was Something About Mary: The National Viewers' and Listeners' Association and Social Movement History', in Nick Crowson, Matthew Hilton, and

James McKay (eds), *NGOs in Contemporary Britain: Non-state Actors in Society and Politics Since 1945* (Palgrave Macmillan, 2009): 182–200

Black, Lawrence, Hugh Pemberton, and Pat Thane (eds), *Reassessing 1970s Britain* (Manchester University Press, 2013)

Bland, Lucy, 'White women and men of colour: Miscegenation fears in Britain after the Great War', *Gender & History* 17.1 (2005): 29–61

———, *Britain's 'Brown Babies': The Stories of Children Born to Black GIs and White Women in the Second World War* (Manchester University Press, 2019)

Blos, Peter, *On Adolescence: A Psychoanalytic Interpretation* (Free Press, 1962)

Brewitt Taylor, Sam, 'Christianity and the invention of the sexual revolution in Britain, 1963-1967', *Historical Journal* 60.2 (2017): 519–46

Brooke, Stephen, '"A new world for women"? Abortion law reform in Britain during the 1930s', *American Historical Review* 106.2 (2001): 431–59

———, 'The Sphere of Sexual Politics: The Abortion Law Reform Association, 1930s to 1960s', in Nick J. Crowson, Matthew Hilton, and Dr James McKay, *NGOs in Contemporary Britain* (Palgrave Macmillan, 2009): 77–94

———, *Sexual Politics: Sexuality, Family Planning, and the British Left from the 1880s to the Present Day* (Oxford University Press, 2011)

Brown, Callum G., 'Sex, religion, and the single woman: The importance of a "short" sexual revolution to the English religious crisis of the sixties', *Twentieth Century British History* 22.11(2011): 189–215

———, *The Battle for Christian Britain: Sex, Humanists and Secularisation, 1945–1980* (Cambridge University Press, 2019)

Bugge, Christian, '"Selling Youth in the Age of Affluence": Marketing to Youth in Britain since 1959', in Lawrence Black and Hugh Pemberton (eds), *An Affluent Society? Britain's Post-war 'Golden Age' Revisited* (Ashgate, 2004): 185–202

Caron, Jean-Claude, Annie Stora-Lamarre, and Jean-Jacques Yvorel, *Les âmes mal nées. Jeunesse et délinquance urbaine en France et en Europe (XIXe–XXIe siècles)* (Presses Universitaires de Franche-Comté, 2008)

Charnock, Hannah, *Girlhood, Sexuality and Identity in England, 1950–1980* (University of Exeter, 2017)

———, 'Teenage girls, female friendship and the making of the sexual revolution in England, 1950–1980', *Historical Journal* 63.4 (2020): 1032–53

Chettiar, Teri, *The Psychiatric Family: Citizenship, Private Life, and Emotional Health in Welfare State Britain, 1945–79*, PhD dissertation, University of Evanston, 2013

———, 'Treating marriage as "the sick entity": Gender, emotional life, and the psychology of marriage improvement in postwar Britain', *History of Psychology* 18.3 (2015): 270–82

Clarke, John, Stuart Hall, Tony Jefferson, and Brian Roberts, 'Subcultures, Cultures and Class: A Theoretical Overview', in Stuart Hall and Tony Jefferson (eds), *Resistance through Rituals: Youth Subcultures in Post-war Britain* (Routledge, 1996): 9–74

Cohen, Stanley, *Folk Devils and Moral Panics: The Creation of the Mods and Rockers* (MacGibbon & Kee, 1972)

Cohen, Deborah A., 'Private lives in public spaces: Marie Stopes, the mothers' clinics and the practice of contraception', *History Workshop Journal* 35.1 (1993): 95–116

Collins, Marcus, 'Pride and prejudice: West Indian men in mid-twentieth-century Britain', *Journal of British Studies* 40.3 (2001): 391–418

———, *Modern Love: Personal Relationships in Twentieth-Century Britain* (University of Delaware Press, 2006)

—— (ed.), *The Permissive Society and its Enemies: Sixties British Culture* (Rivers Oram Press, 2007)
Conekin, Becky, Frank Mort, and Chris Waters (eds), *Moments of Modernity: Reconstructing Britain, 1945–64* (River Oram Press, 2000)
Connell, Kieran, *Black Handsworth: Race in 1980s Britain* (University of California Press, 2019)
Cook, Hera, *The Long Sexual Revolution: English Women, Sex, and Contraception 1800–1975* (Oxford University Press, 2004)
Cook, Matt, '"Archives of feeling": The AIDS crisis in Britain 1987', *History Workshop Journal* 83.1 (2017): 51–78
——, 'AIDS, Mass Observation, and the fate of the permissive turn', *Journal of the History of Sexuality* 26.2 (2017): 239–72
Coote, Anna, and Beatrix Campbell, *Sweet Freedom: The Struggle for Women's Liberation*, 2nd edn (John Wiley, 1987)
Court, Audrey, and Cynthia Walton, *1926–1991: Birmingham Made a Difference: The Birmingham Women's Welfare Centre, the Family Planning Association in Birmingham* (Barns Brook, 2001)
Cox, Pamela, *Gender, Justice and Welfare: Bad Girls in Britain, 1900–1950* (Macmillan, 2003)
Cox, Pamela, and Heather Shore (eds), *Becoming Delinquent: British and European Youth, 1650–1950* (Ashgate, 2002)
Crane, Jennifer, *Child Protection in England, 1960–2000: Expertise, Experience and Emotions* (Palgrave Macmillan, 2018)
Dadzie, Stella, Beverley Bryan, and Suzanne Scafe, *'The Heart of the Race': Black Women's Lives in Britain* (Virago, 1985)
Davidson, Roger, *Dangerous Liaisons: A Social History of Venereal Disease in Twentieth-Century Scotland* (Rodopi, 2000)
Davidson, Roger, and Gayle Davis, *The Sexual State: Sexuality and Scottish Governance, 1950–80* (Edinburgh University Press, 2012)
Davis, John, 'Reshaping the Welfare State? Voluntary Action and Community in London, 19601–975', in Lawrence Goldman (ed.), *Welfare and Social Policy in Britain since 1870: Essays in Honour of Jose Harris* (Oxford University Press, 2019): 198–212
Dean, Mitchell, *Governmentality: Power and Rule in Modern Cociety* (Sage, 2010)
Debenham, Clare, *Birth Control and the Rights of Women: Post-Suffrage Feminism in the Early Twentieth Century* (I. B. Tauris, 2014)
Dixon, Thomas, *Weeping Britannia: Portrait of a Nation in Tears* (Oxford University Press, 2015)
Donnelly, Mark, *Sixties Britain: Culture, Society and Politics* (Routledge, 2014)
——, 'Sixties Britain: The Cultural Politics of Historiography', in Trevor Harris and Monia O'Brien Castro (eds), *Preserving the Sixties* (Palgrave Macmillan, 2014): 10–30
Donovan, Chris, et al. 'Teenagers' views on the general practice consultation and provision of contraception: The Adolescent Working Group', *British Journal of General Practice* 47.424 (1997): 715–18
Duckworth, Sophie, '"Time for Tea": Tea Practices and Care in a British Gospice', in Aaron Parkhurst and Timothy Carroll (eds), *Medical Materialities: Toward a Material Culture of Medical Anthropology* (Routledge, 2019)
Durham, Martin, *Sex and Politics: Family and Morality in the Thatcher Years* (Macmillan International Higher Education, 1991)

Dyhouse, Carol, *Girl Trouble: Panic and Progress in the History of Young Women* (Bloomsbury, 2014)

Elizabeth, Hannah J., *[Re]inventing Childhood in the Age of AIDS: The Representation of HIV Positive Identities to Children and Adolescents in Britain, 1983–1997*, PhD thesis, University of Birmingham, 2016

———, 'Love carefully and without "over-bearing fears": The persuasive power of authenticity in late 1980s British AIDS education material for adolescents', *Social History of Medicine* 34.4 (2021): 131–42

———, '"Private things affect other people": *Grange Hill*'s critique of British sex education policy in the age of AIDS', *Twentieth Century British History* 32.2 (2021): 261–84

———, '"If it hadn't been for the doctor, I think I would have killed myself": Ensuring Adolescent Knowledge and Access to Healthcare in the Age of Gillick', in Jennifer Crane and Jane Hane (eds), *Posters, Protests, and Prescriptions* (Manchester University Press, 2022): 255–80

Finch, Janet, and Penny Summerfield, 'Social Reconstruction and the Emergence of Companionate Marriage, 1945–59', in David Clark (ed.), *Marriage, Domestic Life and Social Change: Writings for Jacqueline Burgoyne* (Routledge, 1991): 6–27

Fink, Janet, and Penny Tinkler, 'Teetering on the edge: Portraits of innocence, risk and young female sexualities in 1950s' and 1960s' British cinema', *Women's History Review* 26.1 (2017): 9–25

Fisher, Kate, *Birth Control, Sex, and Marriage in Britain 1918–1960* (Oxford University Press, 2006)

———, 'Marriage and Companionate Ideals Since 1750', in Sarah Toulalan and Kate Fisher (eds), *The Routledge History of Sex and the Body* (Routledge, 2013)

Foucault, Michel, *La Volonté de Savoir: Histoire de La Sexualité 1* (Gallimard, 1976)

———, *Security, Territory, Population: Lectures at the Collège de France 1977–1978*, trans. Graham Burchell (Palgrave Macmillan, 2007)

Fowler, David, *The First Teenagers: Young Wage-Earners in Interwar Britain* (Woburn, 1995)

Freud, Anna, 'Adolescence', *The Psychoanalytic Study of the Child* 13.1 (1958): 255–78

Geiringer, David, 'Catholic understandings of female sexuality in 1960s Britain', *Twentieth Century British History* 28.2 (June 2017): 209–38

Giddens, Anthony, *The Transformation of Intimacy: Sexuality, Love and Eroticism in Modern Societies* (Stanford University Press, 1992)

Gillis, John R., *Youth and History, Tradition and Change in European Age Relations, 1770–Present* (Academic Press, 1974)

Gilroy, Paul, *There Ain't No Black in the Union Jack* (Routledge, 1987)

Gomersall, Meg, *Working-Class Girls in Nineteenth Century England: Life, Work and Schooling* (St. Martin's Press, 1997)

Grier, Julie, 'A Spirit of "Friendly Rivalry"?: Voluntary Societies and the Formation of Post-War Child Welfare Legislation in Britain', in Jon Lawrence and Pat Starkey (eds), *Child Welfare and Social Action in the Nineteenth and Twentieth Centuries: International Perspectives* (Liverpool University Press, 2001): 234–55

Hadley, Alison, R. Ingham, and V. Chandra-Mouli, 'Implementing the United Kingdom's ten-year teenage pregnancy strategy for England (1999–2010): How was this done and what did it achieve?', *Reproductive Health* 13.1 (2016): 139

Hall, Lesley A., 'Eyes Tightly Shut, Lying Rigidly Still and Thinking of England?: British Women and Sex from Marie Stopes to Hite 2000', in Claudia Nelson and Michelle

H. Martin (eds), *Sexual Pedagogies: Sex Education in Britain, Australia, and America, 1879-2000* (Palgrave Macmillan, 2004): 53-71

———, 'Birds, Bees and General Embarrassment: Sex Education in Britain from Social Purity to Section 2', in Richard Aldrich (ed.), *Public or Private Education?: Lessons from History* (Woburn, 2004): 93-112

———, 'In Ignorance and in Knowledge: Reflections on the History of Sex Education in Britain', in Roger Davidson and Lutz Sauerteig (eds), *Shaping Sexual Knowledge: A Cultural History of Sex Education in Twentieth Century Europe* (Routledge, 2009): 31-48

———, *Sex, Gender and Social Change in Britain since 1880* (Bloomsbury Publishing, 2017)

Hall, Stanley, *Adolescence: Its Psychology and its Relations to Physiology, Anthropology, Sociology, Sex, Crime, Religion and Education* (Sydney Appleton, 1904)

Hall, Stuart, 'Reformism and the Legislation of Consent', *Permissiveness and Control: The Fate of the Sixties Legislation* (Macmillan, 1980): 1-43

Hammond Perry, Kennetta, *London is the Place for Me: Black Britons, Citizenship and the Politics of Race* (Oxford University Press, 2016)

Hampshire, James, *Citizenship and Belonging: Immigration and the Politics of Demographic Governance in Postwar Britain* (Palgrave Macmillan, 2005)

Hampshire, James, and Jane Lewis, '"The ravages of permissiveness": Sex education and the permissive society', *Twentieth Century British History* 15.3 (2004): 290-312

Hampton, Jameel, *Disability and the Welfare State in Britain* (Policy Press, 2016)

Hanawalt, Barbara A., 'Historical descriptions and prescriptions for adolescence', *Journal of Family History* 17.4 (1992): 341-51

Hanley, Anne, 'Migration, racism and sexual health in postwar Britain', *History Workshop Journal* 94 (2022): 202-22

Harding, Alan, and Brendan Nevin, *Cities and Public Policy: A Review Paper* (Government Office for Science, 2015)

Harris, Alana, 'Love Divine and Love Sublime: The Catholic Marriage Advisory Council, the Marriage Guidance Movement and the State', in her *Love and Romance in Britain, 1918-1970* (Palgrave Macmillan, 2015): 188-224

Harrison, Brian, *Seeking a Role: The United Kingdom, 1951-1970* (Oxford University Press, 2009)

———, *Finding a Role: The United Kingdom, 1970-1990* (Oxford University Press, 2010)

Hay, Kristin, *An Oral History of Birth Control Practices in Scotland: Gender, Sexuality and Scottish Society c. 965-1980* (unpublished PhD dissertation, University of Strathclyde, 2022)

Hemming, James, *Problems of Adolescent Girls* (Heinemann, 1960)

Hendrick, Harry, *Images of Youth. Age, Class, and the Male Youth Problem, 1880-1920* (Clarendon, 1990)

Hilton, Matthew, et al., *The Politics of Expertise: How NGOs Shaped Modern Britain* (Oxford University Press, 2013)

Hilton, Matthew, Chris Moores, and Florence Sutcliffe-Braithwaite, ''New Times' revisited: Britain in the 1980s', *Contemporary British History* 31.2 (2017): 145-65

Hirsch, Shirin, *In the Shadow of Enoch Powell: Race, Locality and Resistance* (Manchester University Press, 2020)

Humphries, Stephen, *Hooligans or Rebels? An Oral History of Working Class Childhood and Youth, 1889-1939* (Blackwell, 1981)

Louise Jackson, 'The Coffee Club menace: policing youth, leisure and sexuality in post-war Manchester', *Cultural and Social History*, 5.3 (2008): 289-308

Louise Jackson, 'Childhood and Youth', in H. G. Cocks and Matt Houlbrook (eds), *Palgrave Advances in the Modern History of Sexuality* (Springer, 2005): 231–55

Jackson, Louise, and Angela Bartie, *Policing Youth* (Manchester University Press, 2014)

Jackson, Stevi, and Sue Scott, 'A Sociological History of Researching Childhood and Sexuality: Continuities and Discontinuities', in E. Renold, J. Ringrose, and R. D. Egan (eds), *Children, Sexuality and Sexualization* (Palgrave Macmillan, 2015)

Jefferson, Laura, Karen Bloor, and Alan Maynard, 'Women in medicine: Historical perspectives and recent trends', *British Medical Bulletin* 114.1 (2015): 7

Jobling, Paul, 'Playing safe: The politics of pleasure and gender in the promotion of condoms in Britain, 1970–1982', *Journal of Design History* 10.1 (1997): 53–70

Jones, Cecily, '"Human weeds, not fit to breed?": African Caribbean women and reproductive disparities in Britain', *Critical Public Health* 23.1 (2013): 49–61

Jones, Claire, *The Business of Birth Control: Contraception and Commerce in Britain Before the Sexual Revolution* (Manchester University Press, 2020)

Jones, Emma L., 'The establishment of voluntary family planning clinics in Liverpool and Bradford, 1926–1960: A comparative study', *Social History of Medicine* 24.2 (2011): 352–69

Jones, Katherine, '"Men too": Masculinities and contraceptive politics in late twentieth century Britain', *Contemporary British History* 34 (2020): 44–70

Kelly, Laura, '"Please help me, I am so miserable!" Sexual health, emotions and counselling in teen and young adult problem pages in late 1980s Ireland', *Medical Humanities*, first published online 25 October 2022

———, *Contraception in Modern Ireland: A Social History, c.1922–1992* (Cambridge University Press, 2023)

King, Laura, *Family Men: Fatherhood and Masculinity in Britain, c.1914–1960* (Oxford University Press, 2015)

Koffman, Ofra, *Towards a Genealogy of Teenage Pregnancy in Britain* (PhD submitted to Goldsmith College, University of London, 2008)

———, 'Children having children? Religion, psychology and the birth of the teenage pregnancy problem', *History of the Human Sciences* 25.1 (2012): 119–34

Lambert, Caitlin, '"The objectionable injectable": Recovering the lost history of the WLM through the campaign against Depo-Provera', *Women's History Review* 29.3 (2020): 520–39

Langhamer, Claire, *Women's Leisure in England, 1920–1960* (Manchester University Press, 2000)

———, 'Adultery in post-war England', *History Workshop Journal* 62.1 (2006): 86–115

———, 'Love, selfhood and authenticity in post-war Britain', *Cultural and Social History* 9.2 (2012): 277–97

———, *The English in Love: The Intimate Story of an Emotional Revolution* (Oxford University Press, 2013)

———, 'Everyday advice on everyday love: Romantic expertise in mid-twentieth century Britain', *L' Homme: Zeitschrift Für Feministische Geschichtswissenschaft* 1 (2013): 35–52

Larsson, Anna-Karin L., 'Girls' responsibilities, boys' needs: Sexual health, gender and youth in Sweden 1970–1999', *European Journal for the History of Medicine and Health* 80.1 (2022): 96–118

Laverack, Glenn, *Health Activism: Foundations and Strategies* (Sage, 2013)

Leathard, Audrey, *Fight for Family Planning* (Springer, 1980)

Levi, Giovanni, and de Jean-Claude Schmitt, *L'Histoire des Jeunes en Occident* (Seuil, 1996): 7–19

Lévy, Marie-Françoise, 'Le mouvement français pour le planning familial et les jeunes', *Vingtième siècle Revue d'histoire* 75 (2002): 75–84

Lewis, Jane, 'Family provision of health and welfare in the mixed economy of care in the late nineteenth and twentieth centuries', *Social History of Medicine* 8.1 (1995): 1–16

Lewis, Jane, David Clark, and David Morgan (eds), *Whom God Hath Joined Together: The Work of Marriage Guidance* (Routledge, 1992)

Lewis, Ruth, Clare Tanton, and Catherine H. Mercer, et al. 'Heterosexual practices among young people in Britain: Evidence from three national surveys of sexual attitudes and lifestyles', *Journal of Adolescent Health* 61.6 (2017): 694–702

Loughran, Tracey, 'Sex, relationships, and "everyday psychology" on British magazine problem pages, c.1960–1990', *Medical Humanities*, first published online 22 December 2022

———, '"The Most Helpful Friends in the World": Letters Pages, Expertise and Emotion in British Women's Magazines, c.1960–80', in Laurel Foster and Joanne Hollows (eds), *Women's Periodicals and Print Culture in Britain, 1940s–2000s: The Postwar and Contemporary Period* (Edinburgh University Press, 2020): 133–49

Lynch, Charlie, *Scotland and the Sexual Revolution c.1957–1975: Religion, Intimacy and Popular Culture* (PhD dissertation, University of Glasgow, 2019)

Mahood, Linda, and Barbara Littlewood, 'The "vicious" girl and the "street-corner" boy: Sexuality and the gendered delinquent in the Scottish child-saving movement, 1850–1940', *Journal of the History of Sexuality* 4.4 (1994): 549–78

Marks, Lara, *Sexual Chemistry: A History of the Contraceptive Pill* (Yale University Press, 2010)

Mars-Jones, Adam, 'The book that launched clause 28', *Index on Censorship* 17.8 (1988): 37–40

Marwick, Arthur, *Britain in the Century of Total War: War, Peace, and Social Change, 1900–1967* (Atlantic Little, Brown, 1968)

———, *The Sixties: Cultural Revolution in Britain, France, Italy, and the United States, c.1958–c.1974* (Bloomsbury, 1998)

———, *Sex, Gender and Social Change in Britain since 1880* (Bloomsbury, 2017)

———, 'The 1960s: Was there a "Cultural Revolution?"', *Contemporary Record* 2.3 (1988): 18–20

McRobbie, Angela, *Feminism and Youth Culture: From Jackie to Just Seventeen*, 2nd edn (Macmillan, 2000)

McSmith, Andy, *No Such Thing as Society: A History of Britain in the 1980s* (Constable, 2010)

Mechen, Ben, *Everyday Sex in 1970's Britain* (PhD thesis, University College London, 2016)

Mills, Helena, 'Using the personal to critique the popular: women's memories of 1960s youth', *Contemporary British History* 30.4 (2016): 463–83

Mold, Alex, *Making the Patient-Consumer: Patient Organisations and Health Consumerism in Britain* (Manchester University Press, 2015)

Mold, Alex, and Virginia Berridge, *Voluntary Action and Illegal Drugs: Health and Society in Britain since the 1960s* (Palgrave Macmillan, 2010)

Moore, Martin D., 'Food as medicine: Diet, diabetes management, and the patient in twentieth century Britain', *Journal of the History of Medicine and Allied Sciences* 73.2 (2018): 150–67

———, '"Bright-while-you-wait"? Waiting Rooms and the National Health Service, c.1948–1958', in Jennifer Crane and Jane Hand (eds), *Posters, Protests and Prescriptions: Cultural Histories of the National Health Service in Britain* (Manchester University Press, 2022): 199–228

Moran, Joe, 'Childhood sexuality and education: The case of Section 28', *Sexualities* 4.1 (2001): 73–89

Morgan, Kenneth O., *Twentieth Century Britain: A Very Short Introduction* (Oxford University Press, 2000)

Mort, Frank, *Capital Affairs: London and the Making of the Permissive Society* (Yale University Press, 2010)

Nassy Brown, Jacqueline, 'The racial state of the everyday and the making of ethnic statistics in Britain', *Social Text* 27.1 (2009): 11–36

Odem, Mary, *Delinquent Daughters: Protecting and Policing Adolescent Female Sexuality in the United States, 1885–1920* (University of North Carolina Press, 1995)

O'Neill, Jane, '"Education Not Fornication?": Sexual Morality among Students in Scotland, 1955–1975', in Jodi Burkett (ed.), *Students in Twentieth-Century Britain and Ireland* (Palgrave macmillan, 2018)

Pacione, Michael, *Geographies of Division in Urban Britain* (Routledge, 1997)

Paul, Kathleen, *Whitewashing Britain: Race and Citizenship in the Postwar Era* (Cornell University Press, 1997)

Pikó, Lauren, '"You've never seen anything like it": Multiplexes, shopping malls and sensory overwhelm in Milton Keynes, 1979–1986', *The Senses and Society* 12.2 (2017): 147–61

Pilcher, Jane, 'Gillick and After: Children and Sex in the 1980s and 1990s', in Jane Pilcher and Stephen Wagg (ed.), *Thatcher's Children? Politics, Childhood and Society in 1980 and 1990* (Falmer Press, 1996): 77–93

Praz, Anne-Françoise, 'Gérer la sexualité des jeunes. Stratégies familiales et institutionnelles en Suisse romande (1960–1977)', presentation given at Society for the History of Children and Youth Ninth Biennial Conference, Rutgers University, Camden, New Jersey, June 21–3, 2017

'Professor Cedric Carter', *Journal of Medical Genetics* 21 (1984): 401–3

Rees, Gareth, and John Lambert, *Cities in Crisis: The Political Economy of Urban Development in Postwar Britain* (Edward Arnold, 1985)

Rhodes, James, and Laurence Brown, 'The rise and fall of the "inner city": Race, space and urban policy in postwar England', *Journal of Ethnic and Migration Studies* 45.17 (2019): 3243–59

Robertson, Stephen, 'Age of consent law and the making of modern childhood in New York City, 1886–1921', *Journal of Social History* 35.4 (2002): 781–98

Robinson, Emily, et al. 'Telling stories about post-war Britain: Popular individualism and the "crisis" of the 1970s', *Twentieth Century British History* 28.2 (2017): 268–304

Robinson, Lucy, *Gay Men and the Left in Post-war Britain: How the Personal got Political* (Manchester University Press, 2013)

Rose, Nikolas, *Inventing Our Selves: Psychology, Power, and Personhood* (Cambridge University Press, 1998)

———, *Governing the Soul: The Shaping of the Private Self* (Free Association Books, 1999)

Rusterholz, Caroline, *Deux enfants c'est deja pas mal, Famille et fecondite en Suisse, 1955–1970* (Antipodes, 2017)

———, '"You can't dismiss that as being less happy, you see it is different": Sexual therapy in 1950s England', *Twentieth Century British History* 30.3 (2019): 375–98

———, *Women's Medicine: Sex, Family Planning and British Female Doctors in Transnational Perspective 1920–70* (Manchester University Press, 2020)

———, 'Teenagers, Sex, and the Brook Advisory Centres, 1964–1980', in Siân Pooley and Jono Taylor (eds), *Children's Experiences of Welfare in Modern Britain* (Institute of Historical Research, 2021): 492–540

———, 'Youth sexuality, responsibility, and the opening of the Brook advisory centres in London and Birmingham in the 1960s', *Journal of British Studies* 61.2 (2022): 315–342

———, '"A mechanical view of sex outside the context of love and the family": Contraception, censorship and the Brook Advisory Centre in Britain (1964–1985)', *Journal of the History of Sexuality* 33.1 (2024):33–55.

———, 'A Private Matter? The Brook Advisory Centre and Young People's Everyday Sexual and Reproductive Health in the 1960s–1990s', in Hannah Froom, Tracey Loughran, Kate Mahoney, and Daisy Payling (eds), *'Everyday Health': Embodiment and Selfhood since 1950* (Manchester University Press, forthcoming)

Sandbrook, Dominic, *White Heat: A History of Britain in the Swinging Sixties* (Abacus, 2006)

Saumarez Smith, Otto, 'The inner city crisis and the end of urban modernism in 1970s Britain', *Twentieth Century British History* 27.4 (2016): 578–98

Schofield, Camilla, *Enoch Powell and the Making of Postcolonial Britain* (Cambridge University Press, 2013)

Scott, Joan, 'Gender: A useful category of historical analysis', *American Historical Review* 91.5 (1986): 1053–75

Shapira, Michael, *The War Inside: Psychoanalysis, Total War, and the Making of the Democratic Self in Postwar Britain* (Cambridge, 2012)

Sheldon, Sally, Gayle Davis, Jane O'Neill, and Clare Parker, *The Abortion Act 1967: A Biography of a UK Law* (Cambridge University Press, 2022)

Springhall, John, *Coming of Age: Adolescence in Britain, 1860–1960* (Gill and Macmillan, 1986)

———, *Youth, Popular Culture and Moral Panics: Penny Gaffs to Gangsta-Rap, 1830–1996* (Macmillan Press LTD, 1996)

Stevens, Lorna, '13 Telling Tales of Virago Press', in Stephen Brown (ed.), *Consuming Books: The Marketing and Consumption of Literature* (Routledge, 2006): 160

Szreter, Simon, and Kate Fisher, *Sex Before the Sexual Revolution: Intimate Life in England 1918–1963* (Cambridge University Press, 2010)

Tallon, Andrew, *Urban Regeneration in the UK*, 3rd edn (Routledge, 2021)

Tarrant, Chris, *Ready Steady Go!: Growing Up in the Fifties and Sixties* (Hamlyn, 1994)

Tebbutt, Melanie, *Making Youth: A History of Youth in Modern Britain* (Macmillan Education, 2016)

Thane, Pat, *Happy Families?: History and Family Policy* (British Academy, 2011)

Thane, Pat, and R. Davidson, *The Child Poverty Action Group, 1965 to 2015* (Child Poverty Action Group, 2015)

Thane, Pat, and T. Evans, *Sinners? Scroungers? Saints? Unmarried Motherhood in Twentieth-Century England* (Oxford University Press, 2013)

Thiercé, Agnès, *Histoire de l'adolescence (1950–1914)* (Belin, 1999)

Thomson, Debra, 'The Ethnic Question: Census Politics in Great Britain', in Simon Patrick, Victor Piché, and Amélie A. Gagnon (eds), *Social Statistics and Ethnic Diversity: Cross-National Perspectives in Classifications and Identity Politics* (Springer, 2015): 111–39

Thomson, Matthew, *Psychological Subjects: Identity, Culture and Health in Twentieth Century Britain* (Oxford University Press, 2006)

———, *Lost Freedom: The Landscape of the Child and the British Post-War Settlement* (Oxford University Press, 2013)

Thomson, Rachel, 'Moral rhetoric and public health pragmatism: The recent politics of sex education', *Feminist Review* 48.1 (1994): 40–60

———, 'Prevention, promotion and adolescent sexuality: The politics of school sex education in England and Wales', *Sexual and Marital Therapy* 9.2 (1994): 115–26

Tinkler, Penny, *Constructing Girlhood: Popular Magazines for Girls Growing up in England, 1920-1950* (Taylor & Francis, 1995)

——, 'Are you really living? If not, get with it!', *Cultural and Social History* 11.4 (2014): 597-619

——, 'Going places or out of place? Representations of mobile girls and young women in late-1950s and 1960s Britain', *Twentieth Century British History* 32.2 (2021): 212-37

Tomlinson, Sally, 'Enoch Powell: Empires, immigrants and education', *Race Ethnicity and Education* 21.1 (2018): 1-14

Travis, Alan, *Bound and Gagged: A Secret History of Obscenity in Britain* (Profile Books, 2000)

Turner, Alwyn W., *Crisis? What Crisis?: Britain in the 1970s* (Aurum Press, 2009)

——, *Rejoice! Rejoice!: Britain in the 1980s* (Aurum Press, 2010)

Waites, Matthew, *The Age of Consent: Young People, Sexuality and Citizenship* (Palgrave Macmillan, 2005)

Walkowitz, Judith R., *City of Dreadful Delight: Narratives of Sexual Danger in Late-Victorian London* (University of Chicago Press, 1992)

Waters, Chris, '"Dark Strangers" in our midst: Discourses of race and nation in Britain, 1947-1963', *Twentieth-Century British Studies* 36.2 (1997): 207-38

Waters, Rob, *Thinking Black: Britain, 1964-1985*, Vol. 14 (University of California Press, 2018)

Webster, Wendy, *Imagining Home: Gender, Race and National Identity, 1945-1964* (Routledge, 1998)

Weeks, Jeffrey, *Sexuality and its Discontents: Meanings, Myths and Modern Sexualities* (Routledge, 1985)

——, 'The sexual citizen?', *Theory, Culture & Society* 15.3-4 (1998): 35-52

——, *The World We Have Won: The Remaking of Erotic and Intimate Life* (Routledge, 2007)

——, *Sex Politics and Society, The Regulation of Sexuality since 1800*, 4th edn (Routledge, 2018)

Weeks, Jeffrey, et al., 'Community and contracts: Tensions and dilemmas in the voluntary sector response to HIV and AIDS', *Policy Studies* 17 (1996): 108-10

Wellings, Kaye, *The Role of Teenage Magazines in the Sexual Health of Young People* (London School of Hygiene & Tropical Medicine: Department of Public Health and Policy, November 1996)

Wellings, Kaye, Julia Field, Anne M. Johnson, and Jane Wadsworth, *Sexual Behaviour in Britain: The National Survey of Sexual Attitudes and Lifestyles* (Penguin, 1994)

Index

Note: 'n.' after a page reference indicated the number of a note on that page

Abdullah, Sheila 72, 96, 99
Abortion 33, 39, 57–58, 72, 88–92, 153–160, 192–194
Abortion Act
   Abortion Law Reform Association 42, 50, 63, 72, 83
   Experiential expertise in defence of Abortion Act 91–92
   Legislative changes 83, 88–92
   Opposition 62, 88–92
Abstinence *see* Chastity
Accessibility, Centre 115, 230
Activism
   Abortion 88–92
   Birth Control 71–76, 83–85, 104–105
   Confidentiality 92–100
   Funding 76–82, 104–105
   Legislative change 82–87
   Under-16s 92–100
   Women's position in society 75–76
Agony aunts 20, 48, 85, 216, 221, 240–244
AIDS 81, 136, 189–190, 201, 203–204, 212, 219–228, 236–237, 245–246
Atmosphere 106–108, 116–127, 162–163

Bailey, Caroline 99, 220
Balint, Michael 177–178, 194
Bedford, June 54, 56, 59
Bella see Teenage Magazines
BBCCC *see* Bristol Brook Clinic Campaign Committee
BCC *see* Birth Control Campaign
BCT *see* Birth Control Trust
Birmingham Brook *see* Brook Advisory Centres
Birth Control *see* Contraception
Birth Control Campaign 83–84
Birth Control Trust 71–72, 102, 104, 235
BMA *see* British Medical Association

BPAS *see* British Pregnancy Advisory Service
Brien, Joanna 72, 173, 177–178
Bristol Brook *see* Brook Advisory Centres
Bristol Brook Clinic Campaign Committee 52–53, 58, 61
British Pregnancy Advisory Service 72, 74, 173
British Medical Association 29–30, 31, 239
Brixton Brook *see* Brook Advisory Centres
Brook, Helen 1–2, 36–37, 40–46, 48, 51–54, 57, 59, 64, 75, 131, 170–172, 178
Brook Advisory Centres
   Birmingham Brook 50–51, 57, 60–63, 65–66, 78, 109, 162–163, 172, 175, 178, 190, 213–214, 229
   Bristol Brook 51–53, 57–59, 61, 67, 213
   Brixton Brook 114–115, 117–124, 179–180
   Edinburgh Brook 54–56, 62–63, 78–79, 109–110, 112, 123, 163, 220, 230
   London Brook 50, 111, 140–141, 173, 236–237
   Liverpool Brook 63–64, 119–120
   Tottenham Court Road Brook 79, 106, 111, 117–118, 122, 230
Browne confidentiality case 158, 175
Bury, Judy 79, 95, 99, 163

Campaigns
   Confidentiality 238–240
   Gillick 92–100, 176
   HIV and AIDS 219–228
   Publicity 204–210
   Sex education 210–219 (*see also* Sex education)
   Teenage magazines 240–244 (*see also* Teenage magazines)
   Young men 234–238
Chastity 29–31, 34, 38, 46

Clients' experiences
    Accessing Contraception 87, 97–98, 146–152
    Sex Education 141–145
    Influencing Brook services 161–165
    With FPA Services 147–152
    With GP 146, 149–152
    With Brook 128, 148, 153–161
Cole, Martin 50–51, 57, 65–66, 68, 72
Community groups (*see also* Demographics, User)
    Multiracial communities 112–115
    University students 109–111
    West Indian community 37, 41, 45, 114, 114n.23, 119, 138–141, 186, 188
    Working class communities 111–112
Condom 72, 123, 134, 136–137, 190, 207, 220–223, 228, 235–238, 243–244 (*see also* Sheath)
Confidentiality 92–100, 157–158, 163–164, 174–176, 199–200, 238–240, 245
Consent
    Age of consent 12, 130–131, 174
    Disclosure 238
    Issues of informed consent 94, 185–186
    Parental consent 2, 92–100, 135 (*see also* Campaigns, Gillick)
    Sexual consent 216
Contraception (*see also* Depo-Provera; Condom; IUD; Pill; Sheath; Sterilization)
    Emergency 87, 184–185, 206, 208, 243, 252
    History 5
    Men responsibility 107–108, 190, 234–238
    Statistics 136–137
Cossey, Dilys 72, 76, 83–84, 90, 108, 167, 189, 235
Counselling 167–202
    Abortion 154, 193–194, 214
    Before Brook 36
    Contraception 181–186
    Emotional 155, 164–165, 170–172, 187, 193–194
    Good practice 167–176
    Public emphasis on counselling services 66–68
    Pregnancy 191–194
    Psychosexual 155, 194–198

Sexual Abuse 198–200
Under-16s 95–97, 190–191, 193
Counselling Advisory Committee 174, 178, 189
Court, Audrey 50
Crabbe, Pauline 73, 114, 116, 179, 188–189, 191–192, 214

Demographics, User
    Ethnicity 133, 137–141, 179–180
    Socioeconomic status 135–136
    Typical client 135–136
    Young people 130–133, 135
Department of Health and Social Security
    Challenges to funding 79–80
    Guidance on confidentiality 93–95, 100
    Guidance on family planning 82–85, 93, 176
    The Health of the Nation Report 81, 101–103, 239
    Publication and Education Unit 78, 216–218
Department of Education and Science 218
Depo-Provera 17, 184–186

Edinburgh Brook *see* Brook Advisory Centres
Edwin Brooks Family Planning Bill 52, 54
Emotions
    Counselling *see* Counselling, Emotional
    Emotional labour 173, 194, 200
    Emotive language 92, 103–104, 131, 173, 192
    Feeling in Brook Centres 124–127 (*see also* Atmosphere)
    In activism 92, 104
Ethnicity 137–141, 165–166, 180, 187, 232–234, 250–251
Eugenics Society 40, 44, 55

Fairbairn, Nicholas 56, 67
Family Planning Association 21–22, 36–47, 50–55, 59–61, 87, 119, 170, 200, 210–212, 235
FPA *see* Family Planning Association
Family Planning Act 5, 61, 182
Fraser, Jane 100, 219, 230–231, 238
Frater, Alison 74–75, 90–91, 96, 99–100, 180, 236

General Practitioner 58–59, 86, 95–96, 129–130, 145–146, 149–152, 238–239
Gillick, Victoria 94, 96, 100, 251
Gilmore, Margaret 55, 62, 68
GP *see* General Practitioner

Hadley, Alison 73–74, 164, 239
Hayman, Suzie 98, 201, 207, 209, 217, 221, 241–242
Health Education Authority 208, 210, 212, 221, 239
van Heeswyk, Dorothy 115–119, 124, 179–180, 213
Helpline 243
Homosexuality 35, 130, 212, 219, 232
Humanist Society 51–52
Hutchinson, Fay 89, 94–98, 126, 131, 155, 171, 173, 183, 186–187, 191, 194, 210, 238, 242

Illegitimacy 11–12, 28, 32–36, 39, 44, 57–58, 66
IUD 136–137, 152, 184

Jackson, Janet 54, 56, 59
Just Seventeen see Teenage Magazines

Keeping, Dorothy 117, 230

Lafitte, François 50–51, 57, 63, 109
Layout 116–127
Little Kinsey Report 29, 194
Liverpool Brook *see* Brook Advisory Centres
Liverpool Mother's Welfare Clinic 53
Locality 48–68, 109–115
London Brook *see* Brook Advisory Centres
Look Now see Teenage Magazines

MacGillivray, Ruth 179, 197, 214
Marie Stopes clinics 40–47
Marriage Guidance Centres 36, 40, 170, 211, 212
Materiality 106–107, 116–127
McFadyean, Melanie 221, 242
Medical authority 63–68
Medical Recording Service Foundation 214
Merseyside Young People's Advisory Clinic 53–54, 59
Mizz see Teenage Magazines

Morality 8, 12–13, 25, 28–35, 38, 66, 79–81, 92, 159–160, 168, 172–174, 182–183, 186–187, 211
Morris, Roy 51–53, 58, 59, 63
Mother figure 172–174
Muggeridge, Malcolm 55–56
Music 108, 116, 119, 123, 125–126, 163
MYPAC *see* Merseyside Young People's Advisory Clinic

National Birth Control Association 36, 40
National Marriage Guidance Council 211–212
Nineteen see Teenage Magazines

Oh Boy! see Teenage Magazines
Opposition 60–68
  FPA 60–61
  Medical 63–68
  Moral 48–49, 61–62, 66, 79–80
  Religious 53, 55, 62
  Universities 62–63
Overseas services
  France 3
  Netherlands 3, 164, 239
  Sweden 3
  Switzerland 3

Pawsey, James 80, 217
Penetrative intercourse 133, 156, 189, 204, 222–228, 245
Permissive society 2, 4–8, 21, 54–55, 62, 247
Petticoat see Teenage Magazines
Pill 5–6, 54, 55–56, 85, 110, 133–134, 136–137, 182–184
Population control 55, 56, 83
Promiscuity 1–2, 31–33, 38, 57, 64–65, 170, 196, 208–209

Race 16–18, 27, 45, 112–115, 137–141
Responsible society 79, 92–93, 217
Riche, Valerie 79, 217

Safe sex 187, 206, 214–219, 229
Sex education
  Disability 229–231
  Ethnicity 188–189, 233–234
  Inclusive 228–234

Sex education (*cont.*)
  Premarital 29–30, 36, 59n38
  Resources 210–219
  Sexual Orientation 212, 232
Sex Education Forum 102, 212
Sexual pleasure 66–68, 194–198, 201–202, 227, 249
Sexual responsibility
  Responsible sex 33, 48, 58, 64–67, 83, 110, 168–169, 187, 204, 228, 247–249
Sexual Revolution 6, 19, 129, 247
Sheath 97, 133, 136, 189–190, 235 (*see also* Condom)
Smyth, Margaret 53–54, 59, 61–63
Spicer, Faith 40, 42–46, 64–66, 71, 73, 169, 178–179
Statistics (*see also* Demographics, User; Little Kinsey report)
  Abortion 88, 91
  Adolescent sexual behaviour 31–32, 131–133
  Age of first sexual intercourse 28–29, 133
  Contraception 133–134, 136–137
  Gender 137
  Illegitimacy 28
  Premarital Sex 29, 31–32
  To counter Promiscuity claims 44, 209
  Race and Ethnicity 137–141
  Reason for first visit 136–137
  Referral from friend 153, 162
  Return rate 161
  Social class 133, 135
  Teenage pregnancy 32, 95, 100
Sterilization 18, 55, 83
Stopes, Marie 40

Teenage conception (*see* Teenage pregnancy)
Teenage magazines
  Bella 243
  Just Seventeen 20, 86, 98, 115, 221, 241–243
  Look Now 106
  Mizz 86, 233, 240, 243
  Nineteen 20, 132, 242
  Oh Boy! 241
  Petticoat 223, 241
Teenage pregnancy 9, 12–13, 74, 86, 101–105, 112, 164, 239, 247–248, 252
Thomas, Wendy 117, 150–151, 162
Tottenham Court Road Brook *see* Brook Advisory Centres

Under-16s 85, 100–101, 174, 190–194

Vanhegan, Gillian 173, 179, 187, 198
Venereal Disease 17, 27, 31, 35, 211
Voluntary Sector 14–16, 70

Whitehouse, Mary
  Clean UpTV Campaign 62
Woodroffe, Caroline 69, 71–72, 75–76, 80–81, 83–85, 89–90, 96, 98–99, 108–109, 139–140, 191, 217
Woodside, Moya 54–55, 56, 59
Woodward, Joan 162, 171, 183–184, 195, 197
World Population Crisis Campaign 56